"*The Anarchist Imagination* is more than a comprehensive introduction to anarchist and anarchist-inspired scholarship across the disciplines. It is a clear and unambiguous testament to the vitality of anarchist thought both within and without the academy. I cannot endorse it strongly enough."

– **Nathan Jun,** *Midwestern State University, USA*

"These wide-ranging essays trace anarchism's extensive intersections with academic fields and studies. Anarchism's influence, the essays demonstrate, is impressively wide and appears both directly, in the relevance of recognized authors, texts and events, and indirectly, in the spill-over of anarchist ways of asking questions and pursuing inquiries into key concepts such as power, order, and change."

– **Kathy E. Ferguson,** *University of Hawai'i, USA*

The Anarchist Imagination

This is a broad ranging introduction to twenty-first-century anarchism which includes a wide array of theoretical approaches as well as a variety of empirical and geographical perspectives. The book demonstrates how the anarchist imagination has influenced the humanities and social sciences including anthropology, art, feminism, geography, international relations, political science, postcolonialism, and sociology.

Drawing on a long historical narrative that encompasses the 'waves' of anarchist movements from the classical anarchists (1840s to 1940s), the post-war wave of student, counter-cultural, and workers' control anarchism of the 1960s and 1970s to the DIY politics and Temporary Autonomous Zones of the 1990s right up to the Occupy! Movement and beyond, the aim of this volume is to cover the humanities and the social sciences in an era of anarchist revival in academia. Anarchist philosophy and anarchistic methodologies have re-emerged in a range of disciplines from Organization Studies, to Law, to Political Economy to Political Theory and International Relations, and Anthropology to Cultural Studies. Anarchist approaches to freedom, democracy, ethics, violence, authority, punishment, homelessness, and the arbitration of justice have spawned a broad array of academic publications and research projects. But this volume remembers an older story, in other words, the continuous role of the anarchist imagination as muse, provocateur, goading adversary, and catalyst in the stimulation of research and creative activity in the humanities and social sciences from the middle of the nineteenth century to today.

This work will be essential reading for scholars and students of anarchism, the humanities, and the social sciences.

Carl Levy is a Professor of Politics at Goldsmiths, University of London, UK. He is the author of twelve single-authored and edited books and over 75 journal articles and chapters in books.

Saul Newman (PhD UNSW 1998) is a Professor of Political Theory at Goldsmiths, University of London, UK. His research is in continental political theory, postanarchism and radical political thought. His most recent publication is *Political Theology: A Critical Introduction* (2018).

Interventions

The Series provides a forum for innovative and interdisciplinary work that engages with alternative critical, post-structural, feminist, postcolonial, psychoanalytic and cultural approaches to international relations and global politics. In our first 5 years we have published 60 volumes.

We aim to advance understanding of the key areas in which scholars working within broad critical post-structural traditions have chosen to make their interventions, and to present innovative analyses of important topics. Titles in the series engage with critical thinkers in philosophy, sociology, politics and other disciplines and provide situated historical, empirical and textual studies in international politics.

We are very happy to discuss your ideas at any stage of the project: just contact us for advice or proposal guidelines. Proposals should be submitted directly to the Series Editors:

- Jenny Edkins (jennyedkins@hotmail.com) and
- Nick Vaughan-Williams (N.Vaughan-Williams@Warwick.ac.uk).

'As Michel Foucault has famously stated, "knowledge is not made for understanding; it is made for cutting" In this spirit The Edkins - Vaughan-Williams Interventions series solicits cutting edge, critical works that challenge mainstream understandings in international relations. It is the best place to contribute post disciplinary works that think rather than merely recognize and affirm the world recycled in IR's traditional geopolitical imaginary.'
Michael J. Shapiro, University of Hawai'i at Manoa, USA

Edited by Jenny Edkins, Aberystwyth University and Nick Vaughan-Williams, University of Warwick

Migrant Resistance in Contemporary Europe
Maurice Stierl

EU Democracy Promotion and Governmentality
Turkey and Beyond
Hanna L. Muehlenhoff

Autonomy of Migration?
Appropriating Mobility within Biometric Border Regimes
Stephan Scheel

The Anarchist Imagination
Anarchism Encounters the Humanities and the Social Sciences
Carl Levy and Saul Newman

For more information about this series, please visit: https://www.routledge.com/series/INT

The Anarchist Imagination
Anarchism Encounters the Humanities and the Social Sciences

Edited by
Carl Levy and Saul Newman

LONDON AND NEW YORK

First published 2019
by Routledge
2 Park Square, Milton Park, Abingdon, Oxon OX14 4RN

and by Routledge
52 Vanderbilt Avenue, New York, NY 10017

Routledge is an imprint of the Taylor & Francis Group, an informa business

© 2019 selection and editorial matter, Carl Levy and Saul Newman; individual chapters, the contributors

The right of Carl Levy and Saul Newman to be identified as the authors of the editorial material, and of the authors for their individual chapters, has been asserted in accordance with sections 77 and 78 of the Copyright, Designs and Patents Act 1988.

All rights reserved. No part of this book may be reprinted or reproduced or utilised in any form or by any electronic, mechanical, or other means, now known or hereafter invented, including photocopying and recording, or in any information storage or retrieval system, without permission in writing from the publishers.

Trademark notice: Product or corporate names may be trademarks or registered trademarks, and are used only for identification and explanation without intent to infringe.

British Library Cataloguing in Publication Data
A catalogue record for this book is available from the British Library

Library of Congress Cataloging-in-Publication Data
Names: Levy, Carl, 1951- editor. | Newman, Saul, 1972- editor.
Title: The anarchist imagination : anarchism encounters the humanities and the social sciences / edited by Carl Levy and Saul Newman.
Description: Abingdon, Oxon ; New York, NY : Routledge, 2019. | Includes bibliographical references.
Identifiers: LCCN 2018057716 (print) | LCCN 2019005002 (ebook) | ISBN 9781315693163 (eBook) | ISBN 9781138781184 (hardback) | ISBN 9781138782761 (pbk.)
Subjects: LCSH: Anarchism--Philosophy. | Social sciences--Research--Political aspects. | Humanities--Research--Political aspects.
Classification: LCC HX833 (ebook) | LCC HX833 .A5697 2019 (print) | DDC 335/.83--dc23
LC record available at https://lccn.loc.gov/2018057716

ISBN: 978-1-138-78118-4 (hbk)
ISBN: 978-1-138-78276-1 (pbk)
ISBN: 978-1-315-69316-3 (ebk)

Typeset in Times New Roman
by Taylor & Francis Books
Printed by CPI Group (UK) Ltd, Croydon CR0 4YY

Contents

List of tables ix
List of contributors x
Acknowledgements xi

1 Introduction: Anarchism encounters the humanities and the social sciences 1
CARL LEVY

2 The two anarchies: The Arab uprisings and the question of an anarchist sociology 30
MOHAMMED A. BAMYEH

3 Contesting the state of nature: Anarchism and International Relations 42
ZAHEER KAZMI

4 Anarchism and Critical Security Studies 62
CHRIS ROSSDALE

5 Postanarchism today: Anarchism and political theory 81
SAUL NEWMAN

6 Anarchism and political science: History and anti-science in radical thought 95
RUTH KINNA

7 Toward an anarchist-feminist analytics of power 110
SANDRA JEPPESEN

8 Loving politics: On the art of living together 132
VISHWAM J. HECKERT

9 Black flag mapping: Emerging themes in anarchist geography 146
ANTHONY INCE

10 In dialogue: Anarchism and postcolonialism 163
MAIA RAMNATH

11	What is law? ELENA LOIZIDOU	181
12	Anarchism and education studies JUDITH SUISSA	194
13	Anarchism and religious studies ALEXANDRE CHRISTOYANNOPOULOS	210
14	Aesthetics of tension ALLAN ANTLIFF	229
15	Conclusion in three acts: False genealogies and suspect methodologies? CARL LEVY	240

Index   259

Tables

2.1 Basic features of self-conscious and organic anarchy 32
2.2 Anarchist sociology as synthesis 37
7.1 Toward an anarchist-feminist analytics of power 114

Contributors

Allan Antliff: Associate Professor of Art History and Visual Studies, University of Victoria, Canada.

Mohammed Bamyeh: Professor of Sociology, Department of Sociology, University of Pittsburgh, USA.

Alexandre Christoyannopoulos: Senior Lecturer in Politics and International Relations, Department of Politics, History and International Relations, Loughborough University, UK.

Vishwam Jamie Heckert: Independent Scholar, Yoga Teacher and Healer, UK.

Anthony Ince: Lecturer in Human Geography, School of Geography and Planning, Cardiff University, Wales, UK.

Sandra Jeppesen: Associate Professor in Interdisciplinary Studies/Media Studies and Research University Chair in Transformative Media and Social Movements, Media Studies Programme, Interdisciplinary Studies Department, Lakehead University Orillia, Canada

Zaheer Kazmi: Senior Research Fellow, Mitchell Institute of Global Peace, Security and Justice, Queen's University Belfast, Northern Ireland, UK.

Ruth Kinna: Professor of Politics, Department of Politics, History & International Relations, Loughborough University, UK.

Carl Levy: Professor of Politics, Department of Politics and International Relations, Goldsmiths, University of London, UK

Elena Loizidou: Reader in Law and Political Theory, School of Law, Birkbeck College, University of London, UK

Saul Newman: Professor of Political Theory, Department of Politics and International Relations, Goldsmiths, University of London

Maia Ramnath: Writer, Organizer and Adjunct Professor of History, Fordham University, New York, USA

Chris Rossdale: LSE Fellow in International Relations Theory, Department of International Relations, London School of Economic and Political Science

Judith Suissa: Professor of Philosophy of Education, Department of Education, Practice and Society, UCL Institute of Education, London, UK

Acknowledgements

This book project incurred a number of debts. It arose from a conference ('Anarchism Today': 26 October 2012) at Goldsmiths, University of London, organized by the then Department of Politics (now the Department of Politics and International Relations), the Research Unit in Governance and Democracy, and the Research Unit in Politics and Ethics. The participants included Allan Antliff, Alexandre Christoyannopoulos, Mohammed Bamyeh, David Graeber, Carissa Honeywell, Ruth Kinna, Carl Levy, Saul Newman, Chris Rossdale, and Judith Suissa. The conference received a grant from the Anarchist Study Group of the Political Studies Association (UK) and we would like to thank them for their generosity. We would also like to thank the editors and editorial assistants at Routledge for their patience and help in steering this book to publication, particularly, Nicola Parkins and Ella Halstead. Nick Vaughan-Williams of the Department of Politics and International Studies at the University of Warwick, Commissioning Editor of the Routledge Interventions Series, got the ball rolling and we are grateful for his enthusiastic support.

Carl Levy and Saul Newman, London, September 2018

1 Introduction

Anarchism encounters the humanities and the social sciences

Carl Levy

Anarchism as a methodology and inspiration for the humanities and the social sciences

In 1971, American political scientist, David Apter, and the British historian, James Joll, published an edited book (originally in a special issue of *Government and Opposition* (October, 1970)), on anarchism today, which sported a period-piece, rather lovely, psychedelic Bakunin on its front cover (Apter and Joll 1970; Apter and Joll 1971). In the wake of '1968', with black flags spotted from Paris to Berkeley, and events in Paris which mushroomed from a tiny movement in March in Nanterre to, in May, a strike of an estimated ten million students, white collar workers and the industrial proletariat, with the Gaullist state nearly tottering and the General rallying his troops at their base in Baden-Baden, and his supporters on the Right Bank, too (Berry 2018; Vinen 2018), George Woodcock's earlier obituary for anarchism in his 1962 edition of *Anarchism*, now seemed premature (Woodcock 1962: 468–469). It was the sheer force of 'untimely mobilizations' (Rose 1999: 280),[1] of anarchic protest not within the compass of the prevailing Cold War functionalist settlement, which forced anarchism back onto the academic agenda. By the late 1960s anarchism and syndicalism had become worthy subjects of academic study for historians, social scientists and economists, as the interesting special issue and book version of *Anarchism Today* handily demonstrated.

The waves of student protest, workers' control and rank and file unofficial movements, pioneering gay rights activists and second wave feminism of the 1960s and 1970s were superseded by anti-nuke, Green and squatting movements from the late 1970s to the early 1990s. In all these cases interest in anarchism and syndicalism in the academic world waxed and waned, but never evaporated completely. New Left Marxism, postmodernism and postcolonialism were clearly more evident amongst the leftish academics. In the aftermath of '1968' in West Europe and in a more contested fashion in the USA (due to the vast politicized underground cultural scene), 'it was not libertarianism, but born-again Marxism, of Maoist or Neo-Trotskyist hue which put itself at the head of the campus revolt, replacing real-life self-assertion, with make-believe bids for power' (Samuel 2012: 261). Libertarian free schools and squats could be co-opted into the local state and even here forms of autonomous Marxism were more notable (Katsiaficas 2006). Postmodernism and various forms of postcolonial theory became pathways to university careers; 'automatic Marxism' (Ward 1987: 9) trumped anarchist currents. But in the era after the decline of the Cold War and the seeming triumph of varieties of globalization from neo-liberalism to Chinese capitalism with Leninist characteristics, anarchism or newer variations on the same theme, which in any case had undergone a series of transformations since 1945, steadily gained traction amongst activists and academics. From the 1990s to 2008, the era of the Global Justice Movements, of the alternative lefts in Latin America, of Temporary Alternative Zones and encampments (Feigenbaum, Frenzel and McCurdy 2013), of horizontalist experiments in consensual direct democracy, laid the foundations for an even more notable presence (Maeckelbergh 2011; Levy 2017). These movements drew upon currents outside of anarchism *per se*. Libertarian socialism, libertarian communism, autonomist Marxism, Marxist feminism and postcolonial writings melded with the anarchist tradition as the organized social democratic, Marxist and communist lefts underwent upheavals. Writing in 2016 Alex Prichard and Owen Worth summed up this complex blending:

> In the absence of a party line, social movements and single-issue groups have proliferated and often merged, with some individual members of multiple and contradictory groups coming from radically different ideological and activist backgrounds
>
> (Prichard and Worth 2016: 6).

These movements and associated academic work during the period from the end of the Cold War to the financial crash of 2008 fed into the decline of the neo-liberal model and a spurt of 1968-like activity in the Arab Spring and the grassroots, 'leaderless' movements (Ross 2011) of squares and piazzas from Santiago to Wall Street, from Athens to Madrid, from Barcelona to Tel Aviv and New Delhi (Dupuis-Déri 2018; Sitrin 2018), which made this 'reconfigured anarchism' (Dixon 2014: 5–10) newsworthy again beyond activists and the academic left (Blumenfeld, Bottici and Critchley 2013). The Global Justice Movement and the new or reconfigured anarchism of the Squares were simultaneously both a product and critique of what Peter Mair (2013) identified as the hollowing of liberal democracy. They were the physical embodiments of the phenomena discussed in Simon Tormey's (2015) *The End of Representative Politics*, and were accompanied by the reinvention of a grassroots and cosmopolitan type of social citizenship (Levy 2011). But the period from movements of Occupy and Squares to today has witnessed another switchback: state co-optation, mimesis (the adversary learning the tricks of the digital trade in cyber-space), while the lack of long-term strategic planning and the provisional quality of the tactical emotional politics of the Squares saw an initially contagious strength evaporate (Tufekci 2017: 71–75). The politics of the Square were superseded by battles between forms of right and left parliamentary populism or what Paolo Gerbaudo (2017) has termed, 'citizenism', a hybrid of left-populism and anarchism: an unstable combination of forces manifesting themselves in SYRIZA and Podemos (Sheehan 2016; Feenstra, Tormey, Casero-Ripollés and Keane 2017; Mudde 2017; Ordóñez, Feenstra and Franks 2018). The liminal politics of the Squares in North Africa and the Middle East (Galián 2018) were replaced by bloody power plays between world and regional powers, theocratic nationalisms and remnants of older secular nationalist family-state clans, with the interesting libertarian municipalism of the Rojava experiment in Syrian Kurdistan (a variation on 'citizenism'?) a startling exception to the rule (Knapp, Flach and Ayboga 2016). Latin American alternative left populism, was threatened by imperial hegemonic forces and the internal contradictions between new populist political elites and their allies, unhappy 'backseat driving' ethno-national movements, who felt threatened by natural resource developmental plans issued by the new populist political elites of the capital cities

(Zibechi 2012; Webber 2017). The battle against globalization, in which the cosmopolitan message of anarchism offered an alternative form of world-wide solidarity, was transformed into a battle by right-wing populists against 'globalist elites' and 'interloping' migrants/refugees. Populist billionaires, their minions and imitators, have harnessed the disquiet with neo-liberal globalization to seize the narrative from the populist and anarchist left-wing of '2011', invoking a world of proud, sovereign nation-states as the remedy for the free flow of capital, products and people (or at least certain sorts of people). The hollowing of the liberal democratic world order, the end of the 1945 settlement (Mounk 2018), may not benefit the populist and libertarian left but give life to the hovering ghosts of the Fascist 1930s. It is too early to tell if a left-wing parliamentary populism might still challenge this recent counter-revolution (de la Torre 2015; Müller 2016; Rovira Kaltwasser, Taggart, Ochoa Espejo and Ostiguy 2017).

Dana Williams sums up succinctly the course of anarchism and the new and the newest social movements since 1968 or 1989 (Williams 2018). He differentiates between anarchist and anarchistic movements and argues that the latter are far larger than the former. But anarchist movements fed off and gained credence within these broader movements, which invoked horizontalism, direct action, anti-authoritarianism, anti-capitalism, and actuated mutual aid. In engaging in confrontational and playful street tactics the newest social movements attempt to reclaim urban space for an alternative social world with innovative forms of democratic practice and performative identities. Many participants may be closer to autonomous Marxism or other hybrids, or still feel the label 'anarchist' still carries too much stigma (Prichard, Kinna, Pinta and Berry 2012). Here is David Graeber, who uses the identification 'anarchist' tactically (in the example cited below, in his activist politics) depending whom he is addressing and where he is publishing, and at times overlooks earlier anarchist academic contributors to the social sciences, making himself appear more unique and beleaguered than he is:[2]

> For 'small-a' anarchists such as myself – that is, the sort willing to work in broad coalitions as long as they work on horizontal principles – that is what we'd always dreamed of. For decades, the anarchist movement had been putting much of our creative energy into developing forms of egalitarian political process that actually work; forms of direct democracy that actually could operate within self-governing communities outside any state. The whole project was based on a kind of faith that freedom is contagious. We all knew it was practically impossible to convince the average American that a truly democratic society was possible through rhetoric.
> (Graeber 2013: 89)

In his academic ethnographies (except for *Direct Action* (Graeber 2009) which cannot avoid the labelling), Graeber has only openly invoked anarchism as a central theme in his attempt to flesh a theory of anthropology (Graeber 2004) but otherwise he does so modestly – the indirect linkage of Marcel Mauss to the anarchist tradition, and some references to Peter Kropotkin, in his best-selling study of five thousand years of debt (Graeber 2011). But the essence of his arguments, indeed his telling formulations, have been trailed in books and journals associated with the anarchist and autonomous Marxist press where he is less reticent to discuss the political and intellectual linkages to the ideas and methodologies of the anarchist tradition (Graeber 2007; Shukaitis, Graeber and Biddle 2007). This might be due to the adverse reaction the label 'anarchist' may still have for academics, particularly in the US,[3] but in the UK, the anarchist philosopher, Alan Carter, has held the Chair of Moral Philosophy at the University of Glasgow, a Chair held earlier by Adam Smith! Whatever the merit of this argument, in the UK, even if some of his jealous critics might use political labelling as an excuse to besmirch his impressive corpus of work, on the whole, Graeber has been embraced and celebrated at the London School of Economics and even in the mainstream financial press.[4]

In any case, the new movements (Global Justice and Occupy) chronicled by Graeber have in fact reinforced and validated the growth of anarchism in the academy. Here, anarchism has become increasingly interesting and noticeable and there has been a growth of PhD students in several fields and clusters in certain universities, in the UK at Loughborough, for example: dare I say anarchism is a fashionable topic ('Being an anarchist academic is almost hip' (Shantz and Williams 2014: 176)), and unlike in the previous waves since 1968, this time it seems the tide is still coming in and the academic production is reaching a self-sustaining pitch (Amster, De Leon, Fernandez, Nocella and Shannon 2009; Levy and Adams 2018). Anarchist approaches to freedom, democracy, ethics, violence, authority, punishment, homelessness and the arbitration of justice have spawned myriad academic publications and research projects (Purkis and Bowen 1997; Purkis and Bowen 2004; Gordon 2008; Kinna 2012). Anarchist philosophy and anarchistic methodologies have re-emerged in a range of disciplines from Organization Studies, to Law, Political Economy to Political Theory and International Relations, and Anthropology to Cultural Studies (Havercroft and Prichard 2017: 5).

The anarchist imagination

This volume is the product of a conference originally held in the now distant after-glow of Occupy/Arab Spring, in 2012, at Goldsmiths, University of London[5] (but I hasten to add, radically updated and with other contributors not present at the original gathering and others present not in this volume) to examine how the anarchist imagination (a nod to the sociological imagination of the anarchist-friendly C. Wright Mills), anarchist methodologies and theoretical constructs, have influenced the humanities and the social sciences.

So what is the anarchist imagination? Let us recall that untimely mobilization in May 1968 which wrong-footed Charles de Gaulle and forced George Woodcock to tear up his obituary for anarchism. The anarchist imagination allows the social scientist and historian to undergo such 'moments of madness' during her academic research (Zohlberg 1972). Here is a veteran of 1968 and anarchist-friendly anthropologist Michael Taussig on his arrival at 'Occupy Wall Street' in 2011 describing the 'moment of madness' of social mobilization:

> Welcome to Hakim Bey's Temporary Autonomous Zone. I recall Paris, May 1968: people said they lived in that zone for months, didn't sleep; didn't need to. Out of nowhere a community forms, fuelled by the unforeseen chance to fight back. Decades drift away. Decades of Fox News and Goldman Sachs. Decades of gutting what was left of the social contract. Decades in which kids came to think being a banker was sexy. When that happens, you *know* it's all over – or about to explode, as once again history throws a curveball. Once in a lifetime, the unpredictable occurs and reality gets redefined.
>
> (Taussig 2013: 9)

But moments of madness may also be used to explore the humanities and the social sciences. Many of the most important figures in modernist and postmodernist fiction and poetry relied on this spark from Eugene O'Neill to James Joyce to Ursula Le Guin (Shantz 2011: 10–11).

There is also a link between the humanities and the social sciences, 'the literary imagination can also be powerfully expressed through the social sciences' (Shantz 2011: 121). Paul Feyerabend, the anarchistic methodologist and student of Karl Popper, argued that the scientific worldview must embrace 'contingency and imagination' and reject 'timeless truths' (Stevens 2011: 6). So Feyerabend concluded that a touch of a moment of madness allows the most sober scientist to break paradigms and advance theory: 'My thesis is that anarchism helps achieve progress in any one of the senses one cared to choose. Even law-and-order science will succeed only if anarchistic moves are occasionally allowed to take place' (quoted in Stevens 2011: 18).

The most noted link between the anarchist imagination and the sociological imagination is in the life and work of C. Wright Mills, nostalgic for the IWW and suspicious of bureaucratic 'Big Labor', a self-proclaimed 'Goddamn anarchist' (Levy Forthcoming a). The sociological imagination transcended the self-importance of grand theory on the one hand, and abstracted empiricism on the other; the true purpose of the sociological imagination should be to connect private troubles with political structures (Freedman 2013: 373). And therefore it follows, that 'sociology could be the master discipline of politics, the sociological imagination would feed the political imagination' (Freedman 2013: 374). Anarchist sociologists have recognized the affinity. 'The sociological imagination itself, as defined by Mills, may be one of the most anarchistic ideas ever developed by sociology', so claimed Dana Williams (Heckert 2011). Indeed Williams does not hesitate to argue that, 'Maybe the best anarchist tweaking of the "sociological imagination" is to speak of an "anarchist imagination"' (Heckert 2011). Today there is a crucial if limited overlap between academic anarchist sociologists and 'sociologically-informed anarchists acting within social movements' (Shantz and Williams 2014: 9). In our era of 'immaterial' and symbolic capitalism, this anarchist or radical imagination has become 'a key battleground over what' theorists such as Michael Hardt, Tony Negri or Scott Lasch have termed '"the general intellect" – the sort of baseline knowledges, competencies and understandings that allow us to communicate and work together, and that represent the timbre of our collective creative power' (Haiven 2014: 245). But this anarchist imagination is also an inviting resource for the nimble-footed capitalist or state bureaucrat: the concepts of personal flexibility over the rigidities of institutions, the advantages of networks over hierarchies, and the deep well of personal expression and its linkage to creativity, have and will be cherry-picked by the anarchists' enemies.

Why this volume? An initial panoramic overview of some closer encounters between anarchism, the humanities and the social sciences

There have been a host of edited works on anarchism and postanarchism in the past decade or more, but with the exception of the *Continuum/Bloomsbury Compendium* (Kinna 2012, 2014) and the recently published *Palgrave Handbook of Anarchism* (Levy and Adams 2018), most of these works have focused on one aspect of the social sciences and the humanities, as monographs for the anarchist publishers, PM and AK, and in dedicated series published by Continuum, Bloomsbury and Manchester

University Press, as collections or articles in journals such as *Anarchist Studies, Social Anarchism* or more mainstream and venerable academic journals, especially as Anarchist Studies has been gradually accepted by mainstream academia. Although there have been volumes which address the role of anarchists and anarchist studies in the academy, especially the academy since the 1990s, this volume and especially this chapter examine the ways in which the anarchist imagination, anarchist methodologies, and anarchist ways of seeing have shaped mainstream and radical approaches in the humanities and the social sciences over a longer period of time: it mixes presentism with a longer view (for overviews of the literature see Kinna 2012, 2014 and Levy and Adams 2018).

The exchange of well-known personalities of classical anarchism with, for example, sociology, presents a mixed picture. Proudhon thought Comte's ersatz theology downright silly though they shared interests in cooperation, decentralization, republicanism and anti-feminism. Bakunin and Kropotkin dismissed some sociologists because they treated the state as a given, while Malatesta thought sociology lacked a programme for change in society, the aim of anarchism. Kropotkin admired aspects of Herbert Spencer's sociology but thought he misunderstood Darwin (more on this interchange in the concluding chapter of this volume). However, Voltarine de Cleyre arrived at anarchism through her study of sociology and the libertarian educationalism of Francisco Ferrer. Emma Goldman was sympathetic to sociology's possibilities because it demonstrated the plastic potentialities of human nature (Williams 2013). Nevertheless, as I will discuss in far greater detail further on, the acceptance of or curiosity about anarchist concepts and ideas by the pioneer social scientists (out of fear or attraction), cannot be denied:

> … the history of nineteenth-century social science has as one of its master threads its critical dialogue with anarchism. The 'golden mean' of Spencerian sociology, the 'social solidarity' of Durkheim and the 'iron law of oligarchy' of Michels, these and many more can have little meaning until an accounting of the spectre of anarchism – at least as the most extreme consequence of socialism – is fully made.
> (Horowitz 1964: 64)

It has been argued that flirtations by the infant social scientists with the anarchists were forgotten once these social sciences erected barriers of credentialization and social closure in the twentieth century (Shantz and Williams 2014). This overlooks the importance the social sciences took on in the New Anarchism of the post-war period (1945–1968), after the crushing of the last mass popular movement of anarchists in Spain in 1939. Manifestations of anarchism were near or in the academic and related bohemian worlds. A motley crew of men and women of letters, the self-educated, and anarchist friendly academics within mainstream academic institutions prepared the way for future anarchistic social movements: Ivan Illich (1971), deschooling and tools for conviviality (Illich 1973); Elinor Ostrom (1990) and the commons; Jane Jacobs (1961) and the new urbanism, and of course Patrick Geddes and his disciple Lewis Mumford, patron and later patronizing foe of Jacobs herself (Ryley 2013: 158–178); Richard Sennett (1970) on the city, skill (Sennett 2008), cooperation (Sennett 2012), and human character (Sennett 1999); the previously mentioned Paul Feyerabend (1975) and his radical critique of the scientific method, the disclosure of the 'unscientific subscript' of scientific revolutions; Carole Pateman (1970) and democratic theory. The intellectual heft of the New Anarchism of the post-war years has been characterized as a form of radical sociology or multi-disciplinary radical social science (Honeywell 2011; Pauli 2015), or as Raphael Samuel (2012) put it in his treatment of Colin Ward, 'utopian sociology'. Ward's friend and collaborator, medical doctor, psychologist, gerontologist, sexologist, and novelist, Alex Comfort, announced a 'plan' to followers at an 'anarchist summer camp' in 1950:

> Personally, I would like to see more of us, those who can, take training in social sciences or engaging in research in this field ... I want to see something done which has not been done before – a concerted, unbiased, and properly documented attempt to disseminate accurate teaching of the results of modern child psychiatry, social psychology and political psychology to the general public on the same scale as we have in the past tried to disseminate revolutionary propaganda.
> (Comfort 1951: 13)

This, in effect, anticipates the role of Colin Ward's *Anarchy* magazine in the 1960s. It was a journal of 'constructive antinomianism' (Samuel 2012: 259) or of autonomy, the original chosen name for *Anarchy*. It promoted the works of architects, sociologists, anthropologists, the New Criminologists (Stan Cohen, David Downes, and Jock Young), the new sociology of deviancy (Ian Taylor and Laurie Taylor), the psychiatry and psychology of the aforementioned Comfort, and many other disciplines and most importantly, perhaps, Ward's work on childhood, children in the city and the countryside and a theory of play (Wilbert and White 2011; Levy 2013). Comfort should be linked to Wilhelm Reich's theory of the revolutionary politics of the orgasm, that Paul Goodman had discussed in the 1940s and who then became a promoter of Gestalt therapy: for both, key was a libertarian understanding of the relationship between desire, freedom, and personal autonomy (Honeywell 2011), also found in R. D. Laing and the culture of anti-psychiatry; anti-asylums in Italy, Franco Basaglia (Foot 2015), and the critique of the therapeutic state, the labelling of the marginal, the insane – even radicals – which one finds in Irving Goffman, Thomas Szasz and to a broader audience the novel and film of Ken Kesey's (1962), *One Flew over the Cuckoo's Nest*. These ideas anticipate and advance, perhaps in a more approachable manner, the work of Michel Foucault on madness and asylums (Staub 2011).

Ward's theory of play was advanced through a study of the adventure playground as a parable of anarchy (Samuel 2012: 259), and play or leisure as challenges for industrial society (Burke and Jones 2014) were not absent from the concerns of mainstream sociologists of his generation, albeit with different intentions and ends. Thus Daniel Bell's concept of the end of ideology (Bell 1961), or Seymour Martin Lipset's (1960) belief, enunciated in *Political Man*, that the fundamental discontents of class society had been superseded by the post-1945 form of neo-capitalism, meant for both that the lessening of the Puritan Work Ethic and its replacement by the hedonism of consumerism posed, in turn, a new threat to civilizational values. Later other questions were raised by sociologists about meaningful work, as the Fordist model of industrialism declined, and it is something that Colin Ward discussed decades in advance of present arguments, in light of the work of the sociologist Ray Pahl on household economies on the Isle of Sheppey in Kent. Thus the disappearance of the life-time job defining a person's (in most cases a man's) self-worth was replaced with Ward's arguments about what one might now term the 'gig' economy, which for Ward had inherent possibilities so long as the hierarchies of capital and the state were overthrown or at least mitigated (Honeywell 2013; Williams 2018: 118; also see Graeber's take more recently (2018)).

Anarchy sought to make manifest tribes without rules, architecture without architects, and education without schools: the social sciences and the humanities were enlisted to reveal the heterotopic spaces in the midst of the warfare/welfare state. Ward and his ventures promoted in parallel fashion a theory of everyday life, which Henri Lefebvre discussed in France. *Anarchy* and a plethora of small magazines and discussion groups in the Anglo-American world and elsewhere, served as '"amateur think tanks", seeking to reconstruct radical praxis in light of changing conditions' (Cornell 2016: 247), 'focussing on sexual repression, cultural alienation, and the catastrophic potential of atomic warfare' (Cornell 2016: 208).

It is now appropriate to draw together strands of our argument concerning the exchange of anarchism, the social sciences and the humanities, looking over the past two centuries, by focusing on the formation of doctrines and disciplines, and anticipating arguments found in the chapters of this volume.

1 **Karl Marx and the origins of Marxian thought and Marxism**: Would it be possible to understand this process without Marx's encounters with, assimilation and then sarcastic purging of Stirner, Proudhon and Bakunin and the libertarian currents of the First International? The very model of the future socialist form of governance, the Paris Commune of 1871, also served as the anarchists' template (Thomas 1980; Ross 2015; Stedman Jones 2016).

2 **Herbert Spencer's sociology**: the master themes in his work trace the evolution from a militantly and militaristic hierarchical society to the contractual and minimal state of peaceful competition and spontaneous economic coordination. Although anarchists had little time for the later defender of unbridled capitalism, Spencer's earlier work attracted the 'classical anarchists' and they had no objection to reproducing extracts in their popular newspapers (Williams 2013: 5).

3 **Max Weber's political sociology**: Weber's form of political realism became the reasonable option only once he wrestled publicly with the straw-man friend-enemy embodied in anarchist ethics of ultimate ends and the boundless, the disturbingly close and exhilarating purveyors of antebellum libertarian life-style sub-cultures, particularly that predecessor to Wilhelm Reich, Otto Gross, his critique of the family, and his promotion of a free sexuality as a psychiatric prophylaxis for the neurotic condition of the antebellum Wilhelmine bourgeoisie. Key themes in Weber's sociology – charisma, state legitimacy, war and the persistence of pacifism, religion and utopia, and the role of democracy in modern societies – can only be understood by his life-time engagement with anarchists, syndicalists, and anarchist themes (Whimster 1998). More recently Weberian *verstehen* has been tested to its limits by the anarchist ethnographers of anarchistic movements (more below). Jeff Ferrell poses the effect: 'At its extreme, ethnographic field research can become an anarchic process through which researchers lose themselves – and by losing themselves, find new meanings and emotions' (Ferrell 2009: 81). In his own intimate life, Weber recognized and even at times relished a rather similar effect through Otto Gross and his sexual anarchism, on his friends, family and even himself (Levy 1998)!

4 **Antonio Gramsci**: In some ways, a model for the engagement of a thinker and activist who is at once an adversary and collaborator with anarchism and

anarchists. Thus, as I have shown elsewhere, the early 'libertarian' Gramsci relied on anarchist self-educated workers and skilled technicians in Turin's factories to spread his unique brand of Marxist council communism, and theoretically, his council communism and mature form of voluntarist Marxism relied on his rather unique reading of Georges Sorel throughout his career. But his key concept of *sovversivismo* was a theoretical wall separating him from acceptance of the first premises of anarchism (Levy 1999; Levy 2012).

5 **Political sociology and the theory of elites**: Mosca, Pareto (who admired Proudhon), and Weber's wayward student, Michels (who dabbled in anarchism and syndicalism during his Italian 'exile'), relied heavily on arguments propounded by anarchist and syndicalist contemporaries to craft their deeply pessimistic and jaundiced accounts of parliamentary democracy and mass politics (Nomad 1959: 9–17; Nomad 1961: 10; Levy 1987/2017a; Williams 2013: 8–9). In terms of modern American political science the prevalent pessimistic account of representative democracy was recast in the neutral sounding language of neo-Schumpeterian formulations, yet the problems of possessive individualism and the answers supplied by social anarchism, gave birth to a creative tension in the works of Philip Slater, Christopher Lasch and certainly Benjamin Barber, who anticipated the possibilities of new technology (today the Web and social media, with dubious effects he did not foresee) creating instant feedback and debate by a well-informed citizenry, solving the dilemmas posed by the elitists (Bouchier 1996: 122).

6 **Pragmatism** (Pereira 2009): To recall, C. Wright Mills had great sympathies for the anarchists and the IWW, but so too did his intellectual lodestars: William James, Thorstein Veblen, and John Dewey (Levy Forthcoming a) were also rather sympathetic to anarchist and syndicalist ways of seeing and it might be argued that post-1945–1968 Anglo-American intellectual anarchism is an off-shoot of Pragmatism[6] and even the New Anarchism of our century maintains the tradition. David Graeber self-identifies as a 'Hercalitean social scientist' in which objects are defined as processes and their potentials and society are constituted primarily by actions.[7]

7 **Neo-elitism and New Class Theory**: C. Wright Mills returned to elite theory, viewed through his 'goddam' anarchist squint, in his dissection of the emergent and then rampant US corporate liberal welfare/warfare state (Levy Forthcoming a). New Class theories related totalitarian critiques of State Communism to American concepts of the managerial revolution: Daniel Bell, Lewis Coser and Harold Lasswell were very close to anarchist mavericks such as the self-taught Max Nomad (Max Nacht) (Borgognone 2000) and the small semi-Trotskyist/semi-anarchist intellectual reviews of the 1940s. In this regard, Dwight MacDonald's ventures stand out: the first drafts of C. Wright Mills' *The Power Elite* appeared as 'Powerless People' in 1944 in *politics*, as do the first inklings of Paul Goodman's *Growing up Absurd* (Wreszin 1994: 133–135; Sumner 1996: 18–20, 115–116). They all were intrigued by the semi-anarchist Jan Wacław Machajski (Nomad 1959: 96–117) and his early formulations of social and cultural capital, which could easily be connected to the pivotal concept of bureaucratic collectivism (refined by Bruno Rizzi and James Burnham) (Rizzi 1985), that in any case was foreshadowed by Bakunin's nineteenth-century critique of Marx's concept of the 'dictatorship of the proletariat' and the position of the 'savants' in the revolution: 'There will be a new class, a new hierarchy of real and pretended scientists and scholars and the world will be divided between a minority ruling in the name of knowledge and the immense ignorant minority' (*The Knouto-Germanic Empire and the Social Revolution*, quoted from Szelenyi and

Martin 1988: 646) (also see, Berti 1976; Levy 1987/2017b). This notion was revisited in Alvin Gouldner's dissection of the New Class of the late twentieth century in the 1980s and his Janus-faced 'culture of critical discourse' (CCD) (when is it the CCD of the New Mandarins and when is it the CCD of Noam Chomsky, their anarchist critic?) (Gouldner 1979). In short, this was a reworking of Max Nomad and Harold Lasswell's earlier '"symbol specialists", whose primary capital is their knowledge' (Pels 1998: 283). Noam Chomsky noted the connections between a co-optation by Daniel Bell in his notion of the 'Post-industrial Society' and John Kenneth Galbraith's analysis of the managers of neo-capitalism's technostructures, but he concluded that they did not hold power but in a Gramscian fashion were experts at legitimation:[8] 'The well-bred intelligentsia operates the pump-handle, conducting mass mobilization in a way that is, as Lasswell observed, cheaper than violence or bribery and much better suited to the image of democracy' (Chomsky 1982: 413).

8 **Green Radical Thought** (Price 2018): Although anarchist contributions are brimming with mutually hostile viewpoints – primitivism, Deep Green Anarchism, and Murray Bookchin's social anarchism (Price 2012; Biehl 2015) – the net result for theory and policy were new approaches through the linkages between ecological degradation, technology, capitalism, and the state, highlighting the failures of Marxist theory and practice to address these new issues; detailed if conflicting readings of the emergence of hierarchy and domination since the Neolithic Period and the irrational nature of the modern city, proposing remedies that have been partially embraced by others who are far from being anarchists (Environmentalism, Decentralization, Greening Cities, Sustainable Development, Post Scarcity Anarchism watered down to arguments over Citizen's Income) (Cornell 2016: 295–296).

9 **Second and Third Wave Feminisms**: Sources of inspiration for the more radical Second Wave Feminists included Emma Goldman, Voltarine de Cleyre, Marie Louise Berneri, and others who inspired new reflections on the female body, the nuclear family, new method of child care, economic self-determination, male authority, the liberation from oppressive emotional relationships, and the re-invention of everyday life. The Second Wave Feminists who adapted the older anarchist model of affinity groups for consciousness raising groups in turn fed into arguments about democratic grassroots decision-making and rumination over the 'tyranny of structurelessness' and the 'tyranny of tyranny', given new life in the context of the governance of Square movements more recently (Cornell 2016: 285; Kowal 2018; Nicholas 2018).

10 **Intersectionality**: Anarchists believe that domination is produced through institutions, inter-personal relations and 'situational rituals' (Shantz and Williams 2014: 121). Intersectionality and the concept of a matrix of domination overlaps with anarchism, although Patricia Hill-Collins and Kimberlé Crenshaw did not mention it directly: this has only been noted in the past decade (Dupuis-Déri 2016; Lazar 2018) and is discussed by Sandra Jeppesen in her chapter.

11 **Prefiguration, participatory democracy and the new/newest social movements**: The widespread and somewhat loosely defined uses of the concepts of prefiguration and consensual/participatory democracy (Yates 2015; Franks 2018; Gordon 2018)[9] are joined at the hip with the emergence of the methodologies to study the new and newest social movements (the former in dialogue with the state and the latter dispensing with making demands to, or engaging with, the state) (Williams and Lee 2012). In Europe sociologists such as Habermas, Touraine, Offe, and Melucci,

noted that the New Social Movements of the 1960s and 1970s 'were anti-hierarchal, self-organising and pursued non-instrumental goals that were limited to politicised lifestyles and so-called "post-material" values', and may have posed a symbolic challenge to authority but withered away or produced elite groups that detached from the movements which spawned them, but they did not point to certain resemblances to previous anarchist movements (Purkis 2004: 44). In the United States, where Resource Mobilization and Political Opportunity Structures approaches predominated, Frances Fox Piven and Richard Cloward (1977) used tropes taken from anarchism to explain how poor people's movements failed in the US because well-meaning campaigning groups transformed their rank and file into clients instead of maintaining their activism. More recently, as previously noted, students of the newest social movements (Day 2005) argue that variations on the theme of co-research-based ethnography serve concurrently as templates for the form of consensual participatory democracy revealed in their accounts of the Global Justice Movement or Occupy. Thus Chris Dixon's ethnographies of the movements of 'reconfigured anarchism' are presented as debriefings of comrades, encased in 'acceptable' academic protocols (Dixon 2014: 15). 'The anarchist researcher', Uri Gordon argues, 'is not the participant observer but the participating observer'. She is not joining 'the anarchist milieu periodically for research "among the natives" but an insider and native to this environment'. Thus the researcher is more an organizer 'with a process of collaboration and dialogue which empowers, motivates, increases self-esteem and develops solidarity among those taking part' (Gordon 2012: 86–87). So, as I mentioned previously in discussing Weber's concept of *verstehen*, rather 'than "objectivity" guaranteeing accurate research results, it is *emotional subjectivity* that makes good research' (Ferrell 2009: 80). Others are more sceptical and wary of the power position of the 'anarchist' ethnographer, a theme returned to in the concluding chapter. However, to complete the circle, Dana Williams examines openly declared anarchist movements which work in or in parallel to the larger anarchistic movements (the Newest Social Movements such as Occupy etc.), in which he uses the tools of the first wave social movement researchers (political opportunity structures, social capital, etc.) to reflect back on his subject, the anarchists (Williams 2017).

12 **Social capital**: Another exercise in circular influence brings us to a discussion of origins of the term 'social capital' itself. One of its foremost proponents, Robert Putnam, derived his version from his regional comparisons of the efficiency of public services in Italy, pointing to the medieval roots of trust in the communal civilizations of the North in contrast to the lack of trust and the weak history of communal civilization in the *Mezzogiorno*, which in turn reflected ideas advanced in Kropotkin's *Mutual Aid* and his other works in which the communal civilization of late medieval Europe, and particularly the city-states of Italy, were a source of inspiration (Putnam 1993). A recent study concludes: 'Influenced by the Russian anarchist, Putnam came to the conclusion that cooperation and mutual aid were more important for the development and progress of democratic societies than competition …', and the author, during her post-graduate work, was urged by Putnam to read Kropotkin (Rovná 2013: 55). In a more recent work, *Bowling Alone*, Putnam's concept of the social bonding of bridging social capital (which sadly, he argued, Americans were losing) originated from his reading of the American anarchist, Paul Goodman (Putnam 2000; Rovná 2013: 55; Williams 2015: 21–22).

13 **Transnational labour history**: Yet again, in a similar circular fashion, recent histories of global anarchism and syndicalism set in the era of classical anarchism (1840s to 1940s) (van der Walt and Schmidt 2009; Hirsch and van der Walt 2010) and earlier studies of the secret 'hydrarchy' of the cosmopolitan, antinomian democracy of the Atlantic world of pirate and maroon republics in the eighteenth century, were inspired by or fed into the network analyses of the Global Justice Movement and Occupy/Arab Spring, which have been invoked simultaneously as methodologies and suggested political strategies by several historians and social scientists (Linebaugh and Rediker 2000; Levy 2011; Bantman and Altena 2015). Thus Andrej Grubačić and Denis O'Hearn (2016) apply mutual aid as an 'explanatory and conceptual tool' (248) to understand the role of exilic spaces, which existed before their incorporation into the capitalist world order, thus paralleling the research agenda set by Peter Linebaugh and Marcus Rediker, and more clearly James Scott's (2009) study of Zomia, who investigates the anarchic spaces of upland Southeast Asia. In their case studies of the Zapatistas, the Cossacks and Prison Solidarity movements Grubačić and O'Hearn (2016: 249–250) demonstrate how cooperative exilic practices and direct democracy prevent recapture by the state. Anticipating some of the arguments of Zaheer Kazmi in this volume, but in a different context, they conclude that the politics of world systems theory cannot be reduced to a game of states struggling for power but must include anti-systemic social movements as part of this global 'anarchy'.

14 **Network analysis, chaos and complexity theories**: Network analysis was previously used by the 'anarchist sociologists' of the 1960s and this 'networked anarchy' has been rediscovered quite recently by students of social administration (Wachhaus 2011). Thus Colin Ward defined the anarchic type of organization as voluntary, functional, temporary, and small (Graham 2013). Ward joined this functional theory of organization to a theory of spontaneous order which he claimed could be found in then fashionable theory of cybernetics (Duda 2013), that anticipated the structure of the worldwide-web of the internet (and originally funded as ARPAnet by the US government, to strengthen communications of command and control after a nuclear strike). Thus Ward summarized his arguments in which functional organizations were networked in evolving self-organizing systems:

> Here we have a system of large variety, sufficient to cope with a complex, unpredictable environment. Its characteristics are changing structure, modifying itself under the continual feedback from the environment, exhibiting redundancy of potential command, and involving complex interlocking control structures. Learning and decision-making are distributed throughout the system, denser perhaps in some areas than in others.
>
> (quoted in Graham 2009: 369)

15 In the context of the warfare state the advances in computer sciences, feedback control, and information and systems theory, and within cybernetics, the themes of unpredictability, adaptive systems, and the construction of human/machine/network interfaces, were used to erect a system of Mutually Assured Destruction (MAD) but were concurrently reinterpreted by anarchist writers as models or at least inspirations for self-management. Cybernation, they thought, was a way to replace the distribution of goods and services carried out through the decentralized

capitalist wages/market system, and thereby refute Hayek's criticism of planning (Duda 2013: 68). But within the reconfigured or new anarchism of the newest social movements after the Cold War, cybernation, arising from the imperatives of MAD, seemed an anachronism. These anarchist theorists of the newest anarchism embraced chaos and complexity theories. Thus, reality is understood through non-linearity and non-determining patterns that 'make reductionist scientific explanations impossible', even the ordered patterns of cybernetic networks. In this context Green Anarchism, but even anarchist approaches to International Relations, embraced 'trendy scientific concepts such as complexity, diversity, emergence and self-assembly' (Purkis 2004: 52). Just as anarchist usages of the concepts of 'mutual aid' or 'cybernation' allowed for anarchism to gain some semblance of respectability amongst the mainstream of the humanities and social sciences, so too more recent concepts served as passports from the forbidden world of anarchy and anarchism to a tolerated seat at the academic conversation. But so too do we see a return to the strange coupling of anarchists and the warfare state. After the decline of the Soviet foe, the Rand Corporation (birthplace of MAD) expressed great interest in the international Zapatista network (Ronfeldt and Arquilla 1999), and the swarming techniques of the Black Bloc at Seattle in 1999 (Chesters and Welsh 2006; Thorpe and Welsh 2008), arguing for their adaption and co-optation into anti-insurgency low intensity warfare at the dawn of the Age of Terror; applications suited to miniaturized drone warfare rapidly arose as the technology became available. This odd coupling is also apparent in the rise of the Squares movements. The Serbian Otpor! Movement, which overthrew the Milošević regime and the 'colour revolutions' of the early 2000s, used the non-violent techniques of direct action pacifism, facilitated by the US State Department. 'But the real irony', David Graeber notes,

is that it was these techniques, pioneered by the Global Justice Movement, and successfully spread across the world by the CIA and American-aided groups, that in turn inspired movements that overthrew American client states. It's a sign of the power of democratic direct action tactics that once they are let loose into the world, they become uncontrollable.

(Graeber 2013: 120)[10]

16 **Altruism**: The anarchist imagination has also lurked in the background and foreground of the search for a socio-biological basis for altruism, the basis of mutual aid in Kropotkin's form of anarcho-communism, which curiously also had its Cold War and anarchist linkages. This is a complicated discussion which involves the role of neuro-genetic biology, contending schools of anthropology, game theory, and mathematic modelling, and I will return to this in the conclusion to this volume.

17 **Analyses of ideology**: In my work on social histories of anarchism and cosmopolitanism, I have attempted to understand the difference between anarchism as ideology of a distinct time and place and pre-state forms of state-less social power and conviviality (Levy 2010). Given the fact that anarchist movements were less successful at maintaining bureaucratic continuities and official mouthpieces for the evolution of ideology, more capacious tools of ideological analysis have been employed to capture meaning, most notably, Michael Freeden's notion of core and peripheral elements in ideologies or Quentin Skinner's notion of contextual readings of ideologies and ideas, have helped the explication of the historical movement

(anarchism) fit into the larger cultural and social meanings in a given historical period, rather than remain an odd marginal, irrational, and ahistorical exception (Kinna and Evren 2013; Adams and Jun 2015; Franks, Jun and Williams 2018). Thus, the study of anarchist ideology allows us to re-examine the first principles of the study of the history of ideas more generally, in short, to differentiate between core and adjacent aspects of any given ideology, to map with care intersecting attitudes, beliefs, and opinions without succumbing to anachronisms: all ideologies may possess more similar qualities like 'illusive and liminal anarchism' than the mainstream of Political Science and the History of Ideas have allowed.

18 **Postcolonialism**: In this respect anarchism also shares parallel and intersecting paths with varieties of postcolonial thought (also see Maia Ramnath in this volume): liminal and border-thinking; the different methodologies and epistemologies of the Global South, which until relatively recently have shared a similar fate in academic life to that of the 'irrationalities' of anarchism and its traditions. Whereas the lack of a central authority or hegemonic structure within anarchism may have posed a problem for the social sciences in the past, one could argue that with the hollowing of political institutions and the shifts in political culture witnessed over the past thirty years, the postmodern condition, the qualities of anarchism as movement and ideology, offer much to ponder.

19 **Social history**: Having already mentioned the entangled relationship between the naming of the Newest Social Movements of the post-1989 era and their chroniclers and theoretician-advocates, there is a similar if more guarded relationship between the academic and her subject in the study of subalterns, starting in the 1950s with the pioneering work of Eric Hobsbawm, E. P. Thompson, and (slightly later) in the 1960s by Howard Zinn, expanding rapidly with the rise of new social and feminist histories after '1968' (Levy Forthcoming b). But until recently little has been said in systematic fashion about the role of anarchism as subject and catalyst for the evolution of concepts/methodology in social history. Thompson is an interesting case, as his engagement with William Morris, William Blake, and dissenting sects saw the erstwhile Stalinist 'go native' as he embraced his 'inner antinomian' and by the end of his life declared himself a Muggletonian Marxist (Goodway 2006: 279). James Scott marries an anarchist sensibility with the Marxian and Gramscian approaches of these social historians, so approaches the subject back to front. In his political sociological accounts of peasants, Scott advanced the concept of 'infra-politics': resistance to the state which ignores established politics and the ruling establishment through 'theft, pilfering, feigned ignorance, shirking or careless labor, foot dragging...' (Scott 1990: 188) and 'hidden transcripts': 'the infra-political equivalents of public, radical counterideologies' (Scott 1990: 199). In short, in Scott's works we witness a modification of the Marxist take on the role of subaltern, derived from Gramsci or even Hobsbawm and Thompson, but read through an 'anarchist squint' (Scott 2012: xvii). Here, too, Scott offers another anarchistic-like concept, which relies more on the instruments of domination rather than the dialectics of historical materialism: 'legibility'. Through his critique of high modernist schemes – Haussmann's urban plan for Paris, Russian collectivization, the Great Leap Forward in China, and villagization in Tanzania – legibility is the polar opposite to infrapolitics: it sweeps away the 'ordered disorder' of the 'vernacular city or the variegated rural landscape and imposes a sterile societal monoculture' (Scott 2012: 41). Scott celebrates *mētis*: a form of local, implicit

knowledge 'that can be acquired only by long practice at similar but rarely identical tasks, which requires constant adaptations to changing circumstance' (Scott 1990: 177–178). His quest is for *mētis*- friendly institutions, the sort of quest which the post-1945 anarchist intellectuals (Paul Goodman, Colin Ward, etc.) sought to discover and promote (Shantz 2014). Here, too, the story is one of entanglement. For Scott, the anarchists understood with greater sensitivity than more structurally and bureaucratically freighted ideologists and functional sociologists the moments of madness which make certain historical conjunctures revolutionary: radical uncertainty allowed the authoritarian Bolsheviks to seize their moment in 1917; it was their post-hoc narrative account, which 'eliminated all the contingency, variety, and cross purposes of the real revolution' (Scott 2012: 141) and consigned the anarchists to the memory hole.

Overview of contributors' chapters

Mohammed Bamyeh's, 'The Two Anarchies: The Arab Uprisings and the Question of an Anarchist Sociology', invokes the concept of an 'organic anarchy' to understand the mobilization, in other words, practices in everyday life, which anticipate self-conscious anarchism, without having any direct linkage to it. The method of revolt, a form of spontaneous networking, with minimal organization, the absence of hierarchical guidance and structures with the predominance of local initiative, pointed to anarchistic undercurrents. Rather than the saviour leader or ideologically charged parties, the Mubarak regime was overthrown in a short period of time. In his chapter, Bamyeh differentiates between self-conscious anarchism and organic anarchy by developing a sociology of the Egyptian revolt, which can be applied more broadly to the concurrent Square and Occupy movements in Europe and North America, but the binaries he explores were rather unique to the Egyptian or Arab contexts rather than the Global North and, I believe, have interesting parallels with the work of Asef Bayat (2017) on social 'nonmovements', the subaltern city populace and liminality of Tahrir Square, where briefly, the invisible infrastructural life of the vernacular city compelled the tired post-Nasserite elites to carry out a 'refolution', a revolutionary moment which is restricted to meaningful reforms. Another student of revolution in the Middle East, John Chalcraft (2016) (like Bamyeh), sees the failed movements, as stepping stones to future libertarian hegemonic coalitions of the subaltern 'Street', youth, women, and workers, better able to cope with the Army and the Muslim Brotherhood, by building on the 'untimely mobilizations' of 2011–2013, and presenting an unique offer of participatory democracy founded on social justice.

Zaheer Kazmi's chapter, 'Contesting the State of Nature: Anarchism and International Relations', uses concepts derived from anarchism to challenge the hegemonic term 'anarchy', present in International Relations without endorsing anarchism as ideology. Kazmi is an exemplar of the academic who sees anarchism as a useful non-ideologically loaded catalyst to promote a new paradigm in his/her discipline. Thus he wants to explore anarchism's neglected relevance to International Relations without endorsing the ideology known as anarchism. Thus he takes issue with the new field of Anarchist Studies and more specifically committed anarchist interventions in the field of International Relations. He contends that the leading lights of an Anarchist Studies approach to International Relations (Prichard 2012) are inconsistent, their much vaunted praxis is a recycled and unexamined hagiography of key figures and historical moments in anarchism. In short, Kazmi seeks to interrogate the key concept 'anarchy' in International Relations, invoking a sort of epistemological anarchist methodology, reminiscent, it seems to me, of Feyerabend's sociology of modern science.

In 'Anarchism and Critical Security Studies', Chris Rossdale argues that anarchism can be employed as a radical take of Critical Security Studies itself in interesting and new directions. Thus, like the denizens of Critical Security Studies, the anarchists would argue that the state today is more likely than not the source of insecurity and that naming of threats (terrorism, piracy, illegal migration, and illegitimate social movements), as defined by state fiat, can be redefined with effortless and shocking rapidity (Sartwell 2008; Lindsey 2013). Rossdale suggests that anarchist takes on Critical Security Studies which stress new forms of security founded on the trust of mutual aid rather than the reformed state which manages a 'risk society' may have much to offer.

In 'Postanarchism Today: Anarchism and Political Theory', Saul Newman aligns postanarchism and anarchism, as a renegotiation of anarchism not the transcendence of the anarchist project. This involves a poststructuralist form of anarchism which repudiates what he considers the naïve positivist assumptions of the classical anarchist canon and incorporation from the works of Foucault, Deleuze, and Guattari into a reordered anarchism, which resists unification, totalization, and dogmatism and praises contingency, discontinuity, fluidity, hybridity, and pluralism. But Newman's postanarchism is not a byword for reactionary nihilism, he has no objections to the libertarian, self-critical horizons of the Enlightenment itself: the amoral politics of Carl Schmitt are countered by an unusual melding of Levinas and Stirner: the purged 'singularity', his reading of 'untimely mobilizations' as ethically charged insurrections not traditional revolutions (a theme pursued earlier and throughout this volume) is capable of banishing the false idols of humanism and rationalism. Unlike the dialogical approach of militant ethnographers like David Graeber, Newman's intervention is located purely in the academic world within political theory and political science, albeit his theory draws inspiration and confirmation from events in the street and the square. The aim or condition of these insurrections is an ethical politics not an anti-politics as in recent forms of populism, a condition of autonomy, not postrevolution state sovereignty. Thus Newman claims that postanarchism provides the terrain for a form of political theory that addresses the condition of non-sovereignty and challenges Political Theory's obsession with sovereignty, and in light of the rise of Trump's and cognate worldviews this could not be more relevant.

The focus of Ruth Kinna's chapter, 'Anarchism and Political Science: History and Anti-Science in Radical Thought', is Anglo-American Political Science, and the legitimation of established power relations in the context of anarchist engagement with the emergence of the academic field in the nineteenth and twentieth centuries. Kinna contends that difference about the scope, application, and character of the scientific method complicates the engagement of anarchism. In other words, some of the themes found in Newman's chapter are replicated here but with strikingly different contexts and first premises. Anglo-American Political Science or Politics and Political Studies have had to address the question of its scientific basis, the role of theory and the guiding principles of *realpolitik* (hearkening back to Kazmi's earlier discussion of the overwhelming importance of the concept of 'anarchy' in International Relations). In the inter-war period (reaffirmed by the ensuing Cold War standoff), Anglo-American Political Science sought to differentiate itself from the practices of naked politics and political calculation to see off the challenge of Fascism, its vitalism, and its 'bad' wild ontology (Carl Schmitt, for example), which while in the previous chapter Newman prescribed doses of ethical self-fashioning, the emergent discipline advanced an empirical, non-ideological project linked to the expansion of higher education emphasizing practice-based problem solving within a mixed economy welfare state located in ideologically 'cool' elitist and anti-communist democracies. Kinna engages C. Wright Mills and Peter Kropotkin as her foils. C. Wright Mills sought to merge grand theory and abstracted empiricism, so as to make the personal problem a public and universal problem to help individuals understand their lives. It was a form of autonomy via radical pragmatism, it was found in the practice of urban studies and political sociology in Cold War mavericks such as Jane Jacobs and Richard Sennett, both 'musically' anarchist, or in the 'utopian sociology' of the anarchist Colin Ward.

Kinna presents Kropotkin as a purveyor of epistemological anarchism but rather different than Newman's variety, because the Russian anarchist sought to marry grand theory and empiricism via the inductive-deductive method without relying on Hegelian-Marxist teleology. Thus both Wright Mills and Kropotkin were not anti-science but endorsed the need for a properly constructed methodology in the social sciences. In today's world, Kinna concludes, we are placed in a dilemma; the hottest topics in Political Science are ones dear to the anarchist heart: the newest social movements, participatory democracy, transnational networking, and the nexus of sexuality, gender, and power. If anarchism is proclaimed as an ethics and shuns social scientific methodologies, if it does not offer its own theory of power ('power-with', 'followership', etc.) or in fact refuses to constitutionalize[11] the anarchic practices of the anarchic experiments (encampments, squares, etc.), because this would be 'blue-printing utopia', its chance for relevance will pass it by (Clark 2013: 278; Wilson 2014).

Sandra Jeppesen's chapter, 'Toward an Anarchist-Feminist Analytics of Power', continues the theme of anarchism's encounters with the key issues of Political Theory and Political Science previously discussed in Newman and Kinna's respective contributions. Anarchist-feminists (Jeppesen chooses the formulation anarchist-feminist rather than anarcha-feminist), she argues, have been in the forefront of redefining the parameters of understanding power and oppression, and like the postanarchists, anarchist-feminists have a capacious notion of power including the role of personal power within activist groups themselves, the destabilizing of gender hierarchies, and the root and branch deconstruction of the public-private divide. From the era of classical anarchism to the present, anarchist-feminists have interrogated the politics of marriage, birth control, free love, polyamory, sexual assault, sexual consent and accountability, sex work, trans-inclusion, self-care, mental health, the role of binary sexuality, and the state (the fluidity of sexual identities in the law, the role of the state in coercive gendering, gender assignment, and intentional families (Daring, Rogue, Shannon and Volcano 2012)). Many of these topics, themes, and causes, having begun their lives in the lively sphere of anarchist-feminist politics, became, and increasingly rapidly, mainstream politics. Equally, the anarchist-feminist approach to power has influenced wider discussions. Thus the rich legacy and current activities of anarchist-feminists are perhaps one of the most important influences anarchism has exercised on the humanities and social sciences, hence answering Kinna's plea for relevance.

Vishwam Jamie Heckert's chapter on 'Loving Politics: On the Art of Living Together' discusses a loving politics, the role of politics as a relationship rather than a tactic, a theme which has been broached in Newman's and Jeppesen's chapters and which we revisit in Judith Suissa's chapter on education, philosophy, and anarchism. Central to all forms of anarchism is the autonomous, social and cooperative individual. For Heckert, loving politics is the nurturing of the capacity to love, which brings to mind the 'beloved community' of the anarchist-influenced strands of the civil rights movement in the American South (Polletta 2002), the politics of 'saying no', the militant pacifist anarchist politics of the twentieth century (Cornell 2016), or the affective politics of liminal anti-imperialism in late Victorian London, which merged support for Indian freedom, vegetarianism, Theosophy, sexuality, and anarchism within friendship circles (Gandhi 2006). Anarchist loving politics offers something other than the politics of representation, normativity, and self-policing. Heckert's approach is similar to the realistic utopias of Ursula Le Guin, which tackle jealousy, deceit, and rigidly defined gender expectations, they are not merely presented as simple 'add-ons' to her stories but central to understanding how authoritarian power is resisted or nullified (Davis 2005: 3–36). Heckert wishes to open up this 'loving politics' beyond the rather rigid but necessary formulations of intersectionality, thus he is interested in 'the diverse ways in which anarchism can be opened up by moving from an emphasis on sameness and identity to a recognition of diversity of oppression, contexts, methods and voices' (p. xx). But Heckert's open-ended living politics, employing yoga, meditation, and biodanza, is a useful check on anarchist lifestyles becoming ends in themselves in order to avoid a puritanism of prefigured ethical living in which lifestyle choices (vegetarianism, housing arrangements, clothing, etc.) become boundaries and forms of social closure (Portwood-Stacer 2013; Lagalisse 2017). Heckert's approach, his 'loving politics', is a variation on the theme of ontological anarchism expressed by several authors in this volume.

In 'Black Flag Mapping: Emerging Themes in Anarchist Geography', Anthony Ince outlines the rich and evolving field of anarchist geography. In a similar fashion to sociological and anthropological ethnographies of the Global Justice Movement, urban squatting and anti-roads protests and later Occupy movements, twenty-first-century anarchist geography conceptualized space via networked and rhizomatic patterns of autonomy. While anarchist geographers have been in the forefront of resurrecting the legacies of Kropotkin and Reclus, they also engaged in a broader literature on deregulation and the neo-liberal erosion of public control of urban and rural space (Springer 2016; Ferretti, Barrera de la Torre, Ince and Toro, 2017; Ferretti 2018). The new anarchist geography offers a unique take on the battle against new forms of enclosure refreshed by discussion of older forms of enclosure and thus is linked to the growing literature on commons and communing, and forms, past and present, of exilic space (Ince and Barrera de la Torre 2016; Grubačić and O'Hearn 2016). In our era of mass migration, contested notions of citizenship, and politics of bordering, anarchist geography, Ince argues, is at the heart of key debates in geography and politics more generally (Levy 2018).

Maia Ramnath's 'In Dialogue: Anarchism and Postcolonialism' examines the complex interaction between the two. She is a friendly critic of postcolonialism seeking to free it from increasingly opaque epistemological disputes by applying some anarchist common sense. Usefully, she argues that postcolonialism should be considered an analysis whereas anti-colonialism is an orientation and ethic. She suggests a revisiting of an earlier generation of 'independence intellectuals' who mixed the explication of 'Othering' with elements of Marxist anti-imperialist thought, and who mixed the modernism of Gramsci with the literary poststructuralism of Edward Said. Ramnath argues that new forms of anarchism can bridge the gap between this generation and the academic postcolonialism of the late twentieth and early twenty-first centuries. Anarchism has affinities to postcolonialism, in their joint suspicion of nationalism, the need to break the model of the postcolonial state, the mutual attraction to cultural hybridity and the liminality of nomadic zones of diaspora. All types of anarchists are attracted to travellers and exile, escaping the mind-space of state and capital. They both share the previously mentioned antinomian geographical imaginary, of histories of transnational syndicalism, marronage, and the 'lines of flight' of Deleuze and Guattari, or the political ethnographies of the 'shatter-zones' of James Scott and others. Ramnath see the merging of anarchist and postcolonial themes in a 'decolonized planetarity' which in this writer brings to mind the 'planetary humanism' of Paul Gilroy (2004) or the transcendence of identity politics in the previously mentioned work of Leela Gandhi (2006), whose open-ended friendship model, discussed in reference of Heckert's chapter, was neither based on social closure nor a form of reverse 'Othering'. But self-reflective accounts of post-colonial and anarchist politics and methodologies also reveal weaknesses in each. In the latter, the theorists of subalternity have become remote from the subaltern, while in the former, the Global Justice Movement (Olesen 2005) and Occupy skated over glaring problems of white privilege and heteronormative unspoken assumptions (Gemie 2012 for early formulation of the bigger picture; Pedroso 2016). So just as postcolonialism needs to rediscover the urgency of the independence intellectuals, the long history of anarchism as the suppressed alternative of modernity needs to be recalled but also critically interrogated. Ramnath ends her chapter by pleading for a joint struggle against the racially inflected 'sovereigntist' populism of the Global North and ersatz traditionalism and ethnic triumphalism in the Global South, for a new formulation of the social sciences, a 'New Humanities', urged on by the vision of a utopian postcoloniality.[12]

In 'What is Law?' Elena Loizidou examines the relationship between law and anarchism. Just as the anarchists questioned a world of states and thus posed essential questions in the fields of International Relations and Political Science, the questioning of statist jurisprudence and the attendant institutions (courts, prisons, and police forces) have been central to anarchist interventions in the field of Criminology. Just as Rossdale used anarchism to question the radical nature of Critical Security Studies, Loizidou uses anarchism to interrogate the critical but non-anarchist jurisprudence, which still holds that the law is a necessary prerequisite for freedom. The anarchists see this as beside the point. Loizidou invokes Nietzsche as she proclaims that the anarchists pose the question how shall man (*sic*) overcome? In other words, how shall humans organize life outside legal norms and restrictions? Or to put it another way, how can we live ethical lives outside the law? Loizidou discusses the interventions of Emma Goldman and Peter Kropotkin. Goldman argues that anarchists do not want the just application of law, which would only reveal the insolvable contradictions, inconsistencies, and exclusions, which are inherent in any system of statist jurisprudence. Similarly Kropotkin thought that law was useless and hurtful, whereas customs, habits, and usages, which preceded the state and still persist in daily life outside the reach of the state, are clues to the anarchist way of living. The legal form of life, the anarchists argue is merely protection for private property and state, but many anarchists, most tellingly Proudhon, depart from this rather Marxist reading, because anarchist ethics embodied in equal-liberty means that the concepts of justice and transparency are things in themselves, not merely epiphenomena of the class structure of a given society. Anarchists, Loizidou argues, seek self-mastery not subjugation to the law, an art of living in which human beings solve everyday problems themselves, that untheorized anarchism which Colin Ward or James Scott seek to reveal in everyday life. Loizidou is invoking concepts that are present in Bamyeh's interpretation of anarchistic practices, Newman's communities of ethical singularities and Heckert's 'art of living'. But within the realist strand of the anarchist tradition, the assertion that 'man [sic] had overcome' was simply not enough, in Barcelona in 1936 or an encampment in 2011, the language games the anarchists may invoke to rename or just reinvent the 'State', the 'Law', and the 'Police', did not solve existential problems at hand, and Errico Malatesta, for one, retained a sense of self-awareness which essentially meant that in practice 'full' anarchy was a slow and gradual, multi-generational process of learning 'lawless etiquette' (Levy 2017: 91–92).

Learning a 'lawless etiquette' explains why education and educationalism were and are central for anarchist activists and thinkers alike. In 'Anarchism and Education Studies', Judith Suissa examines how anarchist pedagogy interacts with the academic discipline, Educational Studies, applying the sub-field of the Philosophy of Education as her critical lens. But to her dismay, today philosophers and theorists of education have become sparse due to the general hostility to intellectual enquiry and a distorted form of pragmatism, certainly not John Dewey's earlier anarchist friendly Pragmatism, but a mindless search for 'what works'. Thus the emphasis is on teacher training and the formal institutional setting of schooling. It is assumed that students are customers, education is commodity and processes are understood through markets and market behaviour. Thus today critical academics and teachers defend the vanishing state school model and attack the agenda of the market-makers, who in their more extreme formulations approximate libertarian capitalists. In a similar manner to Loizidou's discussion of the law, Suissa argues that the aim of posing anarchist challenges is to see if educational practice is morally and politically defensible. Thus the very concept of the educational system should be questioned because 'mainstream' critical philosophers of education do not depart very far from a Rawlsian framework.

In a climate that proclaims that there is no alternative to the market, the audit, and the performance, Suissa's take on the anarchist imagination is a useful corrective. She is not defending anarchism as an ideology *per se* but as goad to force us to think outside of the box. Education should not be 'system' but form part of a normative, ethical project for transforming the lives of individuals and society. She disavows the 'free schools' of Coalition and Conservative UK government policy in the 2010s, she is not for a marriage of audit culture, state centralism, and free-market individualism, but she is closer to Paul Goodman's invocation of community of scholars, teachers, and children beyond institutional walls and disciplinary boundaries, perhaps Ivan Illich's convivial learning webs (Suissa 2010: 76–77), in which children learn and adults and children rediscover the art of living, or Colin Ward's form of educational practice, that harnessed and melded children's urban and rural geographical imaginations (Burke and Jones 2014).

In 'Anarchism and Religious Studies', Alexandre Christoyannopoulos engages in multiple conversations necessary to address a vast array of encounters: anarchists revisiting their assessment of religions and/or how specific anarchists approached religion, religious scholars articulating a theology, which engages with anarchism, and also how religious scriptures have been interpreted to point to an anarchist politics. In other words, Christoyannopoulos engages in ontological, epistemological, and methodological approaches. This chapter sketches out how anarchism and Religious Studies intersect and influence each other's imaginations.

Art and anarchism has been a much studied subject. There has been significant work on the relationship between schools of art, styles of art, and the sociological and urban geographies of bohemia and wave of art innovation in Paris, London, Milan, New York, Moscow, Barcelona, and elsewhere. In his chapter 'Aesthetics of Tension', Allan Antliff takes another tack, in which he examines the integral part played by aesthetics in anarchism's politics (also see Antliff 2017). In this regard, he does not divide, as some have done, the success of modernist aesthetics from a failed anarchist politics, nor does he argue that anarchism (as some suggest of Fascism) is a politics of aesthetics and style (also see Leighten 2013). Nor does he propose Jesse Cohn's model in which the self-educated cultures of artisan and peasant anarchism and the anarchism of the avant-gardes are severed by the rise of a class-based mass direct action syndicalism well before the First World War and in a paradoxical fashion a newly revived but less working-class New Anarchism of the 1940s and 1950s borrowed styles developed by the previous and now defunct first anarchist bohemia of the late nineteenth and early twentieth centuries (Cohn 2014: 381–382).

For much of the nineteenth and twentieth centuries, Antliff argues, artworks were adjudicated formally and in splendid isolation. But since then, artwork has grown increasingly conceptual and performance-based. Conceptual art is invested with meaning in situational and relational contexts rather than as an isolated art object as such. This is where anarchism enters today: it is the form of becoming, a passionate attraction, therefore aesthetics are an integral part of anarchism's politics. Antliff's chapter is about the aesthetics of tension within contemporary art production, namely the tension involved between self-actualization and transformative modalities, in the same way that Suissa's utopian anarchist philosophy of education presumes that the first premises of the 'educational system' will no longer apply, or as Loizidou argues, the law will be replaced by the practice of speaking freely. Creativity, as Herbert Read argued, 'is interwoven into everyday life, this grants it a unique epistemological status' (Adams 2015: 90). Through a series of conceptual art works in Canada and elsewhere, Antliff teases out the aesthetics of tension. He concludes that it is a constituent part of the inner life of an artwork to serve as a source of social transformation, but it is open to be applied in a myriad of ways. It is autonomous but at the same time intimately connected with the artist's creative agency. The tension encapsulates both a critique of present capitalist-statist reality with a form of prefiguration. The aesthetics of tension is thus a variation on the theme of 'small-a' anarchism, which several authors in this volume have deployed in their contributions. Prefiguration in these art works escapes the closure of the art system, and promotes an open-ended dynamic, which will give way to further tensions, in which the future is provisional, contingent, and unknown (also Mattern 2016; 2018).

Conclusion

In this volume we could not possibly cover all relevant disciplines with chapters devoted to each, but the reader will have noticed coverage of aspects of Psychology, Criminology, and History. The field of Management and Organizational Studies was obliquely touched upon (networks, chaos theory, etc.) and it was broached by anarchists in the 1950s and 1960s and has become something of a growth field recently (Carson 2008; Wachhaus 2011; Barrington-Bush 2014; Paskewich 2014; Western 2014). The vigorous engagement of philosophers who are anarchists with philosophical, moral, and political anarchism is a vibrant field and we have only touched on it in reference to political theory (Franks and Wilson 2010; Egomenides 2014; Jun 2017). Economics deserves its own treatment and anarchism has interacted via sociology (the commons), political economy (globalization), anthropology (debt and money), and political science (industrial democracy) (Albert 2003; Ness 2014; Shannon 2018; Wilbur 2018). And although the figurative arts have been covered, the literary arts have not been afforded their own chapter (but see the superb overview by Gifford 2018). In the concluding chapter to this volume, I will return with a discussion of anthropology, altruism, mutual cooperation, and language. The aim of this volume is to cover the humanities and the social sciences in an era of anarchist revival in academia, but bearing in mind that there is an older story too, in other words, the continuous role of the anarchist imagination as muse, provocateur, goading adversary, and catalyst in stimulating research and creative activity in the humanities and the social sciences from the middle of the nineteenth century to today.

Notes

1. This is rather similar to the concept of 'eventful democratization' used by Donatella della Porta (2014) in her comparison of '1989' with '2011'.
2. Shantz and Williams (2014: 178) make the point in their survey of anarchism and the social sciences: Not only does he overlook the earlier works of Paul Goodman and Colin Ward who lived largely beyond the walls of academia, he also does not mention Jeff Ferrell or other anarchist academic anthropologists, such as Harold Barclay, albeit he offered a fine endorsement to a collected volume of essays by Brian Morris (2015), Emeritus Professor of Anthropology, Goldsmiths, University of London.
3. For a study of the anarchist sociologist/activist, Harold Ehrlich, see Williams and Shantz (2016).
4. Graeber explained his position in a series of interesting emails to me and I thank him for his insights (6 August 2013, 17:32 and 6 August 2013, 21.28).
5. 'Anarchism Today', Goldsmiths, University of London (26 October 2012), organized by the then Department of Politics (now the Department of Politics and International Relations), the Research Unit in Governance and Democracy, and the Research Unit in Politics and Ethics. The participants included Alan Antliff, Alexandre Christoyannopoulos, Mohammed Bamyeh, David Graeber, Carissa Honeywell, Ruth Kinna, Carl Levy, Saul Newman, Chris Rossdale, and Judith Suissa. The conference received a grant from the Anarchist Study Group of the Political Studies Association (UK), and we would like to thank them for the generous assistance.
6. Proudhon's form of experimentalism and his decentralized federalism has much in common with John Dewey's approaches (Pereira 2009).
7. Graeber (2001: 53).
8. Max Nomad's position evolved, so that by the post-war period he saw the reformist educated elites of the West as a lesser evil, thereby once again anticipating the conclusions of Bell (Borgognone 2000).
9. Luke Yates defines prefigurative politics as experimental politics which encapsulates expressive and emotional tropes; it is community-building and mutual learning (Yates 2015) but it is also in danger of merely describing a method rather than a set of ideas aiming at anarchistic ends. The leaderless and decentralized extreme right has also embraced prefiguration (Gordon 2018).
10. Network analysis has also been used by anarchist transnational histories to track the subjects of their study, for the latest with a theoretical edge, see Hoyt (2015).
11. See the Economic and Social Research Council (ESRC) project led by Ruth Kinna and Alex Prichard on 'Anarchy as a Constitutional Principle: Constitutionalizing in Anarchist Politics' (ESRC Transformative Grant Scheme ES/N006860/1, 2016).
12. The 'New Humanities' approach informs the teaching and researching of postcolonialism in the Department of Politics and International Relations, Goldsmiths, University of London.

References

Adams, M.S. (2015) *Kropotkin, Read, and the Intellectual History of British Anarchism. Between Reason and Romanticism*, Basingstoke: Palgrave Macmillan.
Adams, M.S. and Jun, N. (2015) 'Political Theory and History: The Case of Anarchism', *Journal of Political Ideologies*, 20(3): 244–262.
Albert, M. (2003) *Parecon. Life After Capitalism*, London: Verso.
Antliff, A. (2017) 'Anarchism and Aesthetics', in N. Jun (ed.) *Brill's Companion to Anarchism and Philosophy*, Amsterdam: Brill, pp. 39–50.
Amster, T., DeLeon, A., Fernandez, J. A., Nocella, A. J. II and Shannon, D. (eds.) *Contemporary Anarchist Studies. An Introductory Anthology of Anarchy in the Academy*, London: Routledge.
Apter, D. and Joll, J. (eds.) (1970) 'Anarchism Today', *Government and Opposition*, 5(4): 397–554.
Apter, D. and Joll, J. (eds.) (1971) *Anarchism Today*, London: Macmillan.
Bantman, C. and Altena, B. (eds.) (2015) *Reassessing the Transnational. Scales of Analysis in Anarchist and Syndicalist Studies*, London: Routledge.
Barrington-Bush, L. (2014) *Anarchists in the Boardroom. More Like People*, UK: Self-Published.
Bayat, A. (2017) *Revolution without Revolutionaries. Making Sense of the Arab Spring*, Palo Alto: Stanford University Press.
Bell, D. (1961) *The End of Ideology: On the Exhaustion of Political Ideas in the Fifties*, New York: Collier.
Berry, D. (2018) 'Anarchism and 1968', in C. Levy and M.S. Adams (eds.) *The Palgrave Handbook of Anarchism*, Cham: Palgrave Macmillan, pp. 449–470
Berti, N. (1976) *Anticipazioni anarchiche sui 'nuovi padroni'*, Lyon: Ed. Sante Caserio.
Biehl, J. (2015) *Ecology or Catastrophe. The Life of Murray Bookchin*, Oxford: Oxford University Press.
Blumenfeld, J., Bottici, C. and Critchley, S. (eds) (2013) *The Anarchist Turn*, London: Pluto.
Borgognone, G. (2000) 'Max Nomad tra anarchismo e teoria delle elites', *Rivista storica dell'anarchismo*, 7(2): 33–50.
Bouchier, D. (1996) 'Hard Questions for Social Anarchists', in H.J. Ehrlich (ed.) *Reinventing Anarchy, Again*, Edinburgh: AK Press, pp. 106–122.
Burke, C. and Jones, K. (eds.) (2014) *Education, Childhood and Anarchism. Talking Colin Ward*, London: Routledge.
Carson, K.A. (2008) *Organization Theory. A Libertarian Perspective*, USA: Booksource.
Chalcraft, J. (2016) *Popular Politics in the Making of the Modern Middle East*, Cambridge: Cambridge University Press.
Chesters, G. and Welsh, I. (2006) *Complexity and Social Movements: Multitudes at the Edge Chaos*, London: Routledge.
Chomsky, N. (1982) *Towards a New Cold War: Essays on the Current Crisis and How We Got There*, New York: New Press.
Clark, J. (2013) *The Impossible Community: Realizing Communitarian Anarchism*, London: Bloomsbury.
Cohn, J. (2014) *Underground Passages. Anarchist Resistance Culture 1848–2011*, Oakland: AK Press.
Comfort, A. (1951) *Delinquency: A Lecture Delivered at the Anarchist Summer School, London, August 1950*, London: Freedom Press.
Cornell, A. (2016) *Unruly Equality. U.S. Anarchism in the 20th Century*, Berkeley: University of California Press.
Daring, C. B., Rogue, J., Shannon, D. and Volcano, A. (eds) (2012) *Queering Anarchism. Addressing and Undressing Power and Desire*, Oakland: AK Press.
Davis, L. (2005) 'The Dynamic and Revolutionary Utopia of Ursula K. Le Guin', in L. David and P. Stillman (eds.) *The New Utopian Politics of Ursula K. Le Guin's The Dispossessed*, Lanham: Rowman & Littlefield, pp. 3–36.

Day, R.J.F. (2005) *Gramsci is Dead. Anarchist Currents in the Newest Social Movements*, London: Pluto Press.
De La Torre, C. (2015) (ed.) *The Promise and Perils of Populism. Global Perspectives*, Lexington: University of Kentucky Press.
Della Porta, D. (2014) *Mobilizing for Democracy. Comparing 1989 and 2011*, Oxford: Oxford University Press.
Dixon, C. (2014) *Another Politics: Talking Across Today's Transformative Movements*, Berkeley: University of California Press.
Duda, J. (2013), 'Cybernetics, Anarchism and Self-Organisation', *Anarchist Studies*, 21(1): 52–72.
Dupuis-Déri, F. (2016) 'Is the State Part of the Matrix of Domination and Intersectionality? An Anarchist Inquiry', *Anarchist Studies*, 24(1): 36–61.
Dupuis-Déri, F. (2018) 'From the Zapatistas to Seattle: The "New Anarchists"', in C. Levy and M.S. Adams (eds.) *The Palgrave Handbook of Anarchism*, Cham: Palgrave Macmillan, pp. 471–488.
Egomenides, M. (2014) *Philosophical Anarchism and Political Obligation*, London: Bloomsbury.
Feenstra, R.A., Tormey, S., Casero-Ripollés, A. and Keane, J. (2017) *Refiguring Democracy: The Spanish Political Laboratory*, London: Routledge.
Feigenbaum, A., Frenzel, F. and McCurdy, P. (2013) *Protest Camps*, London: Zed Books.
Ferrell, J. (2009) 'Against Method, Against Authority… for Anarchy', in R. Amster, A. De Leon, L.A. Fernandez, A.J. Nocella II and D. Shannon (eds.) *Contemporary Anarchist Studies. An Introductory Anthology of Anarchy in the Academy*, London: Routledge, pp. 73–81.
Ferretti, F. (2018) *Anarchy and Geography: Reclus and Kropotkin in the UK*, London: Routledge.
Ferretti, F., Barrera de la Torre, G., Ince, A. and Toro, F. (eds.) (2017) *Historical Geographies of Anarchism. Early Critical Geographers and Present-Day Scientific Challenges*, London: Routledge.
Feyerabend, P. (1975) *Against Method: An Outline of an Anarchistic Method of Knowledge*, London: N.L.B.
Foot, J. (2015) *The Man Who Closed the Asylums: Franco Basaglia and the Revolution in Mental Health Care*, London: Verso.
Franks, B. (2018) 'Prefiguration', in B. Franks, N. Jun and L. Williams (eds.) *Anarchism. A Conceptual Approach*, London: Routledge, pp. 28–43.
Franks, B. and Wilson, M. (eds.) (2010) *Anarchism and Moral Philosophy*, Basingstoke: Palgrave Macmillan.
Franks, B., Jun, N. and Williams, L. (eds.) (2018) *Anarchism. A Conceptual Approach*, London: Routledge.
Freedman, L. (2013) *Strategy: A History*, Oxford: Oxford University Press.
Galián, L. (2018) 'Squares, Occupy Movements and the Arab Revolution', in C. Levy and M. Adams (eds) *The Palgrave Handbook of Anarchism*, Cham: Palgrave Macmillan, pp. 715–732.
Gandhi, L. (2006) *Affective Communities. Anticolonial Thought, Fin-De-Siècle Radicalism, and the Politics of Friendship*, Durham: Duke University Press.
Gemie, S. (2012), 'A Consideration of the Nature of Third World Anarchism', in R. Graham (ed.) *Anarchism: A Documentary History of Libertarian Ideas, Vol. III: The New Anarchism, 1974–2012*, Montréal: Black Rose Books, pp. 318–323 (originally published in 2003).
Gerbaudo, P. (2017) *The Mask and the Flag. Populism, Citizenism and Global Protest*, London: Hurst.
Gifford, J. (2018) 'Literature and Anarchism', in C. Levy and M.S. Adams (eds.), *The Palgrave Handbook of Anarchism*, Cham: Palgrave Macmillan, pp. 571–588.
Gilroy, P. (2004) *Between Camps: Nation, Cultures and the Allure of Race*, London: Routledge.
Goodway, D. (2006) *Anarchist Seeds beneath the Snow. Left-wing Libertarian Thought and British Writers from William Morris to Colin Ward*, Liverpool: Liverpool University Press.
Gordon, U. (2008) *Anarchy Alive! Anti-Authoritarian Politics from Practice to Theory*, London: Pluto Press.
Gordon, U. (2012) 'Participant Observation' in R. Kinna (ed.) *The Continuum Companion of Anarchism*, London: Continuum, pp. 86–95.

Gordon, U. (2018) 'Prefigurative Politics between Ethical Practice and Absent Promise', *Political Studies*, 66(2): 521–537.
Gouldner, A. (1979) *The Future of the Intellectuals and the Rise of the New Class: a Frame of Reference, Theses, Conjectures, Arguments, and Historical Perspectives on the Role of Intellectuals and Intelligentsia in the International Class Content of the Modern Era*, New York: Seabury Press.
Graeber, D. (2001) *Toward and Anthropological Theory of Value: The False Coin of our Own Dreams*, New York/Basingstoke: Palgrave.
Graeber, D. (2004) *Fragments of an Anarchist Anthropology*, Chicago: Paradigm Press.
Graeber, D. (2007) *Possibilities: Essays on Hierarchy, Rebellion, and Desire*, Edinburgh: AK Press.
Graeber, D. (2009) *Direct Action: An Ethnography*, Oakland: AK Press.
Graeber, D. (2011) *Debt: the First 5000 Years*, Brooklyn: Melville House.
Graeber, D. (2013) *The Democracy Project: A History, a Crisis, a Movement*, London: Allen Lane.
Graeber, D. (2018) *Bullshit Jobs: a theory*, London: Allen Lane.
Graham, R. (ed.) (2009) *Anarchism: A Documentary History of Libertarian Ideas. Vol. 2. The Emergence of the New Anarchism (1939–1977)*, Montreal: Black Rose Books.
Graham, R. (2013), 'Colin Ward: Anarchy and Organisation', in C. Levy (ed.) *Colin Ward: Life, Times and Thought*, London: Lawrence and Wishart, pp. 106–115.
Grubačić, A. and O'Hearn, D. (2016) *Living at the Edges of Capitalism. Adventures in Exile and Mutual Aid*, Berkeley: University of California Press.
Haiven, M. (2014) *Crises of Imagination, Crises of Power. Capitalism, Creativity and the Commons*, London: Zed.
Havercroft, J. and Prichard, A. (2017) 'Anarchism and International Relations Theory: A Reconstruction', *International Political Theory*, 13(1): 252–265.
Heckert, J. (2011) 'Anarchism and the Sociological Imagination: An Interview with Dana Williams', *The Sociological Imagination*, 9, August: http://sociologialimagination.org/archives/5911 (last accessed 21 September 2018).
Hirsch, S.J. and L. van der Walt (eds.) (2010) *Anarchism and Syndicalism in the Colonial and Postcolonial World, 1870–1940*, Amsterdam: Brill Press.
Honeywell, C. (2011) *A British Anarchist Tradition. Herbert Read, Alex Comfort and Colin Ward*, Continuum: London.
Honeywell, C. (2013) 'Colin Ward: Anarchism and Social Policy', in C. Levy (ed.) *Colin Ward: Life, Times and Thought*, London: Lawrence and Wishart, pp. 88–106.
Horowitz, I.L. (ed.) (1964) *The Anarchists*, New York: Dell Publishing Co.
Hoyt, A. (2015), 'Active Centers, Creative Elements, and Bridging Nodes. Applying the Vocabulary of Network Theory to Radical History', *Journal for the Study of Radicalism*, 9(1): 37–60.
Illich, I.D. (1971) *Deschooling Society*, New York: Harper & Row.
Illich, I.D. (1973) *Tools for Conviviality*, New York: Open Forum.
Ince, A. and Barrera de la Torre, G. (2016) 'For Post-Statist Geographies', *Political Geographies*, 55 (November): 10–19.
Jacobs, J. (1961) *The Death and Life of Great American Cities*, New York: Random House.
Jun, N. (ed.) (2017) *Brill's Companion to Anarchism and Philosophy*, Amsterdam: Brill.
Katsiaficas, G. (2006) *The Subversion of Politics. European Autonomous Social Movements and the Decolonization of Everyday Life*, Edinburgh: AK Press.
Kesey, K. (1962) *One Flew over the Cuckoo's Nest*, New York: Viking Press.
Kinna, R. (ed.) (2012) *The Continuum Companion to Anarchism*, London: Continuum.
Kinna, R. (ed.). (2014) *The Bloomsbury Companion to Anarchism*, London: Bloomsbury.
Kinna, R. and Evren, S. (eds.) (2013) *Blasting the Canon, Anarchist Developments in Cultural Studies*, 1, Brooklyn: Punctum Books.
Knapp, M., Flach, A. & Ayboga, E. (2016) *Revolution in Rojava. Democratic Autonomy and Women's Liberation in Syrian Kurdistan*, London: Pluto Press.

Kowal, D.M. (2018) 'Anarcha-Feminism', in C. Levy and M. Adams (eds.) *The Palgrave Macmillan Handbook of Anarchism*, Cham: Palgrave Macmillan, pp. 265–279.

Lagalisse, E. (2017) '"Good Politics": Property, Intersectionality, and the Making of the Occult Self', McGill University, unpublished PhD diss.

Lazar, H. (2018) 'Intersectionality', in B. Franks, N. Jun and L. Williams (eds.) *Anarchism. A Conceptual Approach*, London: Routledge, pp. 157–174.

Leighten, P. (2013) *The Liberation of Painting. Modernism and Anarchism in Avant-Garde Paris*, Chicago: University of Chicago Press.

Levy, C. (1987/2017a) 'Introduction: Historical and Theoretical Debates', in C. Levy (ed.) *Socialism and the Intelligentsia, 1880–1914*, London: Routledge and Kegan Paul/ Routledge, pp. 1–34.

Levy, C. (1987/2017b) 'Conclusion: Historiography and the New Class', in C. Levy (ed.) *Socialism and the Intelligentsia, 1880–1914*, London: Routledge and Kegan Paul/Routledge, pp. 271–290.

Levy, C. (1998) 'Max Weber, Anarchism and Libertarian Culture: Personality and Power Politics', in S. Whimster (ed.) *Max Weber and the Culture of Anarchy*, New York: St. Martin's Press, pp. 83–109.

Levy, C. (1999) *Gramsci and the Anarchists*, Oxford/New York: Berg.

Levy, C. (2010) 'Social Histories of Anarchism', *Journal for the Study of Anarchism*, 4(2): 1–44.

Levy, C. (2011) 'Anarchism and Cosmopolitanism', *Journal of Political Ideologies*, 16(3): 265–278.

Levy, C. (2012), 'Gramsci's Cultural and Political Sources: Anarchism in the Prison Writings', *Journal of Romance Studies*, 12(3): 44–62.

Levy, C. (ed.) (2013) *Colin Ward. Life, Times and Thought*, London: Lawrence and Wishart.

Levy, C. (2017) 'Anarchism and Leninist Communism: 1917 and All That', *Socialist History*, 52: 85–94.

Levy, C. (2018) 'Anarchism and Cosmopolitanism', in C. Levy and M.S. Adams (eds.) *The Palgrave Handbook of Anarchism*, Cham: Palgrave Macmillan, pp. 125–148.

Levy, C. (Forthcoming a) '"I am a Goddamn Anarchist": C. Wright Mills, the Anarchists and Participatory Democracy'.

Levy, C. (Forthcoming b) 'Anarchist Histories, Social Histories, and "1968"'.

Levy, C. and Adams, M. S. (2018) 'Introduction', in C. Levy and M.S. Adams (eds.) *The Palgrave Handbook of Anarchism*, Cham: Palgrave Macmillan, pp. 1–23.

Lindsey, C. R. (2013) *The Concealment of the State*, London: Bloomsbury.

Linebaugh, P. and Rediker, M. (2000) *The Many-Headed Hydra. The Hidden History of the Revolutionary Atlantic*, Boston: Beacon Press.

Lipset, S. (1960) *Political Man: the Social Bases of Politics*, Garden City, NY: Doubleday.

Maeckelbergh, M. (2011) 'The Road to Democracy: The Political Legacy of "1968"', *International Review of Social History*, 56(2): 301–332.

Mair, P. (2013) *Ruling the Void: the Hollowing out of Western Democracy*, London: Verso.

Mattern, M. (2016) *Anarchism and Art. Democracy in the Crack and the Margins*, Albany: State University of New York Press.

Mattern, M. (2018) 'Anarchism and Art', in C. Levy and M.S. Adams (eds.) *The Palgrave Handbook of Anarchism*, Cham: Palgrave Macmillan, pp. 580–602.

Morris, B. (2015) *Anthropology, Ecology and Anarchism: A Brian Morris Reader*, Oakland: PM Press.

Mounk, Y. (2018) *The People vs. Democracy: Why Our Freedom is in Danger and How to Save it*, Cambridge, Mass.: Harvard University Press.

Mudde, C. (2017) *Syriza. The Failure of the Populist Promise*, London: Palgrave Macmillan.

Müller, J.-W. (2016) *What is Populism?*, Philadelphia: University of Pennsylvania Press.

Ness, I. (ed.) (2014) *New Forms of Worker Organization. The Syndicalist and Autonomist Restoration of Class-Struggle Unionism*. Oakland: PM Press.

Nicholas, L. (2018) 'Gender and Sexuality', in C. Levy and M.S. Adams (eds.) *The Palgrave Handbook of Anarchism*, Cham: Palgrave Macmillan, pp. 603–621.

Nomad, M. (1959) *Aspects of Revolt. A Study of Revolutionary Theories and Techniques*, New York: Noonday Press.

Nomad, M. (1961) *Apostles of Revolution*, New York: Collier Books.
Olesen, T. (2005) *International Zapatismo. The Construction of Solidarity in the Age of Globalization*, London: Zed.
Ordóñez, V., Feenstra, R. A. and Franks, B. (2018) 'Spanish Anarchist Engagements in Electoralism: From Street to Party Politics', *Social Movement Studies*, 17(1): 85–98.
Ostrom, E. (1990) *Governing the Commons: the Evolution of Institutions for Collective Action*, Cambridge: Cambridge University Press.
Paskewich, J.C. (2014) 'Rethinking Organizational Hierarchy, Management, and the Nature of Work with Peter Drucker and Colin Ward', *Ephemera. Theory & Politics in Organization*, 14(4): 659–672.
Pateman, C. (1970) *Participation and Democratic Theory*, Cambridge: Cambridge University Press.
Pauli, B.J. (2015) 'The New Anarchism in Britain and the US: Towards a Richer Understanding of Post-War Anarchist Thought', *Journal of Political Ideologies*, 20(2): 134–155.
Pedroso, J.A. (2016) 'Black Lives Matter, or How to Think Like an Anarchist', *Class, Race and Corporate Power*, 4(2): 1–6.
Pels, D. (1998) *Property and Power in Social Theory: A Study of Intellectual Rivalry*, London: Routledge.
Pereira, I. (2009) 'Proudhon Pragmatist', in N. Jun and S. Wahl (eds.) *New Perspectives on Anarchism*, Lanham: Lexington, pp. 225–240.
Piven, F.F. and Cloward, R.A. (1977) *Poor People's Movements: Why They Succeed, How They Fail*, New York: Pantheon Press.
Polletta, F. (2002) *Freedom is an Endless Meeting. Democracy in American Social Movements*, Chicago: University of Chicago Press.
Portwood-Stacer, L. (2013) *Life-Style Politics and Radical Activism*, London: Bloomsbury.
Price, A. (2012) *Recovering Bookchin. Social Ecology and the Crises of Our Time*, Porsgunn: New Compass Press.
Price, A. (2018) 'Green Anarchism', in C. Levy and M.S. Adams (eds.) *The Palgrave Handbook of Anarchism*, Cham: Palgrave Macmillan, pp. 281–291.
Prichard, A. (2012) *Justice, Order and Anarchy: the International Political Theory of Pierre-Joseph Proudhon*, London: Routledge.
Prichard, A. and Worth, O. (2016) 'Left-wing Convergence: An Introduction', *Capital & Class*, 40(1): 3–17.
Prichard, A., Kinna, R., Pinta, S., and Berry, D. (eds.) (2012) *Libertarian Socialism. Politics in Red and Black*, Basingstoke: Palgrave Macmillan.
Prichard etc. (2016) and Prichard etc (2016) should be reversed in order so they are alphabetised properly.
Purkis, J. (2004) 'Towards an Anarchist Sociology', in J. Purkis and J. Bowen (eds.) *Changing Anarchism. Anarchist Theory and Practice in a Global Age*, Manchester: Manchester University Press, pp. 39–54
Purkis, J. and Bowen, J. (eds) (1997) *Twenty-First Century Anarchism*, London: Cassell.
Purkis, J. and Bowen, J. (eds) (2004) *Changing Anarchism. Anarchist Theory and Practice in a Global Age*, Manchester: Manchester University Press.
Putnam, R. (1993) *Making Democracy Work: Civic Traditions in Modern Italy*, Princeton: Princeton University Press.
Putnam, R. (2000) *Bowling Alone: The Collapse and Revival of American Community*, New York: Simon and Schuster.
Rizzi, B. (1985) *The Bureaucratisation of the World*, trans. and introduction, Adam Westoby, London: Tavistock Press.
Ronfeldt, D.F. and Arquilla, J. (1999) *Networks and Netwars: The Future of Terror, Crime, and Militancy*, Santa Monica, CA: Rand Corporation.
Rose, N. (1999) *Powers of Freedom: Reframing Political Thought*, Cambridge: Cambridge University Press.

Ross, C. (2011) *The Leaderless Revolution. How Ordinary People Will Take Power and Change Politics in the 21st Century*, New York: Simon & Schuster.
Ross, K. (2015) *Communal Luxury: The Political Imaginary of the Paris Commune*, London: Verso.
Rovira Kaltwasser, C., Taggart, P., Ochoa Espejo, P. and Ostiguy, P. (eds.) (2017) *The Oxford Handbook of Populism*, Oxford: Oxford University Press.
Rovná, L. A. (2013) 'Peter Kropotkin and His Influence on Czech Anarchism', *Moving the Social. Journal of Social History and the History of Social Movements*, 50: 53–79.
Ryley, P. (2013) *Making Another World Possible. Anarchism, Anti-Capitalism and Ecology in Late 19th and Early 20th Century Britain*, London: Bloomsbury.
Samuel, R. (2012) 'Utopian Sociology', in D. Poyner (ed.) *Autonomy: The Cover Designs of Anarchy 1961–1970*, London: Hyphen Press, pp. 257–262.
Sartwell, C. (2008) *Against the State: An Introduction to Anarchist Political Theory*, Albany: State University of New York Press.
Scott, J.C. (1990) *Domination and the Arts of Resistance. Hidden Transcripts*, New Haven: Yale University Press.
Scott, J.C. (2009) *The Art of Not Being Governed. An Anarchist History of Upland Southeast Asia*, New Haven: Yale University Press.
Scott, J.C. (2012) *Two Cheers for Anarchism*, Princeton: Princeton University Press.
Sennett, R. (1970) *The Uses of Disorder: Personal Identity and City Life*, New York: Knopf.
Sennett, R. (1999) *The Corrosion of Character: the Personal Consequences of Work in the New Capitalism*, New York: Norton.
Sennett, R. (2008) *The Craftsman*, New Haven: Yale University Press.
Sennett, R. (2012) *Together: The Rituals, Pleasures and Politics of Co-operation*, New Haven: Yale University Press.
Shannon, D. (2018) 'Anti-Capitalism and Libertarian Political Economy', in C. Levy and M.S. Adams (eds.) *The Palgrave Handbook of Anarchism*, Cham: Palgrave Macmillan, pp. 91–106.
Shantz, J. (2011) *Against All Authority. Anarchism and the Literary Imagination*, Exeter: Imprint Academic.
Shantz, J. (2014), 'Seeds beneath the Snow: The Sociological Anarchy of Paul Goodman, Colin Ward, and James C. Scott', *Contemporary Sociology*, 43(4): 468–473.
Shantz, J. and Williams, D.A. (2014) *Anarchy and Society: Reflections on Anarchist Sociology*, Chicago: Haymarket Books.
Sheehan, H. (2016) *The Syriza Wave. Surging and Crashing with the Greek Left*, New York: Monthly Review Press.
Shukaitis, S. and Graeber, D. (with E. Biddle) (eds.) (2007) *Constituent Imagination: Militant Investigations/Collective Theorization*, Oakland: AK Press.
Sitrin, M. (2018) 'Anarchism and the Newest Social Movements', in C. Levy and M.S. Adams (eds.) *The Palgrave Handbook of Anarchism*, Cham: Palgrave Macmillan, pp. 659–676.
Springer, S. (2016) *The Anarchist Roots of Geography. Towards Spatial Emancipation*, Minneapolis: University of Minnesota.
Staub, M. E. (2011) *Madness is Civilization. When the Diagnosis was Social, 1948–1980*, Chicago: University of Chicago Press.
Stedman Jones, G. (2016) *Karl Marx. Greatness and Illusion*, London: Allen Lane.
Stevens, J. (2011) 'Anarchist Methods and Political Theory', in J.C. Klausen and J. Martel (eds.) *How Not to Be Governed. Reading and Interpretations from a Critical Anarchist Left*, Plymouth: Lexington Books, pp. 1–18.
Suissa, J. (2010) *Anarchism and Education: A Philosophical Perspective*, Oakland: PM Press.
Sumner, G. D. (1996) *Dwight Macdonald and the Politics Circle. The Challenge of Cosmopolitan Democracy*, Ithaca: Cornell University Press.
Szelenyi, I. and Martin, B. (1988) 'The Three Waves of New Class Theories', *Theory and Society*, 17: 645–667.

Taussig, M. (2013) 'I'm so Angry I Made a Sign', in W.J.T. Mitchell, B.E. Howard and M. Taussig (eds.) *Occupy. Three Inquiries in Disobedience*, Chicago: University of Chicago Press, pp. 3–44.
Thomas, P. (1980) *Karl Marx and the Anarchists*, London: Routledge and Kegan Paul
Thorpe, C. and Welsh, I. (2008) 'Beyond Primitivism: Towards a Twenty-First Century Anarchist and Praxis Science', *Anarchist Studies*, 16(1): 48–75.
Tormey, S. (2015) *The End of Representative Politics*, Cambridge: Polity Press.
Tufekci, Z. (2017) *Twitter and Tear Gas. The Power and Fragility of Networked Protest*, New Haven: Yale University Press.
Van der Walt, L. and Schmidt, M. (2009) *Black Flame: the Revolutionary Class Politics of Anarchism and Syndicalism*, Edinburgh and Oakland: AK Press.
Vinen, R. (2018) *The Long '68: Radical Protest and its Enemies*, London: Allen Lane.
Wachhaus, T.A. (2011), 'Anarchy as a Model for Network Governance', *Public Administration Review*, 72(1): 33–42.
Ward, C. (ed.) (1987) *A Decade of Anarchy (1961–1970)*, London: Freedom Press.
Webber, J.R. (2017) *The Last Day of Oppression and the First Day of the Same. The Politics and Economics of the New Latin American Left*, London: Pluto Press.
Western, S. (2014) 'Autonomist Leadership in Leaderless Movements: Anarchists Leading the Way', *Ephemera. Theory & Politics in Organization*, 14(4): 673–698.
Whimster, S. (ed.) (1998) *Max Weber and the Culture of Anarchy*, New York: St. Martin's Press.
Wilbert, C. and White, D. F. (eds.) (2011) *Autonomy Solidarity Possibility. The Colin Ward Reader*, Edinburgh: AK Press.
Wilbur, S.P. (2018) 'Mutualism', in C. Levy and M.S. Adams (eds.) *The Palgrave Handbook of Anarchism*, Cham: Palgrave Macmillan, pp. 213–224.
Williams, D.M. (2013) 'A Society in Revolt or Under Analysis? Investigating the Dialogue between 19th Century Anarchists and Sociologists', *Critical Sociology*, 40(3): 469–492.
Williams, D.M. (2015) 'Social Capital in Anarchist Movements', in P.J. Lilley and J. Shantz (eds.) *New Developments in Anarchist Studies*, Brooklyn: Punctum Books, pp. 11–35.
Williams, D.M. (2017) *Black Flags and Social Movements. A Sociological Analysis of Movement Anarchism*, Manchester: Manchester University Press.
Williams, D.M. (2018) 'Contemporary Anarchist and Anarchistic Movements', *Sociology Compass*, 12(1): 1–17.
Williams, D.M. and Lee, M.T. (2012) 'Aiming to Overthrow the State (Without Using the State): Political Opportunity for Anarchist Movements', *Comparative Sociology*, 11(4): 558–593.
Williams, D. and Shantz, J. (2016) 'An Anarchist in the Academy, a Sociologist in the Movement', *Journal for the Study of Radicalism*, 10(2): 102–122.
Wilson, M. (2014) *Rules without Rulers. The Possibilities and Limits of Anarchism*, Winchester: Zero Books.
Woodcock, G. (1962) *Anarchism. A History of Libertarian Ideas and Movements*, Cleveland: World Publishing Company.
Wreszin, M. (1994) *A Rebel in the Defense of Tradition. The Life and Politics of Dwight Macdonald*, New York: Basic Books.
Yates, L. (2015) 'Rethinking Prefiguration: Alternatives, Micropolitics and Goals in Social Movements', *Social Movement Studies*, 14(1): 1–21.
Zibechi, R. (2012) *Territories in Resistance. A Cartography of Latin American Social Movements*, Oakland: AK Press.
Zohlberg, A.R. (1972) 'Moments of Madness', *Politics and Society*, 2(2): 183–207.

2 The two anarchies

The Arab uprisings and the question of an anarchist sociology

Mohammed A. Bamyeh

Is anarchism what anarchists do, or is it a much larger social and historical experience? In the history of anarchist thought, we encounter both perspectives: one that states the principles of anarchism as it ought to be practised, while another considers anarchism to be something that has already been practised, across the world and for generations, without being called by the name. This latter tradition, which might be called 'organic anarchy', includes different approaches, just as does the former tradition, which might be called 'self-conscious anarchism'. While neither is an internally unified tradition, each expresses a general approach to anarchy, and imagines it to be endowed with specific features. The anarchist 'canon' includes representatives of both traditions, with the activists often (but not always) being self-conscious anarchists.

However, organic anarchy is also associated with important social movements, indeed more so than the self-conscious variety. Francisco Pi y Margall saw Spanish anarchism, for example, as an expression of communal and libertarian traditions already familiar to large numbers in the country (Alexander 1999: 8). The implicit assumption of that argument is that it is easier for a 'new' emancipatory idea to become socially established if ordinary people are already familiar with it through their own 'old' traditions (Bamyeh 2012a). In this way, emancipation appears as something that is organic to a familiar tradition, rather than as a novelty requiring a fight against tradition. This more general argument was implicit in Peter Kropotkin's (1902) outline of anarchy as a feature of historical systems of civic ethics (even though he also argued anarchy to be based on the method of modern science). In its basic outline, the arguments for an organic anarchy continue today to be produced especially in anarchist anthropology and geography (Graeber 2004; Macdonald 2009; Gibson & Sillander 2011; Springer 2013): anarchy not so much an acquired ideology, but an already familiar practice or custom.

We can therefore speak of two anarchies: one that is embedded in social traditions and is thus already familiar to large numbers, even though those may not use the word 'anarchy' to describe their life. And another anarchy that is self-conscious, which begins its career from the mid-nineteenth century onwards. How do these two traditions relate to each other? In what follows I will focus on the analytical rather than ethical dimensions as we compare the two anarchies. That is to say, I want to explore how one thinks about anarchy from one perspective or the other, rather than determine whether one perspective may be ethically superior to the other. In the end, I will suggest how this comparison may provide some basis for an anarchist sociology. But I would like to start from earth, notably the Arab uprisings that began in 2011, which should offer rich basis for this comparison and for new learning about the sociology of anarchy, including how it may be defined from different social perspectives. (Here I will not address the 'post-revolutionary' phase, that is, the period following 2011 in most places. The post-revolutionary phase possesses dynamics that are very dissimilar to what may be called the 'revolutionary moment' proper (Bamyeh 2016), even though the two are often confused as if they were the same. Unfortunately, the extraordinary, unique revolutionary 'moment' tends to be forgotten when one fixates too much on the aftermath that has very different sociological attributes.)

Beginning with 17 December 2010, a number of spectacular revolutions erupted throughout the Arab World in short order. Within months genuine revolutionary mobilization and large scale protest movements took place in virtually all Arab countries, and in some cases, notably in Libya and Syria, the revolts turned into armed conflicts. Yet in almost all cases, including the *early* phase of armed conflicts, these revolts shared in common surprising new features – surprising, that is, because they had not been typical of older social movements in the region, except for the first Palestinian *intifada* in 1987 and to a certain extent the Sudanese uprising in 1985. But until 2011, the earlier Palestinian and Sudanese episodes appeared as exceptions to the rule.

What was 'anarchic' about those revolts? The method of revolt was characterized by spontaneous networking, minimal organization, absence of hierarchal guidance and structures, pervasive social solidarity and mutual help, local initiative, individual will, and a broadly shared feeling that the agent of historical change was the ordinary person rather than the great saviour leader. Those qualities were sustained even in conditions that seemed to require more hierarchical structures and central command, such as especially during the early phase of the military campaigns in Libya and Syria. But even in those cases, coordination between autonomous units was explicitly preferred to central leadership, and the partisans never consented to a unified leadership even as outside powers demanded it so that those powers might know who to talk to. Moreover, the anarchic qualities of the uprisings lasted beyond their triumph. Thus even in countries where the head of the old regime was toppled, the revolution itself did not produce its own personnel who were ready to take over. Nor did there seem to be a demand from below to give rise to a charismatic leader who would personify a great collective struggle.

Why those anarchic qualities of revolt appeared at that moment is a theme that requires its own study, especially given that many earlier movements within the same region had possessed non-anarchic attributes. What concerns us here, however, is that the anarchic qualities of the Arab Spring must be based on already familiar traditions, since they were clearly not based on an anarchist political programme or on a conscious anarchist intention (Bamyeh 2013). By 'familiar traditions' supplying tools for a revolutionary method, I refer to a process whereby the already familiar spontaneity of everyday life guides the spontaneity of the revolution; the common, pragmatic solidarity in neighbourhoods and towns supplies the model of revolutionary solidarity, and consequently the will to sacrifice and combat; in revolutionary times traditional distrust of distant authorities, based on the ancient proposition that a claim to help or guide is unverifiable in proportion to the power and distance of the authority that makes it, becomes the basis for distrusting any distant authority that claims to stand in for the revolution; and long-enduring traditions of conflict management supply the basis for a non-violent strategy during at least the initial phase of each revolution, and sustain that strategy in the absence of excessive counter-violence.

These revolutionary practices that are already rooted in known traditions rather than learned from revolutionary textbooks, generally describe the method of the revolution during the Arab Spring in 2011. While they may be based on an organic anarchy, organic anarchy is not usually translated into a conscious anarchist political programme. Organic anarchy exists typically in the form of a social order that appears to its inhabitants to be legitimate and practical, since it is an order which they see themselves as having consented to or voluntarily created. But typically it is not an order that is regarded to be the model for a large collective system, even in a revolutionary climate. However, organic anarchy does supply enough ready ethics and methods by which one is able to orchestrate a rebellion, which may not have the intention of propagating anarchy throughout society.

Here I would like to focus on six basic differences between self-conscious anarchism and organic anarchy, including the definition of each practice; the ethics that inform economic order; the question of authority; the source of knowledge; character of radicalism in each perspective; and finally the comparative expectation from revolutionary activity. In the process, I wish to underscore how anarchist sensibilities live on in different domains of social life.

Since it is embedded in customary life, organic anarchy tends to require minimal doctrinal definition. Individuals tend to think of their social order not as an expression of any specific doctrine, but as an order that is appropriate for their needs, one for which they themselves are responsible, and one that is sustained only by their own collective activity rather than by any external authority. In more recent times, realities of self-created and self-governed social orders have been observed by social scientists studying especially new urban environments in the global south. Several of those studies concentrated on environments that would become hotbeds of the Arab uprisings in 2011 and afterward. Focusing on Cairo, Salwa Ismail (2006) described a form of social governance that consisted of a set of informal rules for conflict management that residents have developed, rules that existed largely outside of state and legal channels but were more effective since they relied on neighbours' knowledge of each other and of local histories. Comparing Cairo and other large metropolitan areas in the Middle East, Asef Bayat (2009) explored 'quiet encroachment' as a pervasive strategy used by ordinary people, before the revolutionary wave, to effectively establish new realities and resist state restrictions. That strategy required no organization and no collective planning, only preparedness for mutual help, reinforcement from neighbours, and willingness of so many others to participate in a myriad acts of quiet encroachment, which defined most of their social activity. In a similar vein, Diane Singerman (1996) demonstrated the pervasive role of informal networks, and

Table 2.1 Basic features of self-conscious and organic anarchy

	Self-conscious anarchism	*Organic anarchy*
Definition of the practice	Maximalist definition	Minimalist definition (voluntary, unimposed order)
Basis of economic analysis	Studious anti-capitalism	Broad conception of social justice
The question of authority	Broad conception of anti-authority	Customary authority
Source of knowledge	Knowledge acquired through ideological acculturation	Knowledge acquired through accretion of historical memory
Character of radicalism	Conceptual radicalism	Pragmatic radicalism
Character of revolution	Revolution = Revolution	Revolution = Revolution + Reform

consequently the informal economy, in making it possible for ordinary people to survive in a political and economic system that was otherwise designed to exclude them.

While none of these studies couch the informal social order they describe as anarchic, it is easy to see organic anarchy as the common thread throughout. That is because, whether geographically concentrated in new neighbourhoods or organized as dispersed networks, we encounter communities that evolve through practices of mutual help, with no support from the state and usually against its rules and regulation, and develop informal rules to govern themselves that are practical in nature and able to accommodate accident and surprise. And it is important to remember that the vast majority of the rebels during the Arab Spring came precisely from those anarchically organized segments of society, who by 2011 had long been accustomed to rely on each other, were familiar with the practical usefulness of spontaneity in their own unpredictable life, and also long accustomed to see the state as an external force from which nothing good was to be expected.

This dimension of organic anarchy, namely the sense of familiarity and ease with which one navigates a known local environment, stands in contrast to the doctrine-rich and often complex debates of self-conscious anarchism. This latter attitude is characteristic of modern ideologies generally. Indeed, it seems that 'modern', as an attribute assigned to any idea, itself calls forth additional layers of justification that local knowledge systems need only when they are confronted by an external force intent on replacing them. By contrast, as a local knowledge system, organic anarchy seems content with only general basic principles. An example of these is the notion of 'social justice', which during the Arab Spring emerged as one the key demands. Left commentators sought to translate that demand, and the whole uprising generally, as protest against 'capitalism' or 'neo-liberalism'. However, these latter terms were not used by the revolutionaries of the Arab Spring, including those who were familiar with them, since it appeared that the generic notion of 'social justice' encompassed the above and also seemed more intuitively acceptable than analytical terms that required more familiarity with doctrine and definition.

From the point of view of organic anarchy, terms like 'capitalism' or 'neo-liberalism' appear too abstract and thus cannot be felt in a way that motivates principled resistance. This is not so with the more generic concept of 'social justice', which became appealing precisely because it summed up better than studious abstractions what the point was all about. Ordinary individuals do not protest 'neo-liberalism' in large numbers but, as in Istanbul's Gezi Park, the disappearance of all free and intimate public spaces, and their replacement with ever more private, cold, profit oriented enterprises. The injury has to be concrete enough, and at the same time appear to be happening everywhere in the country. This kind of injury inspires determined resistance more than any abstraction is ever able to.

Thus while ordinary individuals may be familiar enough with inequalities that they see all around them, they reject most intuitively the absence of countervailing mechanisms to at least ameliorate the effects of inequality, so that it may be tolerable. And this perspective is latent in a traditional reluctance to embrace utopias that no one has empirically experienced. Rather, the organic anarchic perspective seems pragmatic and empirical: it endorses solutions with which it is somewhat familiar via empirical experience, rather than solutions that describe an unknown and never experienced world of, for example, full equality. And the notion of 'justice' combines these two elements, by first rejecting the *absence of mutualism* that among other benefits also makes some form of situational inequality tolerable, and second by positing the solutions along the lines of likely experience rather than an unexperienced, and thus abstract, utopia.

This practically oriented framework of organic anarchy also informs its attitude to the question of authority. Throughout the revolts of the Arab Spring we saw the emergence of a category of activists called 'coordinators', who did not see themselves and were never seen as leaders, although they were trusted with important roles especially in militarized uprisings. The term precedes the Arab Spring, and we can already see it in use in older movements as *Kifaya* and the April 6 movements in Egypt. My own experience in Tahrir Square in Cairo showed that in spite of the egalitarian environment, people generally did solicit advice from those they regarded as knowing better, notably intellectuals who had joined the revolution on the streets, even though they did not need to listen to them. And while they continued to respect certain traditional authorities, for example the Mufti of Egypt, they felt free to ignore such authorities when their instructions did not meet their sentiments. Thus when the Mufti of Egypt issued a *fatwa* prohibiting people from demonstrating against the regime on 4 February 2011, his *fatwa* was ignored by millions, even though he continued to elicit broad respect until his eventual retirement.

The above sums up the organic anarchic approach to the question of authority in general: typically, organic anarchy endorses only one form of authority, which might be called customary authority – something for which the model would be that of a teacher, parent, or arbitrator. Customary authority is defined by a situational rather than permanent need: the teacher's authority ceases when one is no longer a student, that of the parent when one is no longer a minor, that of the arbitrator when the conflict in question has ended. As such, the situational nature of customary authority makes it quite different from the authority of the state over society, since the state is understood as a permanent and general sort of authority with no horizon for its termination. Thus from the point of view of organic anarchy, there is no basis for the classical Aristotelian claim that parental authority in the family provides the model for political authority over society.

In organic processes, an attitude toward authority would be expected to be based on how one has experienced authority, which also means that one is in principle prepared to amend one's attitude depending on what experience has revealed. Thus from the point of view of organic anarchy, it would be a mistake, for example, to approach the question of authority in terms of absolute, unwavering *a priori* principles. That is so since organic processes include the possibility of immediate reversal, as we saw in the case of the Arab Spring when traditional authorities are followed only when they express popular sentiments and are ignored when they do not.

In other words, the question of authority, just like all other conceptual issues, is judged from the point of view of organic anarchy on the basis of whether authority itself has proven to be organic to the social order in which it is exercised. This means that organic anarchy acquires its knowledge not in the form of timeless philosophical principles, but through a constant process of adjustment of historical memory. During the Arab uprisings, for example, the clearest example of how historical memory has worked was most evident in how immense social movements, involving millions of participants, did not give rise to great unifying charismatic leaders, as had been the case with similar movements in the *same* region before. I have argued elsewhere (Bamyeh 2012b) that this difference must be based on historical memory, understood as a summary verdict on the lessons of past protest movements, a verdict that became deposited in an intuitive form in civic culture, whereafter the verdict became organic to that culture. This organicity of memory is evident in how rejection of charismatic and unifying leadership has become so intuitive in regions that had previously generated the exact opposite tendency.

The tendency for organic anarchy to cultivate intuition as a depository of knowledge in place of concepts, distinguishes it from self-conscious anarchism, where intuition itself requires being conceptually justified. One is hard-pressed, for example, to find a term like 'patriarchy' or 'homophobia' in organic anarchic use, but this linguistic absence does not mean the absence of a strategy to deal with the imposition in question. Rather, linguistic absence suggests that the *radical posture* that one requires to resolve an injustice is for the time being of a pragmatic rather than conceptual type. Conceptual radicalism begins with a theoretical proposition and commits to it due to the presumed theoretical rightness of the proposition (e.g.: 'patriarchy represents x, y, z; therefore we have to do a, b, c'). By contrast, pragmatic radicalism organizes social experience or practice not in the form of conceptual propositions, but in terms of opportunities for practical resistance. This resistance, as James Scott (1992) has described, tends to take a minute, everyday form most of the time. Therefore it never appears radical enough from the point of view of self-conscious anarchism, or indeed from the point of view of any analysis that prioritizes large scale, systematic change.

Yet, this same pragmatic radicalism provides the necessary fuel for large scale revolutionary insurrections when the time is right, although it tends to colour that insurrection, too, with its general pragmatic outlook. Invisible but persistent everyday acts of resistance indicate a determined rejection of at least a portion of given reality, namely the portion that intrudes most upon a person's immediate life. But this resistance is designed to be invisible due to a calculation of an unfavourable balance of power, in which the subaltern decides on a daily basis that she has no chance of victory in a direct and open confrontation with a mighty authority. And this means that all it takes for a revolution to break out is first the subaltern's recognition of the vulnerability of authority to open resistance, and second that so many others have joined her in that recognition.

Again, the Arab Spring revolts seem to confirm this principle. The revolutions were evidently expressions of long-enduring and pervasive discontent, but they all broke out suddenly and seemed to require nothing more than one *example* of regime vulnerability. Thus the success of a revolt in Tunisia suggested that it would happen in short order elsewhere, and my own conversations with individuals on the streets of Cairo in January and February 2011 confirm that they tended to look for examples of success of movement elsewhere *before* they moved in the same way in their own environment. And once such revolts broke out they sustained a radical posture throughout, in the sense that they did not accept any compromise short of at least the head of the old regime. Pragmatic radicalism is therefore not any less radical than conceptual radicalism, only more subterranean for most of the time.

Yet, when it breaks out into an open revolution, the pragmatic radicalism of organic anarchy also tends to infuse the spirit of the revolution with reformist tendencies. That is so for two reasons. The first is that pragmatism in general, even in revolutionary situations, is governed by the limits of experience, meaning that few organic anarchists are willing to accept a model of post-revolutionary society that is not based on a model of liberty that is *known* to them even in some elementary way. Until today, for example, few in Egypt can imagine a system without a president, including hard core revolutionaries. The discovery of alternatives itself requires further experimentations until one finally confronts the limits of known models, and only after their limits are confronted may they be abandoned. But other than intellectuals, few would do away with a model of liberty they know in some elementary form for another that they have not experienced in *any* form. An imagination that transcends all known reality requires a sense of profound failure of such reality, including all its known variants.

The second ground for the reformist tendencies of the revolutions of organic anarchy is that a substantial portion of participants in those revolutions are themselves reformist in spirit. Tentative data from Egypt and Libya, for example, suggest that in both societies the original revolution was supported by about 75 per cent of the population.[1] However, that figure may be divided equally between revolutionaries and reformists. By 'revolutionaries' I mean those who, before the revolution, saw a revolution as the only way to destroy a corrupt system. By 'reformers' I mean those who, before the revolution, also wished for a complete destruction of the old system but did not trust revolutions, largely because revolutions for them produced too many uncertainties and were guaranteed to generate a violent regime response that worried them more greatly than the persistence of the status quo.

The revolutions broke out when these two groups, roughly equal in number, joined forces. The revolutionaries struck first, but the reformers immediately joined for two reasons. First, the uncertainties they had worried about all along were going to happen anyway once the revolution was already underway, so there was no longer a point in trying to avoid them. And second, the fact that the regime was certain to respond to its enemies violently if needed created a situation that convinced those who were hesitant reformers that they could best protect themselves from the murderous regime response only if the revolution succeeded.

The combined movement of massive numbers of revolutionaries and reformers meant that the revolution would have a split personality, which is perhaps typical of all popular revolutions. This split personality is further aggrandized by the fact that neither camp is unified internally around a singular post-revolutionary perspective or imagination, and yet all imagine themselves to be united, since during the revolutionary phase all who participate are revolutionaries by definition. But the organic anarchic perspective would be expected to be the one most invested in imagining popular unity, since from the point of view of organic anarchy truth is validated by social consensus. Obviously, this is not necessarily how truth is validated from the point of view of self-conscious anarchism, nor for that matter from the point of view of most social ideologies – except perhaps for the patriotic perspective, whose unsuspected relation to organic anarchy requires a separate study.

The two anarchies and sociology

It may appear from the above that the two anarchies have little ground for mutual communication, and that their strategies and even their assumptions about the nature of social reality may differ substantially enough to preclude the possibility of a synthesis. But this depends on what we understand by 'synthesis': if synthesis is something that is produced by acts of knowledge rather than simply by a structured and determined 'reality' on its own, then synthesis becomes a function of a will, the will to learn something new that is yet to be provided by reality, even though the 'new' may be rooted in an observation of reality. This approach is much more common in artistic and literary experiments than in the social sciences. In a previous work, I did suggest that anarchy as a science of humanity was a particular kind of science that must be practised as an art (Bamyeh 2009: 218). Here I would like to confine my last remarks to how this perspective may be applied in a specific discipline, namely sociology, with specific reference to how an anarchist sociology may approach the question of the two anarchies introduced above.

Sociologists have been aware, at least since Max Weber, of the problems of value neutrality in their work, which are inseparable from the fact that here we are speaking of a science that involves the study of humans, including their values, by other humans who cannot possibly not have values of their own. Some sociologists are quite open about the fact that what they do is simply camouflage their values with the appearance of science, so that instead of their position appearing partisan, it appears as 'data' or other kinds of 'objective' indicators. Addressing the problem that all data are selected so as to answer specifically a question defined as such by the researcher, is entrusted not to any logic that is inherent to sociology, but to the basic dialogic expectations of a scientific community: someone else contests your data or your interpretation of them, or shows how you failed to posit the original research question properly. Many, however, follow in practice what Weber himself thought to be the best ethical practice, and that is to approach the process of scientific inquiry itself as a 'calling', since only in that posture would science transcend our own tendency as ordinary humans to be arrested by the perspectivist limits of our values.

In any case, it was evident to Weber that the question of values may be inescapable in at least one respect, namely in determining the research problem itself. What one eventually learns from pursuing that problem should however follow the ethical model of pursuing a calling. Now if we use this perspective to explore the ways in which anarchism itself may be a 'calling', that is to say, a chosen object of inquiry with no conclusions that presuppose the inquiry itself, we come upon certain elements that offer a broad outline of an anarchist sociology. To begin with, it has to be acknowledged that describing a certain reality as being an expression of an 'organic anarchy' is a *chosen* perspective, since that same reality can be and has been described in other terms. But if all perspectives are in the final analysis chosen, what is left for us is to defend the choice. And defending one's choice of perspective is most coherent when

Table 2.2 Anarchist sociology as synthesis

	Self-conscious anarchism	Organic anarchy	Anarchist sociological knowledge
Definition of the practice	Maximalist definition	Minimalist definition (voluntary, unimposed order)	Middle definition (broad range of voluntary options)
Basis of economic analysis	Studious anti-capitalism	Broad conception of social justice	Mutualism
The question of authority	Broad conception of anti-authority	Customary authority	Situational authority
Source of Knowledge	Knowledge acquired through ideological acculturation	Knowledge acquired through accretion of historical memory	Memory translated from intuitive into conscious forms
Character of radicalism	Conceptual radicalism	Pragmatic radicalism	Practical moves within universal perspective
Character of revolution	Revolution = Revolution	Revolution = Revolution + Reform	Revolution = Enlightenment

that defense reflects not simply partisan political values, but a general philosophy that can be shown to be capable of organizing, in a meaningful way, a large spectrum of social observations. This activity of organizing information into a perspective may also be described as a method of adhering to a 'paradigm'. It is one method by which an act of inquiry may be defended as being more scientific than another, so long as the paradigm itself is defensible. But usually scientists are silent about one crucial aspect of this process of knowledge: one does not simply discover new facts. Rather, the discovery adds something to reality, something that did not exist before it was discovered. Had it existed before, it would have been discovered before. The thing comes into being when we see it, and we see it when we need it. A science of this nature is a science that lives with humanity rather than places humanity at its mercy. It is, in other words, an anarchist science.

When applied to sociology, this perspective has, among other advantages, the capacity to transcend an old, tired debate in the discipline between 'structure' and 'agency'. When we say that a large spectrum of social observations actually express a unified popular philosophy that might be described as 'organic anarchy', we recognize how individuals, restricted as they may be by objective realities that surround them, nonetheless react to these restrictions with creativity and in a way that expands the realm of choices available to them. In other words, individuals are shown not simply to be oppressed by or victims of preexisting structures that mandate obedience to objective conditions. Being oppressed or being a victim is not a particularly interesting human or analytical condition, and simply describing oppression or showing how people are passive, voiceless victims of large global structures, is probably the least inspiring approach to knowledge. When it addresses oppression, a lively science would show how one lives with it in a variety of practical ways, how oppression itself enhances one's creativity, and how oppression leads to an enrichment of our imagination. Thus here we describe a science that, as Nietzsche would put it, would be an ally of rather than an enemy of life. It shows how life is actively lived, rather than simply how one is victimized by it. As a philosophy of life or as a science, the validity of anarchy resides not in its abstract theoretical propositions, nor even in its presumed ethics, but in its evident universality: throughout history and in the present, large numbers have constructed systems of mutual obligations, solidarity, and trust that became organic to their life. That is to say, those systems survived because they appeared unimposed and capable of allowing individuals to navigate creative pathways around structural limits and distant, unchosen authorities.

An anarchist sociology thus would be the perspective that employs this observed universality as a basis for the further development of a self-conscious anarchism. This anarchism, then, is a strategy of knowledge: what one discovers becomes an added part of an ever expansive philosophy of life, and not simply recorded as another 'objective fact'. Consider, for example, the first element of the comparison above, namely how a free and non-coerced social order is understood. Here, when we describe organic anarchy as one in which the social order to which one belongs is regarded to be generally voluntary rather than imposed, we immediately encounter a logical problem that is also social in its implications: the term 'voluntary' can only describe a free choice within a range of known and accessible options. One cannot voluntarily choose what one does not know, or that which is inaccessible with the aid of any currently viable method. From this observation, anarchist sociology constructs a synthesis: first it pays attention to what organic anarchy is already doing, and then outlines how the range of known and accessible options may be expanded. Needless to say, this sociological work cannot offer limitless universal voluntarism. But it can describe something more felt and lively: how to expand the realm of the possible, on the basis of a philosophy of life but also on the basis of what is observed. Here, while it may not make the world anarchist overnight, anarchist sociology contributes to making the world itself more voluntary in nature, and less imposed.

Put otherwise, anarchist sociology may be understood as a method of *adding consciousness* to organic anarchy, in a way that expands the possibilities of the latter while in the process subtracting from the maximalist, abstract, and life-antagonistic theoretical propositions of self-conscious anarchism. If for example we recognize the drive toward social justice as a basic orientation of organic anarchy, we may rediscover the merits of 'mutualism', that forgotten early name of anarchism itself. Mutualism was in effect a more accurate way of capturing the spirit of social justice of organic anarchy than the various macro-critiques of the general system. Those macro-critiques, in retrospect, seemed to have served only to immobilize self-conscious anarchism, since in macro-critique self-conscious anarchism saw itself to be fighting an alien world governed by abstract capitalist relations that could only be destroyed *in their totality* – in other words, according to no readily viable method. In contrast to this abstract orientation, anarchist sociology begins with observing the broadly apparent reasonableness of a more basic orientation to social justice, expressed as a broad interest in mutual obligations that have always made inequalities tolerable. If that is the case, then what anarchist sociology can do is explore how the already extant practices of and orientations to a generic notion of social justice may transcend occasional charity, so that social justice becomes a basic expectation of a social system, whose legitimacy is thereafter based in part on its ever more mutualist character.

Likewise would be the approach of an anarchist sociology to the question of authority. Organic anarchy lives at a distance from authorities that are themselves distant from it, and cultivates only those authorities that are customary. But it does not reject the idea of authority as a principled stand. In its basic form, this orientation to customary authority may be translated from the analytical point of view of anarchist sociology as a practical use of what is sometimes but not always needed: situational authority. This is basically the same as customary authority, albeit with no necessary basis in a custom or tradition. Rather, situational authority emerges in an acknowledgment of what we already do: we not only accept but even solicit authority when there is a reason for it, and that authority, which may be technical or require special skills, does not rule us in the same way a state does, nor represent us collectively. Rather, its tasks are to solve a particular problem, or supervise a particular stage in life, or handle crisis situations. Thus whereas customary authority is habitual, situational authority is rational: an anarchist sociology addresses not simply old customs, but new practices of authority that emerge to handle modern connectivities and complexities.

The above remarks suggest that much is expected of an anarchist sociology, both as a source of new knowledge as well as a descriptive approach of how social knowledge emerges. For example, if we accept the notion that historical memory provides basis for the intuitive character of organic knowledge, we also realize that intuition itself, while supplying knowledge in a form that is always ready for immediate use, is also ill-prepared to handle complex conditions, in which case intuition may yield to confusion. Indeed, one way to understand 'confusion' is as a condition in which intuitive knowledge supplies no persuasive choice among what appear to be equally unpalatable (or equally palatable) options. In such case it helps most when one knows, with the aid of an anarchist sociology, where one's intuition had come from, or what it had sought to accomplish to begin with. Here intuition becomes a conscious principle, grounded in knowing why one has been inclined to choose x rather than y. This ability to justify the choice translates an act that is otherwise anchored in faith into one that is anchored in science – in this case, anarchist science.

This new consciousness translates intuition and memory into awareness of the historical reasons for one's choice, action, and intention. It also supplies the radical posture commonly associated with an anarchist attitude, with a long-term perspective that allows one to assess at each step where one might be along a universal path toward anarchy. Of course, such an assessment does not need to be accurate, even though it may be said to be based on a science. But one can only work with the knowledge tools at one's disposal, and usually that is good enough so long as one knows that there is still much more to be learned, so long as one understands the process in which one is involved to be universal. Employing this perspective, anarchist sociology supplies the radical posture with a means of measurement, if not with a destination: 'I am now exactly here, and here is x away from my universal destination. I can now either die, content that I have arrived at the last possible destination in my lifetime; or live on, if possible, and plan for the next step'.

Radicalism is not a matter of a principled stand here or there, but of a life orientation: one acquires from organic anarchy its pragmatic radicalism, which consists of doing one's work of emancipation in any way possible, even if inaudibly and in small steps. But whether great or small, noisy or quiet, those steps have a universal *orientation*. They do not simply express an amateurish proposition about freedom, but a deep understanding of its complexity and universal nature, and also of the basic principle that acts of freedom are never solitary even when they appear to be so. They add more freedom to the world, even when they only appear to add freedom to a person.

It is often assumed that radicalism is best expressed in revolutionary insurrections. This attitude is informed by a rich tradition of left and Third World literature and experiences that had been accumulating since the late eighteenth century. The target of revolution in modernity has been the usual suspects: despotism, capitalism, colonialism. In one sense, revolution in modernity was justified by a sense that the enemy was total and possessed systemic nature, which meant that the revolution against it should be equally total and systemic. But this of course was a conception of the world, an idea, which would not have emerged without a new paradigm that came to be known as the Enlightenment. Without a new paradigm there can never be a revolution, since oppression alone does not produce a revolution; slavery, after all, survived for centuries. Just as Thomas Kuhn argued in the case of science, social revolutions can be approached as expressions of a new paradigm replacing an old one. They are unthinkable otherwise, especially if their target is an old and entrenched authority.

But when we discuss revolutions, we often focus too much on their dynamics and fortunes, and forget in the meantime the most significant contribution of revolution to world history: revolution as an expression of a new paradigm and new knowledge, in other words, of 'enlightenment' (Bamyeh 2013). If enlightenment proceeds without a revolution in the usual sense, there should be no reason for revolution. There is nothing necessary or inevitable about social or political revolutions. But radical change is unimaginable without a revolution at least in thought, that is to say, without a new knowledge that is *experienced as enlightenment*.

Anarchist sociology may be understood as one vehicle of such enlightenment. And here it should be clear that when we speak of enlightenment in this sense we are not speaking of discovering an ultimate and binding truth or of a set of specific propositions about the nature of knowledge. Rather, anarchist enlightenment consists of acts of knowledge from below, in which one overcomes immaturity, both self-imposed and external, and in the process experiences oneself to have become free and related to others in ever more complex and varied ways. A science that aims to produce this enlightenment will not, in the final analysis, be called 'sociology' or any other name, even though that may be where it had started. It would be called anarchist science, and it will be the potential property of all.

Note

1 For Egypt, this figure is based on tallies from the first round of the presidential elections of 2012, in which candidates associated with different parts of the revolution garnered collectively about three-quarters of the vote. For Libya, the figure is obtained from a rare survey done in 2001 but published only ten years later (al-Werfalli 2011: 124–129). A tabulation of al-Werfalli's figures show that 37.9% of respondents believed that the system could not be reformed and that only radical change would do, whereas 38% supported radical change but were afraid of uncertainty and the consequences of regime response.

References

Alexander, R. (1999) *The Anarchists in the Spanish Civil War*, London: Janus.
Bamyeh, M.A. (2009) *Anarchy as Order: The History and Future of Civic Humanity*, Lanham, MD: Rowman & Littlefield.
Bamyeh, M.A. (2012a) 'The Social Dynamism of the Organic Intellectual', in M.A. Bamyeh (ed.) *Intellectuals and Civil Society in the Middle East*, London: I. B. Tauris, pp. 1–28.
Bamyeh, M.A. (2012b) 'Anarchist Philosophy, Civic Traditions and the Culture of Arab Revolutions', *Middle East Journal of Culture and Communication*, 5: 32–41.
Bamyeh, M.A. (2013) 'Anarchist Method, Liberal Intention, Authoritarian Lesson: The Arab Spring between Three Enlightenments', *Constellations* 20(2): 188–202.
Bamyeh, M.A. (2016) 'Will the Spring Come Again?' *R/Evolutions*, 4(1): 74–86.
Bayat, A. (2009) *Life as Politics: How Ordinary People Change the Middle East*, Stanford: Stanford University Press.
Gibson, T. and Sillander, K. (eds) (2011) *Anarchic Solidarity: Autonomy, Equality, and Fellowship in Southeast Asia*, New Haven: Yale University Press.
Graeber, D. (2004) *Fragments of an Anarchist Anthropology*, Chicago: Prickly Paradigm Press.
Ismail, S. (2006) *Political Life in Cairo's New Quarters: Encountering the Everyday State*, Minneapolis: University of Minnesota Press.
Kropotkin, P. (1902) *Mutual Aid: A Factor of Evolution*, London: William Heinemann.
Macdonald, C.J.H. (2009) 'The Anthropology of Anarchy', Princeton: Institute for Advanced Study, School of Social Science, Occasional Paper, 35.
Scott, J. (1992) *Domination and the Arts of Resistance: Hidden Transcripts*, New Haven: Yale University Press.
Singerman, D. (1996) *Avenues of Participation: Family, Politics, and Networks in Urban Quarters of Cairo*, Princeton: Princeton University Press.
Springer, S. (2013) 'Anarchism and Geography: A Brief Genealogy of Anarchist Geographies', *Geography Compass*, 7(1): 46–60.
al-Werfalli, M. (2011) *Political Alienation in Libya: Assessing Citizen's Political Attitude and Behavior*, Reading, UK: Ithaca Press.

3 Contesting the state of nature
Anarchism and International Relations[1]

Zaheer Kazmi

International Relations (IR) shares an intimate though unusual relationship to anarchism. Anarchy is a foundational concept in IR yet anarchism has been ignored almost entirely by IR scholars. IR also holds a unique position among the academic disciplines under discussion in this volume as, unlike them, much of the subject's distinctiveness has derived from its pivotal focus on anarchy as the fundamental condition of international relations.[2] Moreover, its treatment of anarchy has been peculiar to the discipline, acting more as a 'state of nature' metaphor, which distinguishes the international from the domestic sphere, than a global moral vision. In IR theory, anarchy thus functions chiefly as a descriptive category which denotes the absence above states of the overarching political authority which obtains within them, rather than a prescription about how the world should be ordered. It is perhaps no surprise, therefore, that the emergent sub-discipline of international political theory, in its normative aspect, has been more receptive to activist anarchist scholarship than the traditional core of IR theory.[3] In light of the ambivalence of anarchy in IR, however, as both an analytic and normative category, exploring anarchism in IR can also bring into view the deeper relationship between theory and ideology in academic inquiry. In IR, an anarchist *way of seeing* is not necessarily the same thing as seeing like an anarchist.

Academic volumes on anarchism are, almost without exception and despite the vitality of the debates they exhibit, platforms for advocating anarchism by those sympathetic to it as an ideology or social movement.[4] This is not my aim in this chapter which, in this respect, lies outside the bounded discourse of what has come to be termed 'anarchist studies'. What interests me is the *possibility* of exploring anarchism's neglected relevance to IR while not being normatively committed to arguing for or against it as an ideology. In other words, while acknowledging that all theory has normative implications, can an 'anarchist' approach to IR be something other than a form of critical theory? In keeping with the self-images of anarchism as a fringe sensibility, this seems a more pertinently heretical, albeit counter-intuitive, question to ask. From this perspective, it becomes apparent that the uses of anarchism in academia are not immune to the distorting effects on scholarly framing inherent in the ideological dimensions of intellectual production. When deployed as a form of social praxis with a distinct ideological pedigree, anarchism comes to unavoidably embody the very forms of intellectual closure its proponents seek to subvert. Interrogating anarchy's idiosyncratic place in IR and the nexus between theory and practice deeply embedded in the discipline can help to elucidate this paradox. For much of IR's history, the trajectory of American social science has dominated the contours of the discipline (Hoffman 1977; Smith 2002; Bell 2009). While this influence has not been unusual among the social sciences and humanities more generally, an important corollary particular to IR has been the close relationship between its research and analytical priorities and concerns and US foreign policy imperatives. In fact, IR is largely seen as being born out of the ashes of the First World War in a spirit of inter-war Wilsonian idealism, though its intellectual origins are contested (Schmidt 1998; Sylvest 2009). This 'theory-practice' nexus has been an enduring feature, particularly in the USA. Anarchism too is often thought of by its proponents as the quintessential philosophy of action which seeks to reshape the world: for most anarchists, there can be no anarchist theory without anarchist practice. It is only one of the many paradoxes of anarchism's entry into IR that the missionary zeal often associated with its scholarly activism echoes the instrumentalization of academic knowledge which has been so characteristic of dominant modes of IR theory. This insight can also reveal the often unacknowledged intimacies between discourses of radicalism and conservatism when applied to academic contexts.

This chapter aims to unpack the underlying ideological factors which shape anarchism's potential to shed light on the study of international relations, pointing to anarchism's constraints, as well as benefits, when deployed as an activist ideology. The first part outlines conventional approaches to anarchy in IR theory and gives an overview of the minimal literature on anarchism and IR. The second part addresses the activist dimensions of anarchism's scholarly presence in IR, pointing to the battle over the ownership of anarchist ideas. In doing so, it unearths how the highly abstract and value-laden notion of 'anti-authority' is rhetorically appropriated, mirroring the instrumentalization of knowledge which mines a deep vein in conventional IR theory. Turning to issues of methodology and historiography, the third part interrogates the idea of an anarchist 'tradition' in the context of the salience of traditions of international thought in IR, asking if there can be an authoritative anarchist 'tradition' when anarchism is a thoroughgoing anti-authoritarian doctrine. It illustrates how the uses of history and hagiography by anarchist academics can recycle rather than challenge the constricting notion of traditions of international thought in IR. The final section looks at anarchism as a critical moral discourse and the condition of anarchy as an analytical 'state of nature' concept in IR and the possibility of a non-critical anarchist theory in light of the ambivalence of anarchy as a descriptive and prescriptive category in IR. It suggests how an anarchistic way of seeing the concept of anarchy can challenge the authority-centrism of IR theory without being bound to anarchism as a prescriptive ideology.

International anarchy

Perhaps more so than any other discipline in the social sciences and humanities, IR remains contested as a discrete field of academic enquiry. In the USA especially, but also elsewhere, IR is often still viewed more as a sub-field of Political Science than a discipline in its own right. While it has sometimes struggled to distinguish itself alongside more established, cognate areas of study, disagreements about what IR *is* or *should be* animate the field with peculiar intensity. While such debates are present in other disciplines, in IR they can take a decidedly existential form as there has been little consensus on either the objects of study or the epistemological, ontological, and methodological bases of the field. Metatheoretical debates – in the UK in particular, though, tellingly, not in the USA – have been perennial (Booth & Smith 1995; Smith, Booth & Zalewski 1996). This indeterminacy has also been expressed in the nomenclature associated with the study of something as potentially all-encompassing as the investigation of all human and institutional relations beyond the state: thus, the term, 'international relations', is often placed alongside 'global politics', 'world politics', 'international politics' or 'international studies', to denote the field. These terms are themselves normative as well as descriptive in that each tends to emphasize particular actors and contexts of study, be they individuals, states, transnational actors or structures, for example. Of course, all academic disciplines are, in some senses, fluid intellectual constructs embedded in contingent and varied scholarly practices over time. In this respect, the ambiguous, composite and parasitic aspects of IR have not negated its distinctive contribution to scholarship.

Anarchy in IR

Despite its amorphous nature, one idea in particular has come to be associated with IR: anarchy. Turn to any IR textbook or introductory undergraduate lectures and anarchy is a key concept which distinguishes the discipline. While there is disagreement over the nature and implications of anarchy in IR, there is consensus on its centrality. International anarchy has thus come to characterize the distinctive arena of IR as *sui generis*. The predominant IR view is that the international system is anarchic as there is no world state or permanent global coercive authority above that of states. Anarchy, however, is a multivalent concept in IR. While it acts largely as an *analytical* category which describes the anarchical context for subsequent theorizing, it is also a *normative* concept, not only in its divergent roles in defending realism or mapping causality in war among some liberals, for example, but as the characterization of international relations as anarchical, as opposed to hierarchical, has often been challenged (Dickinson 1916; Mearsheimer 2001). In this respect, IR theorists can be understood as being divided broadly into two camps in their treatment of anarchy: those who assume anarchy as a background condition which sets international relations apart from domestic politics; and those who question the assumption that there can be a clear distinction between an anarchic international sphere and a hierarchical domestic one. The former is usually associated with traditional or positivist IR perspectives – and rationalist assumptions about the centrality of power in international politics often associated with the constructive role of US hegemony – and the latter with critical or post-positivist ones. As anarchy has been so central to the many varieties of IR theory, however, a compendium of approaches to anarchy would stretch to several volumes. The following brief summary is intended for the general reader, to give a flavour of how anarchy is most commonly deployed in IR theory. By necessity, it elides, therefore, much of the complex internal debates within and across divergent IR approaches and the contested nature of these categories of IR theory. On the assumption side, I outline how two prominent approaches to IR theory – 'realism' and 'liberalism' – treat anarchy. On those who question the assumption, I look at critical and constructivist critiques. Realists and liberals in IR theory see anarchy as a system of order which defines international relations, in contrast to the hierarchy which obtains within states marked by variant forms of unitary and centralized governance.[5] Both approaches have predominated in IR circles in the USA, in particular, and there has, arguably, been a close correlation between their academic fortunes and the ambivalent self-images of US foreign policy as both hegemonic and liberal. They differ, however, in notable ways, including their respective views on the possibilities for conflict and cooperation under international anarchy, and their relative emphasis on the importance of state and non-state actors. Realists – both traditional, or classical, realists and neo-realists, or structural realists – see international relations fundamentally as a self-help system (Morgenthau 1948; Waltz 1979). States in this anarchical environment behave as egoists, intent on maximizing their relative power in the absence of a world state arbiter. Thus, the international anarchy is seen as a fundamentally hostile arena where states exist in a perpetual 'security dilemma' (Jervis 1976). For realists, common systemic solutions for stability in this environment have often been devices such as strategic alliance building, the balance of power, and great power hegemony: all of which aim to channel unbounded power under anarchy in some way. As a corollary, realism is often considered to view international politics as an amoral realm. For liberals, the international system is also anarchical. However, it does not follow for them that it is inherently a realm of conflict and amorality. Cooperation, rather than conflict, is not only considered possible under conditions of international anarchy, but desirable by liberals. Contra realists, liberals emphasize the global interdependence made possible through patterns of cooperative assent reflected in, for example, international law, and transnational and international organizations. Some liberals tend to underwrite their theories with reference to a nascent international morality or shared international norms existing under international anarchy. This is sometimes tied to ideas of global justice or, drawing on Kant, the normative bases of democratic peace theory (Beitz 1979; Doyle 1983). Like neo-realists, other liberals, such as so-called neo-liberal institutionalists, base their theories on rational actor assumptions about egoistic behaviour under international anarchy but, unlike them, see international relations as an arena in which rational, self-interested forms of cooperation obtain, constructing 'regimes' which, in turn, have normative force (Krasner 1983; Keohane 1984). From around the end of the Cold War, IR underwent what became known in the discipline as a 'post-positivist' or 'critical' turn which challenged the positivist epistemological and ontological biases of IR theory (Weber 2001; Roach 2007). These biases were tied to behaviouralist and 'problem-solving' theoretical imperatives which were also seen to serve underlying ideological purposes, including legitimating US foreign policy by 'naturalizing' IR as a science. This led to a wave of critically-inclined interventions focused on transformative and emancipatory theory. They drew primarily on the postmodernist, poststructuralist, feminist and Frankfurt School approaches which had already permeated other academic fields. In the conventional historiography of IR, this turn to critical theory is often seen as one of its 'great debates', although the idea of there ever having been 'great debates' is increasingly questioned (Schmidt 1998). Notwithstanding the perennial tendency in IR to debate 'debates', and the fact that IR in the USA tends to ignore important developments in the discipline elsewhere, the proliferation of divergent forms of critical IR theory has, nonetheless, greatly revitalized the discipline in recent decades.[6] Some of the more significant critical challenges to traditional IR theory, however, pre-dated the contributions which followed the Cold War. These included the ground-breaking work of Robert Cox, John Ruggie, and Richard Ashley. Cox drew on Antonio Gramsci, among other Marxian sources, to elucidate the hegemonic dimensions of IR's focus on problem-solving theory (Cox, 1981); while, from a different perspective, Ruggie took aim at the assumption of anarchy in IR theory more directly (Ruggie, 1983). Ruggie was concerned with the ways in which the static implications of the influential neo-realism of Kenneth Waltz – where the anarchic structure of a self-help international system determines the functionally similar behaviour of states – inhibited an understanding of the deeper dynamics of change in the international system (Waltz, 1979). Crucially, Ruggie turned

Waltz's own Durkheimian borrowings back on himself by substituting the fuller implications of 'dynamic density' for the limited prospects for change in Waltz's own theory (Durkheim, 1893). Ruggie's insights anticipated later arguments about how the international system is more amenable to change despite anarchy. In another influential article, Richard Ashley also turned his attention to challenging IR assumptions about 'the fact of anarchy'. Deploying Derrida, Ashley sought to expose how anarchy, as conceptualized in conventional IR theory, was, in fact, 'an arbitrary political construction that is always in the process of being imposed' (Ashley 1988: 229). While such critical interventions sought to deconstruct the conventional assumption of anarchy as a fixed fact of international life, emergent constructivists in IR theory did so from an alternative perspective. Their critical insight was that the identities and interests of actors in international relations were not given, *a priori*, by the material fact of anarchy but were socially constructed. This ideational aspect enabled transformation and meant that international anarchy was not a deterministic strait jacket but a more malleable arena. While Ruggie and several other prominent IR theorists have been influential in promoting constructivism in IR, in the most well-known formulation of this approach, Alexander Wendt epitomized constructivist possibilities in his assertion that 'anarchy is what states make of it' (Wendt 1999; Kratochwil 1989; Ruggie 1998).[7]

Anarchism and IR

Alongside these metatheoretical exchanges, IR scholars, and those working in cognate disciplines, began to challenge received orthodoxies about the centrality of the state in international relations (Held 1995; Linklater 1998; Bartelson 2001). The critique of the state had a deeper history in IR, reaching back not only to 'pluralist' departures from state-centric realism in the early 1970s, but to IR's origins in the scepticism of liberal internationalist claims to the state's absolute sovereignty. The burgeoning field of the history of international thought over the past decade has also highlighted the contingency and fluidity of the state as a historical polity (Armitage 2012). In this milieu of cumulative challenges to the primacy of the state, anarchism also came to be reconfigured as an anti-statist critical IR theory catalyzed by the re-emergence of global anarchist activism. Despite some minor interest in recent years, however, studies which draw on anarchism remain marginal to IR. It is symptomatic of this marginality that the only textbook which has treated anarchism as a distinct approach to IR, giving it a dedicated chapter, has pared down this mention considerably in its recent second edition with only a passing reference and the chapter omitted entirely (Daddow 2009, 2013). There have been only two published English language monographs which address explicitly the relationship between anarchist thought and IR (Kazmi 2012; Prichard 2013). While anarchism has begun to emerge on the IR seminar and conference circuit, there are only a limited number of academic articles published in IR journals. These mainly comprise a special forum in *Millennium* and, depending on how one chooses to define anarchism, a forum on Noam Chomsky in the *Review of International Studies*, though the latter was not framed in terms of Chomsky as an anarchist (*Millennium* 2010; Herring & Robinson 2003). Other notable work which engages with IR includes Alex Prichard's wider writings, focused largely on recovering Proudhon, Saul Newman on postanarchism, and Carl Levy on anarchism and cosmopolitanism (Prichard 2007, 2010c, 2011, 2012, 2013; Newman 2012; Levy 2011). Prior to this recent upsurge, three articles in particular drew explicitly on anarchism (Weiss 1975;

Falk 1979; Turner 1998). While small in number, these academic interventions have been tied overwhelmingly to anarchism as an activist left-libertarian ideology and, more explicitly, critical IR theory. My own work on anarchism in IR, to which I shall return in the final part of this chapter, does not fall within this agenda. However, I regard my approach only as an alternative *way of seeing* the possibilities of anarchism in IR rather than *the* correct way. While I acknowledge the unavoidable normative implications of all theory, including my own, therefore, my approach is not intended as either a defence or critique of anarchism as a doctrine, even as it too draws on anarchist thought. Critical anarchist IR scholarship not only adds a neglected and long-overdue dimension to IR but can play a vital role in addressing pressing issues of domination and hegemony in international relations.

Anarchism first entered IR via peace studies in two essays by Thomas Weiss and Richard Falk respectively (Weiss 1975; Falk 1979). Together with Scott Turner's article nearly two decades later, until very recently, these papers constituted the sum total of anarchist IR theory (Turner 1998). Weiss and Falk were concerned with bringing the moral and social dimensions of anarchism to bear on conceptions of world order and prospects for social change. While Falk focused on the relevance of anarchism's anti-statism to emergent pluralist conceptions of international order, drawing on the utopian visions of 'philosophical anarchism', Weiss argued that its 'general principles' were 'appropriate for the formulation of plans and strategies for the creation of a more humane global political system' (Weiss 1975: 3). Turner's was also an intervention in peace studies concerned with reviving interest in the relevance of anarchism to peaceful forms of world governance. Drawing on a reading of what he termed the 'Kropotkian tradition', he presented an alternative to the realist IR account of world order positing a global civil society beyond Hobbesian state-centrism (Turner 1998).

More recently published contributions, many of which are contained in the *Millennium* special forum, fall broadly into three categories: historical anarchism; activism and resistance movements; and biological and social ecology theory. Alex Prichard is the foremost exponent among critical IR theorists of the first tendency. His writings have focused mainly on resurrecting and rehabilitating the legacy of Proudhon and point to the relevance of Proudhon's thought to issues in contemporary international relations (Prichard 2013). He has also tied this interest in Proudhon to a wider engagement with the history and origins of IR, pointing to the legacies of neglect of anarchism in IR's formation and development as a discipline (Prichard 2011). While most critical anarchist IR theory looks back to historical anarchism in some way, Prichard's work is distinguished by his deep engagement with Proudhon as a historical thinker. In his links to wider scholarly anarchist networks, it is also infused with an activist commitment to embedding anarchist ideology, via Proudhon, as a distinct body of critical theory within IR. Issues of global security and global resistance have loomed large for some critical anarchist IR scholars. These contributions can be situated with reference to the sub-discipline of 'critical security studies' and focus on the nature and forms of anarchist social activism and resistance. Chris Rossdale has contested the language, categories, and boundaries of IR and critical security studies as currently configured. Drawing on Simon Critchley and Gustav Landauer, and applying his insights to a case-study of a group of anti-arms trade activists, he has argued that anarchist conceptions of agency can challenge what he sees as the implicit 'statist ontology' of critical security studies (Rossdale 2010 and see Chapter 4 in this volume). While, through the idea of 'democratic insurrection', Daniel Murray describes what he terms, a 'forum-affinity-network' system as a non-hierarchical model of organization for global resistance movements (Murray 2010). This, he argues, drawing on the organizational notion of the 'rhizome' in the philosophy of Gilles Deleuze and Felix Guattari, 'allows free and open relations between individuals and also proves to be an effective form of resistance as it is nearly impossible to contain' (Murray 2010: 478; Deleuze & Guattari 1987). Erika Cudworth and Stephen Hobden have combined insights from complexity theory and the social ecology of Kropotkin and Murray Bookchin to address questions of organization and world order under anarchy in IR. Drawing on anarchist ideas of spontaneity, self-organization, and order without sovereignty, they challenge conventional IR assumptions about the levels of complexity which co-exist and co-evolve under anarchy in the international system (Cudworth & Hobden 2010). Also drawing on Kropotkin's approach to the co-evolution of the natural and social worlds, Adam Goodwin argues for a more 'holistic ontology' of international relations (Goodwin 2010). There have also been notable contributions from scholars outside IR who have broached IR themes explicitly in their work on anarchism, not least the editors of this volume. From a poststructuralist perspective which draws on a particular reading of Carl Schmitt, the political theorist, Saul Newman, has turned the anti-foundationalism of postanarchism to addressing IR theory explicitly, notably the hegemony of realism (Newman 2012), while Carl Levy has turned to Rudolf Rocker and Gustav Landauer to engage with IR, recovering the 'anarchist roots' of cosmopolitanism and, in doing so, exposing the limits of IR theory and its theoretical purview (Levy 2011).

The above summary has highlighted the breadth and vitality of critical anarchist IR scholarship despite its small presence in the discipline. Two related assumptions shared across this divergent body of work, however, also harbour an ideological undertow which pulls against the potential wider possibilities for anarchism in IR: the first is the assumption of anarchism as an activist ideology; the second is the treatment of anarchism as a transhistorical 'tradition'. It is to these issues I now turn.

Partisans of anarchy

To 'naturalize' contested ideas as intuitive is a potent rhetorical device. The peculiarity of anarchism is that it appropriates the highly abstract and value-laden notion of anti-authority in the service of a particular ideological agenda, or rather, agendas – one aligned to libertarian socialism, the other to anarcho-capitalism. In the process, it seeks the holy grail of ideology by asserting the inherent contiguity between its own culturally and historically situated ideals and the purportedly natural order of things: anarchism as a *sensibility* is thus swallowed up by anarchism as *ideology*. In this respect, it is no accident that the ideology of anarchism has been steeped in utopian ideas of scientism and nature since it emerged in the nineteenth century. This is true of both its left- and right-libertarian forms which arose at similar times. That there will be some readers who will object to the very idea of a right-libertarian anarchism and others to libertarian socialism as anything other than a form of closet communism, is also revealing of the depth of contestation over the ownership of such a potent idea.

Left and right

While the left may attach anti-authority to social justice and the right to free market economics, the fact that libertarian socialists and anarcho-capitalists, nonetheless, share much philosophical ground is seldom acknowledged. Entrenched as they are in opposing ideological camps, it is not surprising that a figure such as James C. Scott, who emanates from a leftist milieu and has signalled his deep affinity to anarchism but is admired by both left- and right-libertarians, is exceedingly rare (Scott 1998, 2012). Yet there are other, sometimes unacknowledged, ambiguities in anarchist scholarship today which reach deeper than Scott's idiosyncratic affections for the petty bourgeoisie, not least in 'post-left-' or 'post-anarchist' critiques of liberalism and the deployment of the ambivalent legacies of Friedrich Nietzsche, Max Stirner, or Carl Schmitt (for example, Huysmans 1999; Chandler 2004; Newman 2012). Only a generation ago, when an anarchist revival was forged in the crucible of 1960s radical politics, a synthesis between the radical left and right was deemed possible, epitomized, for example, in the short-lived journal, *Left and Right: A Journal of Libertarian Thought*. Viewed by some as a conservative Rothbardian attempt at co-opting anarchism, it argued that 'a consistent view of liberty includes concepts that have also become part of the rhetoric or program of right and of left' (Left and Right 1965: 3). Reaching further back, it was unremarkable in their times for William Godwin to cite Edmund Burke or Benjamin Tucker to draw on Pierre-Joseph Proudhon. In what is probably the most widely read contemporary history of anarchism, Peter Marshall delineates the diversity of anarchist thought while concurrently making judgements about whom he regards as being within and outside anarchism as a tradition, while Colin Ward has done much the same, with both throwing out anarcho-capitalists from what they regard as true anarchism (Marshall 1992; Ward 2004). In another commentary, Ruth Kinna remarks on the stark neglect of women from the 'the anarchist movement', where 'the anarchist movement' implies a degree of ideological homogeneity in which right-libertarians, such as Ayn Rand, Rose Wilder Lane and Isabel Paterson, are not included (Kinna 2005: 13). Kinna's reference to anarchism as a libertarian socialist movement here is reflective of its predominance rather than dissidence. The fact that she omits the central role of women in anarchism's less pervasive right-libertarian canon – particularly as she discusses it as a strand of anarchism in the same book – is revealing of the implicit choices which are made in projecting what anarchism is, even, or perhaps especially, when anarchist scholars and their sympathizers survey their field. What is interesting about its uses as a critical IR theory today is that anarchism's status as a contested category of thought is left unaddressed. Perhaps this is reflective of the current global climate of neo-liberal crisis – and abject failures of the market – in which opposing libertarian postures have become ever more ingrained, and, despite shared libertarian objections to the wars in Afghanistan and Iraq, unlike during the Vietnam War they have not elicited the same degree of cross-pollination in concerted opposition to the state. Whatever the cause, in IR terms this lack of self-reflexivity in the treatment of anarchism contrasts with the endless debates over the interpretation and meaning of realism, liberalism and all of the other '-isms' in IR theory. But this lack of contestation is more curious still because of the functions and methods normally associated with critical theory which emphasize contingency and deconstruction. One could argue that there is a double mode of intellectual closure at work in the entry of anarchism to IR, one which ties anarchism to both libertarian socialism and critical IR theory exclusively. While this way of treating anarchism, in its dominant left-libertarian mode, may seem the most self-evident, this discursive strategy, nonetheless, functions as a presumptive prism which constricts anarchistic ways of addressing IR. In this mode, rather than signalling a departure from IR's staid suppositions, the fixed assumption of anarchy in IR is replaced by another fixed assumption about the possibilities of anarchism in IR.

If anarchism is indeed a multivalent category, how you choose to define it, however implicitly, will inevitably have a bearing on who is considered inside or outside its boundaries; the point is someone will always be doing the selecting as anarchism is not a category of nature. The discursive strategies adopted by anarchist academics will thus echo the ideological deployment of alternative conceptions of liberty in antithetical forms of IR theory, such as assumptions of atomized and possessive liberty in neo-realism and neo-liberal institutionalism.

Ideas and action

When she wrote of the characteristic 'practical bent' of American social science in her authoritative intellectual history of the subject, Dorothy Ross may not have had IR at the forefront of her reflections, but her insight certainly bears a particular resonance to the subject (Ross 1991: 1). The birth of IR was driven by the policy imperatives which shaped the inter-war period in Europe following the First World War. This intimacy between theory and practice has been evident ever since, in the USA in particular where IR was consolidated as a discipline only after 1945; not coincidentally, this occurred during a period of remarkable growth in social science there. As Stanley Hoffman observed, IR's expansion 'cannot be separated from America's role in world affairs after 1945' (Hoffman 1977: 47).[8] Knowledge which is useful for action has also been a common refrain in anarchist writings, including in IR. As one fairly recent article has put it, the aim is 'to develop methods that produce both a situated analysis of struggles at the ground level and research that is practically useful for those engaged in political activity' (Murray 2010: 463). In terms of the nature of the relationship between knowledge and power, it matters, of course, that the revolving doors between theory and practice in mainstream American IR have led more directly to government policy circles than grassroots activism, from Henry Kissinger to Condoleezza Rice, through to Anne-Marie Slaughter, for example.[9] Perhaps precisely because of their antithetical positions, however, their intellectual strategies tend, nonetheless, to mirror each other. But, unlike for realists or conservatives, this poses a particularly acute dilemma for anarchists, namely the paradoxical practice of moral advocacy alongside seeking non-domination in all forms. Contra the anti-institutionalism usually associated with anarchism, critical anarchist IR theory has also displayed strong institutional links to networks with clearly defined ideological agendas. These include the Political Studies Association's Anarchist Studies Network (ASN) and the British International Studies Association's Network of Activist Scholars of Politics and International Relations (NASPIR). Critical anarchist IR theory thus falls squarely and self-consciously within what has come to be termed 'anarchist studies', that is, studies of anarchism which self-identify as activist, left-libertarian, and anti-capitalist. As with the leading anarchist journal with which it shares its name, the agenda of 'anarchist studies' has come to dominate the study of anarchism to the extent that it has become almost synonymous with 'the study of anarchism' in academia. Critical anarchist IR is an expansion of this ideological colonization. Not unlike other activist scholarly networks where journals, think tanks and research organizations cluster to promote particular ideological agendas – such as those of the libertarian right where members often straddle like-minded institutions – 'anarchist studies' is relatively small with much overlap in membership of boards and committees. While anarchist ideology does not rule out association, such institutionalized ideological hegemony in practice assorts oddly with anarchism's institutional antipathy in theory. In this aspect, critical anarchist IR theory mirrors the conservatism of its right-libertarian opponents in two ways: in the sociology of its intellectual production where power is concentrated; and in its propagation of doctrinal orthodoxy. This mirroring behaviour locks the study of anarchism in IR implicitly into an ongoing ideological struggle. Certainly, critical anarchist IR scholars see the entry of anarchism into IR as part of a wider ideological battle against the state and neo-liberal globalization. As Alex Prichard has exhorted, for example, 'The (re)emergence of anarchism in this context is nothing less than a signifier that we may well be achieving critical mass. We should also expect a conservative backlash' (Prichard 2010a: 375). This battle to which anarchist IR is joined is intimately tied to the legitimating practices associated with the construction of anarchism as an international tradition.

Constructing international anarchism

A set of essays by anarchist scholars, entitled 'Blasting the Canon', was published in a special issue of the journal, *Anarchist Developments in Cultural Studies* (Kinna & Evren 2013). While not concerned explicitly with anarchism in IR, the tenor of the edition is instructive not only for its rare acknowledgement of the need to address critically the idea of canonization in anarchist thought, but also for the delimiting way it approaches the theme which remains within the ambit of a specific left-libertarian tradition. Taking 'postanarchism' as its point of departure, it is as much an exercise in deepening the ideological bases of an established way of treating anarchism, as in deconstructing it. Despite the fact that variant forms of postanarchism have usefully de-naturalized the foundationalism traditionally associated with anarchism, the strategy of what one might term dialectical expansion, at work in this special issue, is symptomatic of the way in which the anarchist 'canon' is critiqued yet simultaneously bolstered by scholars sympathetic to either of its dominant ideological forms; in other words, among anarchists and their sympathizers, even critiques of the anarchist 'tradition' are often viewed through the prism of contending visions of anarchist orthodoxy.

On a global level, writing others out of history by situating anarchism within a discrete genealogy of Western modernity, be it left or right, also renders anarchism as an ideology a very Western enterprise. If their mutual preoccupation with the idea of anarchy ties anarchism and IR together, both bodies of thought are also bound by their shared global remit but remarkably provincial intellectual proclivities. IR theorists have only belatedly begun to address seriously the neglect of non-Western thought, two decades after the 'postpositivist' turn (Tickner & Waever 2009; Acharya & Buzan 2010; Tickner & Blaney 2012) with religion, including non-Western religion, also a marginal theoretical concern in the discipline (Thomas 2005). Perhaps more surprisingly, anarchist scholars have also only relatively recently given non-Western contexts extended consideration. Yet, even then, while some recent works reflect this development, they are mainly directed at bringing to light the non-West's radical alignment and engagement with global circuits of Western dissident socialism (Anderson 2008; Ramnath 2011). When they have been included in the anarchist 'canon', non-Western contributions have rarely been seen as being ideologically pivotal and those which have been mentioned have frequently pre-dated the nineteenth-century construct of anarchism (Marshall, 1992). This is a function of the paradoxical recycling of anarchism as a modern ideology with a distinctly Western heritage, but one which simultaneously attempts to subsume – transhistorically and transgeographically – the anti-authoritarian sensibilities of others. As such, the non-West often serves an implicitly instrumental, rather than substantive, function in anarchist ideology, displaying a rapacious discursive logic which exoticizes anarchism by 'worlding' its relevance rather than representing any serious intellectual engagement with non-Western thought. This belated recognition among anarchist scholars has not yet encroached upon anarchist scholarship in IR – the very discipline with an inherently global focus. As one prominent IR academic sympathetic to anarchism has observed recently, 'unfortunately the language and cultural associations of the anarchist legacy are so misleading and diversionary as to make an embrace of anarchism a disempowering intellectual and political option in any public discourse' (Falk 2010: 387).

The myth of international relations

In his incisive discussion of Leo Strauss, John Gunnell described a tradition of thought as 'a retrospective analytical construction which produces a rationalized version of the past' (Gunnell, 1978, 132). Gunnell drew attention to the strategic dimensions of traditions and the ideological purposes they serve which permeate the study of political philosophy.[10] The idea of 'traditions' of international thought has also been central to the development of IR and the subject of some, though by no means wide, contestation, particularly since the 'postpositivist' turn with its emphasis on pluralizing the philosophical and methodological contours of discipline (Jeffery 2005; Hall 2012). More recently, IR is seen to have undergone a 'historical' turn which has pluralized received interpretations of key historical figures in IR's 'canon', widened the historical field in terms of neglected thinkers, and focused on reinvigorating the historiography of the discipline (Bell 2001). What is also of note in this development is that, while the turn to history in IR has been largely welcomed as a more sophisticated corrective to IR's perceived abuses of history as crude anachronism, there has been very little reflection since on the renewed potential for ideologizing history which pluralizing the discipline in this way opens up; it is as if by virtue of countering the long-standing methodological ahistoricism of IR, there is an assumption that revisionist IR historians are necessarily postideological or less inclined to instrumentality in historical interpretation. The case of critical anarchist scholarship in IR suggests otherwise and three ways in which history is deployed by its proponents are of particular note: the assumption of anarchism as a tradition; the strategic use of historical methodologies; and underlying hagiographical tendencies. Assuming a tradition of international thought, however implicitly, without recognizing its contested nature is an odd position for a critical IR theory to take in light of the centrality of notions of contingency and deconstruction as strategies for immanent critique and emancipation. Yet, all the examples of critical anarchist IR theory I have cited in the first part of this chapter do just this. None question the premise of an anarchist 'tradition' in light of the salience of traditions of international thought in IR and the recognition within the discipline of the methodological inadequacy and ideological functions of such categories. In a kind of paradoxical hegemonic consensus, anarchism in IR is cited unproblematically as a self-evident international tradition. This is the case even in more innovative departures where postfoundationalist theorists have questioned the reductionism of anarchism as a category. Thus, for example, in an otherwise penetrative analysis in which he argues against anarchism as an alternative paradigm in IR by retaining anarchism's heretical spirit, Newman's description of anarchism, nonetheless, fits this conventional mould. As he asserts, 'In contrast to the motifs of competition and insecurity among sovereign states central to the realist tradition, *anarchism emphasises the possibilities of cooperation and solidarity between workers and ordinary people across national borders*' (Newman 2012: 267).[11] Elsewhere, Cudworth and Hobden deploy the particularities of the approaches of Kropotkin and Bookchin as representative of anarchist theory, while Kropotkin is also collapsed into anarchism as a coherent category by Goodwin (Cudworth and Hobden 2010; Goodwin 2010). The assumption of anarchism in these works is tied to the idea of there being a shared discursive 'world of anarchism' between author and audience coterminous with a distinct and discernible left-libertarian tradition, where the idea of there being an anarchist tradition is oddly immunized from critique. Anarchism, understood as a discrete phenomenon identified with the ideas and social movements associated with distinctive strands of libertarian socialism that came to prominence in the nineteenth century, certainly makes sense as a phenomenological category. But it is not coterminous with the philosophical premises of radical anti-authority and their more wide-ranging potential to shed new light on IR. It does not follow that historical anarchism as a discrete social and ideological phenomenon can subsume this potential. In doing so, its proponents also betray a contradictory ideological manoeuvre in light of the underlying emancipatory intent of critical IR theory. While anarchism as a discrete tradition of international thought is, therefore, largely assumed in critical IR scholarship, the strategic deployment of specific historical methodologies reinforces this assumption. Methodology, as a strategy in the social sciences and humanities, reflects a conscious decision to approach a subject in a particular interpretative fashion. Why we choose particular methodologies over others is often left unaddressed but, through this process of deliberate selection, normative assumptions are imported into our approaches. The way in which contextual and genealogical historical methodologies are selectively deployed by critical scholars in IR in relation to anarchism further reveals the underlying ideological nature of the anarchist enterprise in IR. As its name suggests, what came to be termed 'contextual' history in the study of the history of political thought among so-called 'Cambridge School' scholars, was, in various ways, intended to challenge the ahistorical biases of scholarly treatments of political thinkers and the purportedly 'timeless' wisdom of their writings (Skinner 1969). In doing so, it constituted a critique of the ideological tendencies inherent in constructing transhistorical bodies of thought by reading contemporary concerns back into history. In his writings, which have done much to alert IR to the neglect of anarchism, Alex Prichard consciously invokes Skinnerian contextualism in his reading of Proudhon (Prichard 2007: 627, n. 22). But, despite invoking it as a method, Prichard's aims belie his more instrumental deployment of contextualism.[12] The problem lies in the underlying normative enterprise with which he is engaged. Prichard is self-consciously searching for historical foundations in order to bolster the normative force of his arguments appealing for the relevance of an anarchist tradition to pressing problems of domination in current international relations. As he asserts in relation to anarchist theory: 'What is missing in this literature is a sense of historical antecedent' (Prichard 2011: 1648). He makes his position clearer by stating his 'political aim' in 'bringing to light some of their historical and disciplinary antecedents' (Prichard 2011: 1650).

This approach inevitably functions not only as history, but as prophesy, and is couched in the language of coincidence. Thus, Prichard argues, such a reading of the historical Proudhon reveals a 'surprising echo' of critical IR theory's concerns – though this is perhaps less surprising in light of his underlying intent – and 'when read together, the works and observations referred to above constitute an "I told you so!" of historic proportions' (Prichard 2007: 624; Prichard 2010b: 451). Elsewhere, he opines, 'we are where we are today – licking our 20th-century wounds – precisely because so few listened to the anarchists' warnings regarding the combination of populism, the emerging nation state and economic expropriation in the 19th century' (Prichard 2010b: 441–442). While our readings of history can never be entirely unpolluted of present contexts and concerns, on this view, it is difficult not to infer that history has become, unavoidably to some degree, 'a predetermined site for the empirical verification of abstract claims' (Lawson 2012: 204).

Genealogical methods used by poststructuralists are not immune to this kind of methodological selectivity. Like contextualism, though from a different perspective drawing on different intellectual resources, genealogy serves to puncture received notions of tradition and reveal alternative historical narratives. In postanarchist writings, for example, this has served the useful purpose of pluralizing our horizons of understanding about the past through unearthing discursive practices of domination and hegemony. Drawing in part on Hakim Bey's notion of 'ontological anarchy', Newman has drawn attention to the relevance of Carl Schmitt's thought in this way (Newman 2012; Bey 1991). But even here anarchism appears to enjoy exceptionalist dispensation. What is also notable about Newman's genealogy of anarchy is that he deploys such methods while, at the same time, leaving anarchism as a 'tradition' uncontested, punctuating his analysis with citations of the hallowed 'classical' triumvirate of Bakunin, Proudhon, and Kropotkin. That anarchist ideology can evade ideological critique, even in the context of studies which adopt methods aimed precisely at this kind of critique, reveals its often perfunctory use as a transhistorical category.

The apologetic way anarchism is treated in critical IR is an extension of the ubiquitous hagiographic tendencies associated with it. In critical IR, historical anarchist thinkers lie outside critique as they themselves are the vehicles for critique. Subsequently, their resurrection tends to serve a rhetorical function. The rehabilitation of anarchist thinkers is, in this mode, quite separate from the impulses that have animated the growing historicity in IR which has been directed to re-evaluating hallowed historical figures, often presenting them as far more complex, contradictory, and inconsistent thinkers. Anarchist scholarship, by contrast, is almost always framed in terms of a *defence* of an anarchist tradition, its leading lights, doctrinal coherence, and perennial relevance. But to be guardians of a tradition does not sit well with the spirit of anarchism as it not only privileges, but deifies, the ideas of others.

Morals and metaphors

My argument has been premised on the view that the ideological discourse of 'anarchist studies' can constrict the wider academic 'study of anarchism' in IR. If it is seen as being coterminous with the possibilities for anarchism in IR, we risk foreclosing alternative scholarly avenues which a turn to anarchism may otherwise open up. To see anarchy as an *anarchist*, which presupposes adherence to a specific ideology, is not the same as an *anarchistic* way of seeing. In this final section, drawn from my own work on anarchism and IR, I want to argue briefly for the conceptual, rather than critical, radicalism of anarchism in IR by deploying the 'domestic analogy' and bringing attention to the authority-centric nature of IR theory (Kazmi 2012). Because of space constraints, I can only be illustrative here. IR is a particularly pertinent discipline in which to address this as the ambivalence of anarchy as a concept at the heart of the discipline allows for anarchism to be wrested from a solely ideological to a more analytic rendering.

States of nature

The rigid distinction between empirical and normative theory, once prevalent in IR, has long been contested. This fact-value dichotomy, much beloved of positivists, appears untenable once the normative premises that underlie all theory become apparent – not least, in ontological assumptions about what constitutes 'the stuff' of international relations, and epistemological biases which privilege certain ways of discerning it. All IR theory is thus normative in some dimension but not all IR theory is critical. To suggest that an anarchist IR theory can be non-critical is not, therefore, to imply that it can be non-normative, only that it need not seek actively to transform the world in some moral dimension drawn from a delimited, albeit ecumenical, set of 'critical' approaches.

One prominent normative assumption often made in non-critical forms of IR theory is the 'state of nature' metaphor and its methodological corollary, the 'domestic analogy'. This methodological manoeuvre privileges the state by drawing on the political theory of the state and its internal institutional arrangements, and in interpolating analogous behaviour between citizens in states and among states in the international system (Suganami 1989). The 'state-centrism' associated with the metaphor appears anathema to the anti-statism of anarchism. Yet, by adapting the analogy, an anarchistic approach can turn the discipline's central concept on its head by, counter-intuitively, focusing on how international anarchy is, in fact, generated and defended by states, rather than simply assumed as a background condition.

This approach is at once 'state-centric' and 'anti-statist'. In the context of a volume on anarchism, state-centrism naturally demands some explanation. It is state-centric only in that its empirical focus is on inter-state behaviour. In choosing to focus on state interactions without focusing on the state's role in global practices of domination, it can be argued, of course, that I am abetting the perpetuation of the state's hegemony, in some sense. This is not my intention any more than it is to launch a moral critique of the state here. I acknowledge, nonetheless, that the ontological claim I am making implicitly about the state's pivotal role in international relations embodies unavoidably these wider normative implications. One can recognize that international relations are pluralist, encompassing state and non-state actors, and that the separation of the domestic and international spheres is, in empirical terms, artificial. But it is also of some theoretical use to bracket off certain domains in order to better elucidate discrete layers of international interaction, without necessarily contesting these deeper presuppositions.

The *critical* radicalism of anarchism can, in this way, be complemented by a *conceptual* radicalism, where

> the radical dimension is retained in an anarchistic way of thinking about an individual unit (in this case the state) in its relation to the social world (in this case the states system) where the identification of liberty with anarchy acts against a defence of all forms of domination – hegemonic, imperialist, and authoritarian – over the individual unit.
>
> (Kazmi 2012: 6)

On this view, weak states, as well as strong, can be conceptualized as anarchists. The approach is also anti-statist, however, in that it departs from the political theory of the state as the parasitic and centripetal focus of IR theory. IR theory draws on the domestic political theory of the state as a master metaphor but this is an inappropriate analogy which has led to a concomitant focus on authority-centric political thinkers – 'realist' and 'liberal' – who view anarchy as a problem to be mitigated. This has limited conceptual and theoretical approaches to international anarchy in IR. The state of nature in anarchist thought which embodies various approaches to conceptualizing a 'society without a state' is, in this regard, a more appropriate analogy.

To paraphrase James Scott, it is a sort of anarchistic 'squint' which makes an alternative view of international anarchy a theoretical possibility in IR (Scott 2012: xii). Because of the deeply rooted 'state of nature' presumption which has placed the state at the centre of Western political thought, IR has, by extension, turned to address the origins and development of the international system of states, but not international anarchy, in its reflections. In any other sphere of inquiry, a social system, however large or small, would require explanation for its resilience and the social practices which construct and sustain it. In this respect, in IR there has been a fundamental conceptual rupture between questions about the ontology of the international system and questions about the ontology of international anarchy.

The reasons for this rupture become more apparent when we recognize that for a concept that has been so pivotal to IR, there has been very little theorizing *about* anarchy itself, even as theorizing *around* the concept of anarchy is endemic, be it in relation to hierarchy or to the multiple possibilities for conflict and cooperation under anarchy. And while critical anarchist IR theory has usefully extended understandings of the possibilities for moral and practical action under international anarchy, the conceptual valences of anarchy still remain relatively under-theorized in these interventions. Thus, despite Alexander Wendt's open-ended assertion that 'anarchy is what states make of it', IR theory remains tied to the *negative* definition of anarchy as *absence* which permeates the political theory of the state. It is, in this sense, authority-centric as it assumes international anarchy as a background condition which needs to be mitigated in some fashion, be it through realist hegemonic stability or liberal international organization, for example.

The authority-centrism of IR theory contrasts with an anarchistic conception of anarchy as a *positive* enabling *presence*. As I have argued elsewhere, this insight opens up possibilities for thinking about inter-state behaviour from the perspective of multiple logics of positive anarchy (Kazmi 2012: 51–79). Put differently, it allows for a re-conceptualization of states as anarchist actors who tie their defence of their own liberty to a defence of international anarchy. A constructivist account of state behaviour, in which state identities and interests are bound, as anarchists, can help to elucidate the variant ways in which states not only act to constrain the negative effects of unbounded anarchy but also actively defend anarchy as the milieu in which their sovereignty can be protected. This can reveal how the decentralizing behaviour of states is also constitutive of the anarchic structure of the international system.

Seeing states as anarchists can add a neglected explanatory dimension to our understanding of state behaviour which has been lost to both traditional authority-centric IR theory, tied to the political theory of the state, and critical anarchist IR theory, tied to particularist ideological beliefs, by drawing attention to the constructive bases of international anarchy. This can engage both conceptual and historical modes of inquiry. A turn to anarchist history can thus become a suggestive rather than pedagogic process, mining for conceptual, rather than ideological, insight and necessitating an intermediate level of theory-building drawn from such historical investigation.

Conclusion

It is curious to observe that the approach to IR most concerned with emancipating the individual from domination is also among the most ideologically missionary and sectarian. Once anarchism is deified into an ideology with a hallowed canon, it is compelled by its own belief systems towards closing down and denigrating those of its competitors. The relative neglect and instrumentalization of the intellectual and political history of the non-West in anarchist scholarship and IR is also a function of this tendency. While it may be an unintentional consequence, this recourse to particular ideological commitments and historical narratives also sets limits on how we understand international relations in phenomenological terms. Academic anarchist 'exceptionalism' is steeped in a history of defensive posturing, instrumental hagiography, and selective omission. By immunizing itself from ideological critique, it seemingly seeks less to emancipate politics than to exit from it altogether.

Yet, is there the intellectual space to think about anarchism in IR beyond apologetics or polemics? As the self-image of anarchism is inclusive and pluralist, one would not only hope, but assume so. Far from being the natural home of anarchism as ideology, the ambivalence of the concept of anarchy in IR destabilizes anarchist assumptions about anarchy revealing its multivalent nature. Paradoxically, IR is uniquely placed to make this challenge precisely because of the centrality of anarchy in the discipline. My discussion of critical anarchist IR theory has attempted to draw attention to the often unacknowledged ideological factors and tendency towards intellectual closure that underlie this particular approach to bringing anarchism into IR.

As an ideology, anarchism is not unique in being pressed into academic service in this way: conservatives and liberals do much the same, of course, often to greater effect. While the ideological purposes for which history is deployed may be refracted onto phenomenological understandings of the present, however, historical interpretation can best be evaluated with reference to the strength of historical arguments, not links to normative agendas. It is not that such categories of social and political thought should be dismissed or dismantled, therefore, but that they should be treated with the degree of scepticism and irony befitting post-hoc hegemonic constructs. In being more open to the conceptual, as well as critical, dimensions of anarchist theory in IR, and more self-reflexive about the roles we ourselves play in constructing anarchism, neglected insights buried under the weight of anarchist ideology may yet come to challenge our *ways of seeing* anarchy, rather than serve as echo chambers for our systems of belief.

Notes

1 I would like to thank Duncan Bell and Casper Sylvest for their helpful comments.
2 'International Relations', or IR, refers to the academic discipline, while 'international relations' to the subject matter of the discipline.
3 'International political theory' has come to denote normative theorizing of international politics but it can also have a looser meaning synonymous with international theory or IR theory more generally.
4 For a notable exception, see Pennock and Chapman (1979).
5 There has been a recent rise in interest in hierarchy in IR. See, for example, Lake (2009),
6 For a recent reassessment of anarchy in IR theory, see the special edition of the *Journal of International Political Theory* (Havercroft and Prichard 2017).
7 For an alternative view and survey, see also, Milner (1991: 67–85).
8 For an alternative view, linking to empire and race, see Vitalis (2000: 331–356).
9 The actual influence of academia on government policy is, however, heavily contested. For a pessimistic view, see Nye (2009).
10 For an alternative critique which, at the same time, asserts the ineluctability of tradition, see Bevir (2000: 28–53).
11 The italics are mine.
12 Skinner has written of the political choices involved in doing historical work. See, for example, Quentin Skinner (1998: 101–21). Prichard, in fact, cites Skinner on this but his own ideological deployment of the language of prophecy and coincidence belies the underlying logic of doing contextual history (Prichard 2013: 20).

References

Acharya, A. and Buzan, B. (eds) (2010) *Non-Western International Relations Theory: Perspectives On and Beyond Asia*, Abingdon: Routledge.
Anderson, B. (2008) *Under Three Flags: Anarchism and the Anti-Colonial Imagination*, London: Verso.
Armitage, D. (2012) *Foundations of International Thought*, Cambridge: Cambridge University Press.
Ashley, R. (1988) 'Untying the Sovereign State: A Double Reading of the Anarchy Problematique', *Millennium*, 17(2): 227–262.
Bartelson, J. (2001) *The Critique of the State*, Cambridge: Cambridge University Press.
Beitz, C. (1979) *Political Theory and International Relations*, Princeton: Princeton University Press.
Bell, D.S.A. (2001) 'International Relations: The Dawn of a Historiographical Turn?', *The British Journal of Politics and International Relations*, 3(1): 115–126.
Bell, D.S.A. (2009) 'Writing the World: Disciplinary History and Beyond', *International Affairs*, 85(1): 3–22.
Bevir, M. (2000) 'On Tradition', *Humanitas*, 13(2): 23–58.
Bey, H. (1991) *T.A.Z: The Temporary Autonomous Zone, Ontological Anarchy and Poetic Terrorism*, New York: Autonomedia.
Booth, K. and Smith, S. (eds) (1995) *International Relations Theory Today*, Cambridge: Polity.
Chandler, D. (2004) 'The Revival of Carl Schmitt in International Relations: The Last Refuge of Critical Theorists?', *Millennium*, 37(1): 27–48.
Cox, R. (1981) 'Social Forces, States and World Orders: Beyond International Relations Theory', *Millennium*, 10(2): 126–155.
Cudworth, E. and Hobden, S. (2010) 'Anarchy and Anarchism: Towards a Theory of Complex International Systems', *Millennium*, 39(2): 399–416.

Daddow, O. (2009) *International Relations Theory*, London: Sage.
Daddow, O. (2013) *International Relations Theory: The Essentials*, London: Sage.
Deleuze, G. and Guattari, F. (1987) *A Thousand Plateaus: Capitalism and Schizophrenia*, Minneapolis: University of Minnesota Press.
Dickinson, G. L. (1916) *The European Anarchy*, New York: Macmillan.
Doyle, M. W. (1983) 'Kant, Liberal Legacies, and Foreign Affairs', *Philosophy and Public Affairs*, 12(3): 205–235.
Durkheim, E. (1893) *The Division of Labour in Society*, trans. George Simpson, 1933. New York: Free Press, 1964.
Falk, R. (1979) 'Anarchism and World Order', in J.R. Pennock and J. Chapman (eds) *Nomos XIX: Anarchism*, New York: New York University Press, pp. 63–87.
Falk, R. (2010) 'Anarchism without "Anarchism": Searching for Progressive Politics in the Early 21st century', *Millennium*, 39(2): 381–398.
Goodwin, A. (2010) 'Evolution and Anarchism in International Relations: The Challenge of Kropotkin's Biological Ontology', *Millennium*, 39(2): 417–437.
Gunnell, J. (1978) 'The Myth of Tradition', *The American Political Science Review*, 72(1): 122–134.
Hall, I. (2012) *Dilemmas of Decline: British Intellectuals and World Politics, 1945–1975*, Berkeley: University of California Press.
Havercroft, J. and Prichard, A. (eds) (2017) 'Anarchy in International Relations Theory: A Reconsideration' (Special Issue), *Journal of International Political Theory*, 13(3).
Held, D. (1995) *Democracy and the Global Order*, Cambridge: Polity.
Herring, R. and Robinson, P. (2003) '"Introduction" to Forum on Chomsky', *Review of International Studies*, 29(4): 551–552.
Hoffman, S. (1977) 'An American Social Science: International Relations', *Daedalus*, 106(3): 41–60.
Huysmans, J. (1999) 'Know your Schmitt: A Godfather of Truth and the Spectre of Nazism', *Review of International Studies*, 25(2): 323–328.
Jeffery, R. (2005) 'Tradition as Invention: The "Traditions Tradition" and the History of Ideas in International Relations', *Millennium*, 34(1): 57–84
Jervis, R. (1976) *Perception and Misperception in International Politics*, Princeton: Princeton University Press.
Kazmi, Z. (2012) *Polite Anarchy in International Relations Theory*, New York: Palgrave Macmillan.
Keohane, R. (1984) *After Hegemony: Cooperation and Discord in the World Political Economy*, Princeton: Princeton University Press.
Kinna, R. (2005) *Anarchism: A Beginner's Guide*, Oxford: OneWorld
Kinna, R. and Evren, S. (2013), 'Introduction: Blasting the Canon', in R. Kinna and S. Evren (eds), *Anarchist Developments in Cultural Studies* 1, Brooklyn, NY: Punctum Books, pp. 1–6.
Krasner, S. (ed.) (1983) *International Regimes*, Ithaca: Cornell University Press.
Kratochwil, F. (1989) *Rules, Norms and Decisions: On the Conditions of Practical and Legal Reasoning in International Relations and Domestic Society*, Cambridge: Cambridge University Press.
Lake, David. A. (2009) *Hierarchy in International Relations*, Ithaca: Cornell University Press.
Lawson, G. (2012) 'The Eternal Divide? History and International Relations', *European Journal of International Relations*, 18(2): 203–226.
Left and Right (1965) 'Editorial: The General Line', *Left and Right: A Journal of Libertarian Thought*, 1(1): 3.
Levy, C. (2011) 'Anarchism and Cosmopolitanism', *Journal of Political Ideologies*, 16(3): 265–278.
Linklater, A. (1998) *The Transformation of Political Community: Ethical Foundations of the Post-Westphalian Era*, Cambridge: Polity.
Marshall, P. (1992) *Demanding the Impossible: A History of Anarchism*, London: Harper Collins.
Mearsheimer, J. (2001) *The Tragedy of Great Power Politics*, New York: W. W. Norton.

Milner, H. (1991) 'The Assumption of Anarchy in International Relations Theory: A Critique', *Review of International Studies*, 17(1): 67–85.

Morgenthau, H. (1948) *Politics among Nations: The Struggle for Power and Peace*, New York: Knopf.

Murray, D. (2010) 'Democratic Insurrection: Constructing the Common in Global Resistance', *Millennium*, 39(2): 461–482.

Newman, S. (2012) 'Crowned Anarchy: Postanarchism and International Relations theory', *Millennium*, 40(2): 259–278.

Nye, J. S. (2009) 'Scholars on the Sidelines', *The Washington Post*, 13 April 2009.

Pennock, J. R. and Chapman, J. (eds) (1979) *Nomos XIX: Anarchism*, New York: New York University Press.

Prichard, A. (2007) 'Justice, Order and Anarchy: The International Political Theory of Pierre-Joseph Proudhon (1809–1865)', *Millennium*, 35(3): 623–645.

Prichard, A. (2010a) 'Introduction: Anarchism and World Politics', *Millennium*, 39(2): 373–380.

Prichard, A. (2010b) 'David Held is an Anarchist: Discuss', *Millennium*, 39(2): 439–459.

Prichard, A. (2010c) 'Deepening Anarchism: International Relations and the Anarchist Ideal', *Anarchist Studies*, 18(2): 29–57.

Prichard, A. (2011) 'What Can the Absence of Anarchism Tell Us about the History and Purpose of International Relations?' *Review of International Studies*, 37(4): 1647–1669.

Prichard, A. (2012) 'Anarchy, Anarchism and International Relations', in R. Kinna (ed.) *The Continuum Companion to Anarchism*, London: Continuum, pp. 96–108.

Prichard, A. (2013) *Justice, Order and Anarchy: The International Political Theory of Pierre-Joseph Proudhon*, Abingdon: Routledge.

Ramnath, M. (2011) *Haj to Utopia: How the Ghadar Movement Charted Global Radicalism and Attempted to Overthrow the British Empire*, Berkeley: University of California Press.

Roach, S. R. (2007) *Critical Theory and International Relations: A Reader*, Abingdon: Routledge

Ross, D. (1991) *The Origins of American Social Science*, Cambridge: Cambridge University Press.

Rossdale, C. (2010) 'Anarchy is What Anarchists Make of It: Reclaiming the Concept of Agency in IR and Security Studies', *Millennium*, 39(2): 483–501.

Ruggie, J. G. (1983) 'Continuity and Transformation in the World Polity: Toward a Neorealist Synthesis', *World Politics*, 35(2): 261–285.

Ruggie, J. G. (1998) *Constructing the World Polity: Essays on International Institutionalization*, Abingdon: Routledge.

Schmidt, B. (1998) *The Political Discourse of Anarchy: A Disciplinary History of International Relations*, Albany: State University of New York Press.

Scott, J. C. (1998) *Seeing Like a State: How Certain Schemes to Improve the Human Condition Have Failed*, New Haven: Yale University Press.

Scott, J. C. (2012) *Two Cheers for Anarchism: Six Easy Pieces on Autonomy, Dignity, and Meaningful Work and Play*, Princeton: Princeton University Press.

Skinner, Q. (1969) 'Meaning and Understanding in the History of Ideas', *History and Theory*, 8(1): 3–53.

Skinner, Q. (1998) *Liberty before Liberalism*, Cambridge: Cambridge University Press.

Smith, S. (2002) 'The United States and the Discipline of International Relations: "Hegemonic Country, Hegemonic Discipline"', *International Studies Review* 4(2): 57–85.

Smith, S., Booth, K. and Zalewski, M. (eds) (1996) *International Theory: Positivism and Beyond*, Cambridge: Cambridge University Press.

Suganami, H.(1989) *The Domestic Analogy and World Order Proposals*, Cambridge:Cambridge University Press.

Sylvest, C. (2009) *British Liberal Internationalism, 1880–1930: Making Progress?*Manchester: Manchester University Press.

Thomas, S. (2005) *The Global Resurgence of Religion and the Transformation of International Relations: The Struggle for the Soul of the Twenty-First Century*, New York: Palgrave Macmillan.

TicknerA.B. and Blaney, D.L. (eds) (2012) *Thinking International Relations Differently*, Abingdon: Routledge.
TicknerA.B. and Waever, O. (eds) (2009) *International Relations Scholarship Around the World*, Abingdon: Routledge.
Turner, S. (1998) 'Global Civil Society, Anarchy and Governance: Assessing an Emerging Paradigm', *Journal of Peace Research*, 35: 25–42.
Vitalis, R. (2000) 'The Graceful and Generous Liberal Gesture: Making Racism Invisible in American International Relations', *Millennium*, 29(2): 331–356.
Waltz, K. (1979) *Theory of International Politics*, New York: McGraw-Hill.
Ward, C. (2004) *Anarchism: A Very Short Introduction*, Oxford: Oxford University Press.
Weber, C. (2001) *International Relations Theory: A Critical Introduction*, Abingdon: Routledge.
Weiss, T. (1975) 'The Tradition of Philosophical Anarchism and Future Directions in World Policy', *Journal of Peace Research*, 12(1): 1–17.
Wendt, A. (1999) *Social Theory of International Politics*, Cambridge: Cambridge University Press.

4 Anarchism and Critical Security Studies

Chris Rossdale

Security has become the governing ideology of our contemporary age. In its name bombs are dropped, uprisings suppressed, walls erected, weapons sold, and countless numbers spied upon, imprisoned, tortured, and killed; and yet, despite the monumental economic and political resources expended in pursuit of security, life for most people feels less, not more, secure. Threats – whether economic, physical, environmental, imperial – abound, and a future of perpetual financial, military, and ecological crises beckons. Meanwhile, in a series of cruel ironies which those familiar with radical politics know only too well, the supposed agents of security are frequently those propelling and profiting from these abundant insecurities.

In the post-Enlightenment era, systems of hierarchical authority are legitimated by and through their capacity to provide security, to save us from ourselves and from dangerous outsiders and so create the conditions for lives worth living. Such is the social contract so treasured by liberal theorists. This starting point alone demonstrates that anarchists should be (and always have been) engaged with questions of security, revealing and challenging the myths upon which the state and other forms of authority are based. Such concerns have been magnified significantly in recent times, reaching unprecedented levels in the post-9/11 (in)security environment. Our époque is one of permanent paranoia, of normalized exception, in which abuses of authority and the deployment of military power are always already justified by the unending insecurity caused by the myriad (if vague) threats of international terrorism, cyber warfare, unstable markets, disobedient tyrants, and, of course, anarchists.

Security Studies, as an academic discipline, has traditionally been one which has remained servile to, rather than critical of, extant structures and power systems. Dominated by scholars loyal to variants of the 'realist' tradition, it has proceeded with a model which focuses predominantly on relations between states, viewing these states as unitary, self-interested, and in perpetual, volatile, and zero-sum competition with other states. Such models have tended to view security in minimal terms, as the negotiation of military conflict between states, irrespective of internal conditions, imperial and economic relations or ethical considerations.[1] The status quo has been the objective of these theories, a feature which renders them particularly amenable to those for whom this status quo involves their continued dominance of domestic and international life.[2] As Ken Booth argues, 'realist-derived security studies continues to survive and flourish because the approach is congenial for those who prosper from the intellectual hegemony of a top-down, statist, power-centric, masculinized, ethnocentric, and militarized worldview of security' (Booth 2005b: 9).

Critical Security Studies (CSS) has emerged in response to these 'traditional' approaches, and has sought to ask ethical, conceptual, and systemic questions which develop new ways of analyzing and criticizing contemporary international politics and which seek to inspire new pathways forward. To date, anarchist engagement with CSS has been minimal. In this chapter I outline some points of connection, in order to show two things. First, that scholars working within the broad remit of CSS have developed perspectives which can be of significant use to anarchists in criticizing hierarchical and coercive systems of authority, and which highlight some ways in which discourses and practices of security must themselves be the target of critique for any theory or philosophy which seeks to resist domination and explore new ways of living. I do this by outlining some of the most significant approaches within CSS, pointing towards the ways in which their critiques animate or expand upon themes within anarchism. My second intention is to suggest some ways in which taking anarchism seriously might provoke ways of rethinking security which have been overlooked or ignored by much of CSS. It is here that my own research at these intersections has been focused, thinking about the ways in which anarchists have experimented with forms of security which eschew coercive and hierarchical systems of authority. What is mutual aid, for example, if not an anarchist ethic of security? I outline some ways in which this approach to anarchism might be useful in the context of CSS. In the closing discussion I argue that, beyond advocating a more emancipatory approach to security, anarchism can be more radically employed to undermine the very conceptual and political foundations of security and insecurity, to unsettle their grip on modern political life, and to generate ways of being that disrupt rather than reproduce political authority.

Critical Security Studies

Security Studies is usually classified as a subfield of International Relations (IR), and most of those working specifically on security find themselves in the politics departments of their universities. Despite this (and especially in the case of CSS), the study of security is a genuinely interdisciplinary enterprise incorporating philosophy, sociology, history, anthropology, geography, and more. It has few clear boundaries, drawing scholars from a variety of backgrounds. Those working within its remit have sought to ask a series of questions, notably:

- Who or what should the referent object (i.e., the thing to be secured) of security? Should it be states? Individuals? Social groups?
- Who should do the securing?
- Can we think about security beyond just military considerations? Environmental security? Food security? Human security?
- Does the security of some always entail the insecurity of others?

A significant number of surveys and edited collections have been published, alongside a large number of research monographs on one or more of these themes.[3] In addition several journals regularly publish work relevant to CSS, notably *Security Dialogue, Millennium: Journal of International Studies, Review of International Studies*, and more recently *Critical Studies on Security*. As with all such pursuits, there are few common positions which unite all of those working within CSS, the ambiguity of the term 'critical' and the impossibility of a 'neutral' understanding of security (Smith

2005) setting the stage for perpetual disagreement. Nonetheless a broad tradition of scepticism towards 'official' narratives, practices, and orthodoxies of security engenders at least something of a research community.

Despite the rise in attention to the wider field of IR from anarchists, there have been few contributions on the topic of security more specifically.[4] Nonetheless there exists within CSS scholarship much that is of value for anarchists. In the following few pages I point towards some particular conceptual approaches which demonstrate affinities with and analyses useful for anarchist approaches to security. The various approaches are not mutually exclusive, nor is this list exhaustive, serving only to suggest some useful directions.

One central approach has been the 'Welsh School', which has sought to use Frankfurt School analysis as a critical resource for thinking about security. Derived predominantly from the work of Booth and Richard Wyn Jones, Welsh School approaches are notable for their desire to introduce a more explicitly normative dimension to the study of security than is present in most other accounts. Inspired by the Coxian dictum that 'all theory is for someone and for some purpose', much has been taken from Wyn Jones' insistence that critical security studies must be for 'the voiceless, the unrepresented, the powerless' (Wyn Jones 1999: 159). These sentiments find theoretical expression in the idea that human emancipation should be the aim of security. As Booth argues:

> [e]mancipation should logically be given precedence in our thinking about security over the mainstream themes of power and order ... 'Security' means the absence of threats. Emancipation is the freeing of people (as individuals and groups) from those physical and human constraints which stop them carrying out what they would freely choose to do. War and the threat of war is one of those constraints, together with poverty, poor education, and political oppression and so on. Security and emancipation are two sides of the same coin. Emancipation, not power or order, produces true security. Emancipation, theoretically, is security.
>
> (Booth 1991: 319)

Such a conceptualization challenges received wisdom about the relationship between security and the state. For more traditional accounts, the state is the only conceivable object of security, and security studies is about investigating dynamics which render the state, as a timeless and non-political object, more or less vulnerable to other states. Welsh School approaches refuse this on the counts that states are, at best, the means, not the end, of security, and that for many people around the world their primary source of insecurity is *precisely* their own state (Booth 1991: 320). Alongside the focus on security-as-emancipation and sceptical attitude towards making security about 'the state', Welsh School approaches have borrowed the method of immanent critique from the Frankfurt School (Stamnes 2004; Fierke 2007: 167–185). Together, these features come together to produce an approach to security which judges policies and possibilities based not on whether they strengthen the position of a nation state or simply curb particular threats, but on the extent to which they contribute to human emancipation in a more substantive sense. Such a sensibility holds clear resonances with anarchism.

A second important conceptual approach within CSS has been 'securitization' theory. Originally formulated by Ole Wæver, securitization theory moves away from traditional approaches which view security as a property of a thing (which may be more or less secure), and instead argues that security is more usefully understood as a discursive act, a speech act (Wæver 1995). The act of naming something as a security issue or threat thus 'imbues it with a sense of importance and urgency that legitimizes the use of special measures outside of the usual political process to deal with it' (Smith 2005: 34). Examples of securitized issues include international terrorism, piracy, migration, and social movements. In all of these cases, a particular series of objects have been constructed as a threat which necessitates extraordinary responses.

'Security', in this context, signifies an extra-political state of exception and the process of constructing something discursively within the realm of security 'results in a militarized and confrontational mind-set which defines security questions in an us-versus-them manner' (Smith 2005: 34). CSS scholars focusing on securitization have been wary of attempts to redefine security in an emancipatory fashion as per the Welsh School, cautioning that 'it is important to be aware of the politics one legitimises by endorsing security' (Aradau 2004: 399). That is, that there is something deeply undemocratic, 'Othering', and militarizing about discourses of security, and that attempts to reclaim these discourses run the risk of legitimating autocratic political practices. As such, some scholars have suggested that 'desecuritization', that is, the tactic of taking issues out of the threat-defence, exceptional framework of security, might offer more democratic options (Huysmans 1998; Aradau 2004; Elbe 2006; McDonald 2008).

Feminist approaches to security studies have exposed the patriarchal foundations upon which the politics of security rest. This has involved outlining how the role of women has been obscured in dominant accounts of international politics, and demonstrating how the 'normal' conduct of international relations depends on the subordination of women (Enloe 1989; Tickner 2001). Alongside this focus on exclusion and subordination has been an account of how, far from unimportant or peripheral, women have been active in 'on-the-ground' security politics, whether as guerrilla warriors, peace activists, community leaders and more (Sylvester 1994, 1996; McEvoy 2010; MacKenzie 2010). Their relative marginalization within security studies speaks volumes about sedimented ideas about who should and should not be considered important or meaningful.

Whilst many feminist scholars have focused predominantly on seeking to come to terms with the marginalization of women in the context of security, others have sought to identify the ways in which security politics is 'gendered', that is, in which the particular power relations which make up our contemporary security landscape intersect with certain gendered identities and performances. One important early study here was Carol Cohn's (1987) study of US defense intellectuals, in which she revealed the centrality of gendered understandings to 'strategic' narratives.[5] More recently, scholars have looked at how particular accounts of gender identity underpin different security imperatives. For instance, we might point towards the ways in which Afghani women have been narrated as helpless, as subordinated to inferior (non-Western) masculinities, and as therefore in need of the security which might be provided by heroic Western men (Weber 2005; Shepherd 2006). Or we may look at the ways in which the gender identities of deviant Western soldiers have been called into question as a means of creating distance from their crimes, as with Lynndie England's 'failed' femininity, or Chelsea Manning's 'failed' masculinity.

Such accounts are clearly important for anarchists insofar as they reveal particular power relations in the context of security politics. However, there is a slightly deeper critique here which links feminist scholarship with anarchism. Through much of this work runs a critique of the idea of *protection*, and of the relationship between security and protection. For feminists, the purportedly apolitical concept of protection is problematic because it frequently masks the reality that, for many people, their primary source of danger is precisely the one who claims to be providing protection (whether a family patriarch, employer, state, or 'liberal' international community). V. Spike Peterson (1992: 50) makes such an argument when she likens the (gendered) state to a racketeer who demands 'the exchange of obedience/subordination for (promises) of security'. The 'protected' are then entrapped within a system which sediments their structural servitude:

> ... decision making and threat assessment [are left] to those with particular interests that are only ambiguously related to 'collective interests.' Identification of the protected with their protectors (as opposed to other protectees), as well as identification of protectors with each other, further complicates alliance formation directed at transforming the system itself. Protection systems also distort the meaning of 'consent' by both mystifying the violence that backs up the systemic inequality and perpetuating the illusion of equality among parties to 'contractual obligations'.
>
> (ibid. 52)

Security is cast here as a Faustian pact in which obedience, to both the protector and the system within which the protector is embedded and legitimated, is offered in exchange for 'marginal improvements' within the system.[6] Anarchists have themselves made similar arguments, highlighting the ways in which promises of protection can be duplicitous and tend to incorporate subjects within a hierarchical and exploitative system which depends precisely on the perpetual precarity of its protectees; it is here placed in the context of security and gender in a manner which extends the space for anarchist analyses dramatically.

The final theoretical trend on which I focus here comprises those approaches which have used poststructuralist thought to speak to the politics of security. Drawing on thinkers such as Michel Foucault, Jacques Derrida, Judith Butler, and Giorgio Agamben, poststructuralists have examined the ways in which particular narratives, interpretations, and representations of central concepts associated with security, such as identity, threat, safety, and protection, have been constructed as 'truths' in a manner which underpins (and reproduces) dominant power relations. A great deal of this work has been concerned with identifying those binary logics which function to establish (and depoliticize) particular narratives: the civilized 'us' versus the barbarous 'them', the safe 'inside' versus the anarchic 'outside', the lives worth grieving and those which are expendable (Ashley 1988; Walker 1993; Butler 2009). Our contemporary politics of security (and thus war, violence, and statecraft) depends upon certain truths which render particular responses legitimate, and others illegitimate.

Alongside this focus on narrative and representation, poststructuralists have examined the *practices* associated with security. They have used concepts such as Foucault's analysis of biopolitics to examine the ways in which everyday life is governed and regulated through particular power relations and security imperatives. Security is not solely about sweeping narratives of 'us' and 'them', but signifies the micro-political performances and prohibitions which run throughout the social system, governing who may and may not enter the country, blurring lines between military and police enforcement, rendering political protest nominally legitimate but increasingly subject to repression, and seeing advanced metadata algorithms employed for more 'effective' governance and surveillance (Bigo and Tsoukala 2008; Amoore 2009). All of these (and more) signify a form of political control which is perhaps less centralized and absolute than in previous times, but thereby also more subtle and nearly inextricable.

Such critiques are important for anarchists, and not simply because they reveal crucial processes through which power is exercised in security politics. They also tell us something fundamental about how the contemporary nation state is constituted, and about the role of security in constituting the state. Insisting that the state has 'no ontological status apart from the many and varied practices that constitute their reality' (Campbell 1998b: 12), poststructuralists focus on how particular representations and practices reflect and reinforce dominant power relations. David Campbell argues that discourses of security hold a key role in reinforcing the 'truth' of the state; states must continually justify their existence and relevance, must engage in a perpetual project of rendering unquestionable the borders and bureaucracies which constitute this peculiar social edifice. The place of danger and security are vital here:

> [s]hould the state project of security be successful in the terms in which it is articulated, the state would cease to exist. Security as the absence of movement would result in death via stasis. Ironically, then, the inability of the state project of security to succeed is the guarantor of the state's continued success as an impelling identity.
> (ibid.)

The state's legitimacy depends on the continual production of insecurity. Such a perspective profoundly undermines the liberal notion of the state as a security provider. Much has already been written about the possibilities which emerge from a conversation between anarchism and poststructuralism (May 1994; Call 2002; Newman 2007; Rouselle and Evren 2011; Jun 2012). I would suggest that such possibilities are particularly pronounced when discussing the concept and practice of security, and the critique of contemporary forms of power which is contained within such analyses.

An anarchist response

Thus far, this chapter has focused solely on what perspectives taken from CSS can offer for anarchist thought. However, I want to go on to argue that there is much within anarchism which might enrich how we think about security, beyond the extant terms of CSS. In the second half of this chapter I point towards two possible approaches. This is not to suggest that anarchism might sit as a discrete theoretical approach within CSS, but instead to suggest that anarchist thought and practice could serve as an insurrection against the terms by which security has been understood (and violently imposed).

First, I will suggest that anarchism provides a critique of approaches to security which argue that the state is, or could be, a provider of security (or vehicle for an emancipatory reformulation of security). Anarchists have consistently and persuasively argued that, far from being a security provider, state systems have more generally operated as instruments of domination, and paid scant regard to the (in)security of their citizens. Rather than explore ways in which prevailing systems of authority might be better aligned to provide a more emancipatory form of security, an anarchist approach insists that we focus on ways in which ordinary people create their own forms of security, away from (and often in response to) those who profess to be the natural agents of security. In this sense, anarchism inspires a sort of security from below.

Secondly, I argue that a more radical anarchist account might seek to break out of the confines of thinking and acting in terms of security/insecurity. Building on those insights from CSS highlighted above, I suggest that the concept of security is too deeply woven with authoritarian and statist political forms to serve as a building block for an anti-authoritarian politics. Instead, we might want to think about the ways in which the terms of security/insecurity might be undermined, in which we could explore a politics which disrupts their hold on the contemporary political imagination. I will suggest that, at its best, anarchist theory and practice already engages in such a project.

As noted above, a significant feature of CSS has been the critique of the state-centrism of more conventional approaches towards security. Numerous writers have identified the contradictions involved in analyses which place the state as the central object for security studies (that is, as the thing to be secured), arguing both that many states are simply not in the business of providing security for their citizens, and that the ultimate focus should surely be the security of individuals and social groups (McSweeney 1999: 45–67), with state security, at best, a means rather than an end.

This critique of a field which has traditionally taken the primacy of state security as a firm and self-evident starting principle remains a significant one, opening the door for conceptions of security which are perhaps less tightly bound to militarist and authoritarian precepts, and which might be less readily shaped to serve elite interests. However, despite this move to critique the state-centrism of traditional accounts of security, CSS itself remains deeply state-centric. Whilst the state is displaced as the unquestioned object of security, its status as the presumed *means* of achieving security remains implicit. There exists a faith that, through pressure, enlightenment, pluralism or reform, a more virtuous form of security can be produced through the state (Tickner 2001: 96–125; Thomas and Tow 2002a, 2002b; Kaldor 2003; Linklater 2005; Floyd 2007).

One explicit example of this enduring statism comes from Booth (who, as noted above, was instrumental in mounting the original challenge to the statism of traditional approaches). On the one hand, Booth is relatively firm in his scepticism about the capacities of states to 'provide' security, stating that 'for the most part states fluctuate between the role of gangsters, prostitutes, fat cats, or bystanders' (Booth 2007: 204) and that '[f]or many people on earth, life is "solitary, poore, nasty, brutish, and short" within their state, as a result of government policy or incompetence; such insecurity is in the nature of some states, and not only, as Hobbes famously said, in the state of nature itself' (Booth 2007: 203). On the other hand, he argues that '[a]t this stage of history sovereign states exist at best as necessary evils for human society' (ibid.) and that '[s]overeign states exist, and in some form will continue indefinitely, but they should never be "romanticised"' (Booth 2007: 202). His assertion that states constitute a 'necessary evil' is broadly unqualified, save for the comment that '[l]ocally and globally there is a need for mechanisms for producing redistribution and welfare' (Booth 2007: 205), a comment which does little to substantiate a logic which equates the *existence* of states with a *dependence* on states as the fundamental means (and possibility) of security.

Usefully Booth links his position to anarchism. He asserts that

[f]ew would go *all the way* with the anarchist position that states are an 'extraneous burden' on society, and should be dispensed with, but more might accept Thomas Paine's view that society is 'a blessing' in a way the sovereign state is not.

(Booth 2007: 203, emphasis added)

By miscasting anarchism into an 'all the way' dichotomy, Booth shuts down much of the challenge which anarchism offers (some of which I outline below). More significantly for the purposes here, the dichotomy he erects between dispensing and not dispensing with the state implicitly legitimates the perpetuation of the state as the only reasonable choice in the absence of an immanent and complete utopia. The totality of the state form is presumed (and its mythical status thus reinforced) in a manner which ignores or overlooks the myriad ways in which people across the world are continually working to displace it.

We can see a more particular example of this where Booth discusses various forms of civil society. He has mentioned the progressive role of Amnesty International (Booth 1997: 98–99), the positive impacts of 'donating money to a charity [and] working for an NGO' (Booth 2007: 198), and discussed the global citizenship manifested in the direct action of the 'Seeds of Hope' women, who broke into a military base and damaged a Hawk aircraft which would otherwise have been sold by the UK to Indonesia (Booth 2007: 202–203).[7] These three examples represent a broad spectrum of activism, from the relatively conservative structural position occupied by Amnesty International to the more radical direct action carried out by Seeds of Hope. What is interesting is the way in which Booth has cast these actions as *adjuncts* to statist agency, failing to consider how they might constitute a challenge to the ways in which we think about the state in the context of security. In an introduction to a special issue of *International Relations* in which one of the Seeds of Hope women wrote about her experience, Booth approvingly refers to Tim Dunne and Nicholas Wheeler's call for 'a progressive alliance between the moral awareness of cosmopolitan transnational civil society and enlightened state leaders' (Booth 2004: 6). For him (and Dunne, Wheeler and others), there is a place for 'non-state actors', but it is fully folded into statist metaphysics.

Beyond this focus on the state, there exists a commitment in CSS to what I have called a 'hegemonic ontology of agency'. By this I mean the presumption that 'real' security can only be achieved in the context of a single locus of legitimacy and authority. While there might be contestation over the precise nature of 'the securer' (perhaps a world state, or a workers' state), the core principle remains the same, that is, that the ultimate goal remains totalization, that for security to be achieved, the social sphere must be dominated by a single principle, agent or form. Whilst this commitment remains largely implicit, I suggest that it remains active precisely in the assumption that the state is the only possible means of security, and that to suggest otherwise is to advocate an 'all the way' break into utopia. It can also be found in calls for CSS to develop 'counter-hegemonic' positions which are 'based on different understandings of human potentialities' (Wyn Jones 1999: 161).

My critique of such hegemonic approaches takes its influence from Richard Day's work. He argues that the logic of hegemony has dominated liberal and Marxist approaches to social change. By the logic of hegemony, he means

> a process through which various factions struggle over meaning, identity and political power. To use the words of Antonio Gramsci, a key thinker in this lineage, a social group which seeks hegemony strives to 'dominate antagonistic groups,

which it tends to "liquidate," or to subjugate perhaps even by armed force', at the same time as it attempts to 'lead' kindred and allied groups (Gramsci 1971: 57). Hegemony is a simultaneously coercive and consensual struggle for *dominance*, seen in nineteenth- and twentieth-century marxisms as limited to the context of a particular nation-state, but increasingly being analysed at a global level.

(Day 2005: 6–7, emphasis in original)

Day argues that the response to hegemony, in Marxist and liberal theory and in radical social movements, has traditionally been to seek a *counter*-hegemony, to 'shift the historical balance back, as much as possible, in favour of the oppressed' (ibid.). Significantly he responds to the counter-hegemonic instinct by insisting that

[t]o argue in this way … is to remain within the logic of neoliberalism; it is to accept what I call the *hegemony of hegemony*. By this I mean to refer to the assumption that effective social change can only be achieved simultaneously and *en mass*, across an entire national or supranational space.

(Day 2005: 8, emphasis in original)

Such assumptions, upon which the state form rests, mean that domination is always from the start folded into radical political projects; to achieve liberty, or equality, or security, one must always first dominate (or exclude and cast into the position of a useful enemy) that which does not fit. Such dominations and exclusions return us to uncomfortably militaristic and instrumentalizing conceptions of security.

It would be wrong to suggest that all of CSS falls into this particular line of thought; feminist and poststructural scholars have pointed to just such concerns. For instance, Marieke de Goede argues that '[h]ighlighting the plurality and ambiguity of dissent can contribute to overcoming the "fear and hopelessness generated by monolithic accounts of the 'neoliberal project,'" in which only broad-based counter-hegemonic challenges are considered purposeful' (de Goede 2005: 389, citing Larner 2003: 512). Even in such accounts, however, in the final analysis the figure of the state returns. For example, Kyle Grayson (2008: 394) argues that attention to the biopolitics of human security might guide attempts to 'govern responsibly', and Campbell (1998a: 238) advocates an (admittedly pluralized, non-nationalist) state.

In contrast, anarchists have been consistent (and persistent) in their criticism of the state. Mikhail Bakunin wrote that '[i]f there is a state, then necessarily there is domination and consequently slavery' and that

[s]o-called popular representatives and rulers of the state elected by the entire nation on the basis of universal suffrage … is a lie behind which the despotism of a ruling minority is concealed, a lie all the more dangerous in that it represents itself as the expression of a sham popular will.

(Bakunin 2005a: 178)

Similarly, in a communiqué against the First World War signed by a number of important anarchists including Errico Malatesta, Emma Goldman, and Alexander Berkman, it was stated that 'the anarchists' role in the current tragedy is to carry on proclaiming that there is but one war of liberation: the one waged in every country by the oppressed against the oppressor, the exploited against the exploiter' (Malatesta et al. 2005: 389), and Leo Tolstoy wrote that

> [t]o deliver men from the terrible and ever-increasing evils of armaments and war, we want neither congresses nor conferences, nor treaties, nor courts of arbitration, but the destruction of those instruments of violence which are called Governments, and from which humanity's greatest evils flow.
>
> (Tolstoy 1990: 86)

In criticizing the capacity of the state to cater for human needs, anarchists also mounted a critique of hegemonic approaches more widely, insisting on the space for constant experimentation and change. For instance, Rudolf Rocker argued that

> Anarchism is no patent solution for all human problems, no Utopia of a perfect social order, as it has so often been called, since on principle it rejects all absolute schemes and concepts. It does not believe in any absolute truth, or in definite final goals for human development, but in an unlimited perfectibility of social arrangements and human living conditions, which are always straining after higher forms of expression, and to which for this reason one can assign no definite terminus nor set any fixed goal. The worst crime of every type of state is just that it always tries to force the rich diversity of social life into definite forms and adjust it to one particular form.
>
> (Rocker 2004: 15)

On similar terms Bakunin asks

> what brains are mighty enough and massive enough to encompass the infinite multiplicity and diversity of substantive interests, aspirations, wishes and needs, the sum of which represents the collective will of a people, and mighty and massive enough to devise a social organization capable of satisfying them all? That origination will never be anything other than a Procrustean bed upon which the more or less pronounced violence of the State will compel society to stretch out.
>
> (Bakunin 2005b: 207)

The problem in such a context is not so much the state as it is the fact that the state form constitutes the contemporary source and legitimation of domination. A reliance on a hegemonic imaginary is liable to merely replace one state with another. Instead, in order to avoid bringing the logic of domination back in, an approach which accepts disagreement, diversity, and change is crucial.

Highlighting anarchism's persistent critique of the state must not be the end of the story. Over the past few years there has been some debate about the extent to which 'classical' anarchists fetishized or tended to presume the functional unity of the state to an extent which failed to take account of the underlying power relationships which make the state possible (Franks 2007; Newman 2007: 37–54). Without wishing to retread this well-worn ground, my own approach takes influence from Gustav Landauer's account:

> [a] table can be overturned and a window can be smashed. However, those who believe that the state is also a thing or a fetish that can be overturned or smashed are sophists and believers in the Word. The state is a social relationship; a certain way of people relating to one another. It can be destroyed by creating new social relationships; i.e., by people relating to one another differently.
>
> The absolute monarch said: I am the state. We, who we have imprisoned ourselves in the absolute state, must realize the truth: *we* are the state! And we will be the state as long as we are nothing different; as long as we have not yet created the institutions necessary for a true community and a true society of human beings.
>
> (Landauer 2010: 214, emphasis in original)

Such an understanding demands that resistance must be a creative and prefigurative endeavour. More substantially for the purposes here it challenges us to think about the ways in which everyday forms of desire, dependence and domination themselves work to constitute the state form. This does not, of course, mean that the state itself is therefore rendered irrelevant; displacing its ontology does not mean ignoring the fact that the state is an abstraction for which and through which people obey and kill. As Jamie Heckert argues, 'the state may be considered that name which we give to the oppressive effects produced through decentralized relations of domination, surveillance, representation and control' (Heckert 2011: 199). In the context of an anarchist account of security, identifying the fact that the state form will not provide security is an important step, but limited if we do not simultaneously ask what it is about our everyday social relations which binds us to statist modes of security, and work to identify creative means of forming new security relations.

Alongside a persistent critique of the state, it is here that I suggest anarchism can make significant contributions to the understanding and reconfiguration of security. A key principle of anarchism has always been that of self-liberation. As Goldman (1969: 224) wrote, '[h]istory tells us that every oppressed class gained true liberation from its masters through its own efforts'. Whilst hegemonic forms of politics insist upon an appeal to authority, to a sovereign structure of legitimacy and security which will judge competing claims (usually through a lens of extant privilege), anarchists 'believe with Stirner that man has as much liberty as he is willing to take. Anarchism therefore stands for direct action, the open defiance of, and resistance to, all laws and restrictions, economic, social, and moral' (ibid., 65). Anarchists have recognized that making demands on existing structures of power, whilst perhaps sometimes a useful tactical choice, ultimately tends to reinforce those structures. In Day's terms,

> every demand, in anticipating a response, *perpetuates* those structures, which exist precisely in anticipation of demands. This leads to a positive feedback loop, in which the ever increasing depth and breadth of apparatuses of discipline and control create ever new sites of antagonism, which produce new demands, thereby increasing the quantity and intensity of discipline and control
>
> (Day 2011: 107–108).

The alternative is therefore to transform directly the conditions of our own lives, to search for ways to live and commune in ways which resist, undermine or subvert coercive and authoritarian political structures.

Much of anarchist thought and practice works on precisely this level, exploring different ways of effecting such transformations. Space constraints prohibit a full survey, but examples range from more substantial experiments such as the Kibbutzim movement (Horrox 2009), the Spanish revolution (Dolgoff 1974; Ackelsberg 2005), and the Zapatista National Liberation Army (Krøvel 2010), to more micro-political explorations. Food Not Bombs groups, international solidarity movements, community housing and residents' associations, and community defence projects, whilst perhaps not directly seeking to overturn entire social fabrics in a singular gesture, precisely seek to cope with different forms of human insecurity without recourse to structures of authority, without recasting domination as the condition of possibility of liberation.[8] They can be seen as attempts to build security from below, in a manner which is directly responsive to the needs of those involved. Such projects seek to build security without exclusion, and without ceding to the fiction that liberty must be 'balanced' with security (which, as Mark Neocleous (2007) argues convincingly, is a dichotomy always predisposed to cede liberty to an elite-bound conception of security). What examples along the lines I suggest here do, perhaps, is cast the ethic of mutual aid which has been central to the anarchist imagination as an anarchist ethic and practice of security.

We might also see forms of direct action which seek to limit the conduct of state and corporate power through this lens. On a wide range of different issues, anarchists and fellow travellers have engaged in actions which serve to prevent particular policies and practices. Anti-militarists blockade bases and damage military equipment, environmentalists shut down power stations, and broad-based anti-capitalist coalitions have been remarkably successful in pursuing the WTO and IMF across the globe. As I have argued elsewhere (Rossdale 2010; 2016), such actions can be seen as imagining an alternative response to the politics of security. In a context where the 'official' apparatuses of security might actually be seen to be engendering or facilitating colossal insecurity, there are myriad examples where so-called ordinary people are 'doing' the security work that their governments are not, recasting security as a zone of popular participation without the disciplining and depoliticizing injunctions of representation, (un)due process, or patronizing injunctions that such matters are too important to be constrained by considerations of democracy and popular will. These forms of direct action elude the state, and remind us that a grandmother chained to a military base might know more about her security needs than those who control the missiles within.

This is a brief outline, and clearly different examples, practices and forms of anarchist action work differently along these lines, for better and for worse. What is crucial is to recognize the ways in which the anarchist critique of authority and domination, and focus on creativity and self-liberation, can be read as an exploration of alternative understandings of security. Such explorations occur theoretically in the pages of Goldman and Bakunin and Peter Kropotkin and Landauer, or more recently in the work of Colin Ward, Day, Heckert, and many others, but they are also deeply practical explorations, built with and from the actions of those working together to explore these alternative ways of living, and from the instincts made manifest in these projects.

I do not want to end here, however. Whilst the above explorations are crucial, it is unsatisfying to leave them simply on the terms of seeking a better form of security. As outlined above, the concept of security itself is deeply woven into the metaphysics of the state, into logics of exceptionalism, us/them binaries, and militaristic worldviews. Michael Dillon goes further, suggesting that the contemporary fascination with security reveals something deeper about an instinct to secure the foundations of life, to render the world as something calculable, subject to technology, and controllable, such that it might be mastered, and such that this project of mastery might be depoliticized (Dillon 1996: 14–31). The desire for security reveals and represents a contemporary political imagination which is willing to go to extraordinary, sometimes even genocidal, lengths in order to preserve an image of the social order (in tragic form, precisely engendering insecurity). A central vehicle of this project of security is of course the state, and so for Dillon the defining maxim of modern politics has been 'no security outside the State; no State without security' (Dillon 1996: 14). However, we also have to look beyond the state to think about how deeply interwoven our lives have become with this project of security, of mastery over life, and the instincts and impulses of domination which accompany such projects.

This is not to essentialize security, to suggest that it can only possibly mean one thing, or exist in one form. It does neither. It is, more circumspectly, to suggest that it is dangerous to presume that one can so easily recapture the meaning of a concept and series of practices which are so tightly bound into contemporary power relations. As modern political subjects, we are heavily constituted through dynamics of security. We are governed depending on whether we are in, or out; protected, or expendable; safe, or dangerous. We are regulated, we self-regulate, and we regulate others. We are forced to fight, or we are not. We are forced to flee, or we are not. We desire protection, and sometimes we receive it. We lead others to protect themselves, and we are punished for it. We protect others, and enter into relationships of dependency and vulnerability often without recognizing the complicated power relations we weave. As Dillon and Julian Reid argue, 'the history of security is a history of what it is to be a political subject and to be politically subject' (Dillon & Reid 2001: 51). To question security, then, demands that we come into question as ourselves. It involves interrogating what it means to feel secure, to experience (and respond to) fear, to reduce the political world to a series of friends and enemies. It demands that we subvert sedimented ideas about how we experience order, safety and stability – values which may work more to legitimate the current state of affairs than to signify any more transcendent quality.

We can think about this in terms of trying to break apart the binary formulation of security and insecurity. The two operate (sometimes explicitly, sometimes implicitly) as a couplet, placing enormous imperatives on political life. Do what you are told, or we won't be able to control this situation. Accept these small infringements on privacy, or you may not be alive to enjoy what freedom remains. Look at these terrifying anarchists: this is what happens when people don't respect the law. They form a regulatory binary (alongside others: order/chaos, inside/outside, sovereignty/anarchy) which casts that which threatens to unsettle the status quo into the image of the latter, thereby legitimating the former (Ashley 1988).

Anarchism precisely seeks to undermine these binaries, to relieve them of their totalizing and authoritarian power. On one level, we can see this where the official conduct of security is resisted, where anarchists have sought to refuse their incorporation within the field of security. The best-known contemporary examples here are the tactics of anonymity which have characterized much of the aesthetic of post-Cold War anarchism, exemplified by the Black Bloc tactic. When dressed all in black, indistinguishable from those around you, one is in an important sense *un-securable*. As a leaflet handed out before one anti-militarist Bloc action states, '[w]e cover our faces not to threaten or intimidate, but to represent the faceless victims of the arms trade and to protect ourselves from intrusive surveillance. We will not be numbered, catalogued or controlled.' Such an evasion of security is not only the preserve of Black Bloc tactics. The Clandestine Insurgent Rebel Clown Army (CIRCA), who engage in actions dressed as fun-loving clowns, state that

> [w]e are *clandestine* because we refuse the spectacle of celebrity and we are everyone. Because without real names, faces or noses, we show that our words, dreams, and desires are more important than our biographies. Because we reject the society of surveillance that watches, controls, spies upon, records and checks our every move.
>
> (CIRCA undated, emphasis in original)

We might also look towards the tactic of 'fitwatching', whereby activists use a variety of creative tactics to prevent police intelligence teams from gathering information at protests and demonstrations.

These groups and tactics (and many others) practise a form of anti-security which seeks to evade the ways in which contemporary life is governed. They exemplify a sensibility well summarized by Saul Newman:

> Freedom must be discovered *beyond* security, and this can be achieved only through practices of political contestation, through forms of resistance, through modes of collective indiscipline and disobedience. For instance, the refusal and subversion of surveillance, and even the surveillance of surveillance, become part of a new language of resistance that expresses the desire for a life that no longer seeks to be 'secured'.
>
> (Newman 2011: 171, emphasis in original)

However, it would be too limited to simply see them as resisting security in this linear manner. I would suggest that there is something both more disruptive and more creative at work. Rather than seeking to evade security, we might see in much of anarchism a practice of subverting the security/insecurity binary itself. In refusing to subscribe to axiomatic standards of security (obedience to the police, respect for the law), anarchists frequently insist that this refusal does not simply collapse into the chaos which might be expected. State storytelling depends on the myth that the failure of its security apparatus will lead to insecurity. Anarchism subverts precisely this myth.

It is on such terms that, as David Graeber (2009: 407) has gone to great lengths to demonstrate, the Black Bloc tactic does not demonstrate a nihilistic pure chaos, but is in fact the site of extraordinary sympathy, solidarity, and self-discipline. The crucial point is that it is a site in which the specific nature of these qualities is worked out amongst those involved. Such features are not only the preserve of more spectacular forms of anarchist action (which, as Richard Gilman-Opalsky (2011: 15) points out, can perhaps too easily be recuperated back into images which legitimate the state's security project). More everyday experiments and communities, whether those which attempt to organize non-hierarchically, or which work to undermine international borders, or which educate local communities on the excesses of the police and their rights in response, precisely undermine the foundational logics of security, and do so without collapsing into the domain of insecurity.

These (and many other possible examples) perhaps represent a fracturing of the logic of security/insecurity, and a glimpse of moments and modalities of being which strive to live otherwise.

Whilst anarchists have always insisted that one can have order without hierarchy, there has also persisted a sensibility which posits a space between order and chaos. Order is not a self-evident good, frequently masking the experience of those for whom the status quo is a silent but intense chaos, and always quietly mobilizing an image of chaos as a regulatory Other. Any particular order is always political, but the supposedly apolitical concept of order can quickly mask this reality. We might instead want to think in Martin Buber's more lively terms:

> [s]ocialism can never be anything absolute. It is the continual becoming of human community in mankind, adapted and proportioned to whatever can be willed and done in the conditions given. Rigidity threatens all realization, what lives and glows to-day may be crusted over to-morrow and, become all-powerful, suppress the strivings of the day after.
>
> (Buber 1958: 56)

Ceding neither to order, nor to chaos, is a crucial project for any radical political philosophy which wishes to avoid stasis. Instead, the task (in the words of CIRCA) must be to provoke imaginations 'neither here nor there, but in the most powerful of all places, the place in-between order and chaos' (CIRCA undated). We might tell a similar story with security and insecurity; indeed, as Colin Ward (1982: 31) writes, 'the punitive, interfering lover of order is usually so because of his own unfreedom and insecurity'. Anarchism, at its best, looks to break down security/insecurity as a crucial part of the struggle to undermine conceptual and political systems of authority and to prefigure spaces of creativity in the cracks which emerge. In this sense, anarchism has always been about rethinking security, in ways that go far beyond the purportedly anti-statist project of CSS.

Notes

1 See for example Stephen Walt (1991), John Mearsheimer (1990), and Kenneth Waltz (1990).
2 This does not mean that those involved in more traditional security studies do not challenge state actions. For example, a number of these scholars were deeply opposed to the 2003 invasion of Iraq, on the grounds that it would cause instability, fuel terrorism, and cause long-term harm to the security of those conducting the invasion (principally the USA) (see for example Walt and Mearsheimer 2003). However, it is telling that these objections said little about the ethical and imperial dimensions of the invasion, nor raised the question as a systemic issue of Western and capitalist militarism: thus, the title of their critique, 'An Unnecessary War'.
3 For key surveys and edited collections see Krause and Williams (1997), Booth (2005a), Burke and McDonald (2007), and Vaughan-Williams and Peoples (2010). For introductory texts on CSS, see Fierke (2007), Smith (2005), Booth (2007) and Krause and Williams (1996).
4 For scholarship which highlights connections between anarchism and IR, see Weiss (1975); Prichard (2007; 2010a; 2010b), Goodwin (2010), Falk (1983; 2010), Newman (2011), Kazmi (2012).
5 Cohn's attempt to penetrate the surface of the world of defence intellectuals throws up fascinating results: 'Much of their claim to legitimacy, then, is a claim to objectivity born of technical expertise and to the disciplined purging of the emotional valences that might threaten their objectivity. But if the surface of their discourse – its abstraction and technical jargon – appears at first to support these claims, a look just below the surface does not. There

we find currents of homoerotic excitement, heterosexual domination, the drive toward competency and mastery, the pleasures of membership in an elite and privileged group, the ultimate importance and meaning of membership in the priesthood, and the thrilling power of becoming Death, shatterer of worlds. How is it possible to hold this up as a paragon of cool-headed objectivity?' (Cohn 1987: 717).
6 See also Judith Hicks Stiehm (1982).
7 For a full discussion, see Zelter (2004) and Needham (2016).
8 This is not to suggest that all such practices and groups are explicitly defined as anarchist. Such practices can be found in the organizing of workplace, queer, homeless, indigenous, and many other communities, amongst people who have never even heard of anarchism. The argument here is more simply to suggest the value of an anarchist interpretation of these practices, which tend to emerge as much from the everyday necessities of survival as from any theoretical or ideological edifice. Of course, this is an argument that anarchists have long made about the principle of mutual aid more broadly.

References

Ackelsberg, M.A. (2005) *Free Women of Spain: Anarchism and the Struggle for the Emancipation of Women*, Oakland, West Virginia and Edinburgh: AK Press.
Amoore, L. (2009) 'Algorithmic War: Everyday Geographies of the War on Terror', *Antipode: A Radical Journal of Geography*, 41(1): 49–69.
Aradau, C. (2004) 'Security and the Democratic Scene: Desecuritization and Emancipation', *Journal of International Relations and Development*, 7(4): 388–413.
Ashley, R. (1988) 'Untying the Sovereign State: A Double Reading of the Anarchy Problematique', *Millennium - Journal of International Studies*, 178(2): 227–262. Bakunin, M. (2005a) *Statism and Anarchy*, Cambridge: Cambridge University Press.
Bakunin, M. (2005b) 'The Paris Commune', in D. Guérin (ed.) *No Gods, No Masters: An Anthology of Anarchism*, Edinburgh and Oakland: AK Press, pp. 202–206.
Bigo, D. and A. Tsoukala (eds.) 2008. *Terror, Insecurity and Liberty: Illiberal Practices of Liberal Regimes after 9/11*, London and New York: Routledge.
Booth, K. (1991) 'Security and Emancipation', *Review of International Studies*, 17(4): 313–326.
Booth, K. (1997) 'Reflections of a Fallen Realist', in K. Krause and M.C. Williams (eds.) *Critical Security Studies: Concepts and Cases*, London: Routledge, pp. 83–120.
Booth, K. (2004) 'Realities of Security: Editor's Introduction', *International Relations*, 18(4): 5–8.
Booth, K. (ed.) (2005a) *Critical Security Studies and World Politics*, Boulder and London: Lynne Rienner, pp. 1–18.
Booth, K. (2005b) 'Critical Explorations', in K. Booth (ed.) *Critical Security Studies and World Politics*, Boulder and London: Lynne Rienner.
Booth, K. (2007) *Theory of World Security*, Cambridge: Cambridge University Press.
Buber, M. (1958) *Paths in Utopia*, New York: Macmillan. Burke, A. and M. McDonald (eds.) (2007) *Critical Security in the Asia-Pacific*, Manchester: Manchester University Press.
Butler, J., (2009) *Frames of War*, London: Verso.
Call, L., (2002) *Postmodern Anarchism*, Lanham MD: Lexington Books.
Campbell, D. (1998a) *National Deconstruction: Violence, Identity and Justice in Bosnia*, London and Minneapolis and London: University of Minnesota Press.
Campbell, D. (1998b) *Writing Security: United States Foreign Policy and the Politics of Identity*, Manchester: Manchester University Press.
CIRCA, undated. 'About.' Retrieved from http://web.archive.org/web/20120106084027/http://www.clownarmy.org:80/about/about.html.
Cohn, C. (1987) 'Sex and Death in the Rational World of Defense Intellectuals', *Signs*, 12(4): 687–718.
Day, R.J.F. (2005) *Gramsci is Dead: Anarchist Currents in the Newest Social Movements*, London: Pluto Press.

Day, R.J.F. (2011) 'Hegemony, Affinity and the Newest Social Movements: at the End of the 00s', in D. Rousselle and S. Evren (eds.) *Post-Anarchism: A Reader*, London: Pluto Press, pp. 95–116.
de Goede, M.(2005) 'Carnival of Money: Politics of Dissent in an Era of Globalizing Finance', in L. Amoore (ed.) *The Global Resistance Reader*, London and New York: Routledge, pp. 379–391.
Dillon, M. (1996) *Politics of Security: Towards a Political Philosophy of Continental Thought*, London and New York: Routledge.
Dillon, M. and J. Reid (2001) 'Global Liberal Governance: Biopolitics, Security and War', *Millennium: Journal of International Studies*, 30(1): 41–66.
Dolgoff, S. (ed.) (1974) *The Anarchist Collectives: Workers' Self-Management in the Spanish Revolution 1936–1939*, New York: Free Life Editions.
Elbe, S. (2006) 'Should HIV/AIDS Be Securitized?', *International Studies Quarterly*, 50(1): 119–144.
Enloe, C. (1989) *Bananas, Beaches & Bases: Making Feminist Sense of International Politics*, London: Pandora.
Falk, R. (1983) 'Anarchism and World Order', in R. Falk (ed.) *The End of World Order: Essays on Normative International Relations*, London: Holmes & Meier.
Falk, R. (2010) 'Anarchism without "Anarchism": Searching for Progressive Politics in the Early 21st Century', *Millennium: Journal of International Studies*, 39(2): 381–398.
Fierke, K. (2007) *Critical Approaches to International Security*, Cambridge: Polity.
Floyd, R. (2007) 'Towards a Consequentialist Evaluation of Security: Bringing Together the Copenhagen and Welsh Schools of Security Studies', *Review of International Studies*, 33(2): 327–350.
Franks, B. (2007) 'Postanarchisms: A Critical Assessment', *Journal of Political Inquiry*, 12(2): 127–145.
Gilman-Opalsky, R. (2011) *Spectacular Capitalism*, Brooklyn, NY: Autonomedia.
Goldman, E. (1969) *Anarchism and Other Essays*, New York: Dover Publications.
Goodwin, A. (2010) 'Evolution and Anarchism in International Relations: The Challenge of Kropotkin's Biological Ontology', *Millennium - Journal of International Relations*, 39(2): 417–437.
Graeber, D. (2009) *Direct Action: An Ethnography*, Edinburgh and Oakland: AK Press.
Gramsci, A. (1971) *The Prison Notebooks*, New York: International Publishers.
Grayson, K. (2008) 'Human security as power/knowledge: the biopolitics of a definitional debate', *International Affairs*, 21(3): 383–401.
Heckert, J. (2011) 'Sexuality as State Form', in D. Rousselle and S. Evren (eds.) *Post-Anarchism: A Reader*, London: Pluto Press, pp. 195–207.
Horrox, J. (2009) *Living Revolution: Anarchism in the Kibbutz Movement*, Edinburgh, Oakland and Baltimore: AK Press.
Huysmans, J. (1998) 'The Question of the Limit: Desecuritisation and the Aesthetics of Horror in Political Realism', *Millennium: Journal of International Studies*, 27(3): 569–589.
Jun, N. (2012) *Anarchism and Political Modernity*, New York and London: Continuum.
Kaldor, M. (2003) *Global Civil Society: An Answer to War*, Cambridge: Polity.
Kazmi, Z. (2012) *Polite Anarchy in International Relations Theory*, New York: Palgrave Macmillan.
Krause, K. and M. Williams (1996) 'Broadening the Agenda of Security Studies: Politics and Methods', *International Studies Review*, 40: 229–254.
Krause, K. and M. Williams (eds.) (1997) *Critical Security Studies: Concepts and Cases*, London: Routledge. Krøvel, R. (2010) 'Anarchism, the Zapatistas and the Global Solidarity Movement', *Global Discourse*, 1(2): 20–40.
Landauer, G. (2010) *Revolution and Other Writings: A Political Reader*, trans. G. Kuhn. Oakland: PM Press.
Larner, W. (2003) 'Neoliberalism?', *Environment and Planning D: Society and Space*, 21: 509–521.
Linklater, A. (2005) 'Political Community and Human Security', in K. Booth (ed.) *Critical Security Studies and World Politics*, Boulder and London: Lynne Rienner, pp. 113–131.

MacKenzie, M. (2010) 'Securitization and De-Securitization: Female Soldiers and the Reconstruction of Women in Post-Conflict Sierra Leone', in L. Sjoberg (ed.) *Gender and International Security*, London and New York: Routledge, pp. 151–167.

Malatesta, E., et al. (2005) 'Malatesta, The Anarchist International, and War', in D. Guérin (ed.) *No Gods, No Masters: An Anthology of Anarchism*, Edinburgh and Oakland: AK Press, pp. 387–390.

May, T. (1994) *The Political Philosophy of Poststructuralist Anarchism*, University Park, PA: Pennsylvania State University Press.

McDonald, M. (2008) 'Securitization and the Construction of Security', in *European Journal of International Relations*, 14(4): 563–587.

McEvoy, S. (2010) 'Loyalist Women Paramilitaries in Northern Ireland: Beginning a Feminist Conversation about Conflict Resolution', in L. Sjoberg (ed.) *Gender and International Security: Feminist Perspectives*, London: Routledge, pp. 129–150.

McSweeney, B. (1999) *Security, Identity, and Interests: A Sociology of International Relations*, Cambridge: Cambridge University Press.

Mearsheimer, J. (1990) 'Back to the Future: Instability in Europe after the Cold War', *International Security*, 15(1): 5–56.

Needham, A. (2016) *The Hammer Blow: How 10 Women Disarmed a War Plane*, Peace News.

Neocleous, M. (2007) 'Security, Liberty and the Myth of Balance: Towards a Critique of Security Politics', *Contemporary Political Theory*, 6: 131–149.

Newman, S. (2007) *From Bakunin to Lacan: Anti-Authoritarianism and the Dislocation of Power*, Lanham MD: Lexington Books.

Newman, S. (2011) 'Crowned Anarchy: Postanarchism and International Relations Theory', *Millennium: Journal of International Studies*, 40(2): 259–278.

Prichard, A. (2007) 'Justice, Order and Anarchy: The International Political Philosophy of Pierre-Joseph Proudhon (1809–1865)', *Millennium - Journal of International Studies*, 35(3): 623–645.

Prichard, A. (2010a) 'David Held is an Anarchist. Discuss', *Millennium - Journal of International Studies*, 39(2): 439–459.

Prichard, A. (2010b) 'What Can the Absence of Anarchism Tell us about the History and Purpose of International Relations?', *Review of International Studies*, 37(4): 1647–1669.

Rocker, R. (2004) *Anarcho-Syndicalism: Theory and Practice*, Edinburgh, London and Oakland: AK Press.

Rossdale, C. (2010) 'Anarchy is What Anarchists Make of It: Reclaiming the Concept of Agency in IR and Security Studies', *Millennium: Journal of International Studies*, 39(2): 483–501.

Rossdale, C. (2016) 'Ethical Security Studies: Activism, Resistance and Security', in J. Nyman and A. Burke (eds.) *Ethical Security Studies: A New Research Agenda*, Abingdon: Routledge, pp. 201–215.

Rousselle, D. and S. Evren (eds.) *Post-Anarchism: A Reader*, London: Pluto Press.

Shepherd, L. (2006) 'Veiled References: Constructions of Gender in the Bush Administration Discourse on the Attacks on Afghanistan Post-9/11', *International Feminist Journal of Politics*, 8(1): 19–41.

Smith, S. (2005) 'The Contested Concept of Security', in K. Booth (ed.) *Critical Security Studies and World Politics*, London: Lynne Rienner.

Spike Peterson, V. (1992) 'Security and Sovereign States: What is at Stake in Taking Feminism Seriously?', in V. Spike Peterson (ed.) *Gendered States: Feminist (Re)Visions of International Relations Theory*, Boulder and London: Lynne Rienner, pp. 31–64.

Stamnes, E. (2004) 'Critical Security Studies and the UN Preventative Deployment in Macedonia', *International Peacekeeping*, 11(1): 161–181.

Stiehm, J.H. (1982) 'The Protected, The Protector, The Defender', *Women's Studies International Forum*, 5(3/4): 367–376.

Sylvester, C. (1994) *Feminist Theory and International Relations in a Postmodern Era*, Cambridge: Cambridge University Press.

Sylvester, C. (1996) 'The Contributions of Feminist Theory to International Relations', in S. Smith, K. Booth and M. Zalewski (eds.) *International Theory: Positivism and Beyond*, Cambridge: Cambridge University Press, pp. 254–278.

Thomas, N. and W.T. Tow (2002a) 'The Utility of Human Security: Sovereignty and Humanitarian Intervention', *Security Dialogue*, 33(2): 177–192.

Thomas, N. and W.T. Tow (2002b) 'Gaining Security by Trashing the State? A Reply to Bellamy and McDonald', *Security Dialogue*, 33(3): 379–382.

Tickner, J.A. (2001) *Gendering World Politics*, New York: Columbia University Press.

Tolstoy, L. (1990) *Government is Violence: Essays on Anarchism and Pacifism*, London: Phoenix Press.

Vaughan-Williams, N. and C. Peoples (2010) *Critical Security Studies: An Introduction*, Oxon and New York: Routledge.

Wæver, O., 1995. 'Securitization and Desecuritization', R. Lipschutz (ed.) *On Security*, New York: Columbia University of Press, pp. 46–87.

Walker, R.B.J. (1993) *Inside/Outside: International Relations as Political Theory*, Cambridge: Cambridge University Press.

Walt, S. (1991) 'The Renaissance of Security Studies', *International Studies Quarterly*, 35(2): 211–239.

Walt, S. and J. Mearsheimer (2003) 'An Unnecessary War', *Foreign Policy*, 134: 51–59.

Waltz, K. (1990) 'Nuclear Myths and Political Realities', *American Political Science Review*, 84(3): 731–745.

Ward, C. (1982) *Anarchy in Action*, London: Freedom Press.

Weber, C. (2005) 'Not without My Sister(s): Imagining a Moral America in Kandahar', *International Feminist Journal of Politics*, 7(3): 358–376.

Weiss, T. G. (1975) 'The Tradition of Philosophical Anarchism and Future Directions in World Policy', *Journal of Peace Research*, 12(1): 1–17.

Wyn Jones, R. (1999) *Security, Strategy, and Critical Theory*, Boulder: Lynne Rienner.

Zelter, A. (2004) 'Civil Society and Global Responsibility: The Arms Trade and East Timor', *International Relations*, 18(1): 125–140.

5 Postanarchism today
Anarchism and political theory

Saul Newman

Many speak about an 'anarchist moment' in describing contemporary forms of radical politics and activism. From the emergence of the global anti-capitalist movement in the late 1990s, through to the more recent movements of Occupation recently appearing around the world, we have seen new forms of horizontal or 'networked' organization and direct action that seem to be, if not directly inspired by anarchist principles, at least very much reflective of them. David Graeber (2002), in an early paper, 'The New Anarchists', explored some of the methods employed by anti-capitalists for bottom-up, non-hierarchical organization and consensus-style decision-making, methods that political theorists still have a lot to learn from.

Anarchism as an anti-discipline

Of course, this anarchist moment has also been reflected in a renewed interest in anarchism in the academy. In the past few years we have seen a burgeoning literature on anarchism. This most heretical of political and philosophical traditions is finally being taken more seriously, although, if truth be told, it is still very much on the margins of many disciplines, particularly political theory which, for the most part, is still centred around the exaltation of sovereignty. Indeed, perhaps there is something in anarchism – and this is not necessarily a bad thing – which resists its neat incorporation into disciplines, which resists its *disciplining*. Perhaps anarchism is anti-disciplinary, not only in terms of social and political organization, but in an epistemological and ontological sense as well. And perhaps it is precisely *because* of its marginality to the disciplines that it is able to affect and disrupt them and thus, potentially, to transform them. I am not of course saying that anarchism has no place in the disciplines of the humanities and social sciences – quite the contrary – but its place always has to be regarded as somehow undecidable, paradoxical, liminal, on the borders, which is where it has, as I have suggested, its most powerfully disruptive effect. Anarchism may be understood as both a subject of disciplinary enquiry, as well as an insurrection against all disciplines (social and epistemological). I shall return to this point later.

These developments nevertheless demand a reconsideration of anarchism, indeed a *return* to anarchism. But what kind of return is possible here? This is a complicated question. On the one hand, there has always been a kind of insurrectionary impulse, a will to resist, a libertarian desire – what Foucault would call a kind of 'plebeian quality' (an energy or discharge at the limits of power which resists the production of docile bodies)[1] and what Bakunin would call the 'urge to rebel' – which of course transcends anarchism, yet which the anarchist tradition became the most coherent and forthright expression of.

Anarchism turned the 'urge to rebel' into a theory, an ethics, even a social science, and, above all, a politics. Any kind of renewal of anarchism has to take, as its basic starting point, its ethical point of departure, this resistance to power.

At the same time, to take anarchism seriously today means to make an honest appraisal of anarchism as a tradition of thought and practice that is shaped by certain philosophical coordinates and which is founded on certain assumptions about human behaviour, knowledge, morality, and social relations. Yet, as a political ideology – if that is the right term – it is also unusually heterodox and diverse, indeed, much more so than some of its contemporary exponents – and here I have in mind Michael Schmidt and Lucien van der Walt, who seemed to want to turn anarchism into some sort of orthodoxy (van der Walt and Schmidt 2009) – are prepared to acknowledge. Indeed, the controversial yet, I would say, crucial place that Max Stirner occupies in the anarchist tradition – an uneasiness reflected in his expulsion from the canon in Schmidt and van der Walt's *Black Flame* – points to a certain anxiety about anarchism's own internal deconstruction of itself. As I have argued elsewhere, Stirner pulls down, or least makes problematic, many of the humanist and rationalist foundations that underpinned anarchism as a revolutionary discourse. And it is for this very reason that I have always insisted on Stirner's place within the anarchist tradition. My point is that such deconstructions are a corrective to any rigidifying tendencies within philosophical traditions, and indeed are crucial to their survival. Deconstruction, as Jacques Derrida (1998) says, always works *outside* and *within*, as a *destruction* and a *construction*. In this sense, I would say that deconstruction itself is a kind of anarchism, and that anarchism is a kind of deconstruction.[2]

So if we are to think about the relevance of anarchism today we must not be blind to its tensions, *aporias*, and moments of internal contradiction, to its diverse and at times conflicting strands of thought. We have to become genealogists of anarchism in the Nietzschean or Foucauldian sense. This means more than spending our time amongst the archives. Rather it is to recognize that our common heritage is at the same time 'an unstable assemblage of faults, fissures, and heterogeneous layers that threaten the fragile interior from within or underneath' (see Foucault 2000a: 374). We can see here, also, that the genealogical methodology, as prescribed by Nietzsche and Foucault, is fundamentally anarchic because it resists, or at least is alive to, the authoritarian potential of any impulse towards unification, totalization, and dogmatism.

Therefore, I have argued that anarchism has to take account of theoretical developments that would at the outset pose certain problems for it, and might even seem initially to be at odds with it, but which at the same time force it to think through certain limits, both theoretical and political – for example, the limits of power, discourse, regimes of truth and knowledge, the unconscious, and so on. Here I am referring to the very important implications of psychoanalysis and poststructural theory for politics. And it is in trying to synthesize these with anarchism – trying to bring one to bear on the other, and in thinking one *through* the other – that we can speak of a *postanarchism* (see Newman 2010a; 2016).

This is a term that has led to many misinterpretations; perhaps with hindsight it was an ill-chosen term, but it was never intended to imply that anarchism is somehow over or has been superseded. 'Post' does not refer to a *coming after* but, on the contrary, a renegotiation of anarchism and an attempt to revitalize it and explore its relevance for contemporary struggles, movements, and modes of politics. In the same way that postmodernism is not a 'coming after' modernity, but rather a critical reflection on the limits of modernity, and in the same way that – as Foucault (2000b) suggested – the critique of the Enlightenment embodies at the same time the critical spirit of the very same Enlightenment, postanarchism may be seen as a kind of apparatus that allows a reflection on the limits of anarchism, while at the same time situating itself within it.

What postanarchism regards as problematic is the project of turning anarchism into a sort of social science or science of society – in other words, the attempt to see social relations as determined by an underlying rationality or series of processes tending towards greater forms of community, mutuality, and liberation, processes which are objectively verifiable. We find this tendency, for instance, in Kropotkin, who based his theory of mutual aid on his observations of the natural world and what he believed were evolutionary and biological instincts (Kropotkin 1915). We see something similar in Murray Bookchin's (1982) concept of social ecology, in which the possibilities for liberation and harmonious coexistence were immanent in the principles of the natural world, and which were in a process of unfolding into a rational totality.

Postanarchism has no objection to the ethical and political principles at work here; on the contrary, freedom, solidarity, collective action, ecology, and so on are absolutely central to contemporary radical struggles and indeed have to be seen as their common horizon. Rather, what is difficult to sustain here is the ontological claim that there is a sort of underlying rational truth to society that can be unearthed and observed, from which the possibilities of human liberation are seen to emerge. There is a certain image of society here as a kind of natural body that gives meaning to all identities, that conditions their behaviour, and whose truth must be discerned. In opposition to this image of society – which is something of a 'spook' as Stirner would say – I see social relations as unfixed, contingent and indeterminate and as bearing no underlying rationality or process which makes it intelligible. And rather than seeing the project of human freedom as somehow organically rooted and as unfolding like a flower, to use Bookchin's (1982: 32) Hegelian-inspired metaphor, I find it more convincing to see it as a project without end, as involving an ongoing series of inventions, strategies and 'games' with power; a constant work upon the self as well as on the relations and institutions that surround us and in which we participate.

Four axes of postanarchism

I therefore find it more productive to resituate anarchist thinking along the following four axes: (1) ontological anarchism, (2) epistemological anarchism, (3) the anarchic subject, and (4) revolution or insurrection.

1 Ontological anarchism

'Ontological anarchy' is a term associated with Hakim Bey (2003), but it can also be said to be inspired by a number of other philosophical approaches: Stirner, Nietzsche, Heidegger, Reiner Schürmann, Levinas, Foucault, and many others. We could describe ontological anarchism, or *an-archy*, as the absence of rational first principles. This refers to Reiner Schürmann's claim about the 'withering away' of *arché* invoked in Heidegger's idea of the closure of metaphysics. Unlike in metaphysical thinking, where action has always to be derived from and determined by a first principle, '"anarchy"… always designates the withering away of such a rule, the relaxing of its hold' (Schürmann 1990: 6). Importantly, Schürmann distinguishes this notion of 'anarchy' or the 'anarchy principle' from the anarchism of Proudhon, Bakunin, and others, who sought 'to *displace* the origin, to substitute the "rational power", *principium*, for the power of authority, *princeps* – as metaphysical an operation as there has been. They sought to replace one focal point with another' (Schürmann 1990: 6). In other words, the classical anarchists sought to abolish political authority, yet they invoked another kind of authority in its place, the epistemological authority of science and the moral authority of society. Thus, in place of the state emerges a more rational form of social organization. By contrast, according to Schürmann:

> The anarchy that will be at issue here is the name of a history affecting the ground or foundation of action, a history where the bedrock yields and where it becomes obvious that the principle of cohesion, be it authoritarian or 'rational', is no longer anything more than a blank space deprived of legislative, normative, power.
> (Schürmann 1990: 6)

So we can characterize postanarchism as *post-foundational* anarchism – a way of thinking about anarchism without essential foundations – in the sense outlined above by Schürmann. This dislodging of firm ontological foundations does not deprive anarchism of ethics, of principles; it does not turn anarchism into nihilism, as many have alleged. Rather, what it means is that such principles are never absolute, are not set in stone – are not 'fixed ideas' as Stirner would say – and they can give rise to different interpretations. They are meanings to be fought over and fought for. They are contingent.

2 Epistemological anarchism

Here the scientific and positivist impulse present in certain anarchist theories is called into question. This does not mean, of course, that an anarchist politics should not draw upon scientific knowledge, but it should not seek to establish itself as a science or see scientific rationality as the fundamental basis for its ethical and political claims. Instead, what ought to be interrogated is not simply political and social authority, but the authority of certain established forms of scientific knowledge, whose discourses cannot be separated from power. Here we might reflect on Paul Feyerabend's (2010) anarchist approach to science in his book *Against Method*. His argument is that the methodological rules imposed by science are ultimately arbitrary and historically contingent, that they are not based on any firm claim to truth. Indeed, many of the most important scientific discoveries – the Copernican Revolution for instance – were only possible through a breaking of existing methodological rules. This tells us that the authority of scientific knowledge, based on rigid rules of enquiry, is on much shakier ground than it would like to admit. It is much more productive, according to Feyerabend, and indeed much closer to the truth of scientific enquiry, to take an *anarchist* view of science – to question the authority and legitimacy of scientific knowledge and to violate its methodological rules. Indeed, Feyerabend finds it extraordinary that anarchist political thinkers – and here he cites Kropotkin – while questioning all forms of political authority, uphold unquestioningly the epistemological authority of science, and indeed base their whole philosophy on its rather uncertain claims (Feyerabend 2010: 14).[3] Why should the same freedom of thought, speech and action, and the same scepticism about authority that anarchists demand in the field of politics, not also translate into the field of scientific inquiry?

So rather than trying to establish a scientific basis for anarchism, we should ask Foucault's question, which he posed in response to the scientific aspirations of Marxism:

'..."What types of knowledge are you trying to disqualify when you say that you are a science?"' (Foucault 2003a: 10). In other words, we must interrogate the power effects and discursive gestures of exclusion inherent in laying claim to the status of 'science'. It is not so much a question of whether scientific knowledge is right or wrong, true or false, but rather the way in which it promotes a hierarchization of knowledge and thus a certain discursive authoritarianism. In opposition to this we should assert, as Foucault counsels us to do, a genealogical position, which would be that of an 'anti-science'. This does not mean that we disregard the use of scientific knowledge or celebrate irrationalism, but rather that we retain a critical perspective that is always sensitive to science's power effects: 'Genealogy has to fight the power-effects characteristic of any discourse that is regarded as scientific' (Foucault 2003a: 9). It is a question of *politicizing* knowledge, rationality, and truth: in other words, rather than according truth a universal position of abstract neutrality, such that it can always be proclaimed in absolute opposition to the epistemological distortions of power, it should be seen as a weapon wielded in a battle, spoken from the partisan position of one directly engaged in struggle. We should think in terms of, as Foucault (2003a: 9) puts it, an 'insurrection of knowledges'.

3 The anarchic subject

By 'the anarchic subject' I do not mean a subject who is naturally predisposed to revolution or who, as Kropotkin would claim, has an innate tendency towards mutual aid. This is precisely to beg the question. We need to investigate the conditions under which we become insurrectionary subjects. We also have to recognize the problems associated with the whole notion of the revolutionary emancipation of the subject from the external constraints of power, as if the intricacies of our relationship to power – the way it both imposes limits and at the same time constitutes identities and elicits desires – could simply be overcome in the act of revolutionary emancipation. The question we must pose is: who is the subject who revolts today? It seems to me that we can no longer think in terms of preconceived identities and essential interests, whether ethnic, cultural or sexual. Nor is there any longer a universal signifier of Man or Humanity or the Proletariat around which the great historical revolutionary narrative is constituted. Rather we need to think in terms of hybrid subjectivities, *singularities*, those who cannot be represented in any clear, determined, coherent way. This is why the gesture of anonymity, symbolized by the wearing of masks in protests, is so important to contemporary activism; there is a revolt against identification, not only in the sense of state identification and surveillance, but in the sense of socially and discursively defined identities and predetermined modes of behaviour and agency that exist to channel our desires into the representative structures of the state and towards commodified and regulated social relations.

Furthermore, we need to take fuller account of that enigmatic problem of voluntary servitude, the desire for one's own domination, our psychic and subjective attachment to power, that has long been recognized as an obstacle to revolutionary politics and which cannot be simplistically explained in terms of ideological false consciousness.[4] Anarchism was always much more sensitive to this problem than Marxism, for instance. Kropotkin saw our becoming enamoured of authority as one of the chief factors in the growing domination of the state (Kropotkin 1987). However, we need to think this anew today, and explore not only the network of nodes – economic, technological, communicative – that seem to be producing such dangerous and violent pathologies, but also our internalization of fear, our reactive hatred of difference, and our desire for ever greater levels of security.

4 Revolution or insurrection?

These factors point to the need for a different understanding of revolution, one that not *only* seeks to abolish or transcend the coercive and legal power of centralized political institutions like the state, but one that is also micro-political in the sense that it tackles the more intricate problem of our subjective attachment to this power, our self-subordination, and without which any revolution would be doomed to reinvent the power it has destroyed. This was of course something that was recognized by the German anarchist, Gustav Landauer, when he said that the state was nothing but a social relationship – something that we make and participate in, and that we destroy it by 'contracting other relationships, by behaving differently' (Landauer 2010: 213–214). He proposed a kind of spiritual transformation of ourselves and our relations with others, seeing this as being just as important – indeed the very condition of, and thus inseparable from – any kind of mass, organized confrontation with state power.

This revolution of subjectivities, as opposed to simply a political revolution, was described even more vividly by Stirner, who sought to distinguish between two kinds of radical action, the revolution and insurrection:

> Revolution and insurrection must not be looked upon as synonymous. The former consists in an overturning of conditions, of the established condition or *status*, the state or society, and is accordingly a *political* or *social* act; the latter has indeed for its unavoidable consequence a transformation of circumstances, yet does not start from it but from men's discontent with themselves, is not an armed rising but a rising of individuals, a getting up without regard to the *arrangements* that spring from it. The Revolution aimed at new arrangements; insurrection leads us no longer to *let* ourselves be arranged, but to arrange ourselves, and sets no glittering hopes on 'institutions'. It is not a fight against the established, since, if it prospers, the established collapses of itself; it is only a working forth of me out of the established.
> (Stirner 1995: 279–280)

The focus here is on a sort of subjective rebellion primarily against oneself, against the prescribed identities through which we are attached to power (he says it 'starts from men's discontent with themselves'). It is thus not directly aimed at destroying the state as a political institution, but at destroying the internalized *statism* that perpetuates this institution. It is an assertion of the power of singularities, a reclaiming of the self, through which the structure of power collapses of itself, as if the only thing that was propping it up was our voluntary servitude, our idealization of its power. The power of the state is merely an abstraction and abdication of our own power. Stirner's project of insurrection – as distinct from, although *not necessarily* opposed to, revolution – has often been misinterpreted as a purely individual enterprise. In other words, it is alleged, by many anarchists in particular, that Stirner is taking us away from the genuinely collective project of revolution towards a purely individualistic, egoistic form of action. But this is to look at things the wrong way. It is not a question of egoism versus solidarity, or the individual against the collective. There is nothing in what Stirner says that implies that insurrection is a purely private enterprise; indeed, elsewhere Stirner refers to the possibility of acting in cooperation with others with his notion of the 'union of egos'. His point is, rather, that if any sort of revolutionary action is not at the same time actively affirmed by singularities, if it is not made, as he puts it, 'my own cause', 'my own creation', then it risks becoming a sacred, abstracted Cause alien to the individual and to which the individual is ultimately sacrificed. So in this sense, perhaps we can see insurrection and the revolution as two sides of the same coin.

The axiom of liberty

Furthermore, what is being proposed here with the notion of insurrection – which I see as *the* horizon of radical politics today – is the realization of the *freedom that we already have*. This is also reflected in one of Stirner's (1995: 141–154) other key concepts, *ownness* (as distinct from liberal 'freedom'). That is, rather than seeing freedom as a social and political goal, rather than seeing emancipation as an ideal to be aspired to and a political project to be achieved and as something dependent on the destruction of political authority, perhaps it should be seen as something that we already have – something like *ontological freedom*. It is just that we don't know it; we are not awakened to it. The realization of the freedom that we already have is coextensive with the release from our voluntary servitude to power. It is not a question, then, of seeking a state of freedom as a great prize waiting for us on the other side of power, but rather of affirming and living the freedom that we already have in the here and now.

Jacques Rancière (1991; 1999) sees politics in terms of an *axiom of equality* – in other words, it is a question of staging the political *dissensus* or disagreement by marginalized subjectivities who enact their equality, acting on the presumption that they are already equal, even if this is not recognized by the regime of power, like the slaves in the Haitian revolution who took seriously the message of the French revolution – equality for all – when they rebelled against their French colonial masters; or women during the French Revolution who demanded equal rights and representation on the basis that they *already had this right*, just that it wasn't recognized (see Rancière 2004). Perhaps in similar fashion we can speak of an *axiom of liberty*: we act as though we are already free, even if the forms of power that we confront seem so insurmountable. Indeed, to this end, Stirner found it necessary to develop a different notion of freedom, which he called 'ownness' – the ideology of freedom having been corrupted by liberalism, capitalism, statism, and vanguardism. Whereas freedom depends upon a project of emancipation, usually led and imposed by someone else, and is thus a determination of power, ownness is the assertion of the freedom that we already have in the here and now, even in conditions of intolerable oppression. Thus, for Stirner (1995: 143), while the slave was not free in an objective sense, he was still *his own*, and this realization is the starting point of his rebellion against the conditions of his enslavement. Seeing freedom in these terms – rather than as an abstraction or distant goal of revolutionary politics – is the only way to dispel the illusion of power and authority (an illusion which otherwise has such a grip over our psyche). Todd May recounts a beautiful anecdote about a group of activists at an anti-capitalist demonstration who audaciously manage to force their way through a police barricade, and when asked later why they penetrated the police line, they responded by saying, 'what line?'[5] The realization of freedom lies in acting and living *as though power does not exist*.

So we need to think about what revolution actually means today, and whether it is still conceivable in the classical sense as the great Event of social transformation and liberation, one that comes about through the immanent development of social forces. It seems to me that we should revisit and perhaps rethink Bakunin's (1984: 377) call for the people to 'organize their powers apart from and against the state'. This can only refer to a politics of autonomy, and to the creation of alternative spaces of social organization and life that resist the logic of statism – in other words, which allow for the emergence of non-hierarchical and reciprocal relations. I do not see how this can be conceived as a totalizing, all-encompassing action that occurs everywhere, all at once. Rather, it would refer to localized spaces and situations in which power is resisted and in which autonomous, self-managed relations, forms of exchange and ways of life are organized. This is why I believe the recent movements of Occupation, despite their apparent failure, were so significant. To see them simply as protests – and thus, as some have done, to lament their lack of concrete political agendas – is to fundamentally misunderstand them; what was important was the act of occupying and reclaiming spaces, and the horizontal organization of relations within those spaces. It is not so much a question of the violent confrontation with Power, or the attempt to seize the apparatus of the State – but rather of acting in a joyous affirmation of Power's non-existence. We find similar experiments in a politics of autonomy throughout society – whether in squats, social centres, independent media, land occupations in the global South, hacktivism, experiments in the digital commons and alternative economies, and in many other forms. It seems to me that the notion of revolution – if indeed we can retain this term at all (I have suggested that insurrection or insurrections might be more appropriate) – needs to be rethought in light of these heterogeneous, localized (and at the same time globalized) movements, situations, and spaces of rupture and dissent.

At the same time, while anarchism today – or what I call postanarchism – is the project of autonomy and direct action, this should not be taken in an absolute or purist sense. Indeed, what must be deconstructed is the conceptual distinction between outside and inside. We are always inside and outside institutions simultaneously. Power is not unified and totalizing, and its limits are not always clearly defined. Rather, it is heterogeneous, blurred, differentiated, given to a combination of conflicting forces and tendencies, some of which can even be turned against power. Power often works against itself or against those aspects of power that are more dominating and violent than others. Autonomy is not about always situating oneself outside power in a spatial sense, but rather about a different combination and intensification of relationships and forces that seek to contest, disallow, limit, overturn, and disrupt particular relations of domination, inequality, and violence – autonomy is about opening power to an *exteriority*, to a threshold of destabilization. Anarchism today must be prepared to work on multiple fronts, and in collaboration – as anarchists so often do anyway – with a variety of actors and in a variety of non-institutional and institutional settings.

A politics of anti-politics?

One way to think about this is in terms of the paradoxical relationship between politics and anti-politics. Anarchism, as I understand it, is never really entirely one or the other, but always both. There is an inclusive disjunction between politics and anti-politics, such that one proposition is true only if its opposing proposition is also true. Even Bakunin (1984: 314) while he spoke of the 'total abolition of politics' (as opposed to the socialists who simply wanted to 'pursue a politics of a different kind') at the same time went into considerable detail in discussing revolutionary tactics, questions of organization and the mobilization of people, as well as the shape of post-revolutionary society – all of which are, of course, political questions, indeed questions of power. We have no choice, then, but to formulate anarchism in the following paradoxical way, as a *politics of anti-politics*, or an *anti-political politics*.

This tension generates new and productive articulations of politics and ethics. Politics, at least in a radical sense, only has a consistent identity if an anti-political, we could even say 'utopian', dimension is also present – otherwise it remains caught within existing political frameworks and imaginaries. Conversely, anti-politics only makes sense if it takes seriously the tasks of politics – building, constructing, organizing, fighting, making collective decisions, and so on. Where the political pole imposes certain limits, the anti-political pole, by contrast, invokes an outside, a movement beyond limits. It is the signification of the infinite, of a limitless horizon. This is both the moment of utopia – or as I would put it, the outside – and also the moment of ethics. Anarchism has an important utopian dimension. Indeed, some utopian element – whether acknowledged or not – is an essential part of any form of radical politics. To oppose the current order one inevitably invokes an alternative imaginary; one always seeks an outside. However, we should try to formulate a different approach to utopia here: the importance of imagining an alternative to the current order is not to lay down a programme for the future, but rather to provide a point of exteriority – a move toward an outside – as a way of interrogating the limits of this order. As Miguel Abensour (2008: 418) puts it, 'Is it not proper to utopia to propose a new way of proceeding to a *displacement of what is* and what seems to go without saying in the crushing name of "reality"?' The outside provides an escape from this stifling reality by imagining an alternative to it; it opens up different possibilities, new 'lines of flight' and combinations of intensities, forces. Here, we should think about utopias in terms of action in the immediate sense, of creating alternatives within the present, at localized points, rather than as the outcome of the revolution. The outside is something that opens up in (anti-)political struggles themselves.

Ethics also implies an outside to the existing order, but in a different sense. Ethics, as I understand it here, involves the opening up of existing political identities, practices, institutions, and discourses to an Other that is beyond their terms. Ethics is more than the application of moral and rational norms. It is the continual disturbance of the sovereignty of these norms, and the identities and institutions that draw their legitimacy from them in the name of something exceeding their grasp. Importantly, then, ethics is what disturbs politics from the outside. This might be understood in the Levinasian sense of 'anarchy': 'Anarchy cannot be sovereign like an *arché*. It can only disturb the State – but in a radical way, making possible moments of negation *without any affirmation*' (Levinas 1981: 194).

The point is, however, that politics cannot do without anti-politics, and vice versa. The two must go together. There must always be an anti-political outside, a moment of rupture and excess that disrupts the limits of politics. The ethical moment cannot be eclipsed by the political dimension. Nor can it be separated from it, as someone like Carl Schmitt proposed (see Schmitt 1996). If there is to be a 'concept of the political', it can only be thought through a certain constitutive tension with ethics. At the same time, anti-politics needs to be politically articulated; it needs to be put into action through actual struggles and engagements with different forms of domination, different relations of power. There must be some way of politically measuring the anti-political imaginary, through victories, defeats, and strategic gains and reversals. So while anti-politics points to a transcendence of the current order, it cannot be an escape from it. It must involve an encounter with its limits, and this is where politics comes in. The presupposition or axiom of liberty that I have referred to before – acting as though power does not exist – should not be taken as an escape from reality, but rather that which makes possible a more active engagement with and resistance to power; in the same way that the realization of the freedom that one already has makes possible an ongoing elaboration of new practices of freedom.

Formulating anarchism as a politics of anti-politics highlights anarchism's wholly original and radical contribution to political theory, indeed to the very concept of the political itself. It makes possible a displacement of the political relation from the state. It allows us to see that the state and the principle of sovereignty are not the only site of politics, but more often the site of depoliticization in which the unruly dimension of politics is policed, regulated, domesticated, and held in check. Anarchism forces us to shift our gaze from the state and the principle of sovereignty to an alternate and dissenting world, and to resituate the sphere of politics there. In this sense, it gives us a new understanding of the central notion of the autonomy of the political: for Schmitt (1996), this refers to the friend/enemy distinction, but this is a way of intensifying, sharpening, radicalizing the contours of the state and of affirming sovereignty, as it is the sovereign who decides who is the friend and who is the enemy. For Chantal Mouffe, who is in some ways inspired by Schmitt, the agonistic relation proper to the political is also staged within the state, and is concerned with questions of bordering, inclusion/exclusion – once again of deciding the limits of the sovereign political order (Mouffe 2009). While Hannah Arendt is in some ways closer to anarchism – particularly in terms of her critique of sovereignty and statism – her articulation of the autonomy of the political presupposes a sphere of public activity and membership of a distinct political community clearly delineated from the private and domestic spheres, and thus from questions of work and life (Arendt 1958). By contrast, anarchism or postanarchism contends that the autonomy of the political can only mean a politics of autonomy, in which new possibilities of life and co-belonging can emerge.

Postanarchism and political theory

I think we can see, then, that anarchism – developed and sharpened through a postanarchist paradigm – offers us not only a set of radical practices and modes of organization which might be applied to contemporary struggles, but also new tools for political theorizing. There are at least two main areas of problematization in the modern Western tradition of political theory that a postanarchist analysis contests. The first, as suggested above, is political theory's preoccupation with the question of sovereignty, with the imposition of a legitimate social and political order that will secure us against the 'anarchy' of the state of nature and allow for the possibility of civil coexistence and the rule of law. Obviously this is central – albeit in different ways – to both liberal and conservative traditions of political theory, going back at least to Hobbes. This is the tradition of political thought that emerges with, and as a justification for, the rise in early modernity of the national state.[6] Anarchism constitutes the most violent and radical break with this tradition in insisting that sovereignty has no legitimacy – that it is authorized neither by divine right, rational consent, democratic rituals nor liberal legal frameworks; that it is, on the contrary, an illegitimate and violent imposition of power.

Moreover, anarchism contends that the state is unnecessary, that humans have the capacity to organize their lives cooperatively and autonomously, free from the shadow of Leviathan.

Furthermore, as I have shown above, anarchism shifts the focus of political theorizing away from the state towards autonomous practices and forms of life that organize themselves in ways that are heterogeneous to the rationality of sovereignty. While the question arises about the capacity of nineteenth-century anarchist thought to come to grips with the more diffuse, networked forms of power that surround us today, the spectre of sovereignty remains with us, albeit articulated in different ways, through the governing rationalities of the neoliberal market and the biopolitical mechanisms of the state. Anarchism, it seems to me, offers us the most powerful discursive and conceptual weapons for contesting, and thinking and acting beyond these structures of domination. Anarchism provides the terrain for a genuinely non-sovereign political theory.

The second area of intervention concerns political theory's preoccupation with abstract ideals and norms, like justice, which are seen to be universally intelligible, and which inform debates about the best form of regime or the fairest pattern of distribution. Normative political theory – as a form of moral philosophizing – is concerned with the most legitimate and just form of social arrangement.[7] Clearly, anarchism, in affirming an alternative social order to that of the state, engages with such questions and develops a moral philosophy of its own;[8] indeed, the tradition of philosophical anarchism, going back to William Godwin (1985 [1793]),[9] which proposes the pre-eminence of individual autonomy over legal obligation to the state and affirms the moral right to civil disobedience, is situated within such normative debates. While anarchism cannot avoid moral and ethical questions, there is nevertheless a certain tension here with what I have outlined as the anarchic ontology of anarchism, or what Foucault (2003b: 303) calls an 'untamed ontology' – referring to a kind of vitalist understanding of life and existence, emerging with modernity, where life, in its flux and destructive force, exceeds all fixed identities and forms of representation. This anarchic, wild ontology – exemplified in Bakunin's 'destructive urge' and Stirner's assault on 'fixed ideas' and the Christianized 'spooks' of morality and humanity – are absolutely central to anarchism;[10] yet, at the same time, they are in tension with anarchism's desire to ground itself in firm ontological foundations and normative commitments. The problem, as I see it, with such a desire is that it proposes a certain stable, eternal, and moral image of social relations held up as the legitimate alternative to the state. Furthermore, it lays claim to a universal and neutral position of truth: I have already spoken about the scientific and positivist aspirations of some forms of anarchist thought. As Foucault shows us, however, the position of universality and epistemological neutrality is characteristic of what he calls the 'philosophico-juridical' discourse, a discourse that is closely aligned, at least symbolically, with the legislating authority of sovereignty because it functions to repress the memory of conflict and difference, proclaiming instead eternal, grounding truths. It is in opposition to this that Foucault identifies a 'historico-political' discourse that affirms the continuity of conflict – war becomes the ontological ground for social relations – and, moreover, eschews claims to universality and neutrality, adopting instead a partisan position in which truth is wielded like a weapon. Foucault characterizes this position in the following terms:

> The more I decenter myself, the better I can see the truth; the more I accentuate the relationship of force, the harder I fight, the more effectively I can deploy the truth ahead of me and use it to fight, survive, and win.
>
> (Foucault 2003a: 53)

My point here is that much of normative political theory – and here I am including certain anarchist interventions – still holds on to the position of the philosopher-king, which is a profoundly juridical discourse concerned with imposing an abstract normative framework, whether it takes the form of laws or moral guidelines. There is a certain discursive and epistemological position at work here which stands above the fray of power relations and conflicting perspectives. As a political theorist and an anarchist, I believe it is important to interrogate and contest this discursive position, to explore its genealogies, to unmask the assumptions to power behind it. It is to ask the question, posed most forcefully by Stirner: 'who speaks?' Such a partisan, genealogical engagement with political theory, affirming movement, fluidity and contingency rather than fixed categories, does not lead to nihilism, as many have claimed, but to a more postfoundational, politically-engaged and militant mode of political theorizing that, I would argue, is much closer to the spirit of anarchism.

Notes

1 Foucault says in an interview, 'Power and Strategies': 'there is indeed always something in the social body, in classes, groups and individuals themselves which in some sense escapes relations of power, something which is by no means a more or less docile or reactive primal matter, but rather an inverse energy ... a certain plebeian quality' (Foucault 1980: 134–145).
2 See my discussion of the connections between anarchism and Derrida's project of deconstruction (Newman 2001: 1–20).
3 A similar critique of Kropotkin's view of anarchism as a science was made by the Italian anarchist, Errico Malatesta: 'Anarchy, on the other hand, is a human aspiration which is not founded on any true or supposed natural law, and which may or may not come about depending on human will. Anarchy profits from the means from which science provides human beings in their struggle with nature and against contrasting wills. It may profit from progress in philosophical thought when this serves to educate people to reason better and to better distinguish between the real and imagined, but it cannot, without falling into the realms of the absurd be confused either with science or with any philosophical system' (Malatesta 1995: 45–48).
4 The enigma of our voluntary servitude to power has a long genealogy, going back to the sixteenth-century figure of Étienne de La Boétie and his *Discours de la Servitude Volontaire* (1548), in which he asked the vital question: why do we obey a power whose existence depends entirely on our continued obedience? See also my own investigations of this subject (Newman 2010b; 2015).
5 This was referred to in a talk given by Todd May in a symposium on Postanarchism held in Athens in November 2011.
6 No doubt, state sovereignty has a much longer genealogy, as explored in Kantorowicz's (1957) masterful *The King's Two Bodies*, but Hobbes' *Leviathan* develops the first fully modern concept of sovereignty.
7 Here I am most referring to the normative concerns of Anglo-American analytical political theory, but these have also been the concerns of many continental philosophers, from Kant to Habermas.
8 See here a recent edited collection by Benjamin Franks and Matthew Wilson, *Anarchism and Moral Philosophy* (Franks and Wilson 2010).
9 See also the work of Robert Paul Wolff (1998).
10 This point has also been made by Ben Noys, who connects this 'untamed ontology' with insurrectionary anarchism (Noys 2011).

References

Abensour, M. (2008) 'Persistent Utopia', *Constellations*, 15(3): 406–421.
Arendt, H. (1958) *The Human Condition*, Second Edition, Chicago: University of Chicago Press.
Bakunin, M. (1984) *Political Philosophy: Scientific Anarchism*, (ed.) G.P. Maximoff, London: Free Press of Glencoe.
Bey, H. (2003) *T.A.Z.: The Temporary Autonomous Zone, Ontological Anarchy, Poetic Terrorism*, New York: Autonomedia.
Bookchin, M. (1982) *The Ecology of Freedom: The Emergence and Dissolution of Hierarchy*, Palo Alto, CA: Cheshire Books.
Derrida, J. (1998) *Of Grammatology*, trans., Gayatri Chakravorty Spivak, Baltimore: Johns Hopkins University Press.
Feyerabend, P. (2010) *Against Method*, London: Verso.
Foucault, M. (1980) 'Truth and Power', in Colin Gordon (ed. and trans.) *Power/knowledge: Selected Interviews and Other Writings 1972–1977*, Harlow: Longman, pp. 109–133.
Foucault, M. (2000a) 'Nietzsche, Genealogy, History', in James Faubion (ed.) *Aesthetics: Essential Works of Foucault 1954–1984, Volume 2*, , London: Penguin, pp. 369–391.
Foucault, M. (2000b) 'What is Enlightenment?', in Paul Rabinow (ed.) *Ethics: Essential Works of Foucault 1954–1984*, trans., Robert Hurley et al., London: Penguin, pp. 303–320. Foucault, M. (2003a) *Society Must Be Defended: Lectures at the Collège de France 1975–76*, trans., David Macey, London: Allen Lane.
Foucault, M. (2003b) *The Order of Things: An Archaeology of the Human Sciences*, London and New York: Routledge.
Franks, B. and Wilson, M. (2010) *Anarchism and Moral Philosophy*, Basingstoke, Hampshire: Palgrave Macmillan.
Godwin, W. (1985) *Enquiry Concerning Political Justice, and its Influence on Modern Morals and Happiness*, Harmondsworth: Penguin Books.
Graeber, D. (2002) 'The New Anarchists', *New Left Review*, 13 January-February: 61–73.
Kantorowicz, E. H. (1957) *The King's Two Bodies: A Study in Mediaeval Political Theology*, Princeton, NJ: Princeton University Press.
Kropotkin, P. (1915) *Mutual Aid, a Factor of Evolution*, London: Heinemann.
Kropotkin, P. (1987) *The State: Its Historic Role*, London: Freedom Press.
Landauer, G. (2010) 'Weak State, Weaker People', in G. Kuhn, ed., and trans., *Revolution and Other Writings: a Political Reader*, Oakland, CA: PM Press, pp. 213–214.
Levinas, E. (1981) *Otherwise than Being*, trans., A. Lingis,The Hague, London: Nijhoff.
Malatesta, E. (1995) 'Comments on the Article "Science and Anarchy"', in V. Richards (ed.) *The Anarchist Revolution: Polemical Articles 1924–1931*, London: Freedom Press, pp. 45–49.
Mouffe, C. (2009) *The Democratic Paradox*, London: Verso.
Newman, S. (2001) 'Derrida's Deconstruction of Authority', *Philosophy & Social Criticism*, 27(3): 1–20.
Newman, S. (2010a) *The Politics of Postanarchism*, Edinburgh: Edinburgh University Press.
Newman, S. (2010b) 'Voluntary Servitude Reconsidered: Radical Politics and the Problem of Self-Domination', *Anarchist Developments in Cultural Studies* 1: 31–49.
Newman, S. (2015) '"Critique will be the art of voluntary servitude": Foucault, La Boétie and the Problem of Freedom', in S. Fuggle, Y. Lanci and M. Tazzioli (eds.) *Foucault and the History of Our Present*, Basingstoke: Palgrave Macmillan, pp. 58–73.
Newman, S. (2016) *Postanarchism*, Cambridge: Polity Press.
Noys, B. (2011) 'The Savage Ontology of Insurrection: Negativity, Life, and Anarchy', Available at: http://postanarchistgroup.net/?page_id=343
Rancière, J. (1991) *The Ignorant Schoolmaster: Five Lessons in Intellectual Emancipation*, trans., Kristin Ross, Stanford, CA: Stanford University Press.
Rancière, J. (1999) *Disagreement: Politics and Philosophy*, trans., Julie Rose, Minneapolis: University of Minnesota Press.

Rancière, J. (2004) 'Who is the Subject of the Rights of Man?', *The South Atlantic Quarterly*, 103 (2–3): 298–310.

Schmitt, C. (1996) *The Concept of the Political*, trans., G. Schwab, Chicago: University of Chicago Press.

Schürmann, R. (1990) *Heidegger on Being and Acting: From Principles to Anarchy*, trans., Christine-Marie Gros, Bloomington: Indiana University Press.

Stirner, M. (1995) *The Ego and its Own*, D. Leopold (ed.), Cambridge: Cambridge University Press.

Van der Walt, L. and Schmidt, M. (2009) *Black Flame: The Revolutionary Class Politics of Anarchism and Syndicalism*, Oakland, CA: AK Press.

Wolff, R.P. (1998) *In Defense of Anarchism*, Berkeley, CA: University of California Press.

6 Anarchism and political science
History and anti-science in radical thought

Ruth Kinna

In a book called *Free Speech for Radicals*, Herber Newton, a heretical priest active in New York in the late nineteenth century, claimed that 'Anarchism is in reality the ideal of political and social science, and also the idea of religion' (in Schroeder 1916: 14). Newton's assertion, that anarchism is fundamentally religious, is deeply contested, but from a twenty-first-century perspective his coupling of anarchism and political science is also striking. Even accepting that the link he makes between these two terms is mediated by the reference to an ideal, hinting at a utopian aspiration that many anarchists would embrace, the conjunction jars. This chapter considers some reasons why, juxtaposing conceptions of political science adopted in American and British academia in the course of the twentieth century and anarchist critiques of science. I argue that debates about the relationship between the analysis of politics and the legitimation of established power relations usefully contextualize anarchist engagements with political science and that differences about the scope, application, and character of scientific method complicate anarchist engagement. The continuities and discontinuities between these two currents of analysis help explain some very different anarchist approaches to 'scientific' research. My contention is that Newton's view is a productive one, from which anarchists have much to gain. The final section of the chapter examines some fruitful examples of anarchist political science, drawing on the work of C. Wright Mills and Peter Kropotkin.

A brief history of political science

'Anarch*ism, the political philosophy of anarchy*', Alex Prichard argues, 'does not currently feature in the study of international relations, or political science for that matter'. He explains the absence in international relations in terms of 'the grip that common conceptions of anarchy ... have on the political imagination'. In the mainstream, anarchy describes a lack, a void to be filled or, as Prichard puts it, a 'problem to be *resolved*' (Prichard 2012: 100). In political science, where the imagery is still more dramatic, the absence of anarchism reflects the success with which the problem that anarchy presents has been resolved. When political science emerged in the early twentieth century the *Encyclopedia of Social Reform* described its purpose to be the study of the state, or what it called 'natural society'. Its precise 'province' was 'such activities of society as are organized in the constitution' (Bliss 1908: 910). Political science 'assumes for every nation a national character' and takes 'the fact' and 'phenomena of sovereignty – the obedience-compelling power of the State', as given (Bliss 1908: 911). The premises of political science were found 'in facts of human nature', which were not contested, and the methods veered between the causal analysis of 'the motive forces of political life ... the desire of men' and the discussion of 'the whole mass of primitive political theory' which met elite requirements for the legitimation of state policy (Bliss 1908: 910–911). Identifying Machiavelli as the first modern political scientist, the *Encyclopedia* sealed a relationship between political science, political theory, and *realpolitik* that has endured, notwithstanding the best efforts of a generation of late twentieth-century historians of ideas.

The narrow focus of political science on the operation of government in the modern state is still apparent in the modern academic discipline. At its founding in 1903, the object of the American Political Science Association (APSA) was defined as the 'encouragement of the scientific study of politics, public law, administration, and diplomacy' (Bliss 1908: 38). The Association's current website describes political science as 'the study of governments, public policies and political systems, and political behaviour' (APSA n.d.). Similarly, the benchmarks for politics which shape teaching in UK higher education identify the distinctive concerns of political science to be

> primarily but not exclusively: international organisations; regimes; legislatures; executives; party systems; electoral systems; voting behaviour; public policy; public administration or public management; political communication, political development, urban politics, conflict analysis; peace research; human rights; foreign policy analysis; area studies; security studies; international law; international and economic relations.
>
> (QAA 2007: 4)

By this standard, political science is an approach within politics, distinct both from positive or explanatory political theory and normative political theory or political philosophy. Methodologically, too, political science has acquired a reputation for particular practice. According to David Marsh and Gerry Stoker's well-known introduction to political science theory and methods, the centre-ground of the subject is still concerned with 'the formal operation of politics in the work of government and those who seek to influence it' and it is dominated by behaviouralism, rational choice theory, and institutional analysis (Marsh & Stoker 2002: 9).

In his effort to develop an anarchist approach to international relations, Prichard acknowledges that the currency of the concept 'anarchy', however distorted in orthodox traditions in IR theory, provides an entry point for its re-assessment. Indeed, a growing sense that the world of international states does not measure up to the image of anarchy that realists of various stripes have expounded helps in this respect. In comparison, the statist assumptions of political science appear less hospitable to anarchist approaches. Moreover, the concrete experience of 'anarchy' in parts of the world where states fail suggests that the problems confronting would-be anarchist political scientists are intractable. However, first impressions can be misleading and a history of twentieth-century debates, traced here through a selection of definitive statements, indicates that political science is not only a diverse field but that its purposes are also contested. Indeed, political science has been pulled in different directions in the course of the twentieth century and its objectives, scope, and methodologies have been fiercely disputed.

The objectives of political science were a central focus for Hermann Heller's entry in the 1933 *Encyclopedia of Social Sciences*. His exploration of the field charted a complex relationship with the history of ideas and political philosophy to expose a core conception and, at the same time, highlight the diversity of the discipline. In the modern period, political science revolved 'primarily around the problem of the attainment, consolidation and distribution of political power, whether in an actually existing state or in a hypothetical state' and it was often used as a tool to buttress or undermine entrenched group or class interests. Moreover, there was a growing 'disposition' amongst political scientists 'to apply the methods of natural science' to problems of politics 'and thus to obtain a greater objectivity and ... clearer understanding of political attitudes and behaviours' (Heller 1963: 208). Yet far from mechanically endorsing these approaches, Heller challenged them. It was 'impossible' he argued, 'to formulate any precise definition of either the content or method' of political science. This 'peculiarly comprehensive discipline' was 'lacking in either a clearly delimited set of problems or a definitely prescribed methodology' (Heller 1963: 207). The features treated as essential to the discipline were merely transitory; and the aspiration to mimic natural science was a methodological affectation: 'in fact', Heller argued, 'there is no single method for natural science' (Heller 1963: 208).

Heller considered the purposes of political science sociologically. The meanings that attached to the discipline, he argued, were coloured by the role that analysts carved for themselves and these were inevitably shaped by 'the concrete historical and sociological problems and issues which exist in political life itself' (Heller 1963: 208). There was also an ideational aspect to the framing of the field. The recent absorption of Nietzschean and Bergsonian themes into politics, he observed, had enabled ideologues like Georges Sorel and Vilfredo Pareto to argue that political science was 'merely the sublimation of a highly individualized, thoroughly irrational life situation ... above which thought is incapable of rising to any unified point of view' (Heller 1963: 220). Interpreted in this manner, perspectivism was attractive to a powerful group of ruthless political leaders but dangerously reduced 'thought to the level of propaganda' (Heller 1963: 221). The result was the 'fictionalization' of politics (Barash 2000). Heller's response to the intellectual elites eager to serve the naked ambitions of interwar politicians was to expose the bankruptcy of their philosophical relativism and highlight the socio-historical flux that provided the vacuum for political science in the interwar period. It was important, he argued, to rescue the authoritative voice and theoretical validity of the discipline and in an effort to accomplish this task, Heller argued that its proper subject matter was the analysis of systemic continuities and their ideal, intellectual expressions. Admitting that politics was always subject to cultural influences, he identified human nature as its fundamental constant. Heller understood this concept historically and sociologically rather than abstractly and linked it to creative, popular aspiration and a transformative potential to realize ideal ways of life, expressed in political theory and institutional stability. The framework led Heller to endorse democracy. Indeed the continuity of democratic regimes together with a supporting political philosophy not only reflected public contentment (where democracy existed) but genuine political understanding about the validity of the principle. Armed with this insight into politics, he concluded that the important purpose of political science was to offer 'an accurate and authoritative description, explanation and criticism of political phenomena' (Heller 1963: 222–223). Political science thus became an instrument of critique and a tool for the preservation of values and ideals, even in the midst of an onslaught that threatened their collapse.

Writing in the same period, William Beveridge shared Heller's anxieties about the cynical manipulation of political science by ideologues and political elites and also distinguished the purpose of political science from the practice of politics. However, his concerns about the impact of ideology in politics led him to stake the claims of political science to universalism and objectivity. Moreover, whereas Heller believed that political science was evaluative, Beveridge subordinated this role to the scientific spirit, where the two conflicted. The passion to 'make society work better in the future than it has worked in the past' should be distinguished from the 'patience, detachment, industry, suspension of judgment ... readiness to face facts, readiness to learn and change your views' at the heart of science (Beveridge 1932: f.47). Beveridge's view, which he expressed when he was director of the London School of Economics and Political Science (LSE), harmonized with a tradition that extended back to Beatrice Webb: the purpose of the LSE, which she helped found in 1895, was 'the betterment of society'. This aim, she wrote in her diary, could be achieved only by detaching excellent, empirical scientific research from ideology. One of her concerns was to correct the distortions of socialist argument:

> If there is one thing I have believed 'from the beginning to the end' it is that no progress can be made except on the basis of ascertained fact and carefully thought out suggestion. Despite our theory, bias, creed and prejudice, we are all equally wandering in the labyrinth searching for the clue of true facts to bring us out on the right side of each particular problem. It is pitiful to see the narrow sectarian view most socialists take – binding themselves hand and foot by a series of Shibboleths.
> (Webb 1895: f.1392)

In the aftermath of the Second World War, these debates about the function of political science and the theorization of the relationship between science, reform, and ideology gave way to a practice-based approach to understanding. In 1948 UNESCO brought together a group of international scholars to reflect on political science, publishing their deliberations in 1950 in a volume entitled *Contemporary Political Science*. The meaning of 'science', the report noted, was quite wide. Existing practices included a 'strict sense where science was understood as "acquired knowledge verified by accurate observation and logical thought"' and a 'broader sense of "the sum of co-ordinated knowledge relative to a determined subject."' The report accepted the validity of both, since the latter was inclusive and open to 'countries where political phenomena have given rise to study and research, but where neither study nor research have been pursued in a strictly scientific spirit' (Salvadori 1950: 3). A similar plurality characterized the discussion of methods: international political scientists attached a 'great variety of meanings' to the term: 'philosophical, dialectical, juridical, historical, sociological, psychological, economic and normative methods, methods of liberty and of the natural sciences, experimental, integral and statistical methods etc.' (Salvadori 1950: 3–4). Turning, then, to the meaning of 'political', the group developed a classification which served as an umbrella for a variety of different approaches (Salvadori 1950: 4).

The trends towards a narrower conception of political science and scientific method accelerated in the early 1950s and it was particularly marked in American scholarship. A UNESCO survey of the field in 1952–4 noted that political scientists were divided between those who modelled themselves on the physical sciences and metaphysicians. This division was not even, however. 'The most prominent trend' Dwight Waldo (1956: 34), the author of the report noted, 'is toward "science" i.e. toward conceiving "reality" as that which lends itself to study by the methods of the presumably more advanced sciences'. A celebrated critic of positivist and reductive approaches to public administration Waldo observed that the words key to this trend were 'empirical' and 'behavioural' (Carroll and Frederickson 2001: 2–8). Group theory, decision-making, political participation, comparative government and public policy were identified as the staples of political science (Waldo 1956: 34); and the preferred methodology was to 'seek to study the "real" phenomena of political life, starting with carefully refined hypotheses, using rigorous methods of observation, measuring, counting and using mathematical tools wherever possible, and ending with cautious, modest conclusions' (Waldo 1956: 18–19). David Easton's *The Political System*, first published in 1953 was a central text for writers in this emerging field (Easton 1953).

Easton's entry for Political Science in the 1968 *International Encyclopedia of the Social Sciences* still described the discipline to be 'in search of an identity'. This was a call to standardization. Recognition of political science as 'an independent discipline with a systematic theoretical structure of its own', he argued, depended on 'the reception and integration of the methods of science into the core of the discipline' (Easton 1968: 282). Yet even as the American behavioural revolution gained momentum – following Easton's lead – voices within political science continued to celebrate its scope and diversity. In a report on European trends undertaken in 1961 for the International Political Science Association, Jan Barents, the anti-communist chair of Political Science at the University of Amsterdam (Daalder 1991: 280), remarked on the significance of the subject's cultural variation and berated the tendency of some US political scientists to 'regard the American yardstick as too much a sign of European immaturity' (Barents 1961: 86). In particular, he observed both the intimacy of the connection between political science and other social sciences and how this 'reflected in the diverse ways in which political studies are organized in different European universities'. 'In one place they form an integrated part of the law or history departments, in another they are fostered in a somewhat independent institution. Here they occupy a central position, there they are rather marginal' (Barents 1961: 14). Barents' understanding of 'science' was similarly inclusive and he described *The Authoritarian Personality*, Theodor Adorno's anti-positivist study that used empirical evidence to categorize personality types judged by analysts to be dangerous, as scientific – a controversial view in contemporary scholarship (Martin 2001). Moreover, as if to emphasize the closeness of the relationship to science and philosophy he observed that the 'hundreds of pages of scientific investigation and scholarly analysis' that informed the study dovetailed with Jean Paul Sartre's philosophical reflections on anti-Semitism – indeed, he noted that the authors of the report also acknowledged the similarity (Barents 1961: 22). For Barents, this correspondence had a general significance and he encouraged political scientists to 'look at more than studies of political science in the narrower sense of the word' when undertaking their research.

It is possible to capture the twists and turns of the debates about political science in a comprehensive narrative. Mark Bevir relates such a story using historicism and positivism to construct a bi-polar framework, which captures shifts in conceptions of social science, from developmental historicism in the late nineteenth century to modernist empiricism and radical historicism in the mid- and late twentieth (Bevir 2006). Yet while the broad sweep of the arguments might itself be historicized, what emerges from this brief history of political science debate is a picture of plurality and contestation, not homogeneity and consensus. There is neither agreement about purpose or method, nor about the mapping between the two. The appearance of uniformity probably owes as much to the institutionalization of political science internationally, a process accelerated by the expansion of higher education in the period after the Second World War in the context of de-Nazification and the Cold

War, as it does to the coalescence of ideas. Today, while acknowledging that the centre-ground of political science is focused tightly on the study of government, Marsh and Stoker add that the politics that political scientists study is about 'more than what governments choose to do or not do'. Whatever claims are made about the political science method, the strong historic association with behaviouralism and now rational choice is a poor indicator of the range of approaches that practitioners actually adopt. A recent report on UK political science argued that 'hegemonic practice' in US political science, which boasts the largest population of political scientists and consequently sets the global standards for the discipline, accounts for the characterization of the mainstream. Estimating the proportion of US rational choice analysts to be 5% of the total, even in elite Ivy League institutions, the authors pointed out that the academic field is in fact highly diverse (ESRC 2007). Indeed, whereas the QAA distinguish political science from other areas of politics, APSA use the term as an umbrella and identify 'political theory, political philosophy, political ideology, political economy, policy studies and analysis, comparative politics, international relations' amongst its 'host of related fields' (APSA 2019). This plurality suggests that political science might still accommodate a wide body of research – and perhaps even anarchist approaches.

Anarchism and science

Political science is more than the sum of its parts, but in anarchist studies attention has traditionally fastened on its components rather than the whole; and in the history of anarchist ideas suspicions of 'science' and 'politics', but particularly 'science', suggest that the ground for their relationship is stony. The neglect of anarchism by political scientists that Prichard highlights is thus matched by anarchist suspicions of political *science*. The concerns about science are legion and have typically been advanced in critique of approaches to politics adopted by other anarchists, rather than non-anarchist political scientists: Kropotkin is a favourite target. More generally, the expertise that science supports, the certainties that it seems to imply and the misconception of the natural scientific methods that anarchists are said to have aped, are three recurrent themes. However, because questions about science have often been raised in a range of different contexts, all are multifaceted.

Probably the most deeply-held suspicion about science turns on the power advantages of specialist knowledge. Bakunin's worries about expertise and the potential for technical mastery to become bureaucratized, to serve as a platform for a new form of domination based on a claim to authority that threatened to overwhelm the exercise of individual judgement, was expressed as a critique of science. Science had revealed what religion denied, namely the animal origin of the world. Science was also, consequently, the proper foundation for education. The 'universal laws' of science illuminated the principles of flux and natural co-ordination that underpinned anarchist ethics. Without, then, diminishing the potential value of science based on practical experience, Bakunin was wary of the servility that the institutionalization of science might breed and the laws, elaborated by always fallible and typically sluggish 'savants' in the academy might legitimize.

> What I preach then is, to a certain extent, *the revolt of life against science*, or rather against the *government* of science, not to destroy science – that would be high

treason to humanity – but to remand it to its place so that it can never leave it again.

(Bakunin 1916)

The different meanings Bakunin attached to 'science' have not only provided a soft target for critics eager to highlight his theoretical incoherence, but rich pickings for later anarchists interested in the sociological, ideological, and epistemological dimensions of his discussion. For example, Paul Goodman focused on the first aspect of Bakunin's critique. However, whereas Bakunin adopted a neo-Comtean framework to treat science as a transition from religion, Goodman focused on the commonalities in order to explore the causes of scientific stultification. Modern science, he argued, was Christian. This claim did not mean that science was rooted in Christianity, or that the pioneering natural philosophers of the sixteenth and seventeenth centuries did not rebel against religious orthodoxy. Goodman's more nuanced view was that there was a common psychological affinity between science and Christianity. Goodman described this as 'objective and obsessional, frowning on spontaneous responses and rejecting other methods than the proper ritual discipline as essentially irrelevant if not wicked'. Like Christianity, science proposed 'Truth and Beauty as absolute aims and models' and promised 'happiness for mankind'. Both also shared a 'belief in the progress of an objective abstract entity'. Goodman referred to Weber to consider the sociological significance of this common psychology. In European history science was assimilated into an ethics of self-denial, individualism, and materialism. Weber, Goodman continued, was right to argue that these ethics provided a spur to capitalist accumulation. In addition, Goodman also claimed that the anxieties that science crystallized by challenging the old Church and undermining the communities it had fostered concomitantly rekindled Roman ideas of imperialism. When science became bureaucratized it was, therefore, already enmeshed in authoritarian political systems and harnessed to interests built on prejudicial exclusions and structural inequalities (Goodman 1962: 83–84).

When he looked at America in the 1960s, Goodman diagnosed the cause of social tension in the parallel development of science and religion. While the protestant ethic stimulated production and underpinned the boom in post-war consumption, the religiosity of science served as a repressive brake on experimentation and creativity. Goodman's analysis pointed to the dry, rationalist character of science and the denial of passion, play, spontaneity, and intuition which Bakunin also characterized as antisocial and anti-democratic. Moreover it pointed towards another rich seam for anarchist critique, one based on an ideological conception of science, from which primitivists, advocates of post-left anarchy, anti-civilizationists, anarchafeminists, and postcolonial anarchists have also drawn inspiration.

According to this conception science maps to a mechanistic view of the universe, which might be thought of as religious insofar as it is dogmatic in its truth claims, yet which remains spiritually vacuous. Technology is a central focus for this critique. However, as Lewis Mumford argued, the illusions of science were not linked to any particular technologies or inventions, but to the emergence and uncritical absorption of a particular world view. Specifically,

> since Francis Bacon and Galileo defined the new methods and objectives of technics, our great physical transformations have been affected by a system that deliberately eliminates the whole human personality, ignores the historic process,

overplays the role of the abstract intelligence, and – makes control over physical nature, ultimately control over man himself, the chief purpose of existence. This system has made its way so insidiously into Western society, that any analysis of its derivation and its intentions may well seem more questionable – indeed more shocking – than the facts themselves.

(Mumford 1964)

One strand of the argument, advanced by Wolfi Landstreicher, is that science underscores a desire to 'tame' or in other words dominate nature in order to exploit resources for profit, but his aim is not just to highlight its costs. He also wants to reveal the 'ideological foundations of science'. Science describes a 'relational view of the universe' which challenges the ancient Greek and anti-civilization understanding in which the universe is viewed holistically 'in order to observe the relationships between things, the connections and interactions'. This stance, Landstreicher argues, supports 'those who have no desire to dominate the universe, but rather only want to determine how to interact with their environment in order to fulfil their desires and create their life'. The scientific view works in entirely the opposite direction (Landstreicher 2007).

A second strand is that science elevates reason over the insights of 'mystics, romantics and nationalists' as Murray Bookchin put it (Bookchin 1995: 10). Bookchin shared Landstreicher's relational view of the world, but classifying himself as an advocate of enlightened humanism he was deeply hostile of currents in anarchism that decried reason and rationalism. And insofar as anti-humanists invoked 'science' to do this, he defended the scientific view. Anti-humanists, he argued, 'deprecate or deny humanity's most distinctive hallmark – reason, and its extraordinary powers to grasp, intervene into, and play a guiding role in altering social and natural reality'. Yet '[i]n the end', he argued, 'it is our claim to be able to reason and to rationally intervene in the world around us that' defined human beings 'as a species' (Bookchin 1995: 4–5). One response to this position, John Clark's dialectical holistic view, is that the world, the universe, 'nature' cannot be objectified in ways that Bookchin's rationalism requires (Clark 1997). Another is that the priority attached to reason and anarchism's rootedness in enlightenment traditions is imperialist (Ciccariello-Maher 2010).

There are some overlaps between the ideological and epistemological aspects of anarchist criticism. Specifically, critics argue that the claims to truth associated with the ideology of science are rooted in theories of knowledge that assume the possibility of objectivity or certainty. Traditionally, the anarchist critique attached to Marxist claims about the status of scientific socialism. Gustav Landauer described this claim to science as a claim 'to know the future'.

It presumes to have such deep insight into eternal laws of development and the determinant factors of human history that it knows what is to come, how history will continue and what will become of our conditions and forms of production and organization.

(Landauer 1978: 49)

In part, Landauer's concern resonated with the Mumford's critique of the 'megamachine': cast in this fashion, science would bring about what Landauer understood to be Marx's dystopian dream, namely the eradication of rural idiocy in the name of industrial efficiency and proletarian freedom. In the other part, he argued the idea that 'a science exists that can reveal, calculate and determine the future with certainty from the data and news of the past and the facts and conditions of the present' was 'foolish' and he recommended that it be revealed, mocked and rejected (Landauer 1978: 49). Having stripped this brand of science bare, recent critics have exposed the compulsion it conceals. In place of scientific certainty, associated here with 'reason', Franco Berardi thus substitutes the Kropotkinian idea of the tendency to discuss sociological trends (Kropotkin 1970: 47):

> As Force and Reason have failed as principles of social change and political government, I think that we should adopt the point of view of the tendency, not the point of view of the will. Tendency is not an ideal, a utopia, it is not the projection of a rational order that force would eventually implement. Tendency is a possibility implicated in the present state of things, a possibility that cannot currently be deployed because the present paradigm of social relation ... makes such deployment impossible.
>
> (Berardi 2012: 144)

Tellingly, Landauer's critique of scientific certainty did not extend to science itself. One of the upshots of Marxism's distortions was that 'the meaning of science' was itself devalued. Like Bakunin, he distinguished between scientific laws – 'laws of our mind' – or 'knowledge', meaning 'to have lived, to possess what has been' and life, 'to live, creating and suffering what is to come' (Landauer 1978: 50). Goodman similarly distinguished science as wonder from science as objective technological precision (Goodman 1966: 34–35). Recent anarchist critics are generally less discriminating. The complaints often combine a rejection of the kinds of Comtean sociological schema that Bakunin absorbed (the law of stages), sometimes viewed through the lens of socialist science, with critiques of the proposition that the world is knowable, and the claim that knowledge is accessible through adoption of a single method, based on observation and experiment. Moving between these positions Saul Newman deploys a form of utopian anti-Marxism, similar to Landauer's, to address the first, Foucauldian anti-foundationalism against the second, and Feyerabend's epistemological anarchism to answer the third (Newman 2012: 162; 47; 49). In this way, nineteenth-century discourses about religion and science are bundled up with vulgar Marxist conceptions of historical necessity and militant twentieth-century arguments about verification and the merits of natural scientific methods in social scientific – including political science – research. The 'discourse of Enlightenment humanism' which unites Kropotkin and Bookchin, Newman argues, is no longer sustainable. Enumerating the list of scientistic motifs that run through this discourse, he isolates 'the universality of morality and reason, and the ideas of the progressive enlightenment of humankind; a conception of the social order as naturally constituted (by natural laws, for instance) and rationally determined; a dialectical view of history; and a certain positivism, whereby science could reveal the truth of social relations' (Newman 2012: 6).

Newman has a particular current of anarchism in his sights, nevertheless the totality of this critique suggests that the possibilities of conducting anarchist political science, either in the sense of being able to engage in the full range of sub-fields collected under the APSA umbrella or, in the UK context, to bring anarchist insights into the analysis of government, are quite slim. Yet notwithstanding the robustness of the anarchist critique of science, it is possible to find examples of anarchist political science and to consider the spaces that exist for a different model of scientific engagement.

Anarchism and political science

I have argued that political science offers anarchists more opportunities for engagement than some recent anarchist critiques of 'science' allow. In this section, I outline three defences of constructive political science practice and then consider how political and social science can support anarchist transformation.

In her discussions of community-based activism Martha Ackelsberg gives one reason why anarchists should care about the exclusion from political science research: grassroots feminist activism, she argues, not only exposes the inadequacy of academic conceptions of democracy but also the space that exists to reshape public conceptions (Ackelsberg 2010: 150). Part of her project is to show what anarchist perspectives bring to the understanding of concepts used in academic debate and how these fail to explain or make sense of actual political phenomena; and the bigger purpose is to transform ordinary-language conceptions and bring them into closer alignment with the values of the activist groups with which she is involved. If democracy is about more than electoral participation, if current political institutions are not what democracy looks like and consensus decision-making and local governance are to be preferred; if protest should be understood as an expression of democracy rather than a corruption of a right of free speech dependent on police fiat; and if it is possible to develop institutions in which decision-making power is not always and necessarily concentrated in the hands of an elite, then anarchists might usefully try to persuade their fellow citizens why and highlight the virtues of the alternatives.

In a recent discussion of global warming, Roy Krøvel gives another reason to engage with political science, at the same time touching directly on the meta-theoretical issues that contemporary anarchist political theory raises. Global warming he argues 'is real' and its reality 'exists independently of our discourse about it'. Global warming provides urgent reasons for action because it 'will have real and dangerous consequences for humans and human society' (Krøvel 2013: 22). At the same time, global warming poses a particular problem, namely full knowledge of the processes and consequences. From an eco-anarchist perspective, confronting climate change requires us to 'rethink our relationship with nature and our possible paths to understanding nature and reality in a theoretically serious manner ... that is, in terms of the unity between theory and praxis'. The task is in part ethical, leading Krøvel to re-examine debates between Bookchin and his critics in an effort to reach a synthesis of deep and social ecology, and partly scientific: confronting climate change effectively involves the development of an approach that will support ecophilosophy and stimulate global action, providing confidence for action in a condition of uncertainty. 'Ethical thinking about global warming cannot ... be reduced to the realm of human consciousness, language and discourse' and the imperatives for action require 'that we act before we know everything we want to know about it' (Krøvel 2013: 22). Science can assist, not because it is expected 'to produce certainty' but because

> it can help to guide us to make more or less sound ethical judgements based on the uncertain predictions we have at the time when we need to make 'policy decisions'. This understanding of the role of science would accept that we have no guarantee

that the future will resemble the past, while also accepting that some statements on global warming are less fallible than others.

(Krøvel 2013: 42)

Krøvel does not for a minute suggest a naive form of empiricism will suffice for his project and he instead argues for an anti-foundationalist approach.

In their sociological and philosophical discussion, Charles Thorpe and Iain Welsh similarly defend the role of science in anarchism. Like Krøvel, they contend that anarchism itself provides the starting point. From this perspective, political science is not a conjunction formed by bolting external models of research onto anarchist aspirations but about developing approaches to study consistent with that ethic. Indeed, finding an affinity between the anarchism of nineteenth-century political activists like Kropotkin, and Feyerabend's epistemological anarchism, they challenge the sociological mainstream by refocusing scientific research from elite interests towards grass-roots initiatives shaped 'from below' and defend the possibility of developing a non-authoritarian philosophy of science consistent with diverse and plural practices and the rejection of abstract, universal knowledge claims (Thorpe and Welsh 2008).

How far can political social scientific research support transformative agendas? In a discussion of feminist research, Martineau and Squires note that scholars working in this area have typically advocated methodological pluralism and that this open approach has facilitated 'greater interaction between positivist and post-positivist feminist scholars, and between empirical political scientists and normative political theorists, than is common in the discipline more generally' (Martineau and Squires 2012: 528). Both the pluralism of feminist research and the exchange between empirical analysis and ideal theory is to be encouraged, they argue, because the potential of political theory to support social transformation requires that it is not entirely disconnected from the empirical investigation of contingent realities (Martineau and Squires 2012: 536). Just as empiricism results in conservatism when it is used to generate theory, ideal theory results in abstraction when detached from empiricism. The priority they attach to social transformation is also central to anarchism: the point of research is to help bring about change.

Fredy Perlman advanced a similar argument not un-coincidentally, in the late 1950s in a critical appreciation of C. Wright Mills (Perlman 1970). In 1959, Mills analyzed the scientific trends then taking hold in social science research. He described the state of the discipline by identifying two dominant axes – grand theory and abstracted empiricism. Neither of these, he argued, helped individuals reflect on shifts in cultural values and changes in social structures or helped them understand their own lives, let alone offer them hope of transformation or empowerment: both were sadly devoid of sociological imagination. He responded by calling for a new kind of intellectual engagement informed by his deep appreciation of sociology's historical roots. Indeed, he not only argued that the history of discipline was far richer than modern trends implied but, in addition, that it offered a model that might help redress the shortcomings of the modern trend.

Perlman's assessment of Mills' work was that he was ultimately unable to free himself from the grip of elitism and that his critical analysis of the interwar theorists that Heller had earlier rejected blinded him to the possibility of grassroots action (Perlman 1970: 106–117). Nevertheless, Perlman regarded *The Sociological Imagination* as a work of a 'fully developed twentieth century man attempting to link his practical activity to the history of his time'. Mills' book was an 'attempt to join thought to action, to unite power with sensibility' (Perlman 1970: 88). Might it still provide a model for anarchist political science?

Worryingly for contemporary anarchist theorists, Mills found his inspiration in the sociology of the 'classic' period, notably in the work of Comte, J.S. Mill, Marx, and Weber. For all its flaws, this body of work was shaped by a commitment to values that were clearly stated, by concern to address 'the private troubles encountered ... by a variety of individuals' and to explore them through the formulation of research questions that located these specific, particular issues with reference to 'larger historical and social structures' (Mills 1983: 144). These sociologists were 'craftsmen' who avoided making deductions from grand, conceptual theories and believed that there was more to analysis than 'microscopic study'. Mills explained that in classic social science,

> Practitioners try to build and to deduce at the same time, in the same process of study, and to do so by means of adequate formulation and reformulation of problems and of their adequate solutions. To practice such a policy ... is to take up substantive problems on the historical level of reality; to state these problems in terms appropriate to them; and then, no matter how high the flight of theory, no matter how painstaking the crawl among detail, in the end of each completed act of study, to state the solution in terms of the macroscopic terms of the problem.
>
> (Mills 1983: 143)

Mills' ideas chimed with the project outlined by Heller, though as a result of the context, their ambitions were quite different. The defensive role that Heller assigned to political science was to gauge the negative consequences of the assaults of powerful, aggressive elites on the popular institutions, legitimized by public endorsement and a history of political thought. Mills' idea was to show how sociologists might help citizens rise above the political indifference, apathy, and uneasiness that he perceived in post-war American society, by challenging the intellectual consensus to explain the causes of this malaise (Mills 1983: 18–19).

The calls that Mills made to a new generation of students resonated with a tradition of anarchist thinking which emerged in parallel to the classic sociology Mills celebrated, notably in the work of Kropotkin. One of his projects was to deploy science methodologically against socialist metaphysics (scientific socialism) and to use the methods of empirical analysis so beloved of Victorians to expose the bankruptcy of capitalism and repressive state politics. For example, he looked at data to demonstrate the economic chaos of international trade divisions and the barbarity of prison policy. His critical admiration for Herbert Spencer and August Comte and his ability to master data and to keep up with a wide range of debates in the social sciences informed much of this work. However, it is a mistake to read into this admiration a crudely positivistic conception of the world. Indeed, the comparison to Mills' notion of craftsmanship is illuminating. The purpose of scientific investigation, Kropotkin argued, was to obtain 'an answer to a definite and clearly-worded question. And it is the more fruitful the more clearly the explorer sees the connection that exists between his problem and his general concept of the universe' (Kropotkin 1970: 153). Because anarchism, he argued, 'was born among the people – in the struggles of real life' (Kropotkin 1970: 150), its research values were shaped by the conditions in which individuals lived and struggled, and the means by which their aspirations might be supported. Like Mills, Kropotkin adopted a synthetic approach to research, rejecting both grand theory and empiricism and advocating instead the inductive-deductive method, which bound the generation of theory and data-analysis. In appealing to this approach, Kropotkin was not interested in 'deducing our social ideas from [natural sciences]' (Kropotkin 1970: 115). Nor did he think that the methods adopted in current research could be applied uncritically, since these were moulded by the interests of dominant elites. The study of history, he argued for example, could not continue as an 'old woman's tale about great kings, great statesmen and great parliaments' any more than social economy could remain 'merely the sanctification of capitalist robbery'. It was obvious to him that these disciplines, as well as 'anthropology, sociology, ethics, must be completely recast, and that the natural sciences themselves, must undergo a profound modification, alike in regard to the conception of natural phenomena and with respect to the method of exposition' (Kropotkin 1970: 277).

The prospect that Kropotkin's and, similarly Mills' work presents, is the development of a prefigurative approach to political science: one which frames the objects of analysis with reference to the achievement of more just realities and which applies political science methods in order to illuminate paths of change instead of the maintenance of the status quo. It is interesting to think how the anti-elitist arguments informing the critiques of parliamentary government that Kropotkin published – notably the essay 'Representative Government' – were absorbed in the early twentieth century into a politics of the far right, as Heller's account of political science documents. It was Mills, moreover, who recast the critique of elitism in the analysis of the military-industrial complex. One of the architects of classical elitism, Robert Michels, could not resist treating princely Kropotkin's aristocratic heritage as grist to his mill, but he acknowledged the cogency of the anarchist critique when he formulated his iron law of oligarchy. Refusing the terms of political science debate in the name of anarchist anti-science leaves open a field of research and runs the risk that the space will be occupied by individuals who do not understand anarchist positions or, in seeking to analyse them, dismiss them as mere utopianism.

Conclusion

Herber Newton's statement that anarchism was political science and religion might be read as a defiant affirmation of the potential for social change. Those who subscribed to anarchism stood on the side of dynamic reform. Armed with evidence about the justice and necessity of change and faith in its possibility, they were prepared to confront reactionaries who were willing to deny basic civil rights and, as the judicial murder of Joe Hill in 1915 demonstrated, use the full weight of the law for repressive purposes. Political science was a tool in that struggle, not just available to anarchists, but to all scholars interested in diagnosing the causes of social problems and finding remedies for their amelioration. The title chosen to highlight late nineteenth-century advances in social science – the *Encyclopedia of Social Reform* – seems indicative of this mood. Indeed, the editor, W.D.P. Bliss was another Christian Socialist (somewhat critical of Newton) committed to the '"gradual and careful" transformation of the social system' and 'the reconstruction of the entire economic and industrial order' (Dressner 1978: 70). Arguments about the proper relationship between normative theory and empirical science, rehearsed between Heller and Beveridge, and the post-war social trends that have both elevated particular methods of research and simultaneously dulled methodological reflections about their scientific validity have not extinguished this reforming aspiration. Mills was a mid-twentieth-century advocate and journals such as *New Political Science* are produced in the same spirit (New Political Science n.d.). Prichard might be right that political science tends to ignore anarchism, yet political science research does not require a narrowing of disciplinary focus or critical view or involve a proscription on the selection of methods. It seems clear that anarchism has a place in the discipline. To cast anarchism against any of its sub-fields on the basis of a critique of science is self-defeating.

References

Ackelsberg, M. (2010) *Resisting Citizenship. Feminist Essays on Politics, Community and Democracy*, London: Routledge.
American Political Science Association (APSA) (2019) Online. Available at: https://www.apsanet.org/RESOURCES/For-Students (accessed 17 January 2019).
Bakunin, M. (1916 [1882]) *God and the State*, with a Preface by Carlo Cafiero and Elisée Reclus, First American Edition, New York: Mother Earth Publishing. Online. Available at: http://dwardmac.pitzer.edu/Anarchist_Archives/bakunin/godandstate/godandstate_ch1.html#I (accessed 13 July 2013).
Barash, J.A. (2000) 'Political Mythologies of the Twentieth Century in the Perspective of Herman Heller, Ernst Cassirer, and Karl Löwith', *Bulletin du Centre de recherche français à Jérusalem*, 6: 121–133. Online. Available at: http://bcrfj.revues.org/2882 (accessed 13 July 2013).
Barents, J. (1961) *Political Science in Western Europe. A Trend Report*, London: Stevens & Sons.
Berardi, F. 'Bifo' (2012) 'The Transversal Function of Disentanglement', in F. Campagne and E. Campiglio (eds.) *What We Are Fighting For? A Radical Collective Manifesto*, London: Pluto, pp. 139–145.
Beveridge, W. (1932) 'Draft of the Director's Address to First-Year Students, 5 October 1932', London School of Economics and Political Science Digital Library. Online. Available at: http://lib-161.lse.ac.uk/archives/beveridge_5_10/19.pdf (accessed 12 October 2012).
Bevir, M. (2006) 'Political Studies as Narrative and Science, 1880–2000', *Political Studies*, 54(3): 583–606.
Bliss, W.D.P. (ed.) (1908) *New Encyclopedia of Social Reform*, New York and London: Funk & Wagnalls Co.
BookchinM. (1995) *Re-Enchanting Humanity. A Defense of the Human Spirit against Anti-humanism, Misanthropy, Mysticism, and Primitivism*, London: Cassell.
Carroll, J.D. and Frederickson, H.G. (2001) 'Dwight Waldo1913–2000', *Public Administration Review*, 61(1): 2–8.
Ciccariello-Maher, G. (2010) 'An Anarchism That is Not Anarchism: Notes toward a Critique of Anarchist Imperialism', in J. Klausen and J. Martel (eds.) *How Not to Be Governed*, Lanham MD: Lexington, pp. 19–46.
Clark, J. (1997) 'A Social Ecology', *Capitalism, Nature, Socialism*, 31: 3–33. Online. Available at: http://theanarchistlibrary.org/library/john-clark-a-social-ecology (accessed 13 July 2013).
Daalder, H. (1991) 'Political Science in the Netherlands', *European Journal of Political Research*, 20(3–4): 279–300.
Dressner, R.B. (1978) 'William Dwight Porter Bliss's Christian Socialism', *Church History*, 47(1): 66–82.
Easton, D. (1953; 1971) *The Political System: An Inquiry into the State of Political Science*, 2nd edn. Chicago and London: University of Chicago Press.
Easton, D. (1968) 'Political Science', in D.L. Sills (ed.) *International Encyclopedia of Social Sciences*, vol. 12, New York: Macmillan Co. & The Free Press, pp. 282–298.
ESRC (2007) *International Benchmarking Review of UK Politics and International Studies*. Online. Available at: http://www.esrc.ac.uk/_images/International%20benchmarking%20review%20-%20Politics%20and%20International%20studies_tcm8-4554.pdf (accessed 13 July 2013).
Goodman, P. (1962) *Utopian Essays and Practical Proposals*, New York: Vintage.

Goodman, P. (1966) *The Moral Ambiguity of America*, Toronto: Canadian Broadcasting Corporation.
Heller, H. (1963 [1933]) 'Political Science', in E.R.A. Seligman (ed.) *Encyclopedia of the Social Sciences*, New York: Macmillan, pp. 207–223.
Kropotkin, P.A. (1970) *Kropotkin's Revolutionary Pamphlets*, R.N. Baldwin (ed.), New York: Dover.
Krøvel, R. (2013) 'Revisiting Social and Deep Ecology in the Light of Global Warming', *Anarchist Studies*, 22(2): 22–47.
Landauer, G. (1978) *For Socialism*, trans. D.J. Parent, introduction by R. Berman and T. Luke, St. Louis: Telos Press.
Landstreicher, W. (2007) 'A Balanced Account of the World: A Critical Look at the Scientific World View', *Anarchy A Journal of Desire Armed*, 63. Online. Available at: http://theanarchistlibrary.org/library/wolfi-landstreicher-a-balanced-account-of-the-world-a-critical-look-at-the-scientific-world-vie (accessed 13 July 2013).
Marsh, D. and Stoker, G. (eds.) (2002) *Theory and Methods in Political Science*, 2nd edn. Basingstoke: Palgrave/Macmillan.
Martin, J. L. (2001) 'The Authoritarian Personality, 50 Years Later: What Lessons Are There for Political Psychology?', *Political Psychology*, 22(1): 1–26.
Martineau, W. and Squires, J. (2012) 'Addressing the "Dismal Disconnection": Normative Theory, Empirical Inquiry and Dialogic Research', *Political Studies*, 60(3): 523–538.
Mills, C.W. (1983 [1959]) *The Sociological Imagination*, Harmondsworth: Penguin.
Mumford, L. (1964) 'Authoritarian and Democratic Technics', *Technology and Culture* 5(1): 1–8. Online. Available at: <http://theanarchistlibrary.org/library/lewis-mumford-authoritarian-and-democratic-technics> (accessed 12 October 2012).
New Political Science (n.d.) 'Aims and Scope', *New Political Science*. Online. Available at: http://www.tandfonline.com/action/aboutThisJournal?show=aimsScope&journalCode=cnps20#.UeKqx8xwZCo (accessed 13 July 2013).
Newman, S. (2012) *The Politics of Postanarchism*, Edinburgh: Edinburgh University Press.
Perlman, F. (1970) *The Incoherence of the Intellectual*, Detroit: Black and Red.
Prichard, A. (2012) 'Anarchy, Anarchism and International Relations', in R. Kinna (ed.) *The Continuum Companion to Anarchism*, New York: Continuum, pp. 96–108.
Quality Assurance Agency (QAA) (2007) *Subject Benchmark Statement: Politics and International Relations*, UK Quality Assurance Agency. Online. Available at: http://www.qaa.ac.uk/Publications/InformationAndGuidance/Pages/Subject-benchmark-statement-Polictics-and-international-relations.aspx (accessed 13 July 2013).
Salvadori, M. (1950) 'Introduction. The UNESCO Project: Methods in Political Science', in *Contemporary Political Science: A Survey of Methods, Research and Teaching*, Publication 426 of the United Nations Educational, Scientific and Cultural Organization, Paris: UNESCO, pp. 1–20. Online. Available at: http://unesdoc.unesco.org/images/0007/000725/072539eo.pdf (accessed 13 July 2013).
Schroeder, T. (1916) *Free Speech for Radicals*, New York: Free Speech League.
Thorpe, C. and Welsh, I. (2008) 'Beyond Primitivism: Toward a Twenty-First Century Anarchist Theory and Praxis for Science', *Anarchist Studies* 16(1): 48–75. Online. Available at: http://theanarchistlibrary.org/library/charles-thorpe-and-ian-welsh-beyond-primitivism-toward-a-twenty-first-century-anarchist-theory (accessed 13 July 2013).
Waldo, D. (1956) *Political Science in the United States of America. A Trend Report*, Paris: UNESCO. Online. Available at: http://unesdoc.unesco.org/images/0006/000681/068182eo.pdf (accessed 13 July 2013).
Webb, B. (1895) Typescript Diary, 1 January 1889-[7] March 1898, London School of Economics and Political Science Digital Library. Online. Available at: http://digital.library.lse.ac.uk/objects/lse:wip502kaf#page/390/mode/2up (accessed 13 October 2012).

7 Toward an anarchist-feminist analytics of power

Sandra Jeppesen

Introduction

Anarchist-feminists have been engaged globally in political organizing and theorizing since the outset of the anarchist movement in the late eighteenth and early nineteenth centuries (Farrow 1974; Molyneux 1986; Zarrow 1988; Ackelsburg 1991; Brown 1993; de Heredia 2007; Jeppesen and Nazar 2012). Despite this, Margaret Marsh has found that 'very little scholarly attention has been focused on anarchist women, with the exception of Emma Goldman, who was not fully representative' (Marsh 1978: 533). Deric Shannon (2009: 59) similarly argues that 'articles articulating or utilizing a distinctly anarcha-feminist perspective are rarely found in academic journals', leaving anarchist-feminist theory under-articulated. Writers propose various reasons: Marx has theorized capitalism so anarchist-feminists need not; anarchist-feminists believe theory to be elitist; and anarchist-feminists prefer action to theory. We may also observe that women, especially racialized and colonialized women, have disproportionate responsibilities for work both inside and outside the home, as well as an unequal portion of organizing work falling to them, leaving less time for theorizing. Moreover, anarchist-feminist academics may tend to produce time-consuming collaborative work, whereas anarchist men tend to produce individual work. I would argue, with Shannon, that more cross-pollination is needed between anarchist theories of the state and capital, and feminist theories of gender, queer, trans, race, colonialism, and ecology.

There is a growing emergence of global anarchist-feminist research on a wide range of issues. Drawing on this wealth of material, I will first develop a working definition of anarchist-feminism, and then propose an anarchist-feminist analytics of power.

What is anarchist-feminism?

Anarchist-feminism refers to a meeting of anarchism and feminism. Anarchism is a political theory dating back to the publication of two books: William Godwin's (1793) *Enquiry Concerning Political Justice* and Mary Wollstonecraft's (1792) *A Vindication of the Rights of Woman*. Catherine Eschle (2001: 42) theorizes 'anarchism as opposition to relations and structures of hierarchical and coercive power', emphasizing practices grounded in critiques of domination. Today it is an activist practice gaining global momentum: 'From anti-capitalist social centres and ecofeminist communities to raucous street parties and blockades of international summits, anarchist forms of resistance and organizing have been at the heart of the "alternative globalization" movement' (Gordon 2007: 29).

Feminist theories analyze gendered power inequities in politics, economics, and culture, including: psychoanalytic criticism; eco-criticism; French feminism; Marxist, socialist, and poststructuralist feminisms; liberal, bourgeois, and radical feminisms; antiracist, anticolonial, and transnational feminisms: 'In its assumption of the possibility for fundamental social change, feminist theory is supported by feminist practice' (Iannello 1992: 35). While anarchism 'points toward a model of democratic movement organization even if the general insensitivity to multiple forms of power means that this model remains incomplete' (Eschle 2001: 46), when combined with feminism, this sensitivity to multiple complex forms of power emerges.

Starting by defining anarchism and feminism separately, however, suggests that the two have historically been separate. This is not the case. Rather, 'the anarchist movement has long attracted and has had at its center noteworthy women who have influenced the development of the movement worldwide' (Kramarae and Spender 2001: 46). In Mexico, 'Carmen Huerta became the president of the labor congress as early as 1879, and labor policies always reflected women's concerns as a result of anarchist[-feminist] demands' (49). In Argentina, anarchist women produced a feminist newspaper, *La Voz de la Mujer* (Molyneux 1986), and in Spain anarchist-feminists organized the *Mujeres Libres*, which numbered over 20,000 women at its peak (Ackelsberg 2005: 21). Moreover, in 'Uruguay, Brazil and Mexico, anarchists also promoted anarchist-feminism very early on' (de Heredia 2007). Anarchist women such as Emma Goldman and Voltairine de Cleyre were active in the USA in the early twentieth century, when anarchist-feminists such as He Zhen were also organizing in revolutionary China (Zarrow 1988).

What, then, is anarchist-feminism? Lynne Farrow (1974: 3) famously argued in the 1970s that 'Feminism practices what Anarchism preaches'. Deirdre Hogan (2004) argues that 'anarchists believe that the liberty of one is based on the liberty of all and so there can be no true anarchist society without an end to all existing structures of domination and exploitation, including naturally the oppression of women'. De Heredia (2007: 44) argues that 'anarcha-feminism can serve to "mainstream"[1] gender and feminist struggle[s], thereby making anarchist practice more consistent with anarchist theory, [and] anarcha-feminism can contribute to other feminist critiques of and struggles against gender oppression'. Similarly, Breton and colleagues (2012a) have found that anarchist-feminism attempts to anarchize feminism and make anarchism more feminist. Anarcha-feminist and anarcha-queer movements:

> challenge gender and sex oppressions both in the world at large and within the anarchist movement, pushing non-feminist and non-queer anarchists to consider what are often labelled feminist and queer issues including the body, parenting, sex work, (dis)ability, health and mental health. On the other hand they challenge feminist and queer movements to consider oppressions intersectional with sex and gender such as capitalism, class, poverty, labour and housing, where anarchist analysis and practice are particularly strong.
> (Jeppesen and Nazar 2012: 163)

Anarchist-feminists are engaged in struggles internal to social movements against manarchism (systemic male domination in anarchist movements) and liberal feminism (reformist, classist, white-dominated, or essentialist claims for women's rights), simultaneously struggling within these movements for systemic transformations in the broader society.

Alison Jaggar (1983: 11) argues that anarchist-feminist perspectives may sometimes be subsumed under feminist theories, including: Marxist feminism, in which the state withers away; radical feminist challenges to patriarchy; and socialist-feminist critiques of economic hierarchies. Thus we might assume anarchist-feminism does not have its own forms of thought. But anarchist-feminist theory does not claim ownership over ideas, valuing instead the democratization of knowledge for the benefit of humanity. Anarchist-feminists might thus welcome the fact that elements of anarchist-feminism have been integrated into a diverse range of feminisms. Kathleen Iannello suggests that anarchist-feminists offer a unique 'focus on the development of structures that avoid the kind of coercive power transmitted through hierarchical organization ... While questions of hierarchy and power are important to all feminist frameworks, none address it as specifically as anarchists' (Iannello 1992: 42).

At the same time, historically, anarchist women did not always call themselves feminists, 'reject[ing] a feminist label because feminism was understood to be an ideology of the bourgeoisie' (de Heredia 2007), and of suffragists demanding the vote (Reichert 1976: 175–176). Voltairine de Cleyre famously quipped, 'The ballot hasn't made men free and it won't make us free' (cited in Marsh 1978: 541). Mainstream 'feminism did not, after all, threaten cultural foundations', such as marriage, patriarchy in the family, etc., and instead, 'concentrated on legal and political issues' (Marsh 1978: 534). But anarchist-feminists saw the legal and political systems as sites of gendered oppression, which they organized against. Early anarchist-feminists are thus often left out of feminist histories, despite having been active in campaigns against gender oppression, engaged in direct action, and developed important anarchist and feminist theories. Nonetheless, as De Heredia (2007: 50) argues, 'despite their rejection of the word feminism, Spanish anarchists attempted to address specifically women's cultural, social and economic subordination', and groups such as the *Mujeres Libres* were leading-edge feminists in their time, calling on women to think beyond superficial reforms, and noting connections between issues such as gender, class, the nation-state, race, immigration status, and war – some of which were only taken up in non-anarchist-feminist theory more than half a century later, when Kimberlé Crenshaw (1989) coined the term 'intersectionality theory'.

While some anarchist women did not self-identify as feminists, the reverse may also be true: anti-authoritarian feminists may not always identify as anarchists. Alison Jaggar (1983) argues that anarchist-feminists often organized around issues (war, reproductive justice, the environment, free schools, migrant justice, etc.) or identities (indigenous, queer, black, punk, etc.), rather than adhering to an anarchist ideology. 'Often these women might not even call themselves anarchists; more often, they identify themselves as radical feminists' (Kramarae and Spender 2001: 49). Uri Gordon (2007: 32) has found that 'movement participants often speak of themselves as "autonomous", "anti-authoritarian" or "horizontal" ... words used for the sole purpose of not saying "anarchist" because of its popular connotations of chaos and violence'. The anarchist-feminist *Collectif de recherche sur l'autonomie collective* (CRAC) observed that:

> several reasons were given by activists to explain their refusal to take on the anarchist label: because they don't really feel the need to identify an ideological

belonging, they fear outside judgment, they don't want to scare people away from their organizing work, or they don't want to take on ideological labels that they feel may be dogmatic on the one hand, or on the other hand, somehow predetermined by others.

(Breton et al. 2012a: 157)

With this muddying of the waters, it is sometimes difficult to excavate anarchist-feminist histories.

Nonetheless, we can safely argue that anarchist-feminism was alive and active at the outset of anarchism, has maintained a presence in the anarchist movement throughout, and is increasingly active today. 'Since the 1960s, anarchist-feminism has seen a resurgence of interest. With the emergence of third-wave feminism, there is an anarchist impulse alive and well in the women's movement' (Kramarae and Spender 2001: 49). In the 1970s and 1980s, 'a substantial number of contemporary feminists identif[ied] themselves as anarchists'(Jaggar 1983: 11). Moreover, there is also a feminist impulse alive and well in the anarchist movement, where a substantial number of anarchists identify as feminists or pro-feminists[2] (Ehrlich 1994; de Heredia 2007; Gordon 2007; Shannon 2009; Breton et al. 2012a, 2012b; Rogue 2012; etc.).

Today, matters such as transnational feminisms, sex worker decriminalization, queer and trans rights, reproductive justice, indigenous self-determination, and climate change all have anarchist-feminists working on them, thinking through ways to challenge state and capitalist power from an anarchist-feminist position and engaging in global grassroots community building through mutual aid and direct action. These global actions are increasingly based on complex theories of power from an anarchist-feminist perspective.

Toward an anarchist-feminist analytics of power

In this section I will start to develop a theoretical framework for understanding power dynamics, relationships, politics, and processes of anarchist-feminist organizing – what I am calling an anarchist-feminist analytics of power.

I borrow the term 'analytics of power' from Michel Foucault, whose work has been explored by anarchist theorists such as Todd May (1994) and Saul Newman (2001, 2010). Foucault (1978: 82) suggests that the goal of rethinking power is 'to move less toward a "theory" of power than toward an "analytics" of power: that is, toward a definition of the specific domain formed by relations of power'. He argues that an analytics of power must free itself from the Western juridico-discursive conception of power as inherently repressive, limit-setting, negating, and prohibitive, bounded by legal discourse and the rule of law.

If we rethink power as a mechanism that hides itself to create conformity (Foucault 1980: 86), then unmasking power is key. Anarchist-feminists have long sought to reveal and challenge unequal conditions of power, working to create non-hierarchical power dynamics in activist groups. We see this in their early rejection of nationalist, racist, bourgeois, and capitalist systems. For Foucault, people tend to accept restrictive power because it is not absolute – it limits but does not eradicate desire or agency completely, 'leaving a measure of freedom – however slight – intact' (Foucault 1980: 86). People find this acceptable because power is understood 'as a pure limit set on freedom' (Foucault 1980: 86). Foucault counters this, and I argue that anarchist-feminists have always-already been engaged with countering it too, at least in part because they have rejected juridico-discursive conceptions of power, refusing to petition for legal reforms or expecting profound change to come through the state. The conception of power beyond the state underpins anarchist-feminist rethinking of gender oppression as well.

Following Foucault, we must ask different questions. Rather than asking how anarchist-feminists fight gender oppression, we might ask: How are power relations redistributed, reorganized, and re-characterized by anarchist-feminist collectives in their horizontal, consensus decision-making, cooperative social movement spaces? Or as Marsh (1978: 534) puts it, how do anarchist-feminists 'exercise their power?'

Table 7.1 Toward an anarchist-feminist analytics of power

Axis of theory	Analytics of power	Axes of activism
Gender, sex, sexuality	• patriarchal power relations constructed by state and capital • private/public sphere is a false, gendered, heteronormative binary • anti-heteronormative, anti-patriarchal power sharing • horizontal relational power from feminist centres of influence	• bodily autonomy, polyamory, radical monogamy, reproductive justice, sex workers' rights • queering anarchism, trans activism • non-mixed groups (e.g. Sorcières, APOC, QPOC) • politics of everyday life beyond private/public divide
Capital	• capitalist oppression depends on patriarchal Western property system • capitalist eco-destruction based on anthropocentrism • anarchist-feminist economics • empowerment, cooperation against neo-liberalism and for humanity	• collective gardens, squatting, housing collectives, communes • civil disobedience, direct action, property destruction • anti-capitalist gay shame critiques of corporate pride parades • climate camps, green anarchism
State	• critique of state role in maintaining gender binary (e.g., legal, medical, prison, police, military, education) • critique of monopoly of legitimate violence by the state (police and military) and masculinity • (pro)feminist collective self-determination and autonomy • prefigurative organizational forms	• anti-police brutality, prison industrial complex, military, war • creation of anarchist commons: anarchist day cares, care collectives, free schools, universities, etc. • no-border camps • anarcha-feminist insurrectionists, use of political violence
Colonialism, race	• borders as sites of racialized power • free movement, against all borders • indigenous self-determination; decolonizing minds, methods, actions • intersectionality theory: race and colonialism intersect with gender and capitalism, state, ecology, etc.	• (im)migrant support work: solidarity cities, 'don't ask don't tell' campaigns • forefront global groups in solidarity coalitions • indigenous anarchism, blockades • global anarchist-feminism

Gender, sex, sexuality

Anarchist-feminists historically have been concerned with the 'vexing questions of domestic and economic equality' (Marsh 1978: 535), arguing along individualist lines that 'the primacy of complete individual liberty' (536) in anarchism also applied to women. They insisted that 'women should always be self-supporting' (536), 'decried the sexual double standard' (537), and 'demanded equality of sexual freedom' sometimes in the form of 'varietism' or polyamory, as 'exclusivity implied that lovers held property rights over one another' (537). They believed the female body was not property to be controlled or coerced by men.

We can read Foucault as supporting anarchist-feminist critiques of inter-personal power: 'Relations of power are not in a position of exteriority with respect to other types of relationships (economic processes, knowledge relationships, sexual relations), but are ... the immediate effects of the divisions, inequalities, and disequilibriums' found within all relationships. However, relations of power do not have a prohibitive role but a 'directly productive role' (Foucault 1980: 94). This productive role is seen in nurturing horizontal relationships, wherein horizontalism locates the exercise of mutual power in organizational forms: consensus decision-making, talking and listening structures, participatory power, and mutual aid organizing. Relations of equalizing power are integrated into anarchist-feminist practices.

Reformulating the rejection of power hierarchies, three key sites of action-as-theory emerge for anarchist-feminists: destabilizing gender hierarchies; deconstructing the private-public divide; and re-establishing bodily autonomy.

Gender hierarchies

Historically one of the key gender hierarchies challenged by anarchist women was heterosexual marriage and the nuclear family. In North America,

> Voltairine [de Cleyre] and the anarchist-feminists did not just question the unfair nature of marriage laws of that time, they repudiated institutional marriage and the conventional family structure, seeing in these institutions the same authoritarian oppression as they saw in the institution of the State.
> (Presley 2005: 192)

Anarchist-feminist He Zhen, in China, and later in Japan, organized the 'Women's Rights Recovery Association' (Zarrow 1988: 800), critiquing the triple domination of women by fathers, husbands, and sons: 'She specifically and repeatedly criticized such institutions as polygamy, concubinage, and the authority of the mother-in-law' (806). In Argentina, anarchist-feminists forwarded an anti-marriage

> position on free love, ... [a] rejection of men's traditional authority over women and control of their sexuality. In the context of Southern European *machismo*, in which virginity, fidelity, and the double standard were the common currency of male privilege ...
> (Molyneux 1986: 122)

Despite specific cultural differences (fidelity to fathers, husbands, and sons in Chinese culture vs. *machismo* in Southern European culture, for example), anarchist-feminists universally rejected marriage as a socially constructed gender hierarchy that assigned men power over women.

A strategy rejecting men's participation emerged, 'encouraging the development of a whole movement of autonomous women's only groups across not only the United States, but also in Europe' (de Heredia 2007: 52), Canada (Breton et al. 2012a: 159), Latin America (Molyneux 1986), and beyond. For example, Breton and colleagues argue that:

> Some feminists have experienced sexism within left-wing student organizing and anticapitalist networks, or they might perceive a lack of a feminist analysis of globalization among antiglobalization activists. These experiences among others can be the impetus for the creation of autonomous women-only spaces.
> (Breton et al. 2012a: 159)

Non-mixed groups reduce gendered power dynamics; rather than struggling to assert the importance of developing a gendered analysis of globalization, for example, a non-mixed anarchist-feminist group can simply do this work.

These two strategies – rejection of marriage in the private sphere, and non-mixed organizing in the public sphere – are representative of the way in which anarchist-feminist politics conceives of the two spheres as both political and gendered.

The public and private spheres

Typically when anarchist-feminists have brought up issues in anarchist collectives such as marriage, birth control, free love, polyamory, sexual assault, trans inclusion, day care, self-care, mental health, or intentional families, the response is that these are private issues outside the public sphere of anarchist politics. However, Eschle (2001: 42) argues for 'a more expansive definition of anarchism as opposition to relations and structures of hierarchical and coercive power' including intimate relationships, kinship relations, and other social structures. This definition is taken up today in movements on sexual consent, accountability, and sex work (Jeppesen and Nazar 2012).

Deconstructing the private/public binary using Foucault's notion that power runs through all relations, I propose several arguments. First, following Marsh, we must understand that the private sphere has been deemed the less important of the two spheres, with no place in politics, and beyond the reach of the state. As Sarah Brown (1988: 462) argues, 'The assumption that women have not been ... constitutive of international relations conjoins easily with liberal feminist views of the basis of gender inequality as the expropriation of women's political power through relegation to the private sphere'. The binary private/public is thus hierarchical, with public being political, masculine, and privileged, and private being personal, feminine, and devalued. The dismissal (by men) of the private sphere as feminine can only take place through recourse to masculine power, however, demonstrating that the (heteronormative) private sphere is in fact also male-dominated.

Second, we might argue, with MacKinnon, that in fact the public sphere pre-determines or structures to a great extent the private sphere, so that relations of male hegemony are enacted both in the public sphere through relations of the state, law, policing, and governance, and in the private sphere through relations of marriage, sexuality, parenting, finances, and physical/sexual violence. The public and private spheres are in fact not binary opposites, but rather evidence of similar relations of patriarchal domination enacted in different spaces. Male hegemony may better be understood, according to an anarchist-feminist analytics of power, as the tendency to read masculinity as enacting greater power, and femininity as enacting lesser power. If we can assume that the personal is political, and the private sphere is equal to the public sphere, then the political is also personal, and the public sphere engenders the same unequal power relations as the private sphere. Assumptions regarding gendered power relations affect both types of spaces; therefore macro/public and micro/private spheres are equally important to an anarchist-feminist analytics of power.

Bodies

Bodies, often constructed as belonging to the private sphere, are in fact micro-political spheres of engagement in both public and private spaces. They offer the ultimate return to freedom, control, power-over-self, and the autonomy of the affective internal space.

Anarchist women, queers and trans people have long struggled for bodily autonomy in the context of industrializing capital, advocating relationships unfettered by power dynamics over-determined by ideologies of gender. Having deconstructed the private/public divide, we can define bodily autonomy as a collective political project to exercise self-power. Sometimes this is related to reproductive rights, including abortion (critiqued as white-Western-middle-class feminism), the right to choose to have children or not; to keep children when the state has historically removed them from racialized and colonized women; and to decide how, where, and with whom to raise children (e.g. in multi-generational, multi-parenting, queer, trans and/or same-sex parent households) (Luna 2009).

Contemporary feminist movements understand sex, gender, and sexuality to be three components of liberatory bodily autonomy. If a person's sex is female, their gender is not necessarily feminine, nor is their sexuality necessarily heterosexual. The binaries male/female, feminine/masculine, and heterosexual/homosexual are, like public/private, not neutral but hierarchical, and can be subverted through practices of diverse sexes, genders, and sexualities.

Hierarchical gender, sex, and sexuality binaries are arguably themselves a state form. Jamie Heckert (2012: 66) argues that, 'Whereas a state-oriented LGBT politics tries to challenge the hierarchies of hetero/homo, cis/trans, while keeping the identities, queer politics might ask how the identities themselves might already be state-like with their borders and policing'. Identities have become micro state forms, whereby the state demands that we stabilize our sex/gender/sexuality (on our passports, marriage licenses, birth certificates, etc.), and other people also police the boundaries of our identities. Fluidity of genders is therefore a political act of resistance. 'To become anarchist, to become queer, is not easy. To learn to cross lines, to see that the lines are not even real, is a radical transformation' (Heckert 2012: 72). Similarly, Jerimarie Liesegang suggests that:

> the core of the trans existence and persona is radical and anarchistic, if not insurrectionary, in its embodiment – such that pure liberation of sex and gender will not come through complicit reform within the state but rather through rejecting the state and its many social constructs.
>
> (Liesegang 2012: 88)

Trans, queer, and feminist bodily autonomies 'attempt to "prefigure" a revolutionary future. Thus, for example, self-governing collectives are established before wholesale social transformation has been achieved, to enable individual self-determination in the here and now' (Eschle 2001: 43). The importance of the politics of gender-variant bodies is consistent with the notion that 'the idea of prefiguration involves an assumption that participation in anarchist struggle can generate new ways of being, knowing and identification' (46). Each embodied queer/trans/feminist subject exists in the pre-conditions of liberation for the entire society. Bodily autonomy is crucial if we understand from Foucault that power is everywhere, and each embodied subject, freed from the limits of gender binaries, asserts its autonomy to participate in the collectivity (community, intentional family, partnership, polyamory). Moreover, communities must be anti-capitalist if gender liberation is to be achieved.

Capital

There is a gendered logic to the unequal power relations implicit in capital. Deric Shannon (2009: 63) argues that, 'at the root of anarcha-feminism [i]s an opposition to *power* itself, rather than those who wield it'. If we understand power as the root of oppositional theory, and if power is internal to sexual and gendered relations and simultaneously to capitalist relations, then anarchist-feminists are perhaps in opposition neither to those who wield power, nor to power itself, but rather to the unequal distribution of power across axes of gender and capital. Shannon argues that 'a contemporary anarcha-feminism would actively argue and fight for working class liberation from capitalism' (68).

For Foucault (1978: 94), 'Power comes from below; that is, there is no binary and all-encompassing opposition between rulers and ruled at the root of power relations'. The notion that there is no binary oppositional force within power relations offers a diffuse freedom for labourers, lower socio-economic classes, and those with low cultural capital. We can move from oppositional politics (capitalist vs. working class) to the politics of constructing alternative working arrangements in which participants are neither ruler nor ruled but equals in decision-making and the organization of labour.

However, Foucault's conception of power from 'below' is a binary formulation, contradicting his challenge to the ruled/rulers binary, re-establishing the dichotomy above/below, and discursively constructing power divisions as hierarchical and fixed. If power comes from below, then to exercise productive power must workers remain 'below'? This binary prevents us from integrating a rhizomatic analysis of intersectional oppressions and liberations.

Anarchist-feminism rejects binary conceptions such as male/female, ruler/ruled, above/below, as binary pairs are socially constructed and coercive. '[T]he manifold relationships of force that take shape and come into play in the machinery of production, in families, limited groups, and institutions, are the basis for wide-ranging effects of cleavage that run through the social body as a whole' (Foucault 1980: 94). Power can instead be created by, for, and with those who challenge inequitable power relations by engaging in direct action tactics such as property destruction to demonstrate that the power society believes inheres in particular institutions is not infallible. Marion Crain (1992: 1820) argues that 'labor scholars have unnecessarily cabined the discussion by adopting a patriarchal vision of power as materially based, and of its exercise as synonymous with domination and control'. Anarchist-feminists challenge coercive power, experimenting with ethical practices of creative power-sharing in the organization of work. Crain advances 'an alternative vision of power [in] woman-centered labor unions' (1821), based on 'participatory democracy, and consensus-style leadership' (1823).

Indeed, anarchist-feminists question labour practices as a set of pre-determined power relations. Catharine MacKinnon (1989: 75) argues that, 'Analyses of labor power often proceed as if labor power were produced by and for capital, yet somehow still sprang out of "nature", not out of social relations'. But there is no *a priori* organizational form for work; rather it has been organized by (straight white male) capitalists with the explicit goal of obtaining profits through exploitation, based on the conception of power-over. Crain argues that conventional union organizing today, or business unionism, has taken on a capitalist structure, as 'union structure – hierarchical, bureaucratic, formalistic – has come to mimic the structure of the large companies in opposition to which unions were formed' (Crain 1992: 1835). This failure to challenge power structures disempowers the rank and file (1835), as the 'union becomes simply one more layer in the hierarchy between the individual and the employer, rather than the collective voice of the workers' (1843). Unions can thus be seen as patriarchal structures having adopted the form of capitalism, exercising power-over in similar ways.

Crain articulates the need to engage 'an alternative feminist concept of power as energy, competence, and influence' (1824). Instead of patriarchal unions, based on a patriarchal notion of power-over, Crain argues that unions can be organized along feminist lines, conceiving of power as ability (1851), 'nurturant' (1852), and shaped by experience (1854). Similar to the *Mujeres Libres*, she argues that 'power-with' 'is primarily a capacity or a relation among people' (1851), and thus it can only be exercised through participation in communities, developing 'affiliative relationships of care' (1854). She concludes that 'a feminist theory of power rejects the understanding of power as domination, focusing instead on ability, competence, and the capacity to influence others. Power exercised in a community emanates horizontally, expanding outward in a weblike fashion' (1857). This echoing of Foucault's web of power is consistent with anarchist-feminist prefigurative organizing models.

Moreover Crain argues that 'Those who exercise power may be visualized as positioned at the center of a group, from where they are able to mobilize others' (1857–58), using stereotypically feminine strengths such as nurturing, understanding, compassion, care-giving, inspiration, and interdependence. Women in labour unions who organize according to this model describe their own interactions as 'reaching out rather than down' (1860) in a style of leadership that takes the long view and focuses on the bigger picture (1860). Citing Audre Lorde's famous supposition that 'the master's tools will never dismantle the master's house', Crain argues that people comfortable living in the 'master's house' – union leaders today – are threatened by feminist organizing tactics (1885) that reject the assumption that the house even belongs to the master. Business unionism is therefore not the strongest model of emancipation for working-class women.

Instead, an anarchist-feminist analytics of power relies on anti-heteronormative and anti-patriarchal power-sharing. Through gender, sex, and sexuality campaigns, anarchist-feminists create spaces in which cooperative horizontal power is inspired, produced, circulated, shared, and diffused in communities grounded in mutual care, compassion, survival and resilience. Permissiveness circulates, people experiment and play at deconstructing power, and potential spaces of equal power relations evolve. If we understand that power emanates horizontally from compassionate centres of influence, how might this help us critique the state, and develop horizontal forms of governance?

The state and governance

Catharine MacKinnon asks several important questions about the relationship between women and the state:

> Is the state constructed upon the subordination of women? If so, how does male power become state power? Can such a state be made to serve the interests of those upon whose powerlessness its power is erected? ... [I]s masculinity inherent in the state form as such, or is some other form of state, or some other way of governing distinguishable or imaginable?
>
> (MacKinnon 1989: 161)

Anarchist-feminists draw parallels between the masculinist authoritarianism of the state-form in the public sphere and male hegemony in the private sphere. The state, thus conceived, cannot properly be expected to serve the interests of women, as there is an inherent gendered inequality in its function and form. Indeed, 'anarchist-feminists go further than most radical feminists: they caution that the state by definition is always illegitimate' (Ehrlich 1994: 5) and that 'the very structure of a state creates inequities' (Ehrlich 1994: 5) based in gender, racism, and colonialism. Eschewing the state form, anarchist-feminists self-govern in horizontal collectives, communities, non-mixed groups, affinity groups, coalitions, and other groupings conducive to power sharing.

Anarchist-feminism, like anarchism more generally, is based on 'a commitment to abolishing, rather than capturing, the state – arguing for the state's replacement with horizontally organized trade unions, collectives, neighbourhood associations, etc.' (Shannon 2009: 61). This commitment is in contradistinction to mainstream 'feminism [which] has been caught between giving more power to the state in each attempt to claim it for women and leaving unchecked power in the society to men' (MacKinnon 1989: 161). To understand this critique, Foucault's notion of power as emanative or distributive, rather than inherently hierarchical, is helpful.

Foucault (1978: 93) argues that, 'Power is everywhere; not because it embraces everything, but because it comes from everywhere'. Power can be a strength that groups embrace, engage, encounter, disrupt, channel, absorb, refract or enact. Power can be 'exercised from innumerable points, in the interplay of non-egalitarian and mobile relations' (94). It is precisely non-egalitarian social relations that anarchist-feminists challenge, self-governing from feminist centres of influence, the innumerable points where feminists actively challenge domination. Power is thus 'everywhere' and not *a priori* hierarchical, meaning that all subjects may develop the capacity to share non-hierarchical power.

Whereas systems of domination might enable subjects to exercise power in particular ways skewed to favour the masculine, there is no assumed disempowered position for women, but rather modes of acting that can be changed and challenged by collective subjects. Within anarchist-feminism we see a call to enact power cooperatively to develop what the *Mujeres Libres* called *capacitación*. '*Capacitación* is more than "empowerment" … The *capacitación* of women meant a process of developing the skills and confidence that would enable them to fight for their emancipation' (de Heredia 2007: 51) along three lines – gender oppression, education, and labour (51). This capacity building is crucial to the exercise of collective autonomy and collective self-empowerment in the prefigurative practice of non-state forms of organization and self-governance.

Uri Gordon, for example, develops a typology of power that considers power-over, power-to and power-with. Power-to builds on the *Mujeres Libres*' notion of *capacitación*, where women develop capacities for emancipatory self-determination and collective power. Power-with builds on the work of anarchist-feminist Starhawk (2008: 219), who argues that 'women's empowerment involves acknowledging our anger, owning our rage, allowing ourselves to be powerful and dangerous as well as accommodating and understanding'. In *Webs of Power*, an argument for rethinking power relations through feminist strategies of non-violent direct action, she suggests that we need to go beyond tactics that 'reinforce the system's focus on individuals as isolated actors' (221) to develop strategies where we ask, 'How do we collectively take power?' (221). She advocates for 'activism as empowered or empowering direct action' (231) and maps out ten principles that include using the body in taking action, solidarity and inclusivity, affective positivity found in hope and passion, intentionality of strategies and tactics, prefiguration of direct democracy in horizontal organizing forms, and the practice of direct-action empowerment as a creative expression of freedom (231–233).

Following Starhawk, the *Mujeres Libres*, and other anarchist-feminists, prefigurative politics are taken up not just in bodily autonomy movements but more generally in 'the principle that means must be consistent with ends' (de Heredia 2007: 48) whereby 'in pursuit of a non-hierarchical cooperative society' (de Heredia 2007: 48), anarchist-feminists develop alternatives to state power – in addition to confronting state power directly as it is exercised by the police, government agencies, etc. 'Anarchism ultimately does not provide a narrow path to follow but instead aspires to achieving the time when people make their own choices and work in collaboration with others' (de Heredia 2007: 48). Prefiguration combined with cooperative horizontalism and the intentional absence of a top-down or bottom-up programme reveals an interpretation of power as something that can be redistributed and shared among equals in the construction of the 'anarchist commons' (Sarrasin et al. 2012). Uri Gordon explains it thus:

> Drawing on Foucault and contemporary feminist and queer theorists, May and others argue that the unfreedom of human beings is not reducible to the presence of explicit hierarchical structures and overt coercion, but often an insidious dynamic, reproduced through performative disciplinary acts in which the protagonists may not even be conscious of their roles.
>
> (Gordon 2007: 44)

Opposed to these micro-fascisms, the goal of horizontal power-sharing, consensus decision-making, participatory direct democracy, and affinity group organizing is prefiguratively to 'cultivate the habits of freedom so that we constantly experience it in our everyday lives' (Ehrlich 1994: 5). These habits are political practices of collective organizing integrated into our everyday private and public lives, replacing the internalized masculinist hierarchical individualist state-form with a feminist horizontal collective-self-determination form.

Anarchism's opposition to the state arguably plays out with the greatest stakes in anti-racist and anti-colonial struggles. Here we run up against the limits of the strategy of creating a new world in the shell of the old. Some racialized and/or colonized groups and individuals, locked in struggles for survival against the re-entrenchment of the neo-liberal state and its security forces in a post-9/11 world, have little freedom to experiment with new forms of self-determination. Anarchist-feminists organizing in anti-racist and anti-colonial groups and networks therefore are highly cognizant of the risk of creating informal hierarchies, as horizontal feminist power can often become re-hierarchized along lines of race and colonialism.

Race, colonialism and global anarchist-feminism

Anarchist-feminist movements are improving commitments to anti-racist and anti-colonial struggles, which have always been at the forefront of organizing by anarchist-feminists of colour but not always by white anarchists and/or feminists, who typically prioritize their own struggles. Deric Shannon (2009: 69) notes that 'a contemporary anarcha-feminism would avoid this prioritizing of struggles and recognize the deep connections between all forms of domination' by integrating 'an intersectional approach to our activist praxis'. Rogue argues that 'the multiracial feminist movement developed this approach, which argues that one cannot address the position of women without also addressing their class, race, sexuality, ability, and all other aspects of their identity and experiences' (Rogue 2012: 28). Moreover, 'This is in accordance with the anarchist view that we must fight all forms of hierarchy, oppression, and exploitation simultaneously; abolishing capitalism and the state does not ensure that white supremacy and patriarchy will somehow magically disappear' (Rogue 2012: 28). There is a connection between anti-state, anti-racist, and anti-colonial organizing in that most EuroAmerican states were founded on racism and colonialism, and thus tend to have racist and colonial policies (imprisoning refugee claimants in detention centres, subjecting indigenous children to residential schools or family removal).

This exercise of power is teleological, but when it emerges from apparatuses of capital or the state (gendered, racialized, and colonial apparatuses), it may appear more cohesive and directional than it actually is. Foucault's (1980: 94–95) fourth premise is that 'power relations are both intentional and nonsubjective … there is no power that is exercised without a series of aims and objectives'. There is a logic to the enactment of power, which may be clear, and may yet be unintelligible in its mechanisms, which it hides in order to function. Power-over hides itself; power-with reveals itself. Cognizant of this, how do we extend an intersectional anarchist-feminism?

Anti-racist anarchist-feminism

Intersectionality is a theoretical description of anti-oppression politics (Breton et al. 2012b; Jeppesen and Nazar 2012), critically analyzing interlocking systems of oppression and privilege such as race, class, and gender. Yasmin Jiwani (2006) explores the intersectional mechanisms of gendered racism in the neo-liberal context, where claims we are now in a postracist and multicultural era allow racism to be disguised as a generalized cultural relativism, demarcating who properly belongs to the nation-state, who is violent or non-violent, and whose bodies, intellects, and spirits are then allowable targets for symbolic, physical, or sexual annihilation – both by others in society and by the state itself. This annihilation denies its sexist racism behind discourses of multicultural pluralism. The teleological nature of power, which refuses to take a non-racist society as its goal because it proclaims that such a thing already exists, masks the current lived experiences of racialized women in the West.

Given this masked racialized-gendered power-over, how do we enact power-with, organizing to transgress borders impeding the flow of particular racialized bodies, and resisting illegitimate forms of state power that have systemically dominated or excluded non-white people? State power has explicitly capitalist objectives, such as: generating unfettered profit from resource extraction ventures; maintaining a powerful police force whose illegal actions, including murder, go un-prosecuted; and developing a precarious labour force that keeps austerity wages low and racialized-gendered subjects in dependent relationships to their workplace and often straight-white-male bosses.

Foucault's final premise is 'Where there is power, there is resistance' (Foucault 1978: 95). This is because of the 'strictly relational character of power relationships' (95), wherein the power to act collectively and autonomously 'depends on a multiplicity of points of resistance ... [that] are present everywhere in the power network' (95). This is how we might conceive of anti-racist anarchist-feminist organizing from an intersectional analytics of power. An anti-statist analytics of power, for example, is enacted in groups such as No One Is Illegal (NOII) and Solidarity Across Borders (SAB), where activists oppose the legitimacy of borders, developing campaigns for 'Solidarity cities', campaigning for immigrants, regardless of status, to have access to free health care, education, and other social benefits. Moreover, they insist that the Canadian Border Services Agency (CBSA) 'should not have any right to enter and arrest migrants in hospitals, clinics, shelters, schools, or any space providing essential services' (SAB 2013). They link race to labour, demanding that 'labour and other human rights standards are applied equally to all, without regard to immigration status' (SAB 2013). While SAB is not an anarchist group, it has anarchist and anarchist-feminist organizers; it emphasizes the illegitimacy of the state, borders, and specifically the CBSA. Moreover, some of the Solidarity City signatories are anarchist-feminist groups, such as La Belle Époque, or have anarchist-feminists within them, such as the Convergence des luttes anti-capitalistes (CLAC), which has an anarchist-feminist caucus; the Coalition Opposing Police Brutality (COPB); *homoparentales*; and the Southwest Solidarity Network. The signatory groups, working on issues as diverse as anti-capitalism, police brutality and impunity, same-sex parenting, insurrectionary anarchism, and housing rights, demonstrate an intersectional analysis active within anti-racist anarchist-feminism.

Everyday refusals are examples of struggles against micro-fascisms, where everyone who works in 'the system' – from police to social service providers – knows the rules, which are there to protect people, but contrarily implements an internalized micro-fascist (racialized-gendered) process that contravenes the rights and dignity of individuals. When subjects can resist this teleological power, in these micro moments they are enacting a power-with (with their communities, with other immigrants, with anti-racist activists, with anarchist-feminists, etc.) and simultaneously challenging the stronghold of imperialist, colonial borders. In a series of coordinated micro-direct-actions anarchist-feminist anti-racist politics operate on two levels – the enactment of power from multiple sites of resistance, and an anti-state, anti-capitalist refusal to respect borders and their racialized-gendered restrictions.

Anti-colonialism and anarchaindigenism

Anarchist-feminists theorize decolonization, and support indigenous self-determination movements in 'anarchoindigenist solidarity activism' (Lagalisse 2011: 653). This takes place in the context of poststructuralist feminist critiques of an uncritical 'sisterhood' (women are essentially the same, sharing the experience of being a woman). Linda Tuhiwai Smith ([1999] 2006: 73) suggests that 'Third World women and women of colour also attacked this assumption because it denied the impact of imperialisms, racism and local histories on women, who were different from white women who lived in First World nations'. Anti-imperialist, anti-colonial feminist movements must account for many different perspectives, from Western individualist ideologies that render indigenous collectivities invisible to important distinctions in discourse that reject the notion of an 'authentic' indigenous experience (73–74). How do non-indigenous people participate in solidarity without re-colonizing movements by re-enacting inherited colonialist cognitive, decision-making, and action frameworks?

Colonization has long produced colonial frameworks that privilege pre-existing knowledge structures, using them to document, analyze, and judge indigenous cultures. Colonizers enact power-over to define those colonized through purportedly scientific research. For Tuhiwai Smith, however, the scientific and popular representations (in newspapers, books, and films) of the colonial Other appear indistinguishable and equally inaccurate. Whereas Westerners describe colonization as a process of contact, decline, acculturation, assimilation, and hybridity, indigenous people describe the same process as invasion, destruction and genocide, resistance, survival, and recovery as indigenous peoples (Tuhiwai Smith [1999] 2006: 88). This latter narrative re-centres indigenous peoples as documenters and researchers producing knowledge. Anti-colonial anarchist-feminist solidarity activists are therefore attentive to learning about existing situations from indigenous perspectives and following the leadership of indigenous women, rather than arriving at solidarity actions with cultural assumptions and movement prescriptions.

Anarchaindigenism is gaining traction among anarchists (Lagalisse 2011: 653). Lagalisse details a case where Montreal anarchist indigenous solidarity activists invited an indigenous man and woman from Oaxaca, Mexico, Magdalena and Juan, on a speaking tour. Magdalena, a public health nurse, was active in resisting forced sterilization of indigenous women under colonial government programmes. She spoke of her work in spiritual terms, using narratives that had deeper resonance, particularly when speaking to the indigenous communities of Kahnawake, Six Nations, and Kanehsatake (659). However, the white activists privileged Juan's more masculine, Western mode of speaking:

> Juan spoke of union movements ... and the state repression of his people. He spoke in the third person, assuming the voice of a generalized, objective 'other.' Magdalena spoke in the first person, about specific people who were tortured and what they told her afterward. She told stories about her experience as a community health worker (*promotora*) and described how government representatives tried to persuade her to promote sterilization among indigenous women across the region. Magdalena also spoke of the need to maintain harmonious ways of life among the communities (*pueblos*) and the need to respect all of Creation, land, water, and peoples. ... The anarchist translators largely omitted these references and summed

up her narratives rather than offering the word-for-word translation they granted Juan's discourse.

(Lagalisse 2011: 659)

Lagalisse is critical of the failure of the male anarchists to take Magdalena's spiritual propositions for sustainable lifestyles seriously, an example of sexist re-colonization. Some anarchist-feminists attempted to challenge this, but to little effect. One male apparently said "'F—k Jesus anyway, we're not here to talk about religion, what's important is the struggle!'" (660), imposing a EuroAmerican atheist cognitive framework. Moreover, the male anarchists argued that Juan had "'more of an analysis, he [was] more articulate, educated, and he'[d] had more experience in politics and the union movements'" (661). Union organizing, a shared form of radicalism in the global north and south, was privileged over anti-sterilization movements, particular to indigenous women in the global south. Moreover, Magdalena's organizing is not seen as 'experience in politics', as the affective, gendered labour of women organizers has historically been dismissed by male anarchists. In these examples, Lagalisse also draws attention to the gendering of spirituality as feminine (661–662), and rational secular atheism as masculine, thereby dismissing the former as not properly anarchist and insisting on the circulation of information consistent with what the white male anarchists already knew.

This example points to deeper issues in indigenous solidarity activism. The teleological power of Western colonialism is evident in the male anarchist privileging of Juan, their failure to translate Magdalena's stories, and their dismissal of her work as apolitical. The female anarchists in the group, who saw her struggles as liberation struggles, attempted to decolonize the process of evaluating the speeches, and to demonstrate the power-with or non-hierarchical power processes of harmonization in the community that Magdalena was espousing as important new knowledge.

The commitments of the Oaxacan people as represented by Magdalena, and of anarchist-feminists as represented by women in the collective which organized the tour, are emblematic of the distributive nature of power, the fact that resistance is everywhere, including in struggles against micro-fascisms within our own collectives. If white Western anarchists cannot understand the discourse of an indigenous woman as explicitly anti-colonial, then it will continue to be challenging for anarchists to participate in indigenous solidarity activism where power, respect, and dignity are shared equally. Moreover, this is an example of the development of informal elites in non-hierarchical organizing. The male organizers of the tour, with Juan's complicity, gradually removed Magdalena from the feminist centre of influence she occupies in her own community, putting themselves in her place, and forcing her to the outside of the circle where she was unable to speak or exercise self-determined horizontal power.

Global anarchist-feminisms

Racism and colonialism can also appear in the neglect of non-Western anarchist-feminist histories, of which there are many, historical and contemporary, four of which we will analyze here. Two key issues arise. Firstly, we must consider the specificity of different political contexts in which anarchist-feminism develops. We will analyze the revolution in China, the anti-Franco war in Spain, immigrant uprisings in Argentina, and the Arab Spring in Egypt. The generation of revolutionary geopolitical events in different global cultural contexts will be analyzed. Second is the search for commonalities, as anarchists believe we cannot be liberated until everyone in society is liberated; therefore a strong cross-cultural understanding must be developed in an anarchist-feminist analytics of power that engenders solidarity through creating power-with global struggles.

As early as the nineteenth century, non-Western anarchist-feminists were active in organizing and publishing. In Argentina a newspaper called *La Voz de la Mujer* was published from 1896–97, 'written by women for women, ... an independent expression of an explicitly feminist current within the continent's labour movement' (Molyneux 1986: 119). Molyneux situates the anarchist movement in Argentina in the context of a mass migration from Europe to Argentina of working-class men and women, among whom were notable anarchists. The men supported gender equality on paper but less so in organizing: 'The first issue of *La Voz de la Mujer* seems to have aroused considerable hostility' (Molyneux 1986: 127) in the form of anti-feminist attacks rebutted in subsequent issues by writers insisting they were not attacking good pro-feminist anarchists but rather 'false Anarchists' (128) who did not support the emancipation of women, key to the anarchist project. Like feminist-anarchists in other global locations, they opposed 'coercion implied by the marriage contract' (132) at a time when divorce was still illegal in Argentina, and they advocated 'free love ... through social revolution' (132), arguing for the 'benefits of multiple relationships' (132), and organizing and living in 'free-love communes that had come into existence among the immigrant communities in some Latin American countries' (133).

In addition to bodily autonomy, they struggled against poverty, the church, and domestic slavery, and recommended militant tactics. *Voz* writers noted that having too many children could increase a working-class woman's poverty, but she would nonetheless have strong maternal bonds (133). They denounced the church (136), the labeling of children as illegitimate (135), and women suffering the label of 'damaged reputation' (135). '[E]ditors called for an end to unequal and restricted opportunities for women, discrimination against women at work, domestic slavery, unequal access to education, and men's uncontrolled sexual demands'(141), while also advocating the use of direct action such as 'smash[ing] the machinery' of workplaces (141), focusing predominantly on struggles of working-class women.

Around the same time period in China, as the revolution was growing, anarchist women were also organizing against traditional roles. Radical feminist Jin Yi condemned foot-binding and superficial concerns with appearance, and simultaneously 'demanded a recognition of women's rights to education, business, property, free marriage, and friendship and to become politically involved' (Zarrow 1988: 798), a mixture of anarchist-feminism (free love and intimacies) and state-capitalist feminism (business, property, governance). While economic, familial, and political autonomy were considered key to feminist liberation, anarchist-feminist He Zhen did not tie these to the state but rather 'stressed the centrality of women's liberation in any true revolution' (799) and moreover, joined the predominantly anarchist 'left-wing caucus within the Chinese revolutionary movement' (800) in 'call[ing] for an absolute end to hierarchical social systems' (800). In the state-like, patriarchal family in China, women suffered triple oppression (dominated by father, husband, and sons), as well as subjugation to the mother-in-law, and coerced participation in patriarchal polygamy or the concubine system.

With other anarchist-feminists, He Zhen organized a group called 'The Women's Rights Recovery Association' which opposed capitalism, the ruling elite, and society's hierarchical organization. Their by-laws 'prohibited supporting governments, acting in subservience to men, and becoming a concubine or second wife' (800). She also argued for forefront organizing, as she 'expected women to free themselves; no one would give them their rights' (800). Moreover she drew connections between patriarchy and economics: 'male dominance operated through the unequal distribution of wealth, which led to relationships of dependent and master' (801), arguing for a deeper analysis 'of the relationship between gender and class' (802) as well as sexuality (805). 'He Zhen said, men had thought of women as private property that must be prohibited from loving other men and had established a political system and moral teachings' (805) to institutionalize these social norms.

Although she did in fact marry, 'He Zhen believed', like many anarchist-feminists globally who were her contemporaries, 'that a truly liberated woman would be free to have many lovers' (806). Unlike her contemporaries in the USA and Europe, however, she believed that raising children placed an unfair duty on women, and 'that freeing women from the burden of raising their children was one of the key elements in achieving equality' (806). She proposed children be raised in collective nurseries, thus moving beyond the stereotype of women as nurturers, earth mothers, and 'mothers of the nation', to argue that child care is not a women's issue, but an issue for all of society. She argued that in a liberated society 'the family as an institution marked by biological reproduction, the strict sexual division of labor, and continuation of the family line would no longer exist' (806), proposing an anarchist-feminist model of social transformation that eradicated patriarchal familial and sexual dominance, gendered economic divisions, and the male-dominated state. 'The anarcho-feminist understanding that structural social change was needed was widely accepted after the 1911 revolution' (810); moreover, Zarrow argues, the 'powerful and affecting prose that He Zhen was capable of producing stands as one of the significant achievements of Chinese feminism before the 1911 Revolution' (811).

Several decades later, also challenging the very basis of society, anarchist-feminists in Spain started organizing during the Spanish Civil War (1936–39), forming the *Mujeres Libres*, discussed earlier, emphasizing a politics of capacity building (Ackelsberg 2005). Marta Iñiguez de Heredia provides an insider genealogy of the contemporary *Mujeres Libres*. When the anarchists were defeated, the *Mujeres Libres* went underground only to re-emerge in the 1960s, participating in 'the anti-war and anti-colonial movements' (de Heredia 2007: 52) of the day, and 'advocating gender equality and sexual liberation' (52). The group is currently experiencing a resurgence in Global Justice Movement (GJM) and its anti-austerity protests. They argue that some forms of power are legitimate (e.g., people power) and others are illegitimate (e.g., state power), providing a complex analytics of power that extends intersectionality and resistance theory beyond race, class, and gender to include the environment and inter-generational knowledge. Moreover, de Heredia articulates the anarchist-feminist concept of solidarity organizing across difference, developing shared frameworks beyond identity.

More recently, following the uprisings in Egypt and the appearance of an anarchist black bloc at the Tahrir Square protests, some debate over substance and style of protests has arisen, critiquing the colonizing impulse of Western anarchists who presume that anarchism is Western and male-dominated. In an article on de-colonizing anarchism, Budour Hassan (2013) argues that 'skimming through the US anarchist blogosphere during that period would have given one the impression that the Black Bloc was Egypt's first-ever encounter with anarchism and anti-authoritarianism'. The author argues that American anarchists and Islamists alike reacted in particular but opposing ways due to the black bloc actions and outfits, the former uncritically celebrating the tactic, and the latter denouncing them 'merely because they looked like Westerners' (Hassan 2013). Hassan provides a brief but important history of anarchist organizing in Egypt to dispel the myth that anarchism is new there, arguing that this 'is but one example of how "white anarchism" has yet to break away from orientalist prejudices that plague the Western left'. He shows how women organizers against the Israeli occupation have demonstrated more militant leadership than the 'patriarchal political "leaders" with masculine energy' who, afraid of reprisals from the Israeli police, attempted to disperse a particular protest while the women held strong. He explicitly challenges the framing of non-Western women in anti-colonial struggles as powerless or voiceless, demonstrating their power-with each other to organize and lead at the forefront of their own struggles.

This article generated a great deal of online debate, particularly regarding the characterization of the anarchist movement as 'white anarchism' which is an essentialist notion of anarchism that not only denies the widespread existence of non-white people organizing as anarchists, but also erases the anti-racism of the global anarchist movement. At the same time, a movement may be committed to anti-racism but not effectively practise it; therefore we must recognize the depth and importance of feminist anti-racist, anti-colonial organizing.

Forms of power-with promoted by indigenous feminists and non-Western anarchist-feminists challenge EuroAmerican solidarity activists to exercise horizontal forms of organizing, not just internally in local feminist collectives, but also in relation to collectivities outside of our experience, in the growing emphasis on *glocalization* – acting locally in solidarity with global struggles (Juris 2005: 191).

Conclusion: Beyond an anarchist-feminist analytics of power

We will conclude with three findings. First, what comes into focus is a deep-seated historical and contemporary image of an overwhelming majority of anarchist men who seem to have had profound difficulty in understanding and actively prioritizing struggles against gender oppression. De Heredia (2007: 48) has observed that, 'while gender norms have been challenged, they have not been eliminated. Despite political development, within the anarchist movement people tend to replicate the same behaviours that a broader society imposes on us'. Similarly, Lagalisse has found that 'anarchists' lack of engagement with gendered power within activist collectives and the gendered aspect of neoliberal political economy' (Lagalisse 2011, 653) points to a failure to address gender in internal and external struggles. While de Heredia (2007: 49) characterizes the problem as a 'male dominated anarchist movement', the CRAC has found that the anti-authoritarian movement in Montreal has many key organizers who are women and/or queer and/or trans and/or of colour, who make important contributions in shaping the direction, actions, and analysis within the anarchist movement (Breton et al. 2012b, Eslami and Maynard 2013), despite encountering racialized, gendered, and heteronormative dynamics.

Some important changes are evidenced in a small but crucial trend toward 'men against patriarchy' groups, men taking the role of pro-feminist allies, and some male theorists taking up questions of anarchist-feminism. Nonetheless, the challenge of unlearning oppressive behaviours remains a daunting task for the anarchist movement.

Second is the irrefutable conclusion that an incredible number of anarchist women globally have struggled in a dizzying array of activist, theoretical, ideological, poetic, artistic, sexual, bodily, conceptual, educational, relational, research, organizing, communal, everyday life, and other forms of resistance, confirming that where there is power there is resistance, and perhaps the corollary – where there is resistance, there is power. For these expressions of anarchist-feminism are exercises in the expression of power, of the *Mujeres Libres* notion of *capacitación*. As Margaret Marsh (1978: 539) has found, those anarchist-feminists 'who were lifetime activists, or who adopted the ideology as mature adults, appear to have developed an intellectual framework which emphasized the interrelationships of anarchist theory, the psychological needs of individuals, and a sense of social responsibility'.

Third, intersectionality theory, which provides an excellent theoretical framework for understanding interlocking oppressions based on race, class, gender, or sexual identities, has its limits. As Heckert (2004: 105) argues, 'Identity provides a problematic starting point for any form of political movement', partially because 'identities develop from social movements rather than the other way around' (105). Often identities develop in opposition to institutions, such as punitive state border policies that create racialized or non-status immigrants, or LGBTQ identities 'defined in opposition to institutionalized heterosexuality' (105). Intersectionality runs up against its limits, therefore, in its assumption of pre-existing axes of identity, on the one hand, and on the other hand, its inability to include forms of oppression which may intersect with socially constructed identities but are not themselves identity-based oppressions. Police brutality, for example, is not an identity but rather an axis of analysis that implicates racialized groups, sex workers, trans people, people with mental health struggles, and others. Similarly, ecology is not an identity, but it is an increasingly important axis of exploitation that is intersectional to capital, sexuality, race, colonialism, and the state (Heckert 2004; Shannon 2009; Jeppesen 2012). Green anarchist-feminists have developed complex analyses of power and practices of disruption, from climate camps to earth liberation and animal liberation direct actions. Intersectionality theory must therefore extend its premises or be superseded by an analytics of power that can better account for these axes of domination.

Finally, many spaces of action and theory have been left out here. These include a deeper consideration of diverse sexualities; an emphasis on art, DIY projects, and media; autonomous spaces; and global connections among anarchist-feminist movements, theories and practices. We can only hope that these directions of research and activism will engage with this tentative dialogue and/or make useful departures from it. If each person's liberation depends on the liberation of all others, then anarchist-feminist theories of power might help us better understand the multiplicity of anarchist struggles we are engaged in today as a broad-based global movement.

Notes

1 De Heredia (2007, 45) explains, 'in the context of anarchism, gender mainstreaming means to make the fight against gender oppression, to go hand in hand with the struggle against capitalism and the state'.
2 Cf. RAG on pro-feminist solidarity: 'feminism has led to a growing consciousness of male oppression under patriarchy, such as strict adherence to masculine gender roles, duty to "provide" in the realm of work and lack of equal rights to active parenthood. Male oppression

has been misconstrued as either a product of the feminist movement, or an oversight of it. Yet it is often through feminist dialogue that a space has opened up for discussing these aspects of men's lives and experiences. Pro-feminist solidarity between men and women can make meaningful inroads into these issues' (RAG n.d.).

References

Ackelsburg, M.A. (1991) *Free Women of Spain: Anarchism and the Struggle for the Emancipation of Women*, Bloomington: University of Indiana.

Ackelsberg, M.A. (2005) *Free Women of Spain: Anarchism and the Struggle for the Emancipation of Women*, Oakland: AK Press.

Breton, É., Jeppesen, S., Kruzynski, A. and Sarrasin, R. (Research Group on Collective Autonomy) (2012a) 'Prefigurative Self-Governance and Self-Organization: The Influence of Anti-authoritarian (Pro)Feminist, Radical Queer and Antiracist Networks in Quebec', in A. Choudry, J. Hanley, and E. Shraffe (eds.) *Organize! Building from the Local for Global Justice*, Oakland: PM Press, pp. 156–173.

Breton, É., Jeppesen, S., Kruzynski, A. and Sarrasin, R. (Research Group on Collective Autonomy) (2012b) 'Feminisms at the Heart of Contemporary Anarchism in Quebec: Grass-roots Practices of Intersectionality', *Canadian Woman Studies*, 29(3): 147–159.

Brown, S. (1988) 'Feminism, International Theory, and International Relations of Gender Inequality', *Millennium: Journal of International Studies*, 17(3): 461–475.

Brown, S. (1993) *The Politics of Individualism: Liberalism, Liberal Feminism and Anarchism*, Montreal: Black Rose.

Crain, M. (1992), 'Feminism, Labor, and Power', *Southern California Law Review*, 65(4): 1819–1886.

Crenshaw, K. (1989) 'Demarginalizing the Intersection of Race and Sex: A Black Feminist Critique of Antidiscrimination Doctrine, Feminist Theory and Antiracist Politics', *University of Chicago Legal Forum* 1(8): 139–167.

de Heredia, Iniguez M. (2007) 'History and Actuality of Anarcha-feminism: Lessons from Spain', *Lilith: A Feminist History Journal*, 16: 42–56.

Ehrlich, H.J. (1994) 'Toward a General Theory of Anarchafeminism', *Social Anarchism*, 19: 44–50.

Eschle, C. (2001) *Global Democracy, Social Movements, and Feminism*, Boulder CO: Westview Press.

Eslami, S. and R. Maynard (2013) 'Antiracist and Anticolonial Antiauthoritarian Networks in Montreal', in R. Bellemare-Caron, E. Breton, M.-A. Cyr, F. Dupuis-Déri and A. Kruzynski (eds.) *Nous sommes ingouvernables. Les anarchistes au Québec aujourd'hui*, Montréal: Lux, pp. 203–224.

Farrow, L. (1974) 'Feminism as Anarchism', http://theanarchistlibrary.org/library.

Foucault, M. (1978) *The History of Sexuality: Volume 1, An Introduction*, New York: Random House.

Foucault, M. (1980) *Power/Knowledge: Selected Interviews and Other Writings, 1972–1977*, New York: Vintage.

Godwin, W. (1793) *An Enquiry Concerning Political Justice*, London: Robinson.

Gordon, U. (2007) 'Anarchism reloaded', *Journal of Political Ideologies*, 12(1): 29–48.

Hassan, B. (2013) 'The Colour Brown: De-colonising Anarchism and Challenging White Hegemony', Random Shelling, http://budourhassan.wordpress.com/2013/07/24/the-colour-brown-de-colonising-anarchism-and-challenging-white-hegemony/.

Heckert, J. (2004) 'Sexuality/Identity/Politics', in J. Purkis and J. Bowen (eds.) *Changing Anarchism*, Manchester: Manchester University Press, pp. 101–116.

Heckert, J. (2012) 'Anarchy without Opposition', in C.B. Daring, J. Rogue, D. Shannon and A. Volcano (eds.) *Queering Anarchism*, Oakland: AK Press, pp. 63–75.

Hogan, D. (2004) 'Anarcha-feminism: Thinking about Anarchism', Workers Solidarity, http://struggle.ws/wsm.women.html, accessed 4 August 2013.

Iannello, K. (1992) *Decisions without Hierarchy: Feminist Interventions in Organization Theory and Practice*, New York: Routledge.
Jaggar, A.M. (1983) *Feminist Politics and Human Nature*, New York: Rowman & Littlefield.
Jeppesen, S. (2012) 'DIY Zines and Direct-Action Activism', in K. Kozolanka, P. Mazepa and D. Skinner (eds.) *Alternative Media in Canada: Policy, Politics and Process*, Vancouver: UBC Press, pp. 264–281.
Jeppesen, S. and H. Nazar (2012), 'Genders and Sexualities in Anarchist Movements', in R. Kinna (ed.) *The Continuum Companion to Anarchism*, London: Continuum, pp. 162–191.
Jiwani, Y. (2006.) *Discourses of Denial: Mediations of Race, Gender, and Violence*, Vancouver: UBC Press.
Juris, J. S. (2005), 'The New Digital Media and Activist Networking within Anti-Corporate Globalization Movements', *Annals of the American Academy of Political and Social Science* 597: 189–208.
Kramarae, C. and Spender, D. (eds) (2001) *Routledge International Encyclopedia of Women: Global Women's Issues and Knowledge, Volume 1 Ability-Education: Globalization* [online], London: Taylor & Francis, (accessed 16 July 2013).
Lagalisse, E.M. (2011) '"Marginalizing Magdalena": Intersections of Gender and the Secular in Anarchoindigenist Solidarity Activism', *Signs* 36(3): 653–678.
Liesegang, J. (2012) 'Tyranny of the State and Trans Liberation', in C.B. Daring, J. Rogue, D. Shannon, and A. Volcano (eds.) (2012) *Queering Anarchism*, Oakland: AK Press, pp. 87–99.
Luna, Z., 2009, 'From Rights to Justice: Women of Color Changing the Face of US Reproductive Rights Organizing', *Societies Without Borders*, 4(3): 343–365.
MacKinnon, C. (1989) *Toward a Feminist Theory of the State*, Cambridge MA: Harvard University Press.
Marsh, M.S. (1978) 'The Anarchist-Feminist Response to the "Woman Question" in Late Nineteenth-Century America', *American Quarterly*, 30(4): 533–547.
May, T. (1994) *The Political Philosophy of Poststructuralist Anarchism*, Pittsburgh: Penn State Press.
Molyneux, M. (1986) 'No God, No Boss, No Husband: Anarchist-feminism in Nineteenth-Century Argentina', *Latin American Perspectives*, 13(1): 119–145.
Newman, S. (2001) *From Bakunin to Lacan*, Lanham MD: Lexington.
Newman, S. (2010) *The Politics of Postanarchism*, Edinburgh: Edinburgh University Press.
Presley, S. (2005), 'The Exquisite Rebel: The Anarchist Life of Voltairine de Cleyre', in V. de Cleyre, *Exquisite Rebel: The Essays of Voltairine de Cleyre-Anarchist, Feminist, Genius*, Albany: SUNY Press, pp. 17–27.
RAG (n.d.) ragdublin.blogspot.ca (Accessed, 4 August 2013).
Reichert, W. (1976) *Partisans of Freedom: A Study in American Anarchism*, Bowling Green: Bowling Green University Popular Press.
Rogue, J. (2012), 'De-essentializing Anarchist-feminism: Lessons from the Transfeminist Movement', in C.B. Daring, J. Rogue, D. Shannon and A. Volcano (eds.) *Queering Anarchism*, Oakland: AK Press, pp. 25–32.
Sarrasin, R., Kruzynski, A., Jeppesen, S. and Breton, E. (Collectif de recherche sur l'Autonomie Collective) (2012) 'Radicaliser l'action collective: portrait de l'option libertaire au Québec', *Lien social et politiques*, 68 (Fall): 141–166.
Shannon, D. (2009) 'Articulating a Contemporary Anarcha-Feminism', *Theory in Action*, 2(3): 58–74.
Solidarity Across Borders (SAB) (2013) Solidarity City Declaration. solidarityacrossborders.org/en/solidarity-city/solidarity-city-declaration (accessed 31 July 2013).
Starhawk (2008) *Webs of Power*, Gabriola Island: New Society Publishers.
Wollstonecraft, M. (1792) *A Vindication of the Rights of Woman*, London: Unwin.
Tuhiwai Smith, L. ([1999] 2006) *Decolonizing Methodologies*, New York: Zed Books.
Zarrow, P. (1988) 'He Zhen and Anarcho-Feminism in China', *The Journal of Asian Studies* 47(4): 796–813.

8 Loving politics
On the art of living together

Vishwam J. Heckert

Preface

When I've presented this live, I've invited the participants to join me in a little meditation to start. Meditation helps to calm the mind and improve focus making it easier to take in the ideas being explored. Also, meditation is one example of the kinds of practices which can help people live together. To be able to sit quietly and observe the thoughts, feelings, and images which come into our minds is to be able to live with ourselves just as we are. If we can live with ourselves, it becomes easier to live with others. You might also wish to begin with a simple meditation. If you have your own practice, feel free to follow that.

Otherwise, you can begin by finding a comfortable upright seated position, either in a chair or on the floor. The feet, legs, and pelvis can release downwards, all of the muscles in the lower body letting go. The spine can grow alert and relaxed into its natural s-shaped curve. Belly muscles can soften so the breath can move freely. Shoulders broaden, opening the centre of the chest. The jaw, ears, and eyes soften. The crown of the head is light.

Awareness can come to the breath, simply observing how it flows in and out through the nose. Cool, fresh air coming in; warm, stale air flowing out. Take a minute or two simply observing the breath.

Let the awareness come to the thoughts. Notice how the thoughts rise and fall like waves in the sea. It may seem that some thoughts are very important to follow. Sometimes they seem to tell you something about who you are. See what happens if you allow yourself to simply witness the thoughts for a minute or two.

Come back to the breath for a minute. And then to the physical body. Invite gentle motion in fingers and toes followed by whatever stretch you feel. (Or, for a very beautiful guided heart meditation, visit Heart of Living Yoga, 2018).

Introduction

> Anarchist love can never be phrased in terms of fulfilling one's selfish interests, because it is not mere selfish love between lovers themselves but an outgrowth of respect and love for all people.
>
> (Takamure 2005: 387)

By questioning the focus on politics *as tactic* through the lens of politics *as relationship*, I hope to link a subtle awareness of who we are, how we are in the world, and how we relate to each other to some wider questions about social and political movements. How do they hold together? How do they fall apart? In what ways are they transformative and in what ways to do they reproduce the status quo? In particular, I explore practices that may help nurture the development of more loving politics. What political systems might we love? What politics might nurture our capacity to love: to care for ourselves and each other and to recognize our fundamental equality, dynamic interdependence and inherent beauty? Like Takamure Itsue, I would like to invite a way of being and relating in the world which is continually opening our hearts to love, for the benefit of ourselves and all others.

The representation of politics

We each have ideas or images of what politics means. These representations of politics, in our minds, can change over time. An image may be based on some official idea of politics involving parliaments, politicians, and perhaps corporations. Or it may be based on an alternative ideal of politics as social movements, counterculture, and direct action. Like the feminist slogan that the personal is political, Deleuze and Guattari (1988: 213) write, 'everything is political, but every politics is simultaneously a macropolitics and a micropolitics'. Wanting to move away from the representation of politics (which prioritizes the macropolitical) to a more subtle level (which looks to the micropolitical as that from which the macropolitical emerges), I was struck by a quote from an anarcha-feminist blog about Occupy Wall Street called No Bosses, No Boyfriends.

> [I]t's important to stress that what's happening in the park isn't some sort of culmination, or ending point in our struggle against oppression. Spaces like that are created organically everyday, but *go unrecognized as part of a movement*. Even the police bus that took us off the bridge and to the precinct became a contested space ... I don't want to make light of incarceration, but merely explain that even in the darkest and scariest places there is hope for solidarity and transformation.
> (noboyfriends.org 2011; my emphasis)

I'm moved by those who invite a broad view of what constitutes social movement. For example, bell hooks (2000) has argued for recognizing social movement as a verb. The writers at noboyfriends.org echo this sentiment, emphasizing everyday spaces, relations of care, the power of connection, and the political value of hope and music. By transcending dichotomies of personal/political, art/activism, care/justice, and inside/out, (anarchist) feminist analysis queers social movement, undermining and overflowing dominant representations of radical politics.

Just say no to capitalism

The discursive emphasis in radical politics lies with that which we wish to stop, reject, replace, discard, and disassociate from; it lies with that to which we are saying no. Radical is anti-capitalist, anti-sexist, anti-fascist, anti-authoritarian, anti-racist, anti-heteronormative, anti-state. Saying no can be empowering. It's an important step in learning to care for ourselves, each other and the world of which we are a part (Rosenberg 2003). My concern is when saying no becomes a form of identity. What happens when ways of saying no become normative, standardized? No-normativity, if you like. This bears a striking similarity to different versions of unifying people through a mythic event – The General Strike, The War to End All Wars, etc. – freeing people from the enemy ideology.

I'm concerned that any attempts to promote a sameness of behaviour across a large population are unlikely to be successful. Life functions through difference, not standardization. And yet, a desire for control, perhaps stemming from understandable fear of something which we wish to avoid (like the devastation of capitalism), can lead to advocating sameness. I'm thinking here of Graeber's (2004: 18–19) commentary on one element of the anarcho-syndicalist tradition which evolved into fascism:

> Sorel argued that ... [p]olitics is the art of inspiring others with great myths. For revolutionaries, he proposed the myth of an apocalyptic General Strike, a moment of total transformation. To maintain it, he added, one would need a revolutionary elite capable of keeping the myth alive by their willingness to engage in symbolic acts of violence ... By the end of his life, Sorel himself had become increasingly sympathetic with fascism; in this he followed the same trajectory as Mussolini (another youthful dabbler with anarcho-syndicalism).

While it is true to say the anarcho-syndicalist tradition has brought tremendous benefits to people through organizing unions across divisions of labour, I am troubled when the emphasis is on the moment of revolution and by the understanding of politics as great myth-making. While Ciccariello-Maher (2011) contests that Graeber's reading misses some radical value of Sorel's work, he also offers a queer critique of imperialist forms of anarchism maintaining 'fidelity to anarchism as identity rather than as a series of practices which undermine and attack the state as a structure of inequality' (p. 40). I suggest elsewhere that anarchism may be further queered through deconstruction of 'the state' as external structure (Heckert 2013). What interests me here are the diverse ways in which anarchism can be opened up by moving from an emphasis on sameness and identity to a recognition of the diversity of oppressions, contexts, methods, and voices.

I do?

Are 'gay rights' a similar myth? Here we can see the opposite: many people all saying yes in the same way. Yes to formal equality under the law. Yes to marriage. Stonewall, the UK's dominant LGBT-rights lobbying group, launched their 'Say "I Do" to Equal Marriage' campaign in July 2012. Their website refers to ideological enemies 'who will stop at almost nothing to prevent Britain's lesbian, gay and bisexual people from enjoying this last measure of equality', and then asks for money. The representation of equality is fascinating: 'Equal marriage is the final legislative measure for equality – and will help put an end to public mockery of gay relationships. It will send a crystal clear message to the remaining opponents of equality that in 21st century Britain *all* people truly are equal' (Stonewall 2013). Like the mythic general strike, a singular event is proclaimed to have the power to end the war once and for all, victorious over ideological enemies. Same-sex marriage becomes the symbol for a radically egalitarian society. And yet, as numerous commentators note, marriage is an institution granting privileges of certain kinds to certain people. Duggan (2012), for example, notes 'the right to marry is a very narrow and utterly inadequate solution for the problems that most queer people face. Access to the state-regulated institution of marriage does not provide full equality, universal health care, or expansively reimagined forms of kinship that reflect our actual lives'. Nor does legislative equality guarantee the experience of equality: laws are broken all the time. Meanwhile, legal equality is being used by various Western governments to proclaim the status of being more advanced than those nations from whom they wish to limit immigration or upon whom they wish to drop bombs (Puar 2011).

Queer anarchonormativity

I do not mean to disregard anarcho-syndicalism, General Strikes, gay rights or marriage. Rejection is attachment in disguise. Rather, I want to question how attachment to these and other forms potentially functions to create normative pressure to say either yes or no. Over the past few years, there has been a surge of theorizing at the overlaps of anarchism and queer theory (Heckert 2010a; Heckert and Cleminson 2011; Daring et al. 2012). How do we organize without *either* hierarchies *or* normativities? Portwood-Stacer (2010: 491) has argued that 'Where the disciplinary power of anarchonormativity is used to promote a queer critique of hegemonic sexuality, and thus makes life more livable for those whose desires are repressed by dominant institutions and discourses, it has positive political potential'. She acknowledges the risks of normative, disciplinary critique of domination becoming a new form of domination but feels the risk can be avoided with care. I'm cautious and more inclined to agree with Eribon (2011):

> There is, after all, more normativity ... in all these accusatory discourses than in the struggle for the right to marry ... transforming what had been critical thinking into a policing of thought, after having also transformed it into a policing of the desires and aspirations of this person or that ('subversive' is 'good'; 'conformist' is 'bad').

Queer normativity was raised as a major concern in a discussion I hosted on Queering Anarchism at the 2013 Bristol Anarchist Bookfair. Participants shared numerous examples of expectations to both sound like queer anarchists by citing certain works of queer theory, and to look like queer anarchists by eschewing aesthetics associated with hegemonic gender and sexuality. One person cited her research on young women being excluded from radical environmental politics for not conforming to anarchonormative gender expression (see also Coleman and Bassi 2011). Portwood-Stacer's argument, which I find intriguing for many reasons *including* our disagreement, reminds me of Day's (2005) postanarchist call for an affinity of affinities in order to undermine the hegemony of hegemony. Whereas Portwood-Stacer might be read as calling for an anarchonormative counter-hegemony in order to destabilize hegemonic sexuality, Day's affinity approach encourages relationships of solidarity across identities, movements and cultures (what Carrillo Rowe (2008) calls 'power lines'). In other words, a movement which relies on coalition building and the welcoming of diverse participants might benefit more from 'a careful listening' (Kanngieser 2013) than any expectations of sameness.

The politics of representation

Anarchism offers something *other* than a politics of representation, normativity, and policing. I like to reverse Deleuze's comment on the 'indignity of speaking for others' to say that there is a profound dignity in speaking for ourselves, speaking our own truth, and in listening to others (Heckert 2010b; Feigenbaum, McCurdy and Frenzel 2013; Kanngeiser 2013). Sensitivity becomes important: to become calm, to be aware, and to listen to what feels right within ourselves and to what is coming from others. This can be difficult when we are caught up in our own thoughts, emotions, and desires. In our own pain. Here lies the political power of practices of freedom which release us from the trap of an ego-centric point of view.

I introduced this chapter with an invitation to practice meditation because, in my own experience, it enables a politics of love rather than of representation. Learning to witness the thoughts and judgements, rather than getting caught up in them, helps me see when prejudices are formed about the potential for affinity with someone else. Unexpected connections strike me as fundamentally necessary for profound personal-social transformation. Dropping the borders between people, between nations, between any constructed categories of identity involves dropping the protective barriers built around the heart. Meditation, as a method of inviting consciousness to merge in the heart, allows those barriers to soften, melt, and, with regular practice, disappear (Devi 2007).

Each of us learns to be identified with our persona, our representation of ourselves in the world. We might take our borders very seriously. And when these identities, representations, borders are believed to be the truth of who we are, then both queer theory and anarchism are read as inherently impractical. Fluidity and playfulness are understood as wishy-washy and ineffectual. For example, one of the most common criticisms made of Occupy was its lack of a clear 'message'. Is there really a problem if there's not a singular clear message from a social movement? I turn to Ursula Le Guin (2009: 126–128) who speaks to this question:

> A dance, a landscape painting – we're less likely to talk about *its message* than simply about the feelings it rouses in us. Or music: we know there's no way to say all a song may mean to us, because the meaning is not so much rational as deeply felt, felt by our emotions and our whole body, and the language of the intellect can't fully express those understandings … In fact, art itself is our language for expressing the understandings of the heart, the body, and the spirit.

Loving politics, too, is an art, an experience. Instead of looking for a message, we might relate to politics as Le Guin invites us to look at literature, by thinking, 'Here's a door opening on a new world: what will I find there?' (ibid.: p. 129). Indeed each meeting with person, place, and emotion might be greeted with the same open-hearted curiosity. As Shukaitis (2011) argues, there is a clear link between the effectiveness of social movements and their affectiveness – the loving connections between beings.

The anarchist tradition has long recognized that normativity and representation are intertwined with hierarchy. The declaration of oneself or one's group as superior to another is dependent upon a convincing representation, a narrative in which beings are cast in their roles of superiority and inferiority. Each group must be normatively policed to maintain the representations which are presented as presocial, essential, and natural. This is hierarchy in an overt sense which in turn depends on domination 'in a more subtle psychological sense, of body by mind, of spirit by a shallow instrumental rationality' (Bookchin 1982: 4). Over and over again, direct experience is replaced with representation: the theatrics of the mind, the message, imposed upon bodies and spirits. When we are focused on our identities, our performances, and our image of the 'real world', a certain sensitivity can be lost. And with it, our ability to get along, to love each other. The challenge of ending hierarchy 'poses the need to alter every thread of the social fabric, *including the way we experience reality*, before we can truly live in harmony with each other and with the natural world' (Bookchin 1986: 22–23; my emphasis).

Perhaps there is no identity 'crisis' when identity is recognized as an effect, rather than a truth of the self. If there is a non-attachment to identity, to labels, to the stories we tell about who we are and who other people are, it seems to bring a spaciousness where self-consciousness falls away. When you believe, 'I'm this kind of person, I have to be seen like this or act like that', does it bring a tightness to the body, to the mind, to the emotions? It does in my experience. I propose that freedom between us depends upon freedom *within* each of us. I've noticed over the years declaring oneself an anarchist or queer or whatever doesn't make freedom happen. There is no freedom that comes from an identity. Rather, it seems that the release of identity makes room for freedom. Thus, elements of both queer and anarchist traditions emphasize playfulness, fluidity, and mobility when it comes to questions of identity. To take our roles too seriously is to take the entire theatrical production of hierarchy seriously. We can see this in the normative performativity of gender, long questioned by anarchist feminists (de Cleyre 2004: 101).

The link between the naturalized performativity of gender (hierarchy) and the naturalized performativity of the state is found at the anarchist roots of queer theory. In the opening pages of *Gender Trouble*, Butler (1990: 3) notes that 'The performative invocation of a nonhistorical "before" becomes the foundational premise that guarantees the presocial ontology of persons who freely consent to be governed and, thereby, constituted the legitimacy of the social contract'. In other words, in the theatre of the state, people are cast in the role of those who have already freely consented to being governed in much the same way that people are cast in the role of a gender presumed to pre-exist its enactment. In an interview making her anarchism explicit, Butler later wrote (in Heckert 2011: 95) that:

> My sense is that every time law is reiterated, it is 're-founded' and 're-instituted.' This becomes most important in relation to the general strike, that is, the strike that is not protected by law, but which aims to bring to a standstill an existing regime of law. One could say that we are sometimes under an obligation to pull the brake of emergency on gender norms.

Queer individuality

Butler's approach has been read as an individualistic form of transgression more consistent with capitalism than with social revolution (e.g., Ebert 1996). I suggest, rather, that it is more consistent with an anarchism which queers the distinction between individual and social. Such an anarchism can be found, among other places, in the political theory of Emma Goldman. Goldman (1996: 111–112) was vociferous in her critique of capitalism and advocated radical social movements, while also recognizing the importance of individuality which she described as:

> the consciousness of the individual as to what [s]he is and how [s]he lives. It is inherent in every human being and is a thing of growth ... Individuality is not to be confused with the various ideas and concepts of Individualism; much less with that 'rugged individualism' which is only a masked attempt to repress and defeat the individual and [their] individuality.

Identity logic – seeing through the lens of people as *kinds*, whether prestigious and important or oppressed and marginalized – is deeply intertwined with capitalist individualism. Identifying with a role, rather than following one's evolving consciousness, inhibits the growth Goldman described.

Of course we have our roles in life. We have our jobs or projects, our pleasures, the people we are connected with, our histories of suffering and/or ease. We are playing those roles in a social story. As I argued above, a key element of authority-claims depends on widespread belief that these roles we play are the truth of who we are. A queer strategy is not to necessarily rebel against those roles or responsibilities, though it might include that, but simply to take them less seriously, to hold them lightly, to be playful with them. The power of this is illustrated by the concept *protagonismo* which arose in an outbreak of direct democracy in Argentina. Grassroots, horizontal networks self-organized in order to manage workplaces and coordinate among neighbourhood assemblies. This movement presaged Occupy Wall Street, the Arab Spring and other incarnations of the global movement of movements.

> Many people in the movements speak of themselves as protagonists, of a new subjectivity, and of social protagonism. This reflects not only people's sense of self-activity and action, but of a social phenomenon in which people are deciding for themselves, breaking from a past of political party brokerage and silence. It also refers to a new collective sense of being, where, through direct democracy, new individuals and collectives are being born.
>
> (Sitrin 2006: vii)

The awareness of being someone in the world who is capable of contributing in connection with others is very different from the trapped identity of powerlessness in the face of truth-claims. Individuality and social movement are not opposites. In this example and many more, they are mutually constitutive. This is consistent with the long-standing anarchist analogy of the healthy society as a functioning organism and the individual as a cell within the organism. There is no competition among cells in a body, except in the case of cancer or other forms of dis-ease. Drawing on this analogy in her famous anarchist utopian novel, *The Dispossessed*, Ursula Le Guin (1974: 333) defines cellular function as 'the individual's individuality, the work [they] can do best, therefore [their] best contribution to [their] society. A healthy society would let [them] exercise that optimum function freely, in the coordination of all such functions finding its adaptability and strength'. I will add an even greater emphasis, suggesting that a healthy society *nurtures* individuality, including the individual's capacity for growth and change. In this manner, Starhawk (2011) describes how anarchist and other non-hierarchical groups might be understood as leaderful, rather than leaderless, because each individual offers complementary forms of leadership.

Invisible politics

While the dominant representations of politics focus on the spectacles of statecraft and its discontents, numerous transformative processes go unnoticed. To recognize the possibility of radical social change requires, as I suggested above, a certain sensitivity, a fine-tuning of perception in order to sense what is otherwise invisible. This is not a particularly original argument. Others have, for example, referred to infrapolitics (Scott 1990) or imperceptible politics (Papadopoulos, Stephenson & Tsianos 2008). But it is, I feel, an important one to express in a number of different ways. Essential to any minoritarian politics is the capacity to perceive those injuries kept hidden, whether declared merely personal or in other ways denied significance. In this way, feminist and queer politics have worked hard to make the invisible visible with marches, manifestoes and movements. The risk here, as noted by Wendy Brown (1995: 52–76), is that visible injuries become a basis of identity, tied into state-thought: 'wounded attachments'. It is sometimes necessary for wounds to be acknowledged in order to heal, for attachments to be recognized in order to be released. Neither is visible or political in the conventional sense. In a queer way, they might be all the more transformative.

The magic of mushrooms

Mushrooms are the visible fruit of underground rhizomic networks of mycelial connections. Sullivan (2008a) notes the similarity to global social movements where the fruits (activist convergences, counter-summits, protests, alternative institutions, etc.) are merely the tip of the iceberg. Behind the scenes, everyday relationships, connections, work, and play enable the appearance of what is more commonly called politics. Furthermore, mushrooms and other fungi act to break down dead structures, transforming them into vital nutrients for living systems. If the state and related patterns cannot be smashed, perhaps they can be composted. In other words, rather than simply attempting to abolish or oppose oppressive patterns of relationships, we might ask what can be gleaned from them. What valuable lessons might be learned from simply witnessing the micro-politics of (b)orders, state-thought, normativity? Becoming sensitive to the production of hierarchy/normativity may provide invaluable insights for how to relate otherwise. In doing so, vital energy can be withdrawn from the production of the spectacular and transformed into nourishment for autonomy. Mycelial networks also function to help maintain entire ecosystems. In an experiment where a portion of a forest was covered such that the trees could not receive light and could not create their own food through photosynthesis, mycelial networks transferred nutrients from uncovered trees to those which were covered, from the food rich to the food poor, through the roots (Stamets, 2005). Different species of mushrooms are useful for bioremediation (the use of micro-organism metabolism to remove pollutants), nutrient-rich food for humans and other species, medicine for the treatment of serious illnesses including HIV and cancer, and, of course, the potential transformation (or equally the limitation) of consciousness through psychedelic properties.

Mushrooms as metaphor can remind us of the value of feeding our networks and relationships, social and ecological, recognizing that when they thrive they will bear fruit. To focus on the fruiting body, the visible events of strikes and occupations, means to potentially miss seeing where they come from, how they arise and what sustains them. To tune in to the subtle aspects of social movement allows the possibility of delivering nutrients directly to the roots, especially important for those living on the edge. This is also consistent with the anarchist approach which suggests that the ends do not justify the means. Indeed, there are no ends for every fruit must fade, decomposing to become nutrients for yet more life.

Invisible cities

Italo Calvino's *Invisible Cities* is a series of fantastic descriptions of European cities as told by the explorer Marco Polo. It becomes clear that all 55 cities described are the same city: Venice. The entire book functions as a beautiful example of that which I wish to communicate. For truly, one must love a place deeply in order to describe it in lavish detail in such diverse ways that it appears to be a different place each time. When one is obsessed, rather than in love, the focus is the image of the other, the representation. When one *sees*, many representations are possible. Each hints at different aspects of the beloved, yet none of them are true to the experience of love itself.

In one story, the city is described in its position above an underground lake. The edges of the city perfectly match the edges of the invisible water source. As above, so below. Throughout the city, numerous ingenious devices draw water from deep underground in order to sustain life above. There are two religions in the city. For the majority, the object of worship is that which is visible: the beautiful engineering works which raise the revitalizing waters to the beings above. For a minority, the hidden lake is the focus of devotion.

Personally, I'm immediately drawn to the latter approach. On one level it seems obvious that a direct relationship with the Source of Life itself is more profound than the worship of the mechanisms by which we connect to it. But then, I find myself reconsidering. How is it that I have any awareness of a Source? It is partly through its effects: the wonders of nature, including humanity and all of our creations, or the experience of heart-melting bliss with no apparent cause. And it is partly through the teachers and the teachings which have pointed me in the right direction, guiding me through practices which retune my awareness to that which is invisible.

These teachers also remind me again and again that the practices, the teachings, the images that work for me to help me escape that narrow sense of 'me' to find something greater may be different from what works for other people. Yet they all point to the same Source. The irony is, 'We kill each other over which name to call the Nameless' (Ram Dass 2002). This applies equally to differences in political ideology. Different people are drawn to different ideas at different points in their lives for different reasons. And yet we learn to judge each other based on those ideas, despite their fluidity. Like sexuality, mentality is assumed to be the truth of the self.

It is at the level of representation where conflict arises. When we become attached to our mentality, when we have the idea that we are right and someone else is wrong, the seeds of conflict are present. Marshall Rosenberg (2003), a radical psychologist who developed the practice of Non-Violent Communication (NVC), suggests seeing everyone as always doing the best thing that they can imagine, in any given situation, to serve life. Of course, this imagination may be severely curtailed and great harm to living beings may result. Where judgement is likely to trigger a certain defensiveness, a self-consciousness which tightens the bodymind system, NVC offers an alternative method: to listen for the emotions and the life-serving needs which lie beneath the surface of representation. In other words, it may be possible to not get so distracted by the different mechanisms that people use to seek vitality that you or I forget we are all drinking from the same Source.

Inner work

The next example is inspired in part by Chicana feminist Gloria Anzaldúa on the politics of experiential knowledge.

A form of spiritual inquiry, *conocimiento* is reached via creative acts – writing, art-making, dancing, healing, teaching, meditation, and spiritual activism ... Breaking out of your mental and emotional prison and deepening the range of perception enables you to link inner reflection and vision – the mental, emotional, instinctive, spiritual, and subtle bodily awareness – with social, political action and lived experiences to generate subversive knowledges.

(Anzaldúa 2002: 541–542)

In some, though certainly not all, cultures of radical political activism, taking time for introspective writing or practising yoga or meditation can be seen as having less value than participating in direct action or engaging in intellectual political analysis. Here, I echo Judy Greenway's (2010: 7) call to 'challenge the hierarchical approach which sees writing and fighting vie for place as Top Anarchist Activity [... in order to] investigate other sources, ask different kinds of questions, gain new inspirations'. Spiritual enquiry is another form of direct action, focused not on domination as an external force but in the subtle psychological sense to which Bookchin referred above. There is immediate practical value in learning to give less attention to the representations of ourselves and others and more attention to the reality of our relationships. Numerous commentators have highlighted the detrimental effects of people identifying as activist heroes, saving the world through a certain version of what constitutes activism (Anonymous 2000; Chatterton 2006; Sullivan 2008b; Coleman and Bassi 2011). Likewise, a certain resentful attachment to victim-mentality is disempowering for the individual and challenging for the collective (Brown 1995). And the guilt of identifying as the villain, perhaps in the narrative of privilege, similarly diminishes capacity for contributing to the well-being of the world. Certain practices like yoga, meditation, and biodanza are designed to release us from these mental and emotional cages which lie at the roots of individualism. They can help us queer our experience in order to become unfixed, free (The Nanopolitics Group 2013).

Everyday autonomous spaces

My final example of invisible politics is a return to the everyday autonomous spaces mentioned at the beginning of this chapter which '*go unrecognized as part of a movement*' (noboyfriends.org 2011). By this I mean the everyday ways, the little things between people, that make movement, that nurture autonomy. I'm interested in people like Colin Ward (White and Wilbert 2011) who argues that anarchism is a form of organization which is happening all the time, all around us. Mutual aid is so fundamental to society and ecology that we may take it for granted. Instead, we might learn to tune into these invisible politics, to recognize, nurture, and practise them. And to reflect them back with appreciation to the people enacting these everyday anarchies so they know that they are contributing to the benefit of others. It seems to me we all *mean* to be helpful, and equally, we need feedback to let us know when that is happening. If this is true, then gratitude is fundamental to the functioning of mutual aid.

For example, Gavin Brown (2011) offers his gratitude for a number of queer autonomous spaces which have inspired him, bridging from (1) self-identified queer autonomous spaces to (2) queer alternatives nestled within commercial gay scenes to (3) ethnographic writing about the practice of autonomy in a public sex space. In his conclusion, Brown calls for recognizing and nurturing the diversity of queer autonomous spaces springing forth from everyday experiments in autonomy.

Practising loving politics

So far in this chapter, I've argued that not only is an *other* kind of politics possible (Sullivan 2005), it is always happening all around us. We only need the eyes to see it. I close the chapter here with practical suggestions for learning to see and practise loving politics.

In bell hooks' (2001) book *All About Love*, there is a line that really struck me. I really disagreed with it. It's something like, where there is fear there is no room for love. I think I had an idea of what love is – that it meant caring for someone and recognizing that they are important in life. But often times there can still be fear, control, in a relationship of care. Am I good enough? Are they doing it right? What if they leave me? All these fears that can arise. But there is something else that shines through when the fears drop away, in those moments of connection where we see and accept the other person as they are and ourselves just as we are. That is very different from the everyday ups and downs of romantic, familial, pedagogical, comradely, neighbourly, collegial or other relationships which we might want to be loving. And there seems to be something about having a desire for things to be a certain way and trying to make that happen, that makes it harder to see people as they are, to see the invisible politics already happening. As Lao Tzu so eloquently put it, 'the unwanting soul sees what's hidden and the ever-wanting soul sees only what it wants' (Le Guin 1998: 3). There may also be something about everyday relationships that are taken for granted. Taking time to nurture those connections, to acknowledge fears, feels like one of the most basic forms of politics – the art of living together.

sandra jeppesen (who has chosen to queer grammar by using only lower case letters in her essay) recalls a queer anarchist ethic of

> treat[ing] your lovers like friends and your friends like lovers ... to take one example, a friend and i were both not in any sexual relationship, so for valentine's day, almost satirically, one year she invited me over for a dinner date. she ran me a bath, handed me a glass of wine, and cooked dinner while I relaxed in the tub. the following year I did something similar for her. they were oddly romantic non-romantic, very caring friend-dates.
>
> (jeppesen 2012: 150)

While this might be read as 'merely personal', Marina Sitrin notes the essential nature of relationships to radical politics:

> People doing eviction defense in support of their neighbors even speak of how they might not have 'liked' that particular person, but that they 'felt' a connection to them and cared so much about what happened to them that they were risking possible arrest by putting their bodies between the marshals and the person's home. From these relationships, in dozens and dozens of neighborhoods and communities across the country, networks of support and care have been formed.
>
> (Sitrin 2013)

We might see here how an emphasis on awareness and recognition of each other can allow something else to blossom that is surprising. Seeing others through loving eyes means letting representations, stories, identities fall away, making room to connect.

To me there is something ontological about anarchy, about the fundamental equality of all of us. We can have those fantasies that some people are better and some are worse. We were encouraged to believe that people are identical with our judgements of them. We might let go of these stories to see our interdependence, our ontological oneness. Maybe what's radical is not trying to change the world to our vision of how it should be, but changing our vision by seeing what is already there and listening to how we feel moved to engage with it, just as it is.

Intentional process

Of course, politics is not all poetry and perception. There are still practical tasks. Here, too, the awareness can shift from the image to the experience. Rather than asking what constitutes radical politics, we might ask how to make whatever we do radical: getting to the roots. Feminists, anarchists, and others have long emphasized the importance of process, of means over ends. Rather than allowing eutopia, the good place, to always be in the future – when I'm on holiday, after I retire, after the revolution – the intention can be to practise the good place, the good relationships in the present. After all, the present is all there is. The future never arrives, and the past is only memory. To be sure, there is much to be learned from memory as well as from visions of possible futures. They can be enacted only in the present moment.

At a subtle level, the mindset, the intention, with which we engage in a task or with a person or a group affects the outcomes of that engagement. This applies to any practice, any process. In a political action, the intention may be to show solidarity, to protect living beings from violence, to feed people. In yoga, one intention might be connection: to be in tune with the body, the breath. For non-violent communication (NVC), the intention is always connection – to relate to another person's world and share one's own, as equals. If the intention is otherwise (e.g., to be right) everything will change. Rancière (1991, 72) would agree: 'There are no madmen except those who insist on inequality and domination, those who want to be right'. 'Right' is a representation, an idea, an image. It is a prevalent one in both academia and activism, and, of course, throughout competitive cultures. And in this chapter, I have made a strong argument. Let it be read less as an attempt to convince you of my rightness and more as an attempt to connect, to share what resonates with my experience. Perhaps you have listened, observing what resonates with you and your experience.

Perhaps you also listen to yourself, noticing the ways in which you are called to engage with the world as it is. You may notice the intentions you hold and where they come from (fear? love? fresh anger? stale resentment? self-consciousness? thinking of others?) without judgement, or perhaps with judgements not given too much attention. And in the processes of life, of politics both invisible and named, you might feel inclined to focus your intention in order to bring a certain vitality to projects, to relationships, to life.

References

Anonymous (2000) 'Give Up Activism', *Do or Die*, 9: 160–166. Online: http://www.eco-action.org/dod/no9/activism.htm (accessed 1 May 2013).
Anzaldúa, G. (2002) 'Now Let Us Shift ... the Path of Conocimiento ... Inner work, Public Acts', in G.E. Anzaldúa and A. Keating (eds.) *This Bridge We Call Home: Radical Visions for Transformation*, New York: Routledge, pp. 1–6.
Bookchin, M. (1982) *The Ecology of Freedom: The Emergence and Dissolution of Hierarchy*, Palo Alto: Cheshire.
Bookchin, M. (1986) *The Modern Crisis*, Philadelphia: New Society.

Brown, G. (2011) 'Amateurism and Anarchism: The Creation of Autonomous Querr Spaces', in J. Hekert and R. Cleminson (eds.) *Anarchism and Sexuality: Ethics, Relationships and Power*, London: Routledge, pp. 200–223.

Brown, W. (1995) *States of Injury: Power and Freedom in Late Modernity*, Princeton: Princeton University Press.

Butler, J. (1990) *Gender Trouble*, New York: Routledge.

Carrillo Rowe, A. (2008) *Power Lines: On the Subject of Feminist Alliances*, Durham NC: Duke University Press.

Chatterton, P. (2006) '"Give up activism" and change the world in unknown ways: Or, learning to walk with others on uncommon ground', *Antipode* 38(2): 259–281.

Ciccariello-Maher, G. (2011) 'An Anarchism that Is Not Anarchism: Notes Toward a Critique of Anarchist Imperialism', in J.C. Klausen and J.R. Martel (eds.) *How Not To Be Governed: Readings and Interpretations from a Critical Anarchist Left*, Oxford: Lexington Books, pp. 19–46.

Coleman, L. and Bassi, S. (2011) 'Deconstructing Militant Manhood: Masculinities in the Disciplining of (Anti-)Globalization Politics', *International Feminist Journal of Politics*, 13: 204–224.

Daring, C.B., Rogue, J., Shannon, D. and Volcano, A. (eds.) (2012) *Queering Anarchism: Addressing and Undressing Power and Desire*, Edinburgh: AK Press.

Day, R. (2005) *Gramsci is Dead: Anarchist Currents in the Newest Social Movements*, London: Between the Lines/Pluto Press.

de Cleyre, V. (2004 [1890]) 'Sex slavery', in A.J. Brigati (ed.) *The Voltairine de Cleyre Reader*, Edinburgh: AK Press, pp. 93–104.

Deleuze, G. and Guattari, F. (1988) *A Thousand Plateaus: Capitalism & Schizophrenia* (trans. Brian Massumi), London: The Athlone Press.

Devi, N. (2007). *The Secret Power of Yoga: A Woman's Guide to the Heart and Spirit of the Yoga Sutras*, New York: Three Rivers Press.

Duggan, L. (2012) 'Beyond Marriage: Democracy, Equality, and Kinship for a New Century', *The Scholar & Feminist Online*, 10(1–2). Online: http://sfonline.barnard.edu/a-new-queer-agenda/beyond-marriage-democracy-equality-and-kinship-for-a-new-century/ (accessed 1 May 2013).

Ebert, T.L. (1996) *Ludic Feminism and After: Postmodernism, Desire and Labor in Later Capitalism*, Ann Arbor: University of Michigan Press.

Eribon, D. (2011) 'Borders, Politics and Temporality', Sexual Nationalisms. Online: http://didiereribon.blogspot.co.uk/2011/02/politics-and-temporality.html (accessed 29 March 2013).

Feigenbaum, A., McCurdy, P. and Frenzel, F. (2013) 'Towards a Method for Studying Affect in (Micro)politics: The Campfire Chats Project and the Occupy Movement', *Parallax*, 19(2): 21–37.

Goldman, E. (1996 [1940]) 'The Individual, Society and the State', in A.K. Schulman (ed.) *Red Emma Speaks: An Emma Goldman Reader*, Amherst NY: Humanity Books, pp. 109–130.

Graeber, D. (2004) *Fragments of an Anarchist Anthropology*, Chicago: Prickly Paradigm Press.

Greenway, J. (2010) 'Re/membering Women, Re/minding Men: The Gender Politics of Anarchist History'. Online: www.judygreenway.org.uk/docs/GenderingHistory.doc (accessed 1 May 2013).

Heart of Living Yoga (2018) Heart Practice. Online: http://heartoflivingyoga.com/heart-practice (accessed 29 June 2018).

Heckert, J. (ed.) (2010a) 'Anarchism and Sexuality', *Sexualities*, 13(4): 403–411.

Heckert, J. (2010b) 'Listening, Caring, Becoming: Anarchism as an Ethics of Direct Relationships', in B. Franks and M. Wilson (eds.) *Anarchism and Moral Philosophy*, Basingstoke: Palgrave, pp. 186–207.

Heckert, J. (2011) 'On Anarchism: An Interview with Judith Butler', in J. Heckert and R. Cleminson (eds.) *Anarchism & Sexuality: Ethics, Relationships and Power*, Abingdon: Routledge, pp. 93–100.

Heckert, J. (2013) 'An Other State of Mind is Possible: Anarchism and Psychology', *Social and Personality Psychology Compass*, 7(8): 513–525.

Heckert, J. and Cleminson, R. (eds.) (2011) *Anarchism & Sexuality: Ethics, Relationships and Power*, Abingdon: Routledge.

hooks, b. (2000) *Feminism is for Everybody: Passionate Politics*, London: Pluto Press.

hooks, b. (2001) *All About Love*, New York: Harper Perennial.
jeppesen, s. (2012) 'queering heterosexuality', in C.B. Daring, J. Rogue, D. Shannon and A. Volcano (eds.) *Queering Anarchism: Addressing and Undressing Power and Desire*, London: Routledge, pp. 147–164.
Kanngieser, A. (2013) 'Towards a Careful Listening', in M. Zechner, B.R. Hansen and P. Plotegher (eds.) *Nanopolitics Handbook*, London: Minor Compositions, pp. 235–250.
Le Guin, U.K. (1974) *The Dispossessed*, New York: HarperPrism.
Le Guin, U.K. (1998) *Tao Te Ching*, Boston: Shambhala.
Le Guin, U.K. (2009) 'A Message about Messages', in *Cheek by Jowl: Talks & Essays on How & Why Fantasy Matters*, Seattle: Aqueduct Press, pp. 125–130.
noboyfriends.org (2011) 'Beyond the Bridge'. Online: http://noboyfriends.org/2011/10/04/beyond-the-bridge/ (accessed 1 May 2013).
Papadopoulos, D., Stephenson, N. and Tsianos, V. (2008) *Escape Routes: Control and Subversion in the 21st Century*, London: Pluto Press.
Portwood-Stacer, L. (2010) 'Constructing Anarchist Sexuality: Queer Identity, Culture, and Politics in the Anarchist Movement', *Sexualities*, 13: 479–493.
Puar, J. (2011) '"I Would Rather Be a Cyborg that a Goddess". Intersectionality, Assemblage and Affective Politics', *EIPCP*, available at: EIPCP/net/transversal/0811/puar/en
Ram Dass (2002) *One-Liners: A Mini-Manual for a Spiritual Life*, New York: Bell Tower. Online: http://jodilley.com/books/ol/ol.pdf (accessed 1 May 2013).
Ranciere, J. (1991) *The Ignorant Schoolmaster: Five Lessons in Intellectual Emancipation*, Stanford: Stanford University Press.
Rosenberg, M.B. (2003) *Nonviolent Communication: A Language of Life*, Encinitas: PuddleDuck Press.
Scott, J.C. (1990) *Domination and the Arts of Resistance: Hidden Transcripts*, New Haven: Yale University Press.
Shukaitis, S. (2011) 'Nobody Knows What an Insurgent Body Can Do: Questions for Affective Resistance', in J. Heckert and R. Cleminson (eds.) *Anarchism & Sexuality: Ethics, Relationships and Power*, London: Routledge, pp. 45–66.
Sitrin, M. (2006) *Horizontalism: Voices of Popular Power in Argentina*, Edinburgh: AK Press.
Sitrin, M. (2013) 'Occupy Trust: The Role of Emotion in the New Movements', *Cultural Anthropology Online*, February 14, 2013. Online http://production.culanth.org/fieldsights/76-occupy-trust-the-role-of-emotion-in-the-new-movements
Stamets, P. (2005) *Mycelium Running: How Mushrooms Can Help Save the World*, Berkeley: Ten Speed Press.
Starhawk (2011) *The Empowerment Manual: A Guide for Collaborative Groups*, Gabriola Island: New Society Publishers.
Stonewall (2013) 'Help Us Secure Marriage Equality in Britain!' Online: http://www.stonewall.org.uk/what_you_can_do/donate_to_stonewall/7958.asp (accessed 29 March 2013).
Sullivan, S. (2005) 'Another World is Possible? On Representation, Rationalism and Romanticism in Social Forums', *Emphera*, 5(2): 370–339.
Sullivan, S. (2008a) 'Conceptualising Glocal Organisation: From Rhizomes to E=mc2 in Becoming Post-Human', in M. Kornprobst, V. Pouliot, N. Shah and R. Zaiotti (eds.) *Metaphors of Globalisation: Mirrors, Magicians and Mutinies*, Basingstoke: Palgrave Macmillan, pp. 149–166.
Sullivan, S. (2008b) '"Viva Nihilism!" On Militancy and Machismo in (Anti-)globalization Protest', in R. Devetak and C. Hughes (eds.) *Globalization of Political Violence: Globalization's Shadow*, London: Routledge, pp. 203–243.
Takamure, I. (2005 [1930]) 'A Vision of Anarchist Love', in R. Graham (ed.) *Anarchism: A Documentary History of Libertarian Ideas, Vol 1: From Anarchy to Anarchism (300 CE to 1939)*, Montreal: Black Rose Books, pp. 383–388.
The Nanopolitics Group (2013) *Nanopolitics Handbook*, London: Minor Compositions.
White, D.F. and Wilbert, C. (eds.) (2011) *Autonomy, Solidarity, Possibility: The Colin Ward Reader*, Edinburgh: AK Press.

9 Black flag mapping
Emerging themes in anarchist geography

Anthony Ince

I first realized that I wanted to become a geographer when I read *Tearing Down the Streets*, by the anarchist Jeff Ferrell (2001). Overlooking the fact that he was a criminologist, not a geographer, the powerful message of the book orbited the contestation of public space and the politics of creating truly public and egalitarian spaces for social change. Using a critique (anarchism) and subject matter (public space) that I had never experienced before, Ferrell interrogated the ways in which the urban environment is shaped by, and constitutive of, all manner of political, social, cultural, and economic forces. What gripped me was the way that space is ethereal and elusive – we can't hold a piece of space in our hand, or interview it, or run it through a machine for analysis – but it is also necessarily material and grounded, locked deeply into the core of everyday struggles for survival, expression, wellbeing and social justice. As a disillusioned political science undergraduate who had been taught that the study of politics chiefly involved learning by rote the technocratic systems of Western government, this was an epiphany of considerable magnitude.

It quickly became clear that anarchism and geography could be very happy bedfellows, both offering a view of the world that is holistic, nuanced, insightful, and potentially transformative. The powerful tension that inhabits the anarchist critique is that it incorporates a fundamental and unrelenting questioning of the very basis of society as we know it, and yet, identifies situated practices and relationships that take place every day as potentially embodying future emancipatory worlds. The inescapable omnipresence of space as a primary conditioning factor in all human and non-human relationships and processes, thus, easily links us to a mode of political analysis and action like anarchism that gives us the tools to unearth and recast these relationships and processes in a profoundly radical manner. It is therefore not surprising that two of the most influential anarchists of the nineteenth century – Elisée Reclus and Peter Kropotkin – were also two of the era's most influential geographers. What *is* surprising, however, is that aside from a short flurry of interest in the mid-to-late 1970s, academic geography has hitherto had very little direct contact with anarchism. Only recently has a small band of anarchist geographers reawakened this tradition.

In this chapter, I outline the nature of the contemporary renaissance of anarchist geography, considering how geographers are increasingly applying anarchist ideas, concepts and analytical tools to the critical study of our complex relationships with the spaces and places we inhabit. First, I briefly introduce the historical connections between anarchism and geography, as well as cognate fields such as architecture and planning. I then move to a discussion of how anarchist thought has emerged in contemporary academic geography, and suggest some possible reasons for this, before exploring three key contemporary themes emerging through anarchist interventions in Anglophone geographical scholarship: the relationship between anarchism and 'autonomous' practices, thought, and movements; the anarchist critique of authority and statism in relation to broader geographical debates on the spatialities of governance; and anarchist perspectives on the role, nature and politics of 'publics' and public space.

A short history of anarchist geographies

My primary focus in this chapter is the contemporary relationship between anarchism and geography – conceptually, theoretically, and politically – rather than returning to the rich historical accounts of anarchist geography, discussed in depth elsewhere (e.g. Clark and Martin 2004; Ince 2010a; Ward 2010; Springer et al. 2012; Springer 2013a; Ferretti 2016; 2017). However, it is worth briefly re-tracing this history in order to understand the intellectual trajectory of anarchist geographies.

We can see both Kropotkin and Reclus as figureheads of a counter-offensive against dominant theories of ecology and human society that variously sought to justify and support colonialism, white supremacy, capitalism, and the state. Both men utilized analysis of the natural world in order to directly counteract the naturalization of these man-made social and political institutions and practices. For them, the holistic investigation of ecosystems demonstrated the factual inaccuracy of their counterparts' ideas, and through these investigations they sought to politicize the otherwise depoliticized Social Darwinist theories espoused by the likes of Herbert Spencer and Thomas Huxley (Claeys 2000) which worked to support the colonial capitalist state. Kropotkin and Reclus reasoned that if ecological theories that naturalize competition, white supremacy, and hierarchy are undermined by alternative evidence, then radical political imaginations could flourish with firm scientific backing.

In *La Nouvelle Géographie Universelle* (1876–1894, see Fleming 1987; Ferretti 2013), Reclus outlined in minute detail the myriad ways in which ecological processes, land forms, species, and ecosystems were spatially organized in ways that did not conform to any kind of bordering or territorializations that resembled modern statist territorial spatialities. Although territories and divisions existed in the natural world, they were not discrete, singular, or definable in an orthodox cartographic sense, always shifting and overlapping, making and remaking themselves and each other over time. Reclus could see no justification in the natural world for the static lines on the map that Western civilization had imposed, except as mechanisms of social control, and he explained at length the ways in which European colonialism, for example, was not only a moral abomination but also an ecological anomaly.

Although now the more famous of this pair, Peter Kropotkin was by far Reclus' junior when they first met (Ward, 2010). Kropotkin's legendary work, *Mutual Aid*, arguably developed a similar thematic thread to Reclus' *Nouvelle Géographie Universelle*. Identifying the ways in which mainstream ecologists and naturalists were using Darwinism as a means of justifying capitalistic competition and individualism, Kropotkin embarked on a careful analysis of evolution from the perspective not of competition but of co-operation. His conclusions were clear:

> [T]he vast majority of species ... find in association the best arms for the struggle of life ... The mutual protection which is obtained in this case, the possibility of

attaining old age and of accumulating experience, the higher intellectual development, and the further growth of sociable habits, secure the maintenance of the species, its extension, and its further progressive evolution. The unsociable species, on the contrary, are doomed to decay.

(Kropotkin 1972 [1902]: 246)

Following Reclus' early efforts, Kropotkin took a far keener interest in the ecology of human societies, and much of *Mutual Aid* covered practices of tribal societies in such diverse regions as North America, Australia, Southern Africa, and the Pacific, as well as Roman and mediaeval European cities. At the time of the publication of this work, he was already moving into the study of Western modernity in *Fields, Factories and Workshops* (Kropotkin 1968 [1913]). This volume interrogated the spatial inefficiencies of capitalist production in Britain and its social and intellectual impacts. What we see in Kropotkin's work at this time is the dovetailing of ecology and anthropology – the integrated study of human civilization and its environment – arguably for the first time in such a detailed and systematic manner. One might argue that *L'homme et la Terre*, the final volume of Reclus' *magnum opus*, beat Kropotkin to the prize (Ferretti 2013), but whichever is correct, there is little doubt that it was an anarchist who heralded the birth of human geography as we now know it.

The inter-war period, and the eventual death of both Reclus and Kropotkin, saw a decline in anarchist geographies. However, in other fields such as planning, anarchist ideas had already been transplanted into efforts to create self-sustainable, communitarian neighbourhoods and cities through modernist projects such as the Garden City Movement, led by Ebenezer Howard (Hall 1988). Although many of the ideas of these early planning visionaries were appropriated by colonial interests and used to discipline and segregate colonial subjects from their masters, their efforts denoted a shift from anarchist spatial analysis towards material efforts to produce egalitarian, communitarian spaces.

The Spanish Civil War saw arguably the largest experiment in creating anarchist communities in modern history. Led by the CNT, the anarcho-syndicalist union, huge swathes of both rural and urban Spain were voluntarily collectivized along anarchist lines, before their betrayal by the Soviet-backed communists and eventual victory of the fascist forces. The years of collectivization heralded a considerable shift in the spatialities of everyday life in CNT-controlled Spain, and 1970s geographers' efforts at finding an alternative discourse to the impoverished binary between oppressive state socialism and exploitative market capitalism found inspiration in these highly successful experiments:

> Within hours of the Franco assault, anarchist peasants and workers seized direct control over rural land, cities, factories, and social service and transportation networks ... Collectivisation encompassed more than one-half of the total land area of Republican [non-Francoist] Spain, directly or indirectly affecting the lives of between seven and eight million people.
>
> (Breitbart 1978: 60)

Breitbart and others ushered in a new wave of interest in anarchism in geography, reflecting a keenness on the part of geographers to identify structures of authority and recognize the interlocking system of capital and state in a wide range of spatial inequalities. The journal *Antipode* was a key conduit for this, and although principally a Marxist journal, its openness to anarchist ideas began a long anti-authoritarian tradition in radical geography (cf. Peet 1975). A smattering of contributions throughout the 1980s and 1990s (e.g. MacLaughlin 1986; Cook and Pepper 1990) continued the anarchist tradition, but the potential for anarchist geographies was overshadowed by the dominance of Marxist political economy, feminist geographies, and, later, the rise of poststructuralism. However, although anarchism had once again faded from the geographic milieu as an explicit political perspective, it had made a sufficiently powerful imprint in the early days of radical geography to have an enduring, if indirect, impact on geographical scholarship and imaginations.

Renewing the anarchist tradition in geography

In order to understand the return of anarchism to contemporary geography, we must look beyond the boundaries of the academy altogether. At this point, it is worth noting that this chapter stems largely from a British tradition, both of anarchism and of geography. As we will see, there is considerable overlap between British and other Anglophone literatures, along with some connections with other languages, but, as I outline in this section, a set of geographical conditions largely specific to the UK was a principal (although certainly not the only) driving force in laying the foundations for the emergence of contemporary anarchist geographies.

In the 1970s and 1980s, anarchism as a political tendency was relatively small but gradually incorporated a range of perspectives: small-scale, everyday transformations of relationships and institutions such as education (Ward 1998 [1973]); anti-authoritarian punk subcultures (Gosling 2004); and working class anarcho-communism (Franks 2006). Proto-anarchist subcultures that followed were partly a fusion of these currents and a rejection of them, creating their own distinctive brand of creative refusal. The late 1980s and 1990s saw a large and growing counterculture within British youth, orbiting an amorphous 'DIY' political milieu that incorporated a range of cultural and political currents. Anti-roads, hunt-saboteur, and environmental direct action movements were central to this counterculture, alongside a growing radical and experimental arts movement that included huge squatted 'free parties', guerrilla art installations, and occupations of roads, buildings, and other structures of capitalist accumulation or state authority (McKay 1998; St John 2003). A concerted effort by the British state to criminalize this huge, transgressive, and richly creative counterculture (Halfacree 1996) contributed to a further politicization towards a broad anarchistic politics that foregrounded the creation of autonomous zones as a key tactic (e.g. McCreery 2002).

Discussion of anarchism within contemporary geographical scholarship begins to grow in the late 1990s and early 2000s, following the emergence of DIY movements and projects epitomized by the likes of Reclaim the Streets, a transgressive, carnivalesque fusion of party and protest that targeted commercialized public spaces (e.g. Routledge 1997; Brown 2004). These spaces of creative transgression and radical politics fit perfectly with the growing interest in 'geographies of resistance', which sought to analyze the spatialities of these emergent movements, camps, tendencies, and projects (e.g. Sharp et al. 2000; Featherstone 2003).

The networked, relational nature and horizontalist patterns of organization exhibited by the movement shed new light on the way geographers (and many other social sciences) understood the practice of political mobilization. At the same time, in the USA and Canada, the meteoric rise of the movements instigating vast anti-summit demonstrations that rocked Seattle in 1999 and Quebec in 2001 appeared to catch geographical scholarship unawares (Fannin et al. 2000). The gradual build-up of UK radical countercultures was thus contrasted sharply with what appeared to be the sudden appearance of a new, powerful North American movement, both of which were inspired to a degree by a nebulous web of emergent anarchisms.

With the rise of the variously-titled anti-capitalist or global justice movement came greater emphasis among radical geographers on the movemental qualities of these politics. Not only were geographers exploring the constellations of place-making and subversion that these movements undertook, but they also embarked on insightful analyses of the movement's horizontalist, networked qualities (Routledge 2000; Mamadouh 2004). It was only a matter of time before geographers were making deeper engagements with the philosophy, as well as the strategy, that underpinned this movement, and with anarchists at the helm, there was a growing interest in anarchist thought and practice.

A watershed moment was the publication of Pickerill and Chatterton's (2006) paper theorizing what they term 'autonomous geographies'. Although there had already been some important engagements with the notion of autonomy in geography (e.g. Chatterton 2005) this paper drew together existing work into a theoretically and conceptually solid framework – a framework that relied heavily on classical and modern anarchist philosophy. In it, they outlined a manifesto for a new geographical imagination inspired by, and feeding back into, global justice movements. As they explain:

> [A]utonomy is a contextually and relationally grounded concept in specific networks of social struggles and ideas across different times and spaces ... Autonomous geographies allow us to move beyond the dichotomy of global-bad, local-good. Hence, autonomy can be a tool for understanding how hybrid and interstitial spaces are (re)made and (re)constituted.
>
> (Pickerill and Chatterton 2006: 743)

This paper, then, linked activist priorities with geographical scholarship through the concept of autonomy, discussed in more depth below. Yet, the move towards autonomous geographies made little effort to explore the theory and practice of anarchism as a specific political tradition, since a central notion of autonomy (as they theorized it) is its openness to a diversity of ideas, tactics, and subjectivities, and a rejection of 'the problems of blueprints that plague the contemporary world' (ibid.: 731). However, far from being simply another ideology to follow obediently towards a utopian blueprint, anarchism is distinct from other political philosophies in that it involves an explicit rejection of the absolute blueprints that Pickerill and Chatterton rightly rally against. Nevertheless, in exploring autonomous movements and campaigns, these geographers opened up possibilities within the academy for a deeper exploration of the relevance of anarchist ideas to geographical analysis, methodology, and pedagogy.

Anarchy and/or autonomy

With autonomous practices and structures being key means through which anarchists and others have articulated and practised their prefigurative politics (e.g. Pickerill 2007), the notion of autonomy is a central empirical and conceptual focus of anarchist and related fields of geography. This section thus outlines the intellectual development and contributions of anarchist perspectives in geography through a deeper discussion of notions of autonomy contained within them.

As I have argued elsewhere (e.g. Ince 2012), it is the distinctively prefigurative underpinnings of anarchism that exert potentially the most powerful impact on academic endeavour. The notion that we must organize and relate to one another in ways that are reflective of the kind of future world we wish to create is so anathema to the remainder of the political spectrum that it has vast potential to transform the way we enact research and pedagogy. Exactly *how* and *what* to prefigure, however, has long been a focus of debate among both 'pure' anarchists and the diverse anti-capitalist horizontalist movements out of which autonomous and anarchist geographies have sprung.

Daniel Colson outlines an anarchist conception of autonomy thus:

> [A]narchist autonomy refers to the forces constitutive of beings, to the capacity to develop in themselves the totality of resources which they need in order 1) to affirm their existence, and 2) to associate with others, and to thus constitute an ever more powerful force of life.
>
> (Colson 2001: 47–48)

As such, we can conceive of autonomy, from an anarchist perspective, as an immanent social relationship produced through individual and collective self-governing agency. Enacted alongside the fundamental anarchist principles of mutual aid and voluntary association, autonomy sits on the borderline between individual liberty and collective organization. It nurtures a delicate tension between these two qualities, producing complex 'interstitial' (Pickerill and Chatterton 2006) spatialities that may function through a combination of loose networks and formal organizations, and embody an immanent malleability that has the potential to render autonomous spaces and practices near-ungovernable. The majority of geographers, however, have tended to draw less explicitly from the anarchist tradition, also incorporating elements of autonomist Marxism and contemporary anti-capitalist practices of autonomy, to form a heterodox notion of autonomous politics.

Post-autonomism, exemplified by Hardt and Negri's (2001) *Empire*, has already been explored by critical geographers (e.g. Lepofsky 2009), and their conceptions of autonomy have therefore enjoyed some level of influence. By deploying the idea of a 'multitude' – an amorphous mass of humanity which functions as an unmediated, collective social subject – some geographers have made contributions to the study of geopolitics and migrant politics by exploring the ways in which marginal groups may function as networks of autonomous agents of social change (e.g. Merla-Watson 2012).

The strength of the original class-struggle strains of autonomist Marxism, however, is their emphasis on the primacy of working class agency from the outset, where our everyday activities are appropriated by capital and enveloped into a totalizing 'social factory' (see Thoburn 2003). In this view, all forms of economic, social, and material production and reproduction originate with working class agency. Autonomist Marxists deploy notions such as the 'general intellect' (Spence and Carter 2011), which is the sum total of people's ordinary experiences, knowledges, ideas, and emotions, through which capital parasitically learns and develops. With the working class situated as the prime mover of capitalist development, what some geographers have labeled as 'resistance' is transformed into a new phase of class recomposition that elites must respond to, rather than the other way around

(Cleaver 1979). As such, the (post-)autonomist approach places agency solely in the hands of the working class, or multitude.

This conception of autonomy challenges established schools of thought in left geography, most notably Regulation Theory (see, for example, Lee and Wainwright 2010), which seeks to map the structures through which capitalism regulates and perpetuates itself across space.[1] If we follow the autonomists, however, the capitalist classes in business and government become vulnerable and fragile, pitifully dependent on our agency for their survival.

Anarchist geographers have been careful in their use of Marxist ideas, and have used the concepts of this tradition by transplanting elements of it into a prefigurative anarchistic framework that seeks to cancel out the potentially authoritarian, linear, and statist baggage that Marxisms risk bringing with them. As Clough and Blumberg (2012: 344, my emphasis) note, '[w]e call autonomist Marxist thought a "trajectory" here because it is not so much a school of theory as it is *a current of theorising* that draws on a series of shared concepts'. Indeed, some anarchist geographers have recently moved beyond autonomy as a concept – which can easily be linked to an individualistic liberalism – preferring to explore more explicitly collective, materially grounded practices such as mutual aid (e.g. White and Williams 2017; Ince and Bryant 2018). Moreover, there is a growing body of postanarchist work in geography, which problematizes the notion of class in favour of a poststructuralist perspective, conceiving of capital and state as an interlocking terrain of non-linear power relations that cannot be reduced to dialectical oppositional struggle (Newman 2011; Springer 2013b). Postanarchists are therefore also wary of the influence of Marxism on anarchist geographies, albeit for slightly different reasons than their non-postanarchist counterparts.

The role of autonomist Marxist concepts and critiques has therefore been an ambiguous one, but one that has also supported considerable progress towards understanding the functioning and political significance of autonomous spaces. Using this fusion of anarchist and autonomist thought, geographers are deepening knowledge on the ways in which social movements co-ordinate, organize, and communicate across space and in place-based 'militant particularisms' (Pickerill 2007; Rouhani 2012a); the geographies of militant pedagogy and research methods (Autonomous Geographies Collective 2010; Springer et al. 2016); and deconstructing colonial relationships between Settler and Indigenous activists (Barker and Pickerill 2012), among others.

A common theme within these anarchist considerations of autonomy is their emphasis on creating spaces and spatialities of self-management. Autonomy literally means 'self-management' or 'self-government', although as we have seen, it has become much broader than this. Nevertheless, geographers have been particularly interested in the ways in which self-management functions in and across different geographical contexts. A key finding is the messy, contested nature of autonomous space, which means that making meaningful linkages between the local and transnational is far from straightforward (Pickerill and Chatterton 2006; Ince 2010b).

The complex, mundane nature of self-management practices also plays out in the realm of the emotional and experiential 'affective' structures through which activists build autonomous forms of solidarity in place and across space (Clough 2012). In doing so, activists seek to prevent infiltration by security forces through these 'non-representational' modes of self-managing groups and wider movements. Activist fatigue is a deeply affective element of the practicalities of self-managed spaces, and Rouhani (2012a) illustrates the ways in which the materialities of a space's location, size, and spatial configuration can serve to unite or fragment an outwardly 'tight' political collective. However, it is not only in physical spaces that self-management occurs, with online news and information dissemination claiming networked virtual spaces for self-managed media activities (Pickerill 2007).

We can see that autonomy theorizes a particular kind of spatiality – one that might incorporate a range of political perspectives and ideas. Anarchism constitutes only one such political school of thought represented as part of autonomous projects, yet it is certainly the principal one. Thus, while autonomy is a toolkit of spatial strategies or tactics, anarchism is a mode of theory and analysis as well as an approach to spatial strategy. One can potentially conceive of authoritarian or capitalist configurations of autonomy, or non-autonomous modes of anarchist praxis. The intersections and affinities between anarchy and autonomy have often been assumed by scholars in geography and throughout the social sciences. Yet, a more critical investigation of their relationship might bring to light alternative spatial strategies available to anarchist groups and projects, especially when it is clear that autonomous spaces can sap energy and resources, divide broader movements, expose projects to state aggression and infiltration, tend only to occupy margins, and are hard to sustain over long periods of time (e.g. Clough 2012; Rouhani 2012a; White et al. 2016). Autonomy is, without a doubt, a powerful means of forging spaces of creation and resistance between the cracks in the fabric of state and capital, but these successes can sometimes come at a high price.

Re-theorizing governance: statism, authority, and the territorial imagination

There has been a deep antiauthoritarian current within the field of geography for several decades, and geographers have been at the forefront of analyzing the nature and dynamics of power and authority within modern societies. Whereas anarchist-oriented scholars in traditionally conservative disciplines such as international relations (Prichard 2011) and law (Finchett-Maddock 2010) have fought hard to promote an anti-statist and anti-colonialist perspective within their respective fields, anarchist geographers have enjoyed not only relative freedom to explore these themes, but also a solid conceptual foundation on which to build their perspectives.

The relatively welcoming environment that has been forged within geography has led to a range of critical perspectives on the spaces of governance, influenced most heavily by feminist, Marxist, and poststructuralist schools of thought (e.g. Staeheli and Kofman 2004; Featherstone et al. 2012; Strauss 2013). Since space is such an uneven, contested term, geographers' critical investigations into the geographies of governance have likewise been diverse. Political-economic analyses in geography have often foregrounded the role of economic deregulation in the construction of neo-liberal state spaces, not only in terms of the structure of governance itself (Peck 2001), but also localized experiences and negotiations of deregulation processes (Mackinnon and Derickson 2013), and the erosion of state control over internal and external everyday conditions. The field of geographical political economy has hitherto focused chiefly on the spatial relationships between economic processes and changing forms of governance at multiple scales, exploring the ways in which capital and (various levels and branches of) the state interweave and operate through one another. However, a greater focus on the institutional structures and practices of the state in the broader field of modern society (Brenner et al. 2008) has problematized some of the more sweeping assumptions about the erosion of the state in the context of globalization (e.g. Peck 2004).

Criticizing some of the more supposedly essentialist readings of state governance in geography are poststructuralist scholars, many of whom turn to Foucault and the notion of governmentality as a means of understanding how states govern at a distance through technologies that lead individuals to internalize state authority (Gill 2010; Joronen 2013). Others point to a false dichotomy – the 'separate spheres' assumption – between the state and the rest of society, and instead propose understanding 'stateness' as a form of socialized being in the world (Painter 2006).

A central element of geography's ongoing engagements with the structures and processes of governance is therefore its concern with globalization as a key phenomenon of contemporary economic, political, and cultural organization (Sparke 2006). Although they have made relatively few investigations into the organization of the politico-institutional spaces of economic globalization, anarchist and anarchist-influenced geographers have led the field in their analysis of counter-global networks, organizations, and practices, themselves a form of 'grassroots globalization'. A major facet of their research lies in the everyday constitution of global, self-governing processes among activist groups and individuals, which links strongly to the literatures discussed in the previous section concerning autonomy.

The anarchist-inspired geographer Paul Routledge, for example, has mapped the geographies of the global resistance networks that emerged around the turn of the millennium, theorizing the notions of 'terrains of resistance' (Routledge 1996) and 'convergence space' (Routledge 2003) to explain the uneven ways in which global justice networks function across transnational space and (both through and against) scalar structures of governance. This work, along with other more explicitly anarchist-geographic analyses of horizontalist networks and organizations (e.g. Chatterton 2005; Ince 2012; Rouhani 2012a), problematizes the hegemony of hierarchical organizational structures, and offers a constructively critical analysis of the possibilities of global, popular, self-governing spatial strategies. An important, if inadvertent, function of this work is the exposure of the ambiguous relationship of other critical geographers to the state, whose critiques of the state-capital nexus do not go so far as to advocate its abolition altogether. Until recently, anarchist geographers had taken full advantage of this proverbial elephant in the room that has haunted the discipline for some time, although it was identified as a fruitful avenue to explore early in the recent wave of interest (Ince 2012; Springer 2012). In recent years, texts by Springer (2016), Araujo (2016) and Barrera de la Torre and Ince (2016; Ince and Barrera de la Torre 2016; 2017) have begun explicitly addressing this question. In identifying the state as a contingent, fragmented and shifting set of institutional and power relations underpinned by violent coercion, these writings have begun to dismantle not only the empirical but also the epistemological foundations and assumptions of dominant statist geographical imaginaries.

The topic of colonialism is also an emerging area where anarchist ideas are shaping the way we understand the spatialities of statist-capitalist governance. Barker and Pickerill's work on Settler-Indigenous relationships in North America has carefully picked apart the different spatio-cultural imaginations of the two, outlining how any project of decolonization needs to understand the spatial injustices of colonial power's territorial project in order to provide a genuinely emancipatory programme of change (Barker and Pickerill 2012). Indigenous connections to, and definitions of, land and place in North America are fundamentally different to the spatial imagination of the Settler-colonial project, thus making meaningful communication and shared lexicons very difficult. The failure of Settler-dominated anarchist groups to make this connection in their activist efforts is structured by Settler colonial political (mis)understandings of Indigenous politics that position it as a sub-category of other oppressions such as racism. It is also linked to a process of internalization, through which the colonialist state becomes a mode of acting and relating to individuals, groups, and institutions in ways that (de)legitimize certain positionalities and forms of governance (Barker 2009). Thus, the distinct geographies contained within the Settler-Indigenous relationships identify the statist-colonialist project as a marker not only of capitalist 'primitive accumulation' but also a certain territorial form of governing space (Barker and Pickerill 2012).

Developing this theme at a more primary level, Springer (2012: 1607) has argued that 'there is no fundamental difference between colonialism and state-making other than the scale upon which these parallel projects operate'. This re-framing of the state as a colonial exercise in homogenizing, governing, and extracting capitalist value from diverse spaces and cultures is a powerful act that opens up geographical scholarship for a deeper critique of the state *per se*. In exploring the statist-colonialist governance of space, scholars are returning to the roots of anarchist geography, echoing the calls of Reclus to 'provincialise' Europe and forge a geography 'which has its centre everywhere, and its circumference nowhere' (Reclus 1876, quoted in Ferretti 2013: 1351). These initial forays into questions of state governance and colonialism foreground the role of anarchists in geography to move beyond the mere critique of state practices and towards a dismantlement of the state itself. Already exploring in great depth alternatives to statist and hierarchical human relations, the anarchist perspective has a growing potential to reposition hierarchical statist governance systems as socially produced inventions that were created by humans, and can thus be destroyed by them too.

New publics, new spatialities

We have seen how anarchist perspectives within the field of geography have been pushing beyond the boundaries of established critical geography, not only in terms of their critique of statist, capitalist, and authoritarian ways of organizing society, but also in their extensive explorations of alternative modes of organizing and relating. In this third and final substantive section of the chapter, I draw these, and other, works together in order to explore the various ways in which anarchist geographers have sought to transform notions of *the public*.

Much like the spatialities of governance, the discipline of geography has a long tradition in critical analyses of public space, especially in the urban context. Urban geographers such as Lees (2003) and Smith (1999) have variously sought to interrogate the ways in which the everyday life of the city orbits a struggle for access to various forms of public space and a Lefebvrian 'right to the city' (Mitchell 2003). With the neo-liberalization of economies has come a neo-liberalization of public space, carefully stage-managing (non-)public spaces for consumption and capital accumulation through private security forces, surveillance technologies, as well as designing the very physical structure of spaces such as parks, arcades, and malls in such a way as to maximize consumption and minimize the presence of groups and behaviours deemed unacceptable (Mitchell 2003). The contested public spaces of cities are deemed especially central to the politics of public space in general, due to what some have identified as 'planetary urbanisation', with the world's growing urban population now considerably greater than the population in rural areas (e.g. Madden 2012).

Mirroring the critical scholarship concerning the spatialities of governance discussed above, few geographers critical of this enclosure of the public have made steps towards the reconstitution of a liberatory public space free from state and capital (however, see for example, Pinder 2005). Although there have been numerous studies critiquing the role of state and other institutional actors such as police forces in promoting draconian mechanisms of spatial control, even fewer geographers have taken the logical step to advocate the abolition of, or alternatives to, these authoritarian structures and institutions.

In response, anarchists have made initial progress towards broadening our imaginations of a liberated public-ness, not only with regards to transforming physical public spaces but also our practices and relationships of 'doing' and 'being' public. The autonomous project of occupation – of land, of buildings, and of existing public spaces – has become a principal theme through the geographies of anarchist publics, yet autonomous geographies have been surprisingly light on direct theorizations of the public through an anarchist lens. Nevertheless, a number of contributions have been made, largely concerned with the tensions and complexities of creating public spaces of and for liberation. Ferrell (2012), for example, has explored the notion of 'drift' as a conceptual term to unpack the ways in which anarchist praxis links with the spatial practices of marginalized groups such as homeless people and buskers. While sharing some similar spatial practices, the differences inherent in the underlying causes of their practices are a problematic factor for Ferrell. Some level of affinity between drifters may exist, but there is no denying the privileges associated with drift as a political practice. Likewise, dumpster diving, the anarchic practice of taking edible food from rubbish sites, has been identified as actually skirting around structures of power, discipline, and waste, rather than confronting them or creating alternative patterns of association (Crane 2012). These studies suggest that the production of truly public spaces and spatialities within ostensibly statist-capitalist space is riddled with contradictions.

We find with anarchic frameworks for constructing public space a number of approaches that variously foreground Mouffian notions of radical democracy (Springer 2010), collective pedagogy (Rouhani 2012b), affective structures of collective trust and solidarity (Clough 2012), as well as the appropriation of physical spaces themselves (Pickerill and Chatterton 2006). What unites these diverse approaches is the simple yet powerful anarchist principle of 'voluntary association'; of the collective and democratic, uncoerced being-in-common of groups of people (see Bakunin 1990 [1873]). It implies spatial practices that are contestable from within and without, flexible, and shaped contextually in particular spatio-temporalities (cf. Ince 2012). Voluntary association is a term that is rather out of fashion among anarchists, yet its beauty lies in its simple appeal to the very core of anarchist thought and action.

A key differentiation between anarchist and other critical perspectives on the public orbits the role of state apparatus in the constitution of the public good. Not only do anarchist perspectives critique the monopoly of care claimed by the state as the sovereign order and arbiter of wellbeing, but also the very language of publicness. A recent example is the well-intentioned discussion by critical theorist Judith Butler (2013) on whether we can imagine a citizenship through an anarchist lens. Butler wrestles with how to reconcile anarchism with citizenship as the assumed *sine qua non* of public participation, but fails to come to a solid conclusion. She suggests that '[a]t issue is whether there can be an anti-statist anarchism that does not mobilise the prerogatives of citizenship at the same time that it reproduces a certain nationalism' (Butler 2013: 212).

On the contrary, this is precisely what is *not* at issue. Whether citizenship can be disentangled from nationalism is a moot point. Butler's problem lies in the fact that, as Springer (2012: 1617) has noted, 'alternatives to the state do not arise from the order that they refuse, but from the anarchic profusion of forces that are alien to this order'. In other words, truly anarchistic publics are constructed not through a reappropriation of statist language, nor through simple opposition to statist logics, but by means of the associations that exist *despite* it. Carrie Mott's (2018) anarchafeminist geographies of migration politics on the US-Mexico border illustrate well the solidarities and collectivities that can be created not only in opposition to state action but also far beyond that immediacy of resistance. Butler will never be able to identify an anarchist citizenship because citizenship is necessarily linked to statism as a way of being in the world and as a mode of connecting people in particular (hierarchical, exploitative) constellations.

This point returns us to a common theme throughout the chapter: the role of social relationships in the production of anarchist space. As argued elsewhere by anarchist geographers (Ince 2012; Springer 2016), spatial categories and phenomena are socially produced through everyday relationships – a common thread throughout contemporary anarchist geographical thought on autonomy, governance, and the public alike. In the concluding section, I draw together common themes in the chapter and propose some avenues for the further development of anarchist geographies.

Concluding thoughts: for radical reconstruction

With the flourishing of contemporary anarchist geographies, connections to classical anarchism have been pushed aside somewhat, but they still remain the basis of our thought. Ideas still resonate from past waves as fresh as they were in their own periods. Reflecting on a central theme of the chapter – that of the ways in which structures of both domination and liberation are embedded in our social relationships and the spatialities that we create through them – the century-old passage by Gustav Landauer below still rings true:

> The state is a social relationship; a certain way of people relating to one another. It can be destroyed by creating new social relationships; i.e., by people relating to one another differently. ... We, who have imprisoned ourselves in the absolute state, must realise the truth: *we* are the state! And we will be the state as long as we are nothing different; as long as we have not yet created the institutions necessary for a true community and a true society of human beings.
> (Landauer 2010 [1910]: 214)

This passage brings us to the first of several concluding observations for the nascent field of anarchist geography. Statism is a power relation that can be as oppressive in its own right as racism, class, patriarchy, and so on. Rooted in a sovereign, illegitimate exercise of power by a privileged minority or elite, statist modes of authority intersect through these relationships in such a deep way that scholars have mistaken them as a factor in these other oppressions, rather than an oppressive relationship in its own right. Statism can be read as the internalization of state-like authority in everyday practices, socialities, and spaces – and it is an area of study that anarchist scholars are perfectly positioned to make their own. In geography especially, the possibilities for investigating everyday statisms through the geographical analysis of institutional and social processes across and between spaces and places are myriad.

Second, and following from this call to interrogate the everyday, banal forms of statism, anarchist geographers have been all-too-easily courted by the spectacular, vibrant, and countercultural elements of anarchist movements and initiatives, such as Reclaim the Streets, Occupy, and the early 2000s' global anti-capitalist movements. This may take place at the expense of the less 'glamorous' modes of anarchist praxis such as anarcho-syndicalist labour unions or autonomous community groups and support networks whose stories appear superficially far more mundane, but which may offer even more profound insights into future worlds and our paths towards them. Indeed, it is beneficial to take inspiration from Kropotkin's (1972 [1914]) *Mutual Aid*, which considered not anarchist movements but the countless guilds, co-operatives, voluntary associations and everyday grassroots relationships of trust and support that people have enacted and defended throughout history without any direct reference to political ideologies. The notion that we all 'do anarchy' every day is a revolutionary idea in itself, and one that geographers, and social scientists more generally, are well placed to explore.

With what feels like a critical mass of scholars within geography, another important point to make is more of a strategic one. We find ourselves with great potential to bring anarchist thought and action to the academy, and it is essential to capitalize on this in a number of ways. Collaboration will without a doubt be central to the future flourishing of anarchist geographies, as will be efforts to internationalize the field through translation and forging global connections. Large-scale, transnational research projects could provide the basis for a sustainable and long-term research environment. As Rouhani (2012b) and others (e.g. Shukaitis and Graeber 2007) have noted, anarchist approaches to pedagogy are also essential to a vibrant and confrontational culture of anarchist scholarship, as is a healthy relationship of co-operation and feedback loops with social movements and initiatives.

We have seen how anarchist influences on the discipline of geography are on the ascendancy, with a growing body of work and number of scholars making profound contributions to our understandings of the world and ways to change it. Perhaps the most distinctive feature of anarchism from a geographical perspective is the recognition of the tension between present social organisation and the latent possibilities contained within our everyday (inter)actions within that present social order. They play out within and through one another, creating complex socio-spatial relationships that embody tremendous potential for radical social change from the grassroots. While the history of geography since the 1970s has been characterized by a generalized antiauthoritarianism and a critical gaze on the asymmetrical power relations and uneven patterns of development and wellbeing generated by state and capital, the discipline has fallen frustratingly short of what to anarchist geographers is an obvious conclusion. Geography teaches us, time and time again, the injustices of a statist-capitalist world – a world spatially organized by elites for their own benefit – and it is the anarchist geographer's role to teach the rest of geography that there are paths to a new one.

Note

1 It is worth mentioning, however, that there are a number of formerly 'traditionalist' Marxist geographers who have recently begun to utilize autonomist Marxism in their studies of political economy and economic restructuring (e.g. Cumbers et al. 2010).

References

Araujo, E. (2016) 'What Do We Resist When We Resist the State?', in L.M. de Sousa, R.J. White and S. Springer (eds.) *Theories of Resistance: Anarchism, Geography, and the Spirit of Revolt*, Lanham: Rowman and Littlefield, pp. 79–100.

Autonomous Geographies Collective (2010) 'Beyond Scholar Activism: Making Strategic Interventions Inside and Outside the Neoliberal University', *ACME: An International E-Journal of Critical Geographies*, 9(2): 245–275.

Bakunin, M. (1990 [1873]) *Statism and Anarchy*, Cambridge: Cambridge University Press.

Barker, A.J. (2009) 'The Contemporary Reality of Canadian Imperialism: Settler Colonialism and the Hybrid Colonial State', *American Indian Quarterly*, 33(3): 325–351.

Barker, A.J. and Pickerill, J. (2012) 'Radicalising Relationships to and through Shared Geographies: Why Anarchists Need to Understand Indigenous Connections to Land and Place', *Antipode*, 44(5): 1705–1725.

Barrera de la Torre, G. and Ince, A. (2016) 'Post-Statist Geographies and the Future of Geographical Knowledge Production' in L.M. de Sousa, R.J. White and S. Springer (eds.) *Theories of Resistance: Anarchism, Geography, and the Spirit of Revolt*, Lanham: Rowman and Littlefield, pp. 51–78.

Breitbart, M.M. (1978) 'Spanish Anarchism: An Introductory Essay', *Antipode*, 10–11(3–1): 60–70.

Brenner, N., Jessop, B., Jones, M. and MacLeod, G. (2008) 'State Space in Question', in N. Brenner, B. Jessop, M. Jones and G. MacLeod (eds.) *State/Space: A Reader*, Malden, MA and Oxford: Blackwell, pp. 1–31.

Brown, G. (2004) 'Sites of Public (Homo)sex and the Carnivalesque Spaces of Reclaim the Streets', in L. Lees (ed.) *The Emancipatory City? Paradoxes and Possibilities*, London, Thousand Oaks and New Delhi: SAGE, pp. 91–107.

Butler, J. (2013) 'Palestine, State Politics and the Anarchist Impasse', in J. Blumenfeld, C. Bottici and S. Critchley (eds.) *The Anarchist Turn*, London: Pluto Press, pp. 203–223.

Chatterton, P. (2005) 'Making Autonomous Geographies: Argentina's Popular Uprising and the Movimento de Trabajadores Desocupados (Unemployed Workers Movement)', *Geoforum*, 36(5): 545–561.

Claeys, G. (2000) 'The "Survival of the Fittest" and the Origins of Social Darwinism', *Journal of the History of Ideas*, 61(2): 223–240.

Clark, J.P. and Martin, C. (2004) *Anarchy, Geography, Modernity: The Radical Social Thought of Elisée Reclus*, Lanham, MD: Lexington Books.

Cleaver, H. (1979) *Reading Capital Politically*, Brighton: Harvester Press.

Clough, N. (2012) 'Emotion at the Centre of Radical Politics: On the Affective Structures of Rebellion and Control', *Antipode*, 44(5): 1667–1686.

Clough, N. and Blumberg, R. (2012) 'Toward Anarchist and Autonomous Marxist Geographies', *ACME: An International E-Journal for Critical Geographies*, 11(3): 335–351.

Colson, D. (2001) *Petit Lexique Philosophique de l'Anarchisme de Proudhon a Deleuze*, Trans. Cohn, J. Draft text available from translator.

Cook, I. and Pepper, D. (eds.) (1990) 'Anarchism and Geography', *Contemporary Issues in Geography and Education*, 3(2).

Crane, N.J. (2012) 'Are "Other Spaces" Necessary? Associative Power at the Dumpster', *ACME: An International E-Journal for Critical Geographies*, 11(3): 352–372.

Cumbers, A., Helms, G. and Swanson, K. (2010) 'Class, Agency, and Resistance in the Old Industrial City', *Antipode*, 42(1): 46–73.

Fannin, M., Fort, S., Marley, J., Miller, J. and Wright, S. (2000) 'The Battle in Seattle: A Response from Local Geographers in the Midst of the WTO Ministerial Meetings', *Antipode*, 32(3): 215–221.

Featherstone, D. (2003) 'Spatialities of Transnational Resistance to Globalisation: The Maps of Grievance of the Inter-Continental Caravan', *Transactions of the Institute of British Geographers*, 28(4): 404–421.

Featherstone, D., Ince, A., Mackinnon, D., Strauss, K. and Cumbers, A. (2012) 'Progressive Localism and the Construction of Political Alternatives', *Transactions of the Institute of British Geographers*, 37(2): 177–182.
Ferrell, J. (2001) *Tearing Down the Streets: Adventures in Urban Anarchy*, New York and Basingstoke: Palgrave Macmillan.
Ferrell, J. (2012) 'Anarchy, Geography and Drift', *Antipode*, 44(5): 1687–1704.
Ferretti, F. (2013) '"They Have the Right to Throw Us Out": Élisée Reclus' New Universal Geography', *Antipode*, 45(5): 1337–1355.
Ferretti, F. (2016) 'Anarchist Geographers and Feminism in Late 19th Century France: the Contributions of Elisée and Elie Reclus', *Historical Geography*, 44(1): 68–88.
Ferretti, F. (2017) 'Evolution and Revolution: Anarchist Geographies, Modernity and Poststructuralism', *Environment and Planning D*, 35(5): 893–912.
Finchett-Maddock, L. (2010) 'Finding Space for Resistance through Legal Pluralism: the Hidden Legality of the UK Social Centre movement', *Journal of Legal Pluralism*, 42(61): 31–52.
Fleming, M. (1987) *The Geography of Freedom: The Odyssey of Elisée Reclus*, Montréal: Black Rose Books.
Franks, B. (2006) *Rebel Alliances: The Means and Ends of Contemporary British Anarchisms*, Edinburgh: AK Press.
Gill, N. (2010) 'New State-Theoretic Approaches to Asylum and Refugee Geographies', *Progress in Human Geography*, 34(5): 626–645.
Gosling, T. (2004) 'Not for Sale: The Underground Network of Anarcho-Punk', in A. Bennet and R.A. Peterson (eds.) *Music Scenes: Local, Translocal and Virtual*, Nashville, TN: Vanderbilt University Press, pp. 168–186.
Halfacree, K. (1996) 'Out of Place in the Country: Travellers and the "Rural Idyll"', *Antipode*, 28(1): 42–72.
Hall, P. (1988) *Cities of Tomorrow: An Intellectual History of Urban Planning and Design in the 20th Century*, Oxford: Blackwell.
Hardt, M. and Negri, A. (2001) *Empire*, Cambridge, MA and London: Harvard University Press.
Ince, A. (2010a) 'Whither Anarchist Geography?', in N. Jun and S. Wahl (eds.) *New Perspectives on Anarchism*, Lanham, MD: Lexington Books, pp. 209–226.
Ince, A. (2010b) 'Organising Anarchy: Spatial Strategy, Prefiguration and the Politics of Everyday Life', Unpublished PhD Thesis, London: Queen Mary, University of London.
Ince, A. (2012) 'In the Shell of the Old: Anarchist Geographies of Territorialisation', *Antipode*, 44(5): 1645–1666.
Ince, A. and Barrera de la Torre, G. (2016) 'For Post-Statist Geographies', *Political Geography*, 55(1): 10–19.
Ince, A. and Barrera de la Torre, G. (2017) 'Future (Pre-)Histories of the State: On Anarchy, Archaeology and the Decolonial' in F. Ferretti, G. Barrera, A. Ince and F. Toro (eds.) *Historical Geographies of Anarchism: Early Critical Geographers and Present-Day Scientific Challenges*, London: Routledge, pp. 179–194.
Ince, A. and Bryant, H. (2018) 'Reading Hospitality Mutually', *Environment and Planning D*, doi:10.1177/0263775818774048.
Joronen, M. (2013) 'Conceptualising New Modes of State Governmentality: Power, Violence, and the Ontological Mono-Politics of Neoliberalism', *Geopolitics*, 18(2): 356–370.
Kropotkin, P. (1968 [1913]) *Fields, Factories and Workshops, or, Industry Combined with Agriculture and Brain Work with Manual Work*, New York and London: Benjamin Bloom.
Kropotkin, P. (1972 [1902]) *Mutual Aid: A Factor of Evolution*, New York: New York University Press.
Landauer, G. (2010 [1910]) 'Weak Statesmen, Weaker People!', in G. Kuhn (ed. and trans.) *Gustav Landauer – Revolution and Other Writings: A Political Reader*, Pontypool: Merlin Press, pp. 213–214.

Lee, S.O. and Wainwright, J. (2010) 'Revisiting Regulation Theory for the Analysis of South Korean Capitalism', *Journal of the Economic Geographical Society of Korea*, 13 (4): 562–583.

Lees, L. (2003) 'The Ambivalence of Diversity and the Politics of Urban Renaissance: the Case of Youth in Downtown Portland, Maine', *International Journal of Urban and Regional Research*, 27(3): 613–634.

Lepofsky, J.D. (2009) 'Geographies of the Multitude: Finding the Spatial in Empire and its Counters', *ACME: An International E-Journal of Critical Geographies*, 8(2): 149–160.

Mackinnon, D. and Derickson, K.D. (2013) 'From Resilience to Resourcefulness: A Critique of Resilience Policy and Activism', *Progress in Human Geography*, 37(2): 253–270.

MacLaughlin, J. (1986) 'State-Centred Social Science and the Anarchist Critique: Ideology in Political Geography', *Antipode*, 18(1): 11–38.

Madden, D.J. (2012) 'City Becoming World: Nancy, Lefebvre, and the Global-Urban Imagination', *Environment and Planning D*, 30(5): 772–787.

Mamadouh, V. (2004) 'Internet, Scale, and the Global Grassroots: Geographies of the Indymedia Network of Independent Media Centres', *Tijdschrift voor Economische en Social Geografie*, 95(5): 482–497.

McCreery, S. (2002) 'The Claremont Road Situation', in I. Borden, J. Kerr, and J. Rendell, with A. Pivaro (eds.) *The Unknown City: Contesting Architecture and Social Space*, Cambridge, MA: MIT Press, pp. 228–245.

McKay, G. (ed.) (1998) *DiY Culture: Party and Protest in Nineties Britain*, London and New York: Verso.

Merla-Watson, C.J. (2012) 'Bridging Common Grounds: Metaphor, Multitude, and Chicana Third-Space Feminism', *ACME: An International E-Journal of Critical Geographies*, 11(3): 492–511.

Mitchell, D. (2003) *The Right to the City: Social Justice and the Fight for Public Space*, New York: Guilford Press.

Mott, C. (2018) 'Building Relationships within Difference: An Anarcha-Feminist Approach to the Micropolitics of Solidarity', *Annals of the American Association of Geographers*, 108(2): 424–433.

Newman, S. (2011) *The Politics of Postanarchism*, Edinburgh: Edinburgh University Press.

Painter, J. (2006) 'Prosaic Geographies of Stateness', *Political Geography*, 25(7): 752–774.

Peck, J. (2001) 'Neoliberalising States: Thin Policies/Hard Outcomes', *Progress in Human Geography*, 25(3): 445–455.

Peck, J. (2004) 'Geography and Public Policy: Constructions of Neoliberalism', *Progress in Human Geography*, 28(3): 392–405.

Peet, R. (1975) 'For Kropotkin', *Antipode*, 7(2): 42–43.

Pickerill, J. (2007) 'Autonomy Online: Indymedia and Practices of Alter-Globalisation', *Environment and Planning A*, 39(11): 2668–2684.

Pickerill, J. and Chatterton, P. (2006) 'Notes Towards Autonomous Geographies: Creation, Resistance, and Self-Management as Survival Tactics', *Progress in Human Geography*, 30(6): 730–746.

Pinder, D.J. (2005) *Visions of the City: Utopianism, Power and Politics in 20th Century Urbanism*, Edinburgh: Edinburgh University Press.

Prichard, A. (2011) 'What Can the Absence of Anarchism Tell Us About the History and Purpose of International Relations?', *Review of International Studies*, 37(4): 1647–1669.

Rouhani, F. (2012a) 'Anarchism, Geography, and Queer Space-Making: Building Bridges Over Chasms We Create', *ACME: An International E-Journal of Critical Geographies*, 11(3): 373–392.

Rouhani, F. (2012b) 'Practice What You Teach: Facilitating Anarchism In and Out of the Classroom', *Antipode*, 44(5): 1726–1741.

Routledge, P. (1996) 'Critical Geopolitics and Terrains of Resistance', *Political Geography*, 15 (6–7): 509–531.

Routledge, P. (1997) 'The Imagineering of Resistance: Pollok Free State and the Practice of Postmodern Politics', *Transactions of the Institute of British Geographers*, 22(3): 359–376.

Routledge, P. (2000) '"Our Resistance Will Be As Transnational As Capital": Convergence Space and Strategy in Globalising Resistance', *GeoForum*, 52(1): 25–33.

Routledge, P. (2003) 'Convergence Space: Process Geographies of Grassroots Globalisation Networks', *Transactions of the Institute of British Geographers*, 28(3): 333–349.

Sharp, J., Routledge, P., Philo, C. and Paddison, R. (2000) 'Entanglements of Power: Geographies of Domination/Resistance' in J. Sharp, P. Routledge, C. Philo and R. Paddison (eds.) *Entanglements of Power: Geographies of Domination/Resistance*. London: Routledge, pp. 1–42.

Shukaitis, S. and Graeber, D. (2007) 'Introduction' in S. Shukaitis and D. Graeber (eds.) *Constituent Imagination: Militant Investigations // Collective Theorisation*, Oakland and Edinburgh: AK Press, pp. 11–34.

Smith, N. (1999) 'Which New Urbanism? The Revanchist '90s', *Perspecta*, 30: 98–105.

Sparke, M. (2006) 'Political Geography: Political Geographies of Globalisation (2) – Governance', *Progress in Human Geography*, 30(3): 357–372.

Spence, C. and Carter, D. (2011) 'Accounting for the General Intellect: Immaterial Labour and the Social Factory', *Critical Perspectives on Accounting*, 22(3): 304–315.

Springer, S. (2010) 'Neoliberalism and Geography: Expansion, Variegation, Formations', *Geography Compass*, 4(8): 1025–1038.

Springer, S. (2012) 'Anarchism! What Geography Still Ought to Be', *Antipode*, 44(5): 1605–1625.

Springer, S. (2013a) 'Anarchism and Geography: A Brief Genealogy of Anarchist Geographies', *Geography Compass*, 7(1): 46–60.

Springer, S. (2013b) 'Violent Accumulation: A Postanarchist Critique in Neoliberalising Cambodia', *Annals of the Association of American Geographers*, 103(3): 608–626.

Springer, S. (2016) *The Anarchist Roots of Geography: Toward Spatial Emancipation*, Minneapolis: University of Minnesota Press.

Springer, S., Ince, A., Brown, G., Pickerill, J. and Barker, A. (2012) 'Anarchist Geographies: A New Burst of Colour', *Antipode*, 44(5): 1591–1604.

Springer, S., de Sousa, M.L. and White, R.J. (eds.) (2016) *The Radicalisation of Pedagogy: Anarchism, Geography, and the Spirit of Revolt*, London: Rowman and Littlefield.

St John, G. (2003) 'Post-rave Technotribalism and the Carnival of Protest', in D. Muggleton and R. Weinzierl (eds.) *The Post-Subcultures Reader*, Oxford and New York: Berg, pp. 65–82.

Staeheli, L. and Kofman, E. (2004) 'Mapping Gender, Making Politics: Toward Feminist Political Geographies', in L. Staeheli, E. Kofman and L.J. Peake (eds.) *Mapping Women, Making Politics: Feminist Perspectives on Political Geography*, New York and London: Routledge, pp. 1–13.

Strauss, K. (2013) 'Unfree Again: Social Reproduction, Flexible Labour Markets and the Resurgence of Gang Labour in the UK', *Antipode*, 45(1): 180–197.

Thoburn, N. (2003) *Deleuze, Marx, Politics*, London: Routledge.

Ward, C. (1998 [1973]) *Anarchy in Action*, London: Freedom Press.

Ward, D. (2010) 'Alchemy in Clarens: Kropotkin and Reclus, 1877–1881', in N. Jun and S. Wahl (eds.) *New Perspectives on Anarchism*, Lanham, MD: Lexington Books, pp. 281–302.

White, R.J., Springer, S. and de Sousa, M.L. (eds.) (2016) *The Practice of Freedom: Anarchism, Geography and the Spirit of Revolt*, London: Rowman and Littlefield.

White, R.J. and Williams, C.C. (2017) 'Crisis, Capitalism, and the Anarcho-Geographies of Community Self-Help', in A. Ince and S.M. Hall (eds.) *Sharing Economies in Times of Crisis: Practices, Politics and Possibilities*, London: Routledge, pp. 175–191.

10 In dialogue

Anarchism and postcolonialism

Maia Ramnath

No discussion of anarchism or colonialism is ever apolitical. And any discussion of either today may bump up against a tight cluster of posts (colonial, modern, structural) linked together with barbed wire to fence a neutralized academic field off from a wild flock of antis. I write as a partisan. This means that I want to untangle the wire, separate the posts, articulate relationships between them, flush out the antis and range beyond the academic enclave into positions against and among them.

Theorists (and skeptics) of postcolonialism have asked whether this particular academic discourse still has any explanatory utility or oppositional effectiveness as a vehicle of emancipatory, counter-hegemonic thought. Having encountered the texts I now know as canonical postcolonial theory, as I did for the first time as a partisan, not an academic, I recognized much in their ideas that felt personally resonant and politically useful, while blithely ignoring other aspects that did not. It did not occur to me that they would not speak powerfully to a reality pervaded with neocoloniality in the form of globalized capitalism compounded more or less overtly (less in 1999, more in 2003) by American militarism. Later, once disabused of my happy ignorance of the bitter debates between the materially and epistemologically inclined among the post-bound theorists, it seemed to me that the Gordian knot could easily be cut by the sword of anarchist common sense. And that meant simply resituating knowledge production in political commitment.

Whereas postcolonialism is an analysis, anti-colonialism is an orientation, ethic, affect (hope, rage, desire), praxis. It also implies that *post*colonialism is a misnomer. In what follows I place postcolonial alongside globalization and anarchist theories, as related approaches to understanding the condition of the world and what to do about that. To this end, I attempt an idiosyncratic and selective review of these overlapping fields, drawing on a number of illustrative authors to examine affinities of theme and vocabulary, along with differences of location and valence. I end by running a red and black flag up the post, cutlass in hand.

Neo, paleo, post

The world has changed since postcolonialism was solidified as an academic field: the collapse of the 'second world', the rise of neo-liberalism, and the debut of the planetary War on Terror caused those invested in the tropes of the discipline to question their premises. An important theme for postcolonial theory in the early twenty-first century then is whether postcolonial theory is still relevant, or whether other sorts of theory – in particular, globalization theory – are better suited to explain and respond to current relations of power, production, culture, and economy, on a global scale.[1] In order to propose an answer to that, it's necessary not only to refer to the history of colonialism and anti-colonialism, but also to historically contextualize postcolonialism as a discourse. That is, we can either talk about when colonialism may have begun or ended in a given location, or when the field of postcolonialism did.[2] For example, Vilashini Cooppan (2005), in her contribution to *Postcolonial Studies and Beyond*, proposes a strict boundary for the discourse in its most characteristic form, dating it from Edward Said's (1978) *Orientalism* to Michael Hardt and Antonio Negri's (2000) *Empire*; yet intellectual and political engagement with colonialism extends well past both limits.

Whether or not we need (and how we use) postcolonial theory depends on whether we think we are postcolonial. The simple answer is no, we are not. (And by 'we', I mean the life forms of planet Earth.) It's just that colonization – or if you like, the imperial projection of power toward wealth accumulation and control of access to resources – takes different forms at different stages of capitalist development, each with its characteristic disciplinary techniques, legitimizing ideologies and deep logic structures, with or without total cultural, psychological, and/or physical saturation. Different modalities of power generate correspondingly different modalities (theories, tactics, and identity formations) of resistance.

When used as historical shorthand, 'postcolonial' is a convenient way to periodize the end of formal colonial rule, political exit from an empire, and the establishment of a self-governing state. But it's only useful as such when speaking very specifically, since its date is different for each country, ranging from the early nineteenth century to yet unattained. For the majority of current African and Asian states, the era of decolonization occurred with the breakup of the great nineteenth-century empires following the two world wars, with sovereignty validated through a seat at the newly created United Nations.

But aside from the difficulty of pinpointing a postcolonial era even on such narrowly defined grounds, the transition to formal political independence rarely entailed economic self-sufficiency; merely a different mode of subjection to the same global economic system in which the society in question had been embedded in a state of dependency through the classical colonial relationship. Moreover, even within one country there could be no such thing as a singular 'postcolonial condition' that represented the variety of experiences of people of all classes, genders, education levels, and geographic locations, despite coexisting within the unfolding aftermath of conquest.

Still others object to the periodization of postcolonialism on the grounds that it is linear and derivative, a reductive self-definition yoked to colonial power.[3] Yet anyone born since the late fifteenth century was born within the polymorphously perfidious, internally uneven force field of modern coloniality, and warped by it in some way. A more useful suggestion, then, seems to be to consider the *advent* of colonization as the significant horizon (which, if all sites of power are sites of resistance, is simultaneously the advent of decolonization, even if the moment when the balance of power shifts may be much later).

The way that knowledge has been produced – where and by whom – about subordinated areas was deeply implicated in colonial history, power structures, and political interests and motivations (though surely people in the areas in question were also producing knowledge, known at least to themselves). Loomba and colleagues (2005b) point out that elite British and French institutions such as the School of Oriental and African Studies yielded heavy emphasis on the respective empires of Britain and France: Asia (specifically India), North Africa and the Middle East. Only later did Latin America, the Caribbean, and sub-Saharan Africa receive comparable attention.

Area Studies programmes in United States academe then reflected Cold War strategic interests in all those regions, contemporaneous with the major post-war decolonization period. (This expansion in focus is also reflected, though from the opposite direction, in the development of the Tricontinental from the Bandung movement.)

Meanwhile, scholars hailing from the global south working in Western academic settings began to stake out a professional identity that supporters say contributed to subverting the racial and cultural Eurocentrism of the Western canon, and detractors say capitalized on glamourizing a self-serving mantle of exotic marginality. These assessments locate 'postcolonial studies' as much in the self-identification of the people producing the theory, as in its subject matter – as if the two could be fully separated. Amongst such scholars, Ania Loomba and Leela Gandhi have each sketched out an intellectual genealogy of postcolonial theory as an interdisciplinary field, and/or a history of oppositional thought. Before moving forward, then, let me back up.

As precursors Leela Gandhi cites, on the left side of the spectrum, a generation of politically engaged 'independence intellectuals' from Asia, Africa, and Latin America who were more often than not advocates of modernity and development, and at the same time concerned in intensely experiential ways with 'motifs of cultural difference, epistemological othering, colonial subjectivity, and social contradiction – all common in later postcolonial studies' (Gandhi 1998: 38). In other words, there was as yet no dichotomy between the concerns later associated with Marxism and poststructuralism. In fact, Leela Gandhi (1998) suggests, often overlooked or unacknowledged amid the supposed novelty of colonialism as a theme, was postcolonialism's 'genealogical debt' (24) to the 'long history of specifically Marxist anti-imperialist thought' (23) which, despite its limitations, did theorize capitalism as a globally encompassing system that inevitably required the subjugation of ever more distant territories in its need for expansion. Aijaz Ahmad (prominent on the Marxist/materialist side of the feud) rejects the whole idea of postcolonialism as a separate field, saying 'we should speak not so much of colonialism or postcolonialism but of capitalist modernity, which takes the colonial form in particular places and at particular times' (Ahmad 1995: 7). Robert Young (2001) too has described postcolonialism as the innovative application of Marxian thought to the colonized regions of the world (despite earlier being associated with literary poststructuralism).

Given the very real historical ways in which colonial governmentality was implemented textually through ethnographic and archival records, it was perhaps inevitable for postcolonial studies as an anti-colonial project to intersect with the poststructuralist turn in scholarship since the mid-1980s. This was particularly evident within Indian Subaltern Studies, originally a historiographical intervention marked by an innovative dialogue with Gramsci, aimed at producing counterinsurgent narratives of resistance, thus restoring a history from below and outside of colonial and nationalist master narratives.

On one side, Fredric Jameson and others offer an 'account of the postcolonial bias against Marxism', or to be more accurate, of twentieth-century Marxist-Leninist orthodoxy, for its failure to deal adequately with race as a category of oppression, the 'exploitative relationship between the West and its Others', or the 'cultural and political alterity ... of the colonized world' (Jameson 1998: 24–25).[4] On the other side, materialist critics[5] targeted what had by then crystallized into a field with its own orthodoxies, namely 'its preoccupations with the discursive and rhetorical aspects of oppression and exploitation (to the exclusion and mystification of their historical and material causes and effects)', with the result of 'drag[ging the] subaltern subject ... into the abyss of incommensurable language games' (Gupta et al. 2005: 242).

It would be easy to compile endless quotations along similar lines. Yet arguably it is this very tension between poststructuralism/postmodernism and Marxism that has given postcolonial theory as a whole its distinct signature. Neither pole alone is sufficient for understanding the colonial encounter: one is required for postcolonial theory, and the other for postcolonial politics. This pairing indicates postcolonialism's dual constituencies and projects: counteracting racism in the academy and the Eurocentric Western canon, and participating in the decolonization of the same countries therein unrepresented.

Perhaps a similar bifurcation is detectable in the emerging notion of 'anarchist studies': one goal is to legitimize anarchism as a topic of history, political philosophy, and social theory, and as an acceptable lens of critical interpretation within the academy; the other is to promote movement-based intellectual work with the goal of furthering emancipatory practice, by applying the tools of anarchist thought to the tasks of collective liberation. Anarchist scholars, like postcolonial ones, are often positioned in such a way that the two overlap. (Oppositional thinkers too have to make a living somehow!)[6]

In any case, the ideological polarization within the field – which to be sure, rests on different bases than the old anarchist vs. Marxist vendettas – seems to me unnecessary and unfortunate, preventing what could be its greatest contribution to oppositional knowledge: namely the possibility of encompassing the insights and priorities of both in one multidimensional framework. I myself have drawn much value and inspiration from people on both sides of the divide. Is this because I approach this polarity along a separate tangent, with the assumptions of an anarchist, dialogically critiquing (rather than negating) the orthodox left from a place of left heterodoxy?[7] Or because I'm an 'authentic' diaspora-spawned liminal mestizajified hybrid? Or because the academic portion of my intellectual training includes degrees in both World History and Interdisciplinary Humanities & Social Thought? Or because I am a practitioner of the circus arts, in whose world it is not such a strange thing to think of attempting to ride two horses at once, perhaps while performing astounding feats of balance and tantric flexibility?[8]

To the marvel of Nagesh Rao (2003), writing in the collection *Rethinking Modernity*,

> [w]hereas reconciliatory postcolonial thought finds its intellectual/political origins and allegiances within a broadly-defined 'postmodern Left,' critical postcolonialism maintains in various ways a commitment to materialist, realist and Marxist analyses. Crucially, even the theorists most critical of the field ... find themselves uneasily occupying the same shelf-space as those whose attitude towards postcolonialism has been nothing short of celebratory.
>
> (Rao 2003, 241)

The unspoken nemeses here are such canonical theorists as Gayatri Spivak and Homi Bhabha (1994), who, after Edward Said, have been held perhaps most synonymous with the field. To me this shelving arrangement indicates that both sorts of author, while making opposed arguments, are involved in the same conversation. The point of contention always amounts to the inescapable conditions of what is described as late capitalism, postmodernity, or globalization, depending on where you are and to whom you are speaking. And so we come to the encounter of postcolonial theory with globalization theory.

An intellectual genealogy of globalization theory, as a mode of talking about macro-scale economic and political relations and their accompanying social/cultural phenomena – often assumed to be in a celebratory mode, though that need not automatically follow from analysis – draws from world systems theory and related dependency theory, which in the hands of Immanuel Wallerstein, Andre Gunder Frank, and Giovanni Arrighi, proffer a structural explanation of the evolution of capitalism into a global system through several successive phases of expansion constituting modernity as we know it.

Revathi Krishnaswamy and John Hawley, introducing the anthology *The Postcolonial and the Global*, attempt to articulate a relationship between these two new modes of discussing centuries-old questions of global integration, transregional connections, colonial and anticolonial practices (Krishnaswamy and Hawley 2007: 2).[9] Although both use 'the vocabulary of deterritorialization, migrancy, difference, hybridity and cosmopolitanism' and the categories 'universal and particular, global and local, homogeneity and heterogeneity' (3), in terms of methodology, postcolonialism 'tends to be hermeneutic or deconstructive, problematizing the issues of representation', while globalization 'tends to be more brazenly positivistic, taking its representational ability for granted' (2). Where postcolonialism emerged from the humanities, and 'focuses largely on a Eurocentric colonial past and examines how subaltern practices and productions in the non-Western peripheries responded to Western domination', globalization emerged from the social sciences and 'concentrates largely on a post/neocolonial present and examines how contemporary Western practices and productions affect the rest of the world' (2).

The question for globalization theory has been whether globalization – whether celebrated or decried – is an unprecedented phenomenon or if it is but the latest phase of capitalist imperialism, melting all that was solid into polluted, greenhouse gas-laden air. In other words, is it postcolonial or neo-colonial?

Like many anarchists of the generation radicalized in the late twentieth century who received our elementary political education in the streets and convergence spaces of the alterglobalization movement, I am of the opinion that it is unambiguously neo. The symbiosis of neo-liberal capitalism with military force, temporarily camouflaged, was again rendered explicit by the declaration of unending war after 2001. In other words, the reference point for both postcolonial and globalization theorists was out there in the world to be confronted, the proverbial vampire-squid; the debates that mattered concerned the tactics of opposition, and what alternatives to imagine in its place.

Here is where the self-interrogators within both bodies of theory begin to converge upon what I would consider to be an anarchist common sense, including, perhaps, the revival of a more actively oppositional stance to colonialism as something alive and well:

> From the turn of this century, the previous assumptions of colonialism, which corresponded to the shape of postcolonial studies, were being reshaped by newer developments, the most urgent of which is globalization, at once an extension of the world-systems of modern capitalism and colonialism and a newer network that presents a complicated picture of national and transnational agents, capital and labor, suppliers and markets, NGOs and multilateral agencies.
> (Loomba et al. 2005b: 2)

'The War on Terror' then rendered even those arguments about the field's relevance moot: here was a blatantly imperial moment overshadowing the post-Cold War window of end-of-history triumphalism, and sidestepping the dichotomy of those who had remained stubbornly committed to the anti-colonial nationalisms of the erstwhile independence intellectuals 'versus [the] poststructural hegemony' enveloping the field. But now, 'the rapid pace at which globalization is revealing its imperialist structure and ideologies throws our past debates into new relief, reminding us anew why we need to go beyond a certain kind of postcolonial studies' (2–3). So perhaps in the last decade we have entered a new, post-*Empire* chapter in postcolonial theory's social/intellectual history

In the wake of 9/11, Krishnaswamy and Hawley (2007: 12) suggested a concept of 'imperiality' to describe a new mode of globalism, 'to suggest both a break [and] a continuity with older forms of formal imperialism; [and] to establish a theoretical affiliation with the notion of coloniality'. Unlike Hardt and Negri's concept of Empire, (which they have since updated and to some degree modified in *Multitude* and *Commonwealth*; Hardt and Negri 2005, 2011) Krishnaswamy's and Hawley's imperiality continues to operate in terms of hierarchy and dependency, which they consider to be euphemized under the names of 'interdependence and globalization' (12), even while the nineteenth century centre/periphery split is being remixed into interpenetrated 'new geographies' (12). The logic of this imperiality can be seen in 'the ideology of permanent intervention and preemptive war' and 'the systematic use of various forms of extreme violence and mass insecurity to prevent collective movements of emancipation' (12). Whatever terminology is used, evaluation seems quite simple if the analysis behind it stems from committed practices in a real world context: if one believes that colonialism exists, then one is against it. Krishnaswamy and Hawley conclude, 'we have tried to make it possible for all those who believe in the possibilities of a decolonized planetarity to clarify the connections, acknowledge the conflicts, and recognize the complicities between the postcolonial and the global' (16).

A *decolonized planetarity*: if I were to imagine an anarchist organic intellectual passing through the movement of movements via the tropes of the 1990s (neo-liberal globalization), 2000s (war on terror), and 2010s (occupation/decolonization) she could not have put it better. She might add that the resurgence of far-right nationalisms in the 2010s, positioning themselves as the counterforce to a demonized globalism by asserting the sanctity and purity of an imagined homogenous, traditional local over a vilified globality suffused with racism and anti-Semitism, is an indication of the dangers of opposing globalization without recognizing its relationship to colonialism; it thereby misidentifies both scapegoats and solutions.

Anarchism and postcolonialism: shared themes, shared tensions

Neil Lazarus (2005) reports that since the mid-1990s, a materialist critique of the 'epistemological and ideological tendencies … predominant in postcolonial studies since its consolidation as an academic field of inquiry in the universities of Europe and North America' – note the indictment implicit in this phrasing, of the cooptation and neutralization of anticolonial praxis in the global south – has included these issues:

> a constitutive anti-Marxism; an undifferentiating disavowal of all forms of nationalism and a corresponding exaltation of migrancy, liminality, hybridity, and multiculturalism; a hostility toward 'holistic forms of social explanation' (toward totality

and systematic analysis); an aversion to dialectics; and a refusal of an antagonistic or struggle-based model of politics.

(Lazarus 2005, 423)

One assumes these materialist critics are leftists committed to actual resistance. But the list is curious to me, because while some of its points do resemble some of the critiques anarchism has posed to Marxism-Leninism, other points seem quite arbitrary to this logic.

Here are some themes shared by anarchism and anti-colonialism.

Alterity and subalternity

The term subalternity is defined as a power relation of subordination and domination not limited to class (based on relations of production), but also incorporating gender, race, caste, ethnicity; and capable of imagining spaces external to or autonomous from the dominant system. The meaning of anarchism might be encapsulated as opposition to the existence of all subalternity; opposition to any unequal power relation, which means hierarchy, whether maintained by coercion or hegemony. Here, the Hegelian recognition between master and slave as existentially dependent on each other makes no sense: true recognition can only be between equals, just as liberation is only meaningful in the context of equality, and vice versa.

But must equals be identical? And is the 'Other' always subaltern? Freedom, it seems to me, must include the simultaneous possibility of both equality and difference. Is this a paradox, both asserting and refuting universality? Any time the word 'universal' comes into play, postcolonial hackles rise: the controversial category of the human is to be challenged on the grounds that it is not at all universal, but rather a restrictive particularity.

The idea of Orientalism emphasizes the interpellation of the other, as that which is excluded from, rendered alien to, the Western self; when in actuality, these very categories are mutually constitutive and semantically interdependent. This (mirroring? mimicking?) mutual gaze is spatialized less in terms of above and below, than of inside and outside. And whereas the below is something to despise, the outside is something either to fear or fetishize. As an extreme case, the 'Other' inside is enslaved or incarcerated; the 'Other' outside is eliminated.

In 'The Problem with Privilege', decolonial theorist Andrea Smith (2013: 265–267), updates the demands of the subjugated in the face of exclusion from humanity: where previously there was a quest for recognition and inclusion in the human family, now instead she sees a rejection of the very definition of the human specifically marked as white, male, and so forth. But in place of the national or racial family model, might we not adopt an ideal of friendship or comradeship as a model for self-other relations? It does not require sameness – it may in fact thrive on difference – and like freedom, it is only truly possible among equals. I do think that the frequently implied equivalence between sameness/difference and unity/fragmentation is a false one. It is certainly possible to imagine a culture or society that, while stable and coherent, is diverse rather than homogenous, and dynamic rather than static.[10]

Nationalism

Of interest to anarchists is this additional implication: Leela Gandhi (1998) argues that humanist thought has historically 'accompanied and supported the emergence of unified and centralised nation-states' such as Italy and Germany (50), which served to 'bolster [its] fallacious claim to universality' (51). Yet within the same moments, she counters, 'popular aspirations' toward freedom and equality 'threatened to overspill those new boundaries', i.e. of the emergent state which sought to contain them. In this way, she contrasts the urge toward collective liberation with a nationalistic, state-sponsored 'totalitarian humanism' indicative of twin anxieties, each a 'potential anarchism': one 'the willful and uncontainable "populace" at home', the other 'abroad in the colonies'. (51–52)

The postcolonialist suspicion of nationalism is an obvious point of convergence with anarchism. For Edward Said (whose credentials as a proponent of real-world decolonization, Anglophone Palestinian in privileged exile that he was, cannot be faulted), a critique of nationalism was a moral imperative (Curthoys and Ganguly 2007). But the reasons for the two criticisms are not quite the same. Postcolonial theory criticizes nationalist thinking in the process of deconstructing the deep structures of colonial thought, of which nationalism is said to be a derivative. Rejecting the colonial episteme then requires rejecting nationalism. For anarchists, a critique of nationalism in no way requires a retreat from committed action to abstract theory (as anticolonial leftists accuse postcolonialists of doing), but rather a lateral move toward creating alternate forms of social structures and collective identities.

Postcolonial theory criticizes nationalist thinking for positing 'good' and 'bad' nationalisms, with the distinction stemming from Western prejudice and fear of anti-colonial insurgency: one's own is the vehicle of reason and progress, but the other's is the release of frightening atavistic energies. Another way of putting this is a bias toward liberal and away from cultural nationalism – as if there were no liberal nationalisms in the colonial world, and no cultural nationalisms in the north/West. The latter of course has manifested as fascism, deemed the worst of bad nationalisms precisely because it is supposed to be out of place, a racial logic brought into the home from the outside.[11]

A related criticism regards the connection of 'good' nationalism to modernity. Gellner made it inseparable from the shift to industrial economies, as 'the only form of political organization ... appropriate to the social and intellectual condition of the modern world' with its need for a 'homogenous and cooperative workforce and polity' (Gandhi 1998: 104). Anderson considered nationalism a new secular church to replace the rapidly obsolete 'old systems of belief and sociality embedded in the chimeral mysteries of divine kingship, religious communities, sacred language and cosmological consciousness' (Gandhi 1998: 104).[12] In Leela Gandhi's gloss, both accounts assume 'the teleological necessity – indeed, inevitability' of the Hegelian doctrine of history's progression from primitive darkness to the zenith of universal freedom and reason, conveniently identified with the very specific form of the modern European nation-state.

Anarchism has different reasons for rejecting nationalism. There is no question of good or bad: it is always bad, unsalvageable as a model for liberation. Along with capitalism, nationalism, once it has ripened from opposition to institution, requires imperial expansion in order to survive and fulfil its functions and interests. And it requires ethnic exceptionalism to guard the gates qualifying members for its benefits and participation in its demos.

Continuing her earlier theme, Leela Gandhi notes that while the stirring of national consciousness among the colonized may activate 'a teleology of inexorable rationality and development which finds its completed form in the regulative economy of the State', nevertheless the liberatory imaginaries and insurgent energies unleashed in such a struggle will inevitably spill over the nation-state's institutional and ideological apparatus (120). Distinguishing society from state in this way creates space within the liberated or decolonizing zone for 'the recalcitrant elements, characters, and actions invoked and energized by anti-colonial nationalism' that can never be contained within the postcolonial state's 'generic closure' (ibid.). Obviously there is a lot that anarchism would recognize in this.

Some celebrated anti-colonial activist-artists (who may be considered more postcolonial than postcolonialist, though perhaps subjected to postcolonialist readings in comparative literature departments) eloquently concur. Nigerian dissident playwright Wole Soyinka hoped his postcolonial homeland would represent, more than political geography, 'a humanized space of organic development'; 'a space within which I am bound to collaborate with fellow occupants in the pursuit of justice and ethical life'. It meant a duty, an opportunity, a promise and a responsibility to continue to challenge authoritarian governments and revitalize liberatory action well beyond its own boundaries. 'Our function', he concluded, 'is primarily to project those voices that, despite massive repression, continue to place their governments on notice' (Soyinka 1996: 133–134). This refusal of the totalitarianism and violence of postcolonial governments could hardly be called a retreat from radical political commitment. Instead both recognized the continuity of their anti-colonialism, through both literature and movement organizing, across the line of formal political independence.[13]

Hybridity, diaspora

In recognizing Gandhi and Fanon as seminal revolutionary 'independence intellectuals', those inadvertent forerunners of postcolonial theory, Leela Gandhi notes that both developed their signature ideas while in a third country (South Africa, Algeria), after a time studying in their respective colonial metropoles (London, Paris); specifically, while involved in anti-colonial/anti-racist organizing in another part of the same imperial structure as their own (India, Martinique). Accordingly they learned to value, 'creativity over authenticity'. This may be, she suggests, why neither developed into a true nationalist, even while tactically utilizing the mobilizing force of nationalism to channel decolonizing energies, at least temporarily, at a certain phase of the struggle. However, beyond this strategic moment, both expressed a healthy skepticism of elite parties and favoured 'a more decentralised polity closer to the needs and aspirations of the vast and unacknowledged mass of the Indian and Algerian peasantry' (Gandhi 1998: 122).

When that moment had passed, then, what did each propose to come afterward? Could the 'postcolonial desire for extra- or post-national solidarities' (ibid.) be found perhaps in a space of diaspora, where hybridities, impurities, liminalities, nomadisms, dislocations, and migrations are descriptions of actual experience, not abstract theoretical concepts? Could this be where Homi Bhabha's mysterious 'third space' or 'indeterminate zone' of translation, negotiation, modified reiteration, and innovation through encounter, is a reality? Ania Loomba lists as postcolonialist preoccupations 'issues of hybridity, creolisation, mestizaje, in-betweenness, diasporas and liminality, with the mobility and cross-overs of ideas and identities generated by colonialism' (Loomba 1998: 173). These make sense to me. They describe the experiential realities of my subject position. Does that make me a postcolonial scholar, even if not a postcolonialist one? Does it make me a poststructural anarchist, even if not a poststructuralist one?

I should note here the difference sometimes overlooked by high postcolonial theory between the migratory exile of privileged intellectuals and that of subaltern labourers. Here we might find mestizaje recast as a radically liberating force, as Gloria Anzaldúa (1987) does, or Paul Gilroy's double consciousness of the black Atlantic, crucible of 'cultural mutation and restless (dis)continuity that exceed racial discourse and avoid capture by its agents' (Gilroy 1993: 2). Or we might recognize Carter and Torabully's (2002) Coolitude – a riff on Cesaire's (2001) Negritude but with an emphasis on the dynamically hybrid rather than on the mystically essential.

Those of the poststructuralist anarchist persuasion may turn to Deleuze and Guattari or Negri and Hardt, in search of lines of flight; more traditionalist anarchists may turn to James Scott, or to dreams of marronage or piracy. Anarchism of all stripes shares the attraction to travellers and exiles who have escaped from the map- and mind-space of state and capital, of racial regimes, labour regimes, gender regimes, any regimes, to live outside their laws, with all outlaws as equals. I do not think this is depoliticizing.

Yet Brennan accuses both postcolonial and globalization theories of normatizing poststructuralism by promoting:

> the striving for ambivalence as a matter of principle; the ardent belief that answering a question 'forecloses' it; the elision of meaning in pursuit of epistemological doubt; and most of all, the deployment of a variety of tropes such as 'migrancy,' 'nomadism,' 'hybridity,' and 'decentering,' which are marshaled in order to make the case that mobility and cultural mixing – not as contingent historical experiences but as modes of being – are states of virtue ...
> (Brennan 2008: 46)

Yet, such, virtues render sociopolitical life all too easy to recuperate, he warns, by American corporate globalization. As with Lazarus' list, this one too sparks both recognition of the terms listed, and mystification at the implications attributed to them, as not just risks but inevitabilities. But I would hope that those who draw upon them in the process of proposing an alternate globalization from below are smart enough to spot and evade the American corporate juggernaut.

It also seems to me that what we should be most concerned with in assessing the postmodern/poststructuralist turns and counterturns in both anarchism and anti-colonialism, is *what these ideas do*. Are they useful for emancipatory praxis or are they depoliticizing? This can vary considerably according to context and application.

While it's been proposed that anarchism is perhaps the form of left theory most suited to our moment, the editors of *The Post-Anarchist Reader* suggest further that the form of anarchism most suited to our moment is poststructuralist. Rousselle and Evren (2011), in their introduction, contrast a classical anarchism based in humanist rationalism, with a 'postanarchist' critique of Enlightenment reason. In this formulation, postanarchism could refer to an anarchist engagement with poststructuralism, or to the form of anarchism reflective of late capitalism, of which postmodernism is the proverbial cultural manifestation, with a relationship to classical anarchism roughly comparable to that between the New Left of the 1960s-1970s and the Old Left of the 1860s-1930s.

Todd May's contribution takes the former course, asking whether anarchist philosophy can be imputed to the French poststructuralists, or whether anarchism – unlike the traditions he considers definitive of the twentieth-century political theories against which poststructuralist theory has reacted, namely liberalism and Marxism – simply provides the poststructuralists with a framework capable of supplementing their approach with a political practice. While both poststructuralism and anarchism are 'often dismissed in the same terms ... for being an ethical relativism or a voluntarist chaos' (May 2011: 41), he claims, the comparison marks a split within anarchism itself, since poststructuralism 'subvert[s] the humanist discourse which is the foundation of traditional anarchism' (42). Even so, he allows, a rejection of such discourse should not preclude 'the anarchist project of allowing oppressed populations to decide their goals and their means of resistance within the registers of their own oppression'. Instead of rendering struggles interchangeable from one area to another, a non-universalizing logic is compatible with 'decentralized resistance and ... local self-determination' (44). Such a poststructuralism can only exist at the level of 'local values that allow for resistance along a variety of registers', beyond which 'there is no theory, only combat' (44).

May thus concludes that poststructuralist theory is not only anarchist, but 'in fact more consistently anarchist than traditional anarchist theory has proved to be'.[14] Ultimately though, 'What both traditional anarchism and contemporary post-structuralism seek is a society – or better, a set of intersecting societies – in which people are not told who they are, what they want, and how they shall live, but ... will be able to determine these things for themselves' (ibid.). Here is a valourization of difference which has no need of mutual recognition.

This is well applicable to decolonization, although I would question the obvious omission here – there is also contemporary anarchism which is neither traditional nor necessarily poststructuralist. There are problems inherent in positing all the posts as something new against a narrowly defined model of classical anarchism which is limited to a tightly bounded historical narrative and set of canonical texts. As Rousselle and Evren point out, it's not necessary to postulate a new thing called postanarchism if we just broaden the definition of anarchism. On the other hand, there are anarchist advocates of the narrower definition, whose project is to decolonize it not conceptually but geographically, by expanding it beyond the realm of north Atlantic male proletarians to encompass workers' movements in Africa, Asia, Latin America, and elsewhere (Hirsch and van der Walt 2010). (Here's another echo of the Subaltern Studies debates: is syndicalist social history or epistemic deconstruction more decolonizing?)

In the same volume, Sandra Jeppesen points out that continuing to limit the definition of anarchism to a nineteenth-century form ill serves contemporary anarchist theorists and practitioners of many ethnicities and genders (Jeppesen 2011: 151). She asserts that the 'variety of interrelated anti-authoritarian practices' that are important in 'the cultural production of anarchism' today are 'informed, directly and indirectly, by post-structuralism', including not only the usual Frenchmen, but also postcolonial feminists such as Anzaldúa and Spivak; and that poststructuralism has itself been equally influenced by contemporary anarchism (151). Echoing the concerns of decolonizing knowledge production, she also notes that:

> [the] omission of issues such as anarcha-feminism, black anarchism, queer anarchism, disability anarchism, etc. from post-anarchist theorizing, as well as the omission of such a wide range of theorists (contemporary post-structuralist white and non-white women writers, and both historical and contemporary anarcha-feminists and/or anti-racists, etc.) results in a serious misrepresentation of both

post-structuralist and anarchist philosophy, theory and practice in contemporary times.

(Jeppesen 2011: 151)

Jeppesen proceeds to redefine contemporary anarchism by debunking a series of myths, namely that anarchism is a white, masculinist, and heteronormative philosophy/protest movement, merely a lesser-known variant of Marxian workerism. Rather, she defines it as a practice of unlearning multiple modes of domination, through sustained, participatory collective practice, characterized by creativity and diversity of tactics; and last but not least, 'a movement toward decolonization'. Here she cites anarchism's alliances with indigenous movements for sovereignty and self-determination in the Americas and Palestine, while noting that the language of colonization, occupation, subalternity, and representation is also applied to the context of gender. Although she does not expand here upon this conflation of physical/territorial and academic/epistemic 'colonizations', she concludes that 'Post-structuralist anarchism needs to engage this kind of intersectional analysis of decolonization as it is taken up in contemporary social movements involving indigenous and other non-white anarchists' (154–155).

Tadzio Mueller (2011) too insists on the need to get unstuck from nineteenth-century definitions. Scholars who want to know what anarchism is 'need only ask today's self-described anarchists what they think it is and they are', as it dynamically evolves.[15] Drawing examples from the alter-globalization movement, namely the People's Global Action, social *consultas* since 1998, and Strasbourg No Border camp in 2002, Mueller concludes that a suitably humble and 'modest' poststructuralist anarchism, i.e. one capable of acknowledging its inescapable involvement in power relations, is our least problematic option, because if still problematic, at least it is honest. He writes,

> The uncertainty of any action undertaken from such unavoidable entanglements – which is to say all action – might be used productively to recognize that all our politics are guided by our ethics, and that ethics, not historical truth or destiny, becomes the essence of political work...
>
> (Mueller 2011: 91)

And this leads to rejection of any sense of future triumphalism or historical mission, or at least blind faith therein. For Mueller, a daily ethical practice is the only level on which to engage with other people: 'From there ... it is only a short step towards accepting the necessity and ethical acceptability of an anarchist counter-hegemony, or the creation of sustainable communities of resistance' (92) such as could be found in the sites mentioned above (which might be updated to include the euphoric social spaces and autonomous zones briefly glimpsed in 2011's Arab Spring and Occupy). Such acceptance might also enable us to 'find a route that negotiates between two types of oppression: that of too few rules/identities, and that of too many' (92). Given the failures of the organized left, 'this uncertain and modest post-structuralist anarchism' – thus named because of its refusal of faith in a predestined historical mission – 'seems to be our best shot at a new emancipatory project' (92).

Jason Adams too takes the alterglobalization movement as his reference point for the emergence of this mode of thinking and practising anarchism.[16] Drawing on Hardt and Negri, as well as Andre Gorz and Alberto Melucci, he describes a contemporary 'post-hegemonic constellation of singularities' as a mode of counter-hegemonic alliance, replacing the model of 'a universal revolutionary consciousness unified across many locations, whether based in an industrial working class or in some other foundationalist form of identity politics' (Adams 2011: 135). If power, as Foucault tells us, is dispersed throughout a field of linked nodes, then Adams hopes to apply the same principle to resistance (135). Each constituent element of the constellation is 'historically constructed by power' in a unique and multidimensional way; each in all of its fragmentary, nomadic glory, can join forces with all the other singularities, finding a balance somewhere in the wide space between total atomization and 'officialistic organizations', yielding a productive tension which may be a 'source of immense power and possibility' (137).

Conclusion: anticolonial theories

'Imperialism hijacked millions of people across the world away from local processes and into a world in which capitalist Europe pioneered the single coercive script of historical transformation' (Loomba 1998: 13). It is now the task of postcolonial scholars to be responsible anti-imperialists, to 'interrogate, perhaps even interrupt, the forms of globalization now dictated by politicians, military strategists, captains of finance and industry, fundamentalist preachers and theologians, terrorists of the body and the spirit, in short by the masters of our contemporary universe' (13). What this kind of theory can and must do, they urge, is to:

> raise with new urgency ... questions about the shifting and often interrelated forms of dominance and resistance ... the search for alternative traces of social being ... the interdependent play of race and class ... the significance of gender and sexuality ... the complex forms in which subjectivities are experienced and collectivities mobilized.
> (Loomba 1998: 13)

An anarchist agenda would agree.

Loomba and colleagues (2005b) conclude that the time has come to restore postcolonial studies to its original vocation, by 'reasserting the historical urgency' that was generated by the 'oppositional political energies' of the mid-twentieth-century decolonizing intellectuals, but got lost somewhere along the way amid the 'institutionalization of postcolonial studies as a cultural discipline dedicated to the analysis of discourse, and the ... problematization of such central – and centrally imperial – Enlightenment concepts as "development" and "modernity"' (5). Thus it can regain the ability to creatively 'represent the relation between the cultural and the state, between the imagination and the economy, between ideas and facts, evidence and interpretation', and moreover to 'mov[e] beyond ... [the] binarized intellectual genealogy' (5) that places the historical-materialist and poststructuralist dimensions of postcolonial theory in opposition to each other. Agreed, again.

From the perspective of this particular postcolonial anarchist, what's needed is already present within the theory, awaiting recommitment to practice. This means recognizing how imperialism manifests now. It also means engaging with multiple expressions of oppositional knowledge engaged in parallel or converging conversations.

Let me give a few examples. One can be found within anarchism, which also seems to be engaged these days in a reorientation towards the concept of decolonization. Andrej Grubačić recounts his own discovery of a working definition of anarchism while growing up in then-Yugoslavia. For him, anarchism is explicitly a 'project of the South' – which for him (as with the Non-Aligned Movement's Third-Worldist project) includes the Balkans – and thus distinct from hegemonic European Marxism (Grubačić 2013: 189, 198).[17] Grubačić notes the simultaneity of the classical 'anarchist moment' with the zenith of high imperialism at the turn of the 20th century, often called the moment of 'first globalization', a time in which the world seemed rife with migratory anti-colonialists. But he highlights above all the ideas of Serbian anarchist Svetozar Markovic, as rooted in local specificities and the realities of practice on the ground, rather than in universalized historical laws.[18] Clearly this is no relinquishment of revolutionary commitment through an embrace of fragmentation that refuses consistency as totalizing – a gesture that he calls 'postmodernism before the fact' (193) – but rather an embrace of diversity of tactics toward consistent goals and principles in the form of bottom-up federalism: in a word, Balkanization reclaimed. This is for him a homegrown emancipatory imaginary not based in nation-states (197), an exemplar of anarchism as a 'suppressed tradition' of Western modernity and a critical corrective to a Eurocentric left tradition; one uniquely suited to 'guide us in the construction of an anti-capitalist, non-colonialist intercultural dialogue' (199).

Another important example is elaborated in Chela Sandoval's (2000) *Methodology of the Oppressed*. She recounts that during the period of 'cultural breach' between the 1850s and 1970s, the old dominant systems were being challenged on multiple levels (economy, politics, language, psychology, science, gender). Along with this 'onslaught of transformative forces' (Sandoval 2000: 8) came an emergence of transgressive knowledge formations that combined to produce a 'post-traditional' world. These new conditions generated a vein of 'oppositional consciousness' that in all times has been 'most clearly articulated by [those whom it] subordinated' (9). For Sandoval, there is no doubt this is a neo-colonial condition; transnational capitalism 'colonizes and subjectifies' all.

Invoking Jameson, Sandoval then dubs postmodernism 'a neocolonizing global force' (though I think she means postmodernism as the cultural logic of late capitalism, which is a neo-colonizing global force) hypertrophied and hypostatized into a dangerous new phase in which former modes of 'resistance, oppositional consciousness and social movement are no longer effective' (2), although we should still seek guidance from those who developed 'methods of the oppressed ... under previous modes of colonization, conquest, enslavement, and domination', as a key to imagining '"postcoloniality" in its most utopian sense' (9): namely one that is finally a true post, beyond the centuries-old force field of colonization-globalization-imperialism. Therefore we need 'new radical cultural politics' and 'alternate forms of globalization' adequate to the task. While Jameson posed this question in the 1980s, Sandoval notes that US Third World Feminism beat him to it, offering a cognitive map of both 'inner and outer technologies' (2), meaning both psychological and social interventions, for a decolonized twenty-first century.

This 'methodology of the oppressed' will be 'transform[ed] into a methodology of emancipation' through various techniques of interpretation and application, finally combining into an 'apparatus' of love as a 'technology for social transformation',[19] while forging different sites of resistant thought into a 'dissident and coalitional consciousness' (5). Sandoval detects 'decolonial lines of force and affinity' among various 'postmodern, poststructuralist, global feminist and ethnic' tendencies in critical and cultural theory, linking them to 'the theories, hopes, desires, and aims of decolonizing sex, gender, race, ethnic, and identity liberationists' (5). Thereby, she aims to clarify a '"decolonizing theory and method" that can better prepare us for a radical turn during the new millennium, when the utopian dreams inherent in an internationalist, egalitarian, non-oppressive, socialist-feminist democracy can take their place in the real' (5). Sandoval thereby locates our source of hopeful futurity in a 'utopian postcoloniality' – a structure of feeling not unlike the stubborn anarchist demand for the impossible. Similarly, Leela Gandhi (1998) suggests that joining postcolonial studies to other modes of oppositional knowledge (including that described by Said and Foucault), might constitute a 'new humanities' that would be 'life-enhancing and constitutively opposed to every form of tyranny, domination, and abuse; its social goals are non-coercive knowledge produced in the interests of human freedom' (52). Sandoval doesn't speak of anarchism, but surely it fits into her open-hearted list of oppositional thought-streams.

Sandoval, Loomba et al., Krishnaswamy and Hawley, Rousselle and Evren: all are applying their respective theoretical frameworks – anarchism, postcolonialism, US Third World Feminism – to the question of what forms of resistance and emancipatory thought are most appropriate to understanding and confronting the current form of imperialism, colonialism, capitalism? In other words, how do we keep decolonizing now?

Notes

1. See for example Loomba et al. (2005a); Krishnaswamy and Hawley (2007); Nayar (2015); Loh and Sen (2018).
2. As Robert Brennan reminds us, 'Theories of globalization … are not necessarily "globalization theory", just as studies of colonialism, anti-colonialism, and imperialism are not necessarily postcolonial studies' (Krishnaswamy and Hawley 2007: 46).
3. In more optimistic days of the Arab Spring uprisings, some years ago, Hamid Dabashi (2012), suggested that perhaps this phenomenon indicated the end of the postcolonial and the beginning of the post-postcolonial, meaning the emergence of a new self-awareness defined by autonomous forces rather than defined in terms of historical relationship to the west. Although the optimism has dissipated in the wake of ongoing violence and conflicting aspirations, Dabashi's observation still seems pertinent, namely that the antagonists in these conflicts refer largely to each other whereas the role of the USA or any other Western power is largely irrelevant to people's desires or dilemmas, if not to their geopolitical prospects.
4. The culprits include, to use Nagesh Rao's list, theorists such as Gyan Prakash, Partha Chatterjee, Dipesh Chakrabarty, R. Radhakrishnan, Sangeeta Ray, Stephen Slemon, Carol Breckenridge et al. (Gupta et al. 2005: 242).
5. Amongst these, S. Shankar includes Arif Dirlik, Aijaz Ahmad, E. San Juan, Benita Parry, Barbara Harlow, Timothy Brennan, Satya Mohanty and Neil Lazarus (Gupta et al. 2005: 57).
6. Different positions on the spectrum range among, for example, the North American Anarchist Studies Network; UK Anarchist Studies Network; Institute for Anarchist Studies, and various research groups, conferences and fellowships now appearing at universities including the New School, Cornell, Haverford, and Loughborough, among others.
7. Of course I realize some anarchists would reject any identification with any sort of left; that is another conversation.
8. I am referring to the debate between Gyan Prakash ('Writing Post-Orientalist Histories of the Third World: Perspectives from Indian Historiography'; 'Can the "Subaltern" Ride? A Reply to O'Hanlon and Washbrook'), and Rosalind O'Hanlon and David Washbrook ('After Orientalism: Culture, Criticism and Politics in the Third World'). All these may be found in Chaturvedi (2000). For a more recent iteration of this theme, see Chibber (2013), with heated rejoinders by Partha Chatterjee and others; see Warren (2016).
9. See also (Brennan 2008: 37–38, 45–46).
10. Here too contemporary trends are clues to how thinking on these things can be distorted, on progressive as well as reactionary grounds. The commonly invoked formulation of the desire to see 'someone who looks like me' in media representations, political and professional institutions sounds empowering when used by racial or sexual minorities, chilling when used by white supremacists. So what's the distinction? Just context? Of course 'just' context is

actually of deep significance: it means no less than the very weight of history and the map of current power. Beyond this though, the point in the reflexive phrase is (or should be) not really to slot ourselves into ever-proliferating bubbles of separatist homogeneity but to redress persistent patterns of marginalization, erasure, and disenfranchisement; to upend inequitable access to the means of narrative production and material control, which would radically transform the character of the society in which all kinds of people live together – which is ultimately what the white supremacists fear. I would hate and cannot imagine seeing only people who 'look like me'. Instead of this phrase, troubling in its ambivalent implications, we should all rather say what we mean.

11 This discussion draws upon Lloyd (1997) and of course refers to Hannah Arendt (1973), *The Origins of Totalitarianism*.
12 I am taking the expedient route of quoting Gandhi here rather than Gellner and Anderson directly, because what I am primarily interested in right now is the postcolonial theorist's application of these theories of nationalism, which Gandhi aptly summarizes.
13 See also, for inspiration, Pablo Neruda, Faiz Ahmad Faiz, and many more.
14 According to May, 'The theoretical wellspring of anarchism – the refusal of representation by political or conceptual means in order to achieve self-determination along a variety of registers and at different local levels – finds its underpinnings articulated most accurately by the post-structuralist political theorists' (44). I would suggest that postcolonialism, on the other hand, far from being a simple cognate of poststructuralism, is extremely concerned with just the opposite: claiming the rights of representation in both symbolic and material, aesthetic and political, senses.
15 Mueller then walks us through a logical syllogism defining it out of existence: if resistance is counter-power (including the construction of counter-identities and counter-cultures), and power is ubiquitous and unavoidable in all practices and utterances, and assuming anarchism rejects all forms of power, then it is an impossibility as a political project. This to me seems comparable to the writing-into-a-corner of the postmodernist wing of subaltern and other postcolonial studies. Mueller finds an alternative though in actual activist practice, just as I would suggest the way out of the postcolonial theory bind lies in actual anti-colonial practice.
16 As it happens, relevant to the matter of decolonizing anarchist knowledge, Adams is probably most known for his pamphlet on non-Western anarchisms (Adams 2000).
17 Compare Robert Young (2001), who in *Postcolonialism: An Historical Introduction* suggests a definition of postcolonial theory as the location of Marxist theory in a Third World/anti-colonial context; and that context's contribution to global left thought.
18 Grubačić (2010) reclaims this word in his book, *Don't Mourn, Balkanize*. Reinforcing the comparison with the lot of postcolonial/anti-colonial intellectuals, it's telling that Markovic's ideas are far less familiar to most Western anarchists than those of Bakunin, Kropotkin or Malatesta.
19 Despite the sometimes muddled mobius-strip quality of Sandoval's semantic constructions and her fuzzy articulation, repeatedly grouping together apples and eating as comparable categories, Sandoval is getting at something very important politically and ethically.

References

Adams, J. (2002) *Non-Western Anarchisms: Rethinking the Global Context*, Johannesburg: Zabalaza Books.
Adams, J. (2011) 'The Constellation of Opposition', in D. Rousselle and S. Evren (eds.) *Post-Anarchism: A Reader*, London: Pluto Press, pp. 117–138.
Ahmad, A. (1995) 'The Politics of Literary Postcoloniality', *Race and Class*, 36(3): 1–20.
Anzaldúa, G. (1987) *Borderlands/La Frontera*, San Francisco: Spinsters/Aunt Lute Books.
Arendt, H. (1973) *The Origins of Totalitarianism*, New York: Harcourt Brace Jovanovich.
Bhabha, H. (1994) *The Location of Culture*, London: Routledge.
Brennan, T. (2008) 'Postcolonial Studies and Globalization Theory', in R. Krishnaswamy and J. C. Hawley (eds.) *The Postcolonial and the Global*, Minneapolis: University of Minnesota Press, pp. 37–53.

Carter, M., and Torabully, K. (2002) *Coolitude: An Anthology of the Indian Labour Diaspora*, London: Anthem Press.
Cesaire, A. (2001) *Discourse on Colonialism*, New York: Monthly Review Press.
Chaturvedi, V. (ed.) (2000) *Mapping Subaltern Studies and the Postcolonial*, New York: Verso.
Chibber, V. (2013) *Postcolonial Theory and the Specter of Capital*, New York: Verso.
Cooppan, V. (2005) 'The Ruins of Empire: The National and Global Politics of America's Return to Rome', in A. Loomba, S. Kaul, M. Bunzi, A. Burton and J. Esty (eds.) *Postcolonial Studies and Beyond*, Durham, NC: Duke University Press, pp. 80–100.
Curthoys, N. and Ganguly, D. (eds.) (2007) *Edward Said: The Legacy of a Public Intellectual*, Melbourne: Melbourne University Press.
Dabashi, H. (2012) *The Arab Spring: The End of Postcolonialism*, London: Zed Books.
Gandhi, L. (1998) *Postcolonial Theory*, New York: Columbia University Press.
Gilroy, P. (1993) *The Black Atlantic*, Cambridge: Harvard University Press.
Grubačić, A. (2010), *Don't Mourn, Balkanize!*, Oakland: PM Press.
Grubačić, A. (2013) 'The Anarchist Moment', in J. Blumenfeld, C. Bottici, and S. Critchley (eds.) *The Anarchist Turn*, London: Pluto Press, pp. 187–202.
Gupta, S., Kar, P.C. and Mukherji, P.D. (eds.) (2005) *Rethinking Modernity*, New Delhi: Pencraft International Publishing.
Hardt, M. and Negri, A. (2000) *Empire*, Cambridge, MA: Harvard University Press.
Hardt, M. and Negri, A. (2005) *Multitude: War and Democracy in the Age of Empire*, New York/London: Penguin.
Hardt, M. and Negri, A. (2011) *Commonwealth*, Cambridge, MA: Harvard University Press.
Hirsch, S. and van der Walt, L. (eds.) (2010) *Rethinking Anarchism and Syndicalism: The Colonial and Post-colonial Experience, 1870–1940*, Leiden: Brill.
Jameson, F. (1998) *The Cultural Turn: Selected Writings on the Postmodern, 1983-1998*, London: Verso.
Jeppesen, S. (2011) 'Things to do with Post-Structuralism in a Life of Anarchy: Relocating the Outpost of Post-Anarchism', in D. Rousselle, and S. Evren (eds.) *Post-Anarchism: A Reader*, London: Pluto, pp. 151–159.
Krishnaswamy, R. and Hawley, J.C. (eds.) (2007), *The Postcolonial and the Global*, Minneapolis: University of Minnesota Press.
Lazarus, N. (2005), 'The Politics of Postcolonial Modernism', in A. Loomba, S. Kaul, M. Bunzi, A. Burton and J. Esty (eds.) *Postcolonial Studies and Beyond*, Durham, NC: Duke University Press, pp. 423–438.
Lloyd, D. (1997) 'Nationalisms Against the State' in D. Lloyd and L. Lowe (eds.) *The Politics of Culture in the Shadow of Capital*, Durham: Duke University Press, pp. 173–198.
Loh, L. and Sen, M. (eds.), (2018) *Postcolonial Literature and Challenges for the New Millennium*, London: Routledge.
Loomba, A. (1998) *Colonialism/Postcolonialism*, New York: Routledge.
Loomba, A., Kaul, S., Bunzi, M., Burton, A. and Esty, J. (eds.) (2005a) *Postcolonial Studies and Beyond*, Durham: Duke University Press.
Loomba, A., Kaul, S., Bunzi, M., Burton, A. and Esty, J. (2005b) 'Beyond What? An Introduction?', in A. Loomba, S. Kaul, M. Bunzi, A. Burton and J. Esty (eds.) *Postcolonial Studies and Beyond*, Durham, NC: Duke University Press, pp. 1–40.
May, T. (2011) 'Is Post-structuralist Political Theory Anarchist?', in D. Rousselle and S. Evren (eds.) *Post-Anarchism: A Reader*, London: Pluto, pp. 41–45.
Mueller, T. (2011), 'Empowering Anarchy: Power, Hegemony and Anarchist Strategy', in D. Rousselle and S. Evren (eds.) *Post-Anarchism: A Reader*, London: Pluto, pp. 75–94.
Nayar, V. (ed.) (2015) *Postcolonial Studies: An Anthology*, Chichester: Wiley-Blackwell. Rao, N. (2005) 'Modernity Redux: Empire and the End of Postcolonialism', in S. Gupta, P.C. Kar and P.D. Mukherji (eds.) *Rethinking Modernity*, New Delhi: Pencraft International Publishing, pp. 233–239.

Rousselle, D. and Evren, S. (eds.) (2011) *Post-Anarchism: A Reader*, London: Pluto Press.
Said, E. (1978) *Orientalism: Western Conceptions of the Orient*, London/New York: Routledge and Kegan Paul.
Sandoval, C. (2000) *Methodology of the Oppressed*, Minneapolis: University of Minnesota Press.
Smith, A. (2013) 'The Problem with Privilege', in F.W. Twine and B. Gardener (eds.) *Geographies of Privilege*, New York: Routledge, pp. 263–280.
Soyinka, W. (1996) *The Open Sore of a Continent*, Oxford: Oxford University Press.
Warren, R. (ed.) (2016) *The Debate on Postcolonial Theory and the Specter of Capital*, New York: Verso.
Young, R. (2001) *Postcolonialism: A Historical Introduction*, Chichester: Wiley-Blackwell.

11 What is law?

Elena Loizidou

Critical jurisprudence

The question of, *what is law?*, has been addressed by a plethora of legal and political theorists and philosophers over time. The aim of this chapter is *not* to engage with this question. The critical legal theorists Costas Douzinas and Adam Gearey, in their book *Critical Jurisprudence* (2005), provide us with an apt presentation and critique of the legal theory approach to this question. As they explain, legal theorists (i.e. Kelsen, Hart) who extensively addressed this question ended up with providing us with a restricted jurisprudence or theory of law, one that focuses only upon '... [interrogating] ...the essence or substance of law' (Douzinas and Gearey 2005: 10) and, moreover, '... [assumes] that there [are] a number of markers or characteristics that map and delimit the terrain and define what is proper to law' (Douzinas and Gearey 2005: 10). More significantly, they point out that restrictive jurisprudence fails to relate to questions of justice, rights, subjectivity (gender, race, sexuality, and class), ethics, politics, aesthetics, colonialism, and the economy. I would suggest, along with Douzinas and Gearey, that restrictive jurisprudence utilizes the question of *what is law?*, to create a *pure* uncontaminated understanding of what law is, and in doing so it forgets and ignores that law is relational. Restrictive jurisprudence subtracts from its reflections on the essence of law, that law is a mechanism that is supposed to *relate* to the subjective, social, political, etc., concerns and disputes of a polity. In *Critical Jurisprudence*, Douzinas and Gearey (2005) propose a different theoretical understanding of law. They propose, not just that legal theory engages with critique (exposes the limits of law, i.e., law fails to relate to the concerns of the subject before it), a point that Douzinas and others within the UK legal studies movement have been making since the late 1980s, but moreover they suggest that legal theory turns its attention to general concerns. Such legal theory, a general and critical jurisprudence, encourages an engagement with law that returns legal theory to 'all those issues that classical philosophy examines under the titles of law and justice' (Douzinas and Gearey 2005: 10). By this the authors mean that a general jurisprudence will move away from, 'the *what is law?* question', a question that cuts off serious theoretical reflections on law and on law's relational aspects. Douzinas and Gearey anticipate that by turning to the relationship between law and justice for example, we will be able to redress what restrictive jurisprudence excludes from its reflections, questions of rights, subjectivity, the social, etc. Moreover they anticipate that a general jurisprudence will open up law to the 'ontology of social life' (Douzinas and Gearey, 2005: 11) and show how legality is prolific and 'touches all aspects of existence and leads to the modern versions of the classical *ars vivendi*, the art of living, of which law and ethics was a central part' (Douzinas and Gearey 2005: 11). A general jurisprudence, therefore, challenges a restricted jurisprudence approach – based merely on the analysis of principles, rules, and legislation – by pointing to its inadequacy and non-relationality. In this general jurisprudence's observations are in agreement with observations made by contemporary critical philosophers. For example, Giorgio Agamben and Judith Butler have noted that law does not work merely in a vacuum, nor is it 'free' from political influences (Agamben 1998, 2005; Butler 2004). On the contrary they show that law, and more specifically the operations of law, relate to an outer world, drive political agendas, and produce differential consequences on subjects and populations (refugees, women, precarious workers, etc.). In taking account of the limits of restrictive jurisprudence (non-relationality), the notion of general jurisprudence that I propose instead engages with the philosophical question that asks us to consider *who is law?*; who is recognized within law and who is excluded: who in other words becomes law. By pointing to differential treatments in law, and instances of non-recognition, general jurisprudence reacts to restrictive jurisprudential claims that see any injustices within law as internal to law and capable of correction through the alteration of rules. General jurisprudence, instead, points to the impossibility of such claiming by pointing to the relationality of law, that there is a *who* before the law (Goodrich 1990; Aristodemou 2000; Fitzpatrick 2001; Haldar 2007; Wall 2011). General jurisprudence's contribution to law and legal theory is significant. Indeed it fleshes out the skeletal and inadequate understanding of law and its operation that the very dominant restrictive jurisprudence has given to legal theory scholarship and, moreover, at least opens the way to redressing social, political, and economic imbalances by pointing to our relation to law. Nevertheless, I would like to argue that both of these schools of legal theory share one thing in common, an attachment or investment in law (Goodrich 1999). Restrictive jurisprudence is concerned with describing, correcting, and preserving law in this form, while general jurisprudence conserves law and petrifies life within its ambit, through its analysis of our relation to law. Consider Douzinas' and Gearey's words above. They bring to our attention that all aspects of life relate to law. They also point to the exclusionary practices of law; who is not a legal subject, how that exclusion comes about, how we demand through, for example, claims to rights, justice, subjective indicators (gender, race, sexuality, etc.). This proximity to law is necessary, they argue, because by keeping law at our horizon we achieve freedom (Douzinas and Gearey 2005: 354–362). Why? Because, as they aphoristically point out, '[t]he time spent before the law, the time of law's revelation, is the infinitesimal time between infancy, absence of law, and entry to the symbolic – always a deferred entry which is being acted out in the whole lifetime' (Douzinas and Gearey 2005: 361). For general jurisprudence, therefore, law is a necessary condition for our freedom. The critique of law offered by critical legal scholars does not demand a destruction of law or a creation of a life bereft of law. On the contrary, it needs law, the boundary of law in order to sustain a space of freedom for the social, economic and political demands of the polity. Irrespective of the merits of this critical theory of law it is evident that it does not aspire to 'release' life from law. In both of these legal theoretical perspectives 'life' doesn't exist outside the legal imagination. Indeed they both paint us a picture of life organized by the legal imagination.

Anarchists, however, are preoccupied neither with the '*what is law?*' question, nor with the '*who is law?*' question, but rather with the Nietzschean question: 'how shall *man* be overcome?' (Nietzsche 2003). Nietzsche's question wants us to imagine a world, a life, which thinks, organizes and creates itself outside normative, and indeed legal, restrictions. As Deleuze points out in relation to Nietzsche's question 'how shall man be overcome?', it directs us to *'a new way of thinking'*, *'a new way of feeling'*, and *'a new way of evaluating'* (Deleuze 2013: 154). It directs us to a way of life other than that formed in, through and before the law; to a way of life and not a formed life (legal in essence). If man or man's life, as general jurisprudence suggests, is legally formed, then we can say that man can overcome him/herself simply by not placing law at the centre of his existence. And in doing so s/he creates a way of life that operates without the law, without an organization of life that is based on what law allows or disallows, a factor that is not present as we have seen in either restrictive or general jurisprudence. Anarchism, I would like to propose, takes us towards such a life, a new way of evaluating, thinking and feeling. It is important also to note that such a way of life is not future oriented, but rather takes place in parallel to the dominant way of describing life, one that is 'captured' by law. Indeed, even anarchists' addressing the question, *'how shall man be overcome?'*, is indicative of the existence of subjects that think, feel, and evaluate anew the present beyond the terrain of the law. How, then, do anarchists live the question *'how shall man be overcome?'* In order to demonstrate this, I will turn to two anarchist figures of the twentieth century, Emma Goldman and Peter Kropotkin. I will show that the way these anarchists account for law, demonstrates both a *critique* of law (limits of law) that paints law as useless, injurious, unable to account for the ever-changing rhythms of life and a *way* of life that does *not* rely upon law for its existence. In the latter instance, we will be able to observe that this way of life is opened through practices such as self-mastery, frankness and *parrhesia*, to provide us with an anarchist art of living.

Why not *law*

Just as general jurisprudence reveals the limits of law, so too does an anarchist critique: both approaches demonstrate that law perpetuates injustices, that law excludes from its legal categories certain subjects, that law is fictional (Goodrich 1990; Aristodemou 2000). Unlike general jurisprudence, however, anarchist critics of law, such as Emma Goldman and Peter Kropotkin, through their courthouse speeches and published work, contend that since law cannot live up to its aspirations and protect us from the perils of the world, or provide us with justice and truth, call for its destruction. It is to these anarchists, their writings and speech acts, that I will turn now to demonstrate why deferring the destruction of law does not ensure our freedom, as Douzinas and Gearey (2005) suggest in *General Jurisprudence*, but on the contrary sustains our enslavement to the very inequalities that they hope to address in their work.

In 1917 Emma Goldman and her fellow anarchist Alexander Berkman were placed on trial for conspiracy against the *Selective Service Act 1917*. The *Selective Service Act* authorized the Federal government to conscript young men between the ages of 21 and 30 into the armed forces in preparation for the US entry into the First World War. Goldman and Berkman, along with other anarchists, lawyers, and academics, had organized various events, including a debate at the Harlem Casino on the eve (8 May 1917) of the passage of the Bill, which was attended by around 10,000 people, in order to inform citizens of the perils of war and of the devastation that the First World War was already inflicting upon Europe and why they opposed conscription. They had also published on 1 June and 2 June 1917 in their respective magazines, *The Blast* and *Mother Earth*, an essay written by Goldman against conscription (Goldman 2000:

398–399). As they both insisted at the trial, the aim of their gathering at Harlem Casino and Goldman's essay 'No Conscription League' (Goldman 2000: 398–399) was not to discourage or influence young men from enlisting. Rather, they wanted to create the space whereby they could disseminate information about the perils of the First World War and conscription to the general public, as well as enable young men to make an informed decision regarding the draft. In his closing speech to the jury, for example, Berkman categorically denied that he would encourage anyone not to register, as he himself was not of conscription age and thus would not face punishment if he decided not to register, and therefore it would be irresponsible of him to make others do what he was not compelled to do:

> I would never advise anyone to do a thing which does not endanger me. I am willing to resist tyranny. I am willing to resist tyranny if I were willing and ready to resist tyranny, I might advise others to do so, because I myself [sic] would do it. I would be with them and the responsibility. But I was exempted from that registration business. I did not have to register. I was beyond the age. I was not in danger. And would I advise anyone to do the thing which does not put me in danger?
>
> (Berkman and Goldman 2005: 54)

He also pointed out that, as an anarchist, he would leave the choice to the conscience of each man (Berkman and Goldman 2005: 28). Similarly, Goldman, in a letter sent to Mary E. Fitzgerald, her secretary and associate, and read at the first non-conscription meeting on 23 March 1917, explains why she will not urge young men not to register: 'I do not advise or urge young men to refuse to register; as an anarchist, I could not do that, because that would be taking the same position as the Government, by telling someone to do this or that. I refuse to advise young men to register, it must be left to the individual' (Supreme Court of the United States 1917: 241). Goldman and Berkman were found guilty as charged. Berkman and Goldman were sentenced to two years imprisonment and a $10,000 fine each. They were subsequently deported to Russia in 1919. The trial transcript, along with statements surrounding the trial, offers an insight into Goldman's and more generally the anarchists' relationship to law. Goldman was not afraid of the law or of punishment. Goldman never saw law as the author of her life. She did not seek, in other words, legal recognition. Law was only useful for her as a stage upon which she could express her beliefs. Thus, in 1916, she was convicted of breaching the Comstock Law of 1873 which forbade the dissemination of information on birth control. As K. Shulman writes:

> On April 20 Emma's case went to trial. Emma defended herself. Three staid judges presided over an overflowing courtroom. Emma, as always, was expected to put on the best show in town.
>
> After some witty exchanges with the prosecution, Emma turned her trial into an eloquent defence of birth control. Her closing speech to the court lasted for one rapturous hour. 'If it is a crime', she concluded with passion, 'to work for healthy motherhood and happy child-life, I am proud to be considered a criminal'.
>
> (Shulman 1971: 170)

Foreseeing 'that [they] could expect not justice' (Goldman 1970: 613) from their 1917 trial Goldman had decided to turn the courtroom and the trial into a space where anarchism would be propagated. Goldman used to conceive of the law as 'something', a stage that she could stand on and over – not by and or before (as advocates of general jurisprudence propose) – and account for a way of life that was *not* grounded on law. Goldman's attitude to law was elaborated in the 1917 trial. Indeed in this trial Goldman gave a remarkable speech to the jury where she propagated her anarchist beliefs as much as she demonstrated the limits of law (Berkman and Goldman 2005). She provides us primarily with two characteristics of law that effectively are also limits of law. The law, she argued, was hypocritical. The case against herself and Berkman rested on a 'trumped-up charge' (Berkman and Goldman 2005: 61). Furthermore, the law, she argued, was unable to capture the flow of change in life demonstrating in this way that non-relation between law and life (Berkman and Goldman 2005: 62–63). I would like to suggest that, by characterizing law as being hypocritical, Goldman demonstrates that law is grounded on deceit, on illegality. How does she then arrive at this conclusion?

For somebody to be charged with conspiracy it is required to be proven that there is an agreement between two or more parties to commit an offence and at least one of the parties performs an action in that direction. Berkman and Goldman were charged, as I have already noted, with conspiring to encourage men of conscription age not to register for military service. They were charged with section 37 of the *Criminal Code*. To be found guilty of the charge, it required firstly to be proved that they agreed amongst themselves to encourage men of conscription age not to register. This would have fulfilled one part of the *actus reus*, or conduct of the charge, that required evidence of an agreement to do as such. Furthermore, the charge required the proof of a breach of US law. They would have been in breach of US law because on 18 May 1917 the Congress had passed *The Selective Service Act 1917*. The prosecution would have needed to prove at least one overt act, or that one of them would have done something (e.g., circulating pamphlets that said so) that would have demonstrated that they were encouraging young men not to register. The prosecutor, Mr Content, addressed the charge to the jury precisely in the way I described above (Berkman and Goldman 2005: 23). In making his case the prosecutor, presented as evidence of their 'overt acts' the gathering at the Harlem Casino on 18 May, and the publication of the essay, 'No Conscription League' in *Mother Earth* on 1 June and *The Blast* on 2 June 1917.

Goldman considered the charge hypocritical. There were two main reasons that provoked her to characterize the law as such.

Firstly, it was a well-known fact that, as anarchists, both she and Berkman were against militarism, nationalism, and war. As she aptly puts it herself:

> To charge people with having conspired to do something which they have been engaged in doing most of their lives, namely their campaign against war, militarism and conscription as contrary to the best interest of humanity, is an insult to human intelligence.
>
> (Berkman and Goldman 2005: 57)

This to her eyes proved that they did not have to come to an agreement as to the dissemination of information against militarism. Recall that the charge of conspiracy against the draft requires the proof of an agreement. The second reason refers directly to whether they had breached *The Selective Service Act* itself. On 18 May when they were talking at the Harlem Casino the legislation had not passed. The Act had passed while they were in 'conference'. So on 18 May, at least, they could have not committed an offence as *The Selective Service Act* had not yet been passed. Even if we suppose that they did find out while in 'conference' that the draft had been passed, Goldman contended that they never suggested to men eligible for conscription to resist compliance, but rather as she and Berkman repeatedly stated, they merely presented them with their views against conscription in order to enable them to make their own decisions as to whether they would register or not (Supreme Court of the United States 1917: 241). Even in her essay, 'The No-Conscription League' (Goldman 2000), which was presented as evidence against her, she explained that the role of the No-Conscription League was a platform whereby support could be provided to those who have already or were about to make the decision not to register and a space where opposition to militarism, and the killing of fellow human beings, could be debated (Goldman 2000: 398). Furthermore, as she writes in the essay on the 'No- Conscription League', the platform was a legitimate matter of democratic politics, which would result in the recognition of conscientious objector status by US law, a recognition already granted by such European countries as the UK (Goldman 2000: 398).

The method of critique advanced by general jurisprudence is not dissimilar to Goldman's. Like Goldman's approach, general jurisprudence points to the inconsistencies within the law. For example, in an early essay, Costas Douzinas and Ronnie Warrington (1991) noted the paradoxical and contradictory manner in which the law delivers justice. Here they focused on the asylum seeker and the legal asylum process. The law on such occasions demands that refugees need to prove that they were persecuted and, moreover, that their fear of persecution was 'well founded'. In other words a 'well-founded' fear would need to be 'satisfied by showing (a) actual fear and (b) good reason for this fear' (Douzinas and Warrington 1991: 121). They argue that it is paradoxical that law is demanding that 'fear', an irrational emotion, be proved through reason. In other words, law's formula for delivering justice for the asylum seeker is inherently corrupted by the disparity between how law describes the ground for seeking asylum and how it asks proof to be advanced. Inevitably, they argue that legal inconsistency leads to injustice. In conclusion, they propose that for the balance to be redressed, for justice to be done, law would need to have the refugee who is seeking asylum be judged on her own terms. Law would need to understand that fear is irrational. Pointing to the inconsistencies and paradoxes of law, as we have seen, is also part of Goldman's way of critiquing law. Nevertheless it can be distinguished from the critique offered by general jurisprudence. Unlike general jurisprudence, Goldman does not merely expose the inconsistencies of the law. She goes a step further to show that law is based on untruth, that law is at its core deceitful. While general jurisprudence points to the exclusive practices of law, Goldman points to the illegalities that law engages with. There is a fundamental difference between these two critiques. The first, general jurisprudence, accuses law of being exclusionary and aspires to 'correct' the law through pointing to its exclusions. The second, the anarchist critique, does not aspire to correct the law. On the contrary, the inconsistency and illegal aspect of law becomes for anarchists a platform from which they can argue and show that the organization of society, bereft of law, may create a better life. It is not only the fictitious, deceitful aspects of law that make Goldman desire its elimination. As she points out in her closing speech to the jury, 'Progress is ever renewing, ever becoming, ever changing –

never is it within the law' (my emphasis) (Berkman and Goldman 2005: 63). Law is not imagined as the space where radical ideas and practices can be accommodated, but rather a space where the status quo is preserved. Why? Goldman eloquently suggests that,'[t]he law is stationary, fixed, mechanical, "a chariot wheel", which grinds all alike without regard to time, place and condition, without ever taking into account cause and effect, without ever going into the complexity of the human soul' (Berkman and Goldman 2005: 62–63). The law, as Peter Goodrich (1990) has shown in *Languages of Law*, is tradition or rather it preserves tradition. Goldman points out that if the jury looks into all the significant social, scientific, and cultural transformations that have taken place over time they will note that all of them took place against the law. On the contrary, the law always considered new ideas and the individuals propagating them to be criminal, as it does anarchists:

> we are criminals even like Jesus, Socrates, Galileo, Bruno, John Brown and scores of others. We are in good company, among those whom Havelock Ellis, the greatest living psychologist, describes as the political criminals ..., as men and women who out of deep love for humanity, out of a passionate reverence for liberty and an all-absorbing devotion to an ideal are ready to pay for their faith even with their blood.
> (Berkman and Goldman 2005: 63)

Goldman is not alone amongst anarchists in pointing to the law's deceitfulness, its unfairness and inability to accommodate changes in social life, to the renewal of norms. Peter Kropotkin held similar beliefs. In his essay 'Law and Authority' (2002) Kropotkin provides us with an analysis as to why law is both *useless* and *hurtful* for society (Kropotkin 2002: 212) through a brief survey of how modern law was formed. Like most modern political theorists he contrasts the relation between society and law today with the way society functioned in the state of nature, before modern law appeared. In the state of nature, Kropotkin suggests, humans did not need law. Instead of law their everyday affairs were arranged through 'customs, habits and usages' (Kropotkin 2002: 201). Humans in the state of nature were social beings that recognized that their survival necessitated interdependence, the dependence of one human on another (Kropotkin 2002: 202). His presentation of the state of nature is very different from those painted by contractarian political theorists such as Hobbes. As Saul Newman (2012) notes, Kropotkin's understanding of the state of nature is diametrically opposed to that offered by Hobbes. The state of nature was not seen as a threat to humanity. On the contrary, Kropotkin and 'anarchists see [it] as the basis of ethical community' (Newman, 2012: 313). Indeed, Kropotkin, in this particular essay, suggests the 'state of nature' operates to sustain and maintain sociality. In contrast, the introduction of law is seen as a disturbance to social cohesion. The law becomes useless and hurtful, as it does not serve society; it serves 'the ruling class' (Kropotkin 2002: 203). He demonstrates the uselessness and injurious character of law by unpacking law's operation. Kropotkin divides law 'into three principal categories: protection of property, protection of persons, protection of government' (Kropotkin 2002: 212). All three categories of law, he argues, stabilize and petrify (inscribe) customs that accommodate the ruling class at the expense of society (Kropotkin 2002: 205–206). The law is presented as injurious or hurtful because its serves the interests of few and not society at large. If we take, for example, one of the categories of laws that Kropotkin discusses, the category of law that protects the government, we will agree with him that indeed all administrative laws, from tax laws to the 'organisation of ministerial departments and their offices' (Kropotkin 2002: 214) serve to create and sustain agencies of the state, which in turn will be invested in protecting the 'privileges of the possessing classes' (Kropotkin 2002: 212). If we also turn to laws protecting the person, primarily criminal laws that are supposed to appeal to the whole social body or cater for the security of all, one must agree with him that they mainly protect personal property, and these crimes occur because wealth is unequally distributed (Kropotkin 2002: 215). Indeed even if we look at something as crude as the British Crime Survey 2013, we note that more than half of offences committed between 2012 and 2013 were property related offences (ONS 2013: 42). If indeed the law protects those who possess power, that is it protects private property and not the social body, then Kropotkin's description of law as useless and injurious offers a succinct critique of law and its aspirations to deliver justice and equality. The problem can be redressed, Kropotkin argues, by creating a society where the solution to crimes against persons does not lie in better laws or in more severe forms of punishment, but rather in the abolition of private property, which he considers as the root cause of most crimes. (Kropotkin 2002: 215–216). Thus, if law cannot protect society, but instead sustains and expands the power of the ruling class, for Kropotkin it becomes injurious. Why? It subtracts from the social body the equal distribution achieved in the state of nature and, moreover, it denigrates the positions and welfare of those who are ruled. And as law cannot deliver what it promises, Kropotkin proposes, 'No more law! No more judges!' (Kropotkin 2002: 315). Unlike the critique of general jurisprudence offered by critical legal theorists, a critique that, as Newman (2012) aptly observes, 'aim[s] at the anarchic deconstruction of law and propose[s] a contestation of legal authority and violence' (Newman 2012: 310) but does not take this critique further, anarchists, or at least the examples of early twentieth-century anarchists that I have discussed above, seek the disappearance of law. Anarchists call for the complete destruction of law because they understand that law's very constitution is steeped in its inability to follow the flow and changes in life. Why? Because '[t]he law is stationary, fixed, mechanical' (Berkman and Goldman 2005: 62–63). As Kropotkin argued, because law is an apparatus for the ruling classes, it provides 'permanence to customs imposed by themselves for their own advantage' (Kropotkin 2002: 205). Moreover law is deceptive (Goldman); law is useless and injurious (Kropotkin). Goldman and Kropotkin, through their critique of law, clearly point to the fact that a legal form of life does not correspond to the practices or ethos of law itself (truth, justice, transparency, equality). While critical legal scholars such as Douzinas and Gearey may point to this non-correspondence, to the non-correspondence between legal form and legal operation, they at the same time believe that the violence created by the gap between legal form and legal operation can only be redressed through differing justice; by constantly challenging the borders of law. For this purpose the boundary of law, and consequently the existence of law and not its destruction, is necessary for the achievement of freedom and justice. Their response is not necessarily paradoxical. Let us not forget that Derrida's philosophical writings have been extremely influential to this movement (Fitzpatrick 2001). And Derrida never saw himself as an anarchist despite the fact that he put to task the very idea of *arche*. In an interview given to Lorenzo Fabbri in the journal of *Critical Inquiry*, Jean-Luc Nancy explains that Derrida was not concerned to rehabilitate a certain type of politics, or to propose a new politics, but rather to undo the foundations of politics. Derrida was in search of another way of thinking through the questioning of authority, freedom and sovereignty:

> Not one more politics, but another thought of politics, or else another thought than politics, if politics is inextricably linked to the arche in general (or else one must re-interrogate from top to bottom the theme of the arche in general – the anarchy of the arche...)
>
> (Nancy 2007: 435)

For Derrida, pre-packaged political theories, such as anarchism and Marxism, were a constraint to his thought: '[h]e tried to be truly philosophical in politics, rather than applying or reconstructing a "political philosophy." It could be said that, for him ... communist politics, anarchist politics, and so on were outdated' (Nancy 2007: 433). Nevertheless, while Derrida may have not been attracted to anarchism as ideology, he was deeply interested in finding a different way of thinking and being in the world, even an ethos, something that as we will see below is very much at the heart of an anarchist way of life, and very absent from general jurisprudence or critical legal studies, which holds to a way of life and thinking that is hostage to law. Goldman and Kropotkin demonstrate that there is a way of life that is lived without the law. As we shall see below, such a life requires self-mastery, rather than subjugation to law. Such a life requires frankness as opposed to hypocrisy; such a life requires free-speaking as opposed to legal speech.

The art of living: anarchism

Anarchism's critique of law, and particularly the anarchist insistence on the destruction of law, obliges us to look for the specific ways in which anarchists lived their lives or for specific practices that enable us to understand how they lived their lives beyond the law. What does an anarchist way of life consist of? I have argued elsewhere (Loizidou 2011) that such a way of life does not articulate a coherent set of values that one has to follow in order to have such a life. In order to understand an anarchist way of life we need to observe the way actual anarchists lived their lives. In doing so we will be able to formulate an ethics of existence or an art of living akin to what Foucault identified as being present in Greek and Roman life: *parrhesia* ('freely speaking' or self-mastery) (Foucault 2005: 373). An anarchist ethical self is concerned with mastering oneself and not subjugating oneself to a juridical order (Foucault 1991: 348). It is impossible in this chapter to demonstrate the array of practices that lead to an anarchist art of existence. Instead I will focus on two vignettes, which are indicative of self-mastery and parrhesia. The first vignette draws on Kropotkin's understanding of how self-mastery can be achieved. The second draws from Emma Goldman's life which exhibits how parrhesia or 'freely speaking' is integral to an anarchist ethics of existence.

Kropotkin, in 'Law and Authority', proposes that, '[l]iberty, equality and practical human sympathy are the only effectual barriers we can oppose to the anti-social instincts ...', the very bad habits that law itself perpetuates (Kropotkin 2002: 218). At the start of this essay Kropotkin also writes:

> In existing States a fresh law is looked upon as a remedy for evil. Instead of themselves altering what is bad, people begin by demanding a law to alter it. If the road between two villages is impassable, the peasant says: 'There should be a law

about parish roads'. If a park-keeper takes advantage of the want of spirit in those who follow him with servile observance and insults one of them, the insulted man says, 'There should be a law to enjoin more politeness upon park-keepers.' ... In short, a law everywhere and for everything! A law about fashions, a law about mad dogs, a law about virtue, a law to put a stop to all the vices and all the evils which result from human indolence and cowardice.

(Kropotkin 2002: 196–197)

Kropotkin provides us with a cursory insight into an anarchist ethics of existence. An anarchist ethics of existence, Kropotkin argues, requires that humans solve everyday problems by themselves, without routinely and habitually turning to law. His references to 'liberty, social practical sympathy and equality' should be read not as ideals but rather as practices that express our self-mastery and dispense with the law. 'Liberty' is one of the antidotes to the perils of law: it can be achieved precisely through self-mastering our everyday disputes; it can be achieved through thinking together (practical social sympathy) what is at stake in a dispute and in turn this self-mastery over our own affairs will make the law irrelevant. The practice of self-mastery undoes our reliance on law, and it undoes the habitual ways of solving our social disputes that tend automatically to turn to law.

Kropotkin's call for self-mastery finds a paradigmatic advocate in Emma Goldman. Her attitude towards the laws expressed in her speech to the jury during the trial in 1917 is an example of parrhesiatic speech or 'speaking freely' (Loizidou 2011: 175–183). But before introducing another instance where Goldman talks truth to power let us turn to Foucault's interpretation of *parrhesia*. Foucault writes:

> [*parrhesia*] refers both to the moral quality, the moral attitude or the ethos, if you like, and to the technical procedure or techne, which are necessary, which are indispensable, for conveying true discourse to the person who needs it to constitute himself as a subject of sovereignty over himself and as a subject of veridiction on his own account. So, for the disciple really to be able to receive true discourse in the correct way, at the right time, and under the right conditions, the master must utter this discourse in the general form of parrhesia ... What is basically at stake in parrhesia is what could be called somewhat impressionistically, the frankness, freedom and openness that leads one to say what one has to say, as one wishes to say it, when one wishes to say it, and in the form one thinks is necessary to say it. The term parrhesia is so bound up with the choice, decision, and attitude of the person speaking that the Latins translated it by, precisely, libertas.
>
> (Foucault 2005: 372)

In another vignette from her life, Goldman demonstrates that the first premises of her anarchist belief address the law's practices. Goldman proposes a new way of thinking and new way of life that embodies the notion of parrhesia described above. On 6 April 1908 Emma Goldman was returning to the US from Canada. At the border she was stopped and questioned by the Board of Special Inquiry for Immigration. The purpose of the questioning was to establish if Goldman held US citizenship. The US government wanted to deport Goldman, who was born in Königsberg in the German Empire, on the basis that her US citizenship was invalid, because it was granted through her marriage to Jacob A. Kersner (whom the US government denaturalized because he presented a false birth certificate in his application of naturalization). The hearing concluded that no matter what the status of her husband's nationality, Goldman was not an alien and therefore not in breach of the US naturalization act. Inspector Robbins, one of the three inspectors, who questioned her found that Goldman was telling the truth because, 'from the general attitude of Miss Goldman before the Board, and her evident willingness to answer questions, and her manner of answering those questions, I am inclined to the belief that she is telling the truth' (Goldman 2005: 311). Emma Goldman's answers were indeed open, honest and frank, hiding nothing, and being afraid of nothing. Let us consider some of the answers that she gave to the board. When Emma Goldman was asked by the Chairman of the Board Carr whether she can 'swear to tell the truth' (Goldman 2005: 307) she answered: 'Being an atheist, I will only affirm, not swear'. Upon hearing this Carr pressed with a further question:

Q. Do you consider an affirmation binding both legally and morally?

And to this Goldman answers.

A. I certainly do. It is just like giving my word of honor, and I would stick to it (Goldman 2005: 307).

Goldman was asked about her beliefs.

Q. As an anarchist, I understand that you believe in no Government? Is that correct?

A. Exactly. I believe in man governing himself. Each man.

Q. Do you believe in the overthrow of existing governments by force or violence or otherwise?

A. I believe in the method laid down by the Constitution of the United States, that when the government becomes despotic and irksome the people have the right to overthrow. You will have to hold the Government of the United States responsible for that. The Government of the United States was formed by the people uprising to crush a despotic power.

Q. You refer to the Declaration of Independence rather than the Constitution do you not?

A. It is in the Declaration of Independence instead of the Constitution but the Constitution provides for it too.

Q. Do you believe that the Government of the United States has reached such a stage you describe now?

A. Well, the people haven't reached the stage of overthrowing it and therefore I suppose they are satisfied (Goldman 2005: 307)

In her answers Goldman suggests that anarchist politics requires an anarchist ethos – an ethos that requires one to speak the truth, as the auditor sees it, irrespective of whether the receiver of truth may be power or law *per se*. Goldman embodies in these answers how life could be lived without law. It is of course a life that is parallel to the one offered by law; it is a life that cannot be absorbed by the juridical order, and cannot be seen as a corrective to law, as proposed by the discipline of critical legal studies. Anarchism, Goldman believes, means each individual governing him/herself.

Afterthoughts

As I suggested at the start of this chapter, in the words and writings of Kropotkin and Goldman I find that the questions of *what is law?* or *who is law?* are displaced. Instead we find an engagement with the question of 'how shall man be overcome?' It is in the engagement, the battling with this question, that the law is destroyed. We can even say that the very engagement that does not address law, that does not put law at its centre of inquiry, will enable the quiet destruction of the law and the birth of 'a new way of thinking', 'a new way of imagining', 'a new way of creating'. It gives way to an anarchist way of living whose companions are self-mastery and parrhesia. The law is displaced by this form of imagination.

References

Agamben, G. (1998) *Homo Sacer, Sovereign Power and Bare Life*, trans. D. Heller-Roazen, Stanford: Stanford University Press.
Agamben, G. (2005) *State of Exception*, trans. K. Attell,Chicago: Chicago University Press.
Aristodemou, M. (2000) *Law & Literature: Journeys from Her to Eternity*, Oxford: Oxford University Press.
Berkman, A. and GoldmanE. (2005) *Trial and Speeches of Alexander Berkman and Emma Goldman: In the United States District Court, in the City of New York, July, 1917*, New York: Elibron Classics.
Butler, J. (2004) *Precarious Life: The Powers Of Mourning and Violence*, London, New York: Verso.
Deleuze, G. (2013) *Nietzsche and Philosophy*, trans. H. Tomlinson,London: Bloomsbury.
Douzinas, C. and Gearey, A. (2005) *Critical Jurisprudence: The Political Philosophy of Justice*, Oxford: Hart Publishing.
Douzinas, C. and Warrington, R. (1991) '"A Well-Founded Fear of Justice": Law and Ethics in Postmodernity', *Law and Critique*, 2(2): 115–147.
Fitzpatrick, P. (2001) *Modernism and the Grounds of Law*, Cambridge: Cambridge University Press.
Foucault, M. (1991) 'On the Genealogy of Ethics: An Overview of Work in Progress', in P. Rabinow (ed.) *The Foucault Reader*, London: Penguin, pp. 340–372.
Foucault, M. (2005) *The Hermeneutics of the Subject Lectures at the College de France 1981–82*, trans. G. Burchell, New York: Palgrave Macmillan.
Goldman, E. (1970) *Living My Life: Volume Two*, New York: Dover Publications.
Goldman, E. (2000) 'No Conscription League' in P. Glassgold (ed.) *Anarchy! An Anthology of Emma A. Goldman's Mother Earth*, New York: Counterpoint, pp. 398–399.
Goldman, E. (2005) *A Documentary History of the American Years: Volume 2: Making Speech Free, 1902–1909*, C. Falk (ed.), Berkeley: University of California Press.
Goodrich, P. (1990) *Languages of Law: From Logics of Memory to Nomadic Masks*, London: Weidenfeld and Nicolson.
Goodrich, P. (1999) 'The Critic's Love of the Law: Intimate Observations on an Insular Jurisdiction', *Law and Critique*, 10(3): 343–360.
Haldar, P. (2007) *Law, Orientalism and Postcolonialism: The Jurisdiction of the Lotus-Eaters*, London: Routledge Cavendish.
Kropotkin, P. (2002) 'Law and Authority' in R.N. Baldwin (ed.) *Peter Kropotkin: Anarchism a Collection of Revolutionary Writings*, Mineola, NY: Dover Publications, pp. 195–218.

Loizidou, E. (2011) 'This is What Democracy Looks Like', in J. Martel and J.C. Klausen (eds.) *How Not to Be Governed: Reading and Interpretations from a Critical Anarchist Left*, New York: Lexington Books, pp. 167–187.
Nancy, L.J. (2007) 'Philosophy as Chance: An Interview with Jean Luc Nancy', in L. Fabbri (ed.) *Critical Inquiry*, 33(2): 427–440.
Newman, S. (2012) 'Anarchism and Law: Towards a Post-Anarchist Ethics of Disobedience', *Griffith Law Review*, 21(2): 307–329.
Nietzsche, F. (2003) *Thus Spoke Zarathustra*, London: Penguin.
ONS (2013) *Crime in England and Wales, Year Ending March 2013*, http://www.ons.gov.uk/ons/dcp171778_318761.pdf (accessed 15 August 2013).
Shulman, K. A. (1971) *To the Barricades: The Anarchist Life of Emma Goldman*, New York: Crowell.
Supreme Court of the United States (1917) *Goldman [&] Berkman v United States*: Transcript of Record, Sept. 25, 1–531.
Wall, R.I. (2011) *Human Rights and Constituent Power: Without Model or Warranty*, London: Routledge.

12 Anarchism and education studies

Judith Suissa

Introduction

Education has been a central theme in anarchist thought and practice at least since William Godwin famously expressed his misgivings about the prospect of state-controlled education in 1793: 'Before we put so powerful a machine under the direction of so ambiguous an agent, it behoves us to consider well what it is that we do' (Godwin 1986: 147). The historical tradition of experiments in anarchist and libertarian education is an integral part of the anarchist movement (see Smith 1983; Avrich 2006; Suissa 2006), and today one can find anarchist ideas and approaches in many of the alternative educational projects that exist outside the state system. Meanwhile, the flourishing of contemporary social movements opposing dominant political and cultural narratives has gone hand in hand with a commitment to exploring and developing pedagogical practices that are often either explicitly or implicitly anarchist (see Haworth 2012; Springer et al. 2016; Haworth and Elmore 2017). Yet while the conceptual and political connections between educational practice and anarchist revolutionary praxis have been clearly articulated, what role – if any – is there for anarchists within the academic field of education? In the following discussion I will explore this question from the point of view of my own discipline, philosophy of education. To begin with, it will be helpful to consider the changing role of the disciplines within the field of educational studies.

The status and role of the foundation disciplines in education is currently the subject of intense debate, largely as a result of broad political currents that are changing the very nature of higher education. The future of university-based teacher education is unclear given, amongst other things, the recent introduction of Teach First, Schools Direct and other school-based models, which aim to shift the control of teacher training to schools, who will purchase training courses and other 'products' from universities and private providers in a competitive market. Yet as John Furlong (2013: 3) points out, there is a long history of debate over the role of university-based knowledge within professional education. While many theorists talk of education not as a discipline with its own epistemological coherence and rigour but as a field informed by and drawing on a range of different disciplines (see Peters 1977), Furlong makes the case for regarding education as a discipline in its own right, arguing that it functions as a discipline institutionally and politically (Furlong 2013: 4). The reason this has not historically been the case is that 'education has always been dominated by its involvement with teacher education' (Furlong 2013: 4). Following the Robbins Report of 1963, which recommended that initial teacher education become a degree level course, teacher education was fully incorporated into higher education, first in specialist colleges, and eventually as part of the university system. In keeping with the Report, which recommended that teacher education programmes be 'liberal in content and approach' (Furlong 2013: 24) and emphasize academic, rather than practical, training, 'the "foundation" disciplines of psychology, sociology, philosophy and history of education provided the academic content which degree-level work was deemed to require' (Oancea and Bridges 2010: 55). This in turn led to an expansion and flourishing of these disciplines within departments and schools of education.

However, following the 'turn to the practical' in the 1980s (Furlong and Lawn 2010: 6), the role of the disciplines in teacher education has been somewhat more precarious. Unlike in the heyday of the disciplines, there are now very few dedicated academic posts in the philosophy, sociology, history, and psychology of education, and very little support in the way of research funding for scholars working in these disciplines. Yet in spite of these broader political currents, the disciplines have continued to flourish through academic networks, specialist journals, conferences and other activities beyond institutional structures (Oancea and Bridges 2010; Furlong 2013). Is there, then, in this shifting landscape of educational studies, and within a higher education system increasingly dominated by neo-liberal agendas, a role for academics sympathetic to libertarian and anarchist educational values and practices? And how, if at all, can philosophy of education contribute to this project? There is, of course, a familiar scepticism from within the anarchist movement towards the very idea of anarchist studies within state-controlled higher education systems. However, my own view is that we need to regard the university, as Kaltefleiter and Nocella (2012: 201) suggest, 'not only as an instrument of state power but also as a site of cultural resistance'. Trying to maintain a commitment to anarchist positions and activism within the academy is bound to sometimes lead to difficult compromises, not to mention regular attacks of self-doubt, as eloquently articulated by Nathan Jun (2012). Yet as Jun reminds us, the life of academics, especially young and mid-career academics in the current climate, is far removed from the image of the lone scholar in the ivory tower. Academics in public universities are increasingly subject to restrictive and narrowly-defined funding regimes and research priorities and find themselves grappling on a daily basis with the realities of neo-liberal economic policies. There is surely a role for anarchist academics, alongside other critical colleagues, in offering alternative narratives and collective strategies for resistance to the repressive effects of this regime on our working lives (e.g. the managerial governance of daily activities; the casualization of the labour force; instrumental conceptions of teaching, learning, and research). It is indeed the very possibility of collegial and collective action that is so under threat in the modern university. Yet this aspect of life in the academy is not what I want to focus on here.

Partly as a result of current changes in funding, a major part of the work-load of academics is teaching and, as Jun notes, questions about the value of our work as anarchist praxis are crucially connected to questions of what, how, and why we teach (Jun 2012: 290). I believe that philosophy of education is uniquely placed in this regard. As philosophers, our academic work involves the systematic attempt to explore, articulate, and develop the fundamental moral, conceptual, and political assumptions underlying educational policy and practice, and to demonstrate how at the heart of all serious questions about education are deep philosophical questions: What is knowledge? What values are worth promoting and why? How should we organize society and how should we bring children up to play a role in our society? At the same time, as many of our students are themselves teachers, these questions are never abstract intellectual exercises, but involve a rigorous engagement with the realities of educational practice and policy as reflected in the world of schools and other formal and informal educational settings in which many of our students are immersed. For in spite of the growth of educational research as a distinctive area of enquiry (and a significant source of funding), it remains the case that teacher education is the main business of education faculties in both the UK and the USA. Although teacher education is currently in flux, it is still likely that significant numbers of people going on to become teachers will attend university, whether on education courses or other programmes. And given this reality, it is important that, in the course of their studies, these students encounter educational ideas that challenge the dominant, mainstream discourse. It would be both intellectually and politically worrying if young people training to be teachers, coming back to university to do a Masters as part of their professional development, or pursuing an academic interest in education, did not get the opportunity to engage with the rich world of educational ideas provided by the history of radical and alternative educational experiments. There is, then, a clear role for philosophers of education in articulating the conceptual and normative underpinnings of these ideas, and in ensuring that the challenging moral and political questions raised over the years by these dissenting and critical voices remain alive and vibrant. There are however some serious obstacles to fulfilling this role. First, there are external obstacles to do with the position of philosophy of education within faculties and schools of education, some of which I have already touched upon. Second, there are internal obstacles to do with the intellectual focus and dominant paradigms within the discipline. I shall discuss both these sets of obstacles in what follows, as well as defending the critical role of philosophy of education.

The discourse of 'what works?'

Summing up the changes described in the above historical account, Richard Pring (2010: 21) remarks, 'Thirty or more years ago, philosophy was an essential and much needed component in the education of teachers. Now it is no longer regarded as such.' Clearly, this shift in itself signals a reluctance on the part of educational policy makers to engage in, or to encourage teachers to engage in, deep philosophical thinking about education, 'its aims and purposes, its content or its links with the wider preoccupations of society' (Pring 2010: 21). Thus philosophers of education – along with other colleagues engaged in theoretical research – are up against a cultural climate of hostility towards certain forms of intellectual enquiry. The implication of much educational theory and policy discourse is that the big questions about education – 'What is the purpose of education?'; 'Who should educate?'; 'Who should control education?' – have already been answered. This hostility is itself symptomatic of a neo-liberal ideology in which the supreme question is 'what works?', and which has very real ramifications for the working conditions of academics. Institutional demands and priorities are, to a large extent, dictated by the funding regime of the Research Excellence Framework (REF), which now requires that academics demonstrate the 'social and economic impact' of their research. It thus is becoming practically, if not intellectually, more difficult for academics to engage in the kind of critical scholarship that develops sustained analyses of the conceptual underpinnings of our current educational institutions and practices and questions their legitimacy, rather than demonstrating or disproving the 'effectiveness' of specific policy-driven interventions.

As Edwin Keiner explains, the state mechanisms of educational policy and political control of education and the state funding regime on which many academic researchers are dependent demand

> 'applicable' and 'useful' knowledge in order to justify decisions scientifically and, at the same time, hide their own weaknesses and produce 'cover' for politically justified decisions. From this point of view, scepticism, doubt and questioning –constitutive for modern science and research – is perceived more and more as ineffective, a non-productive outcome of the academic discipline. Other concepts i.e. usefulness, accountability, applicability, prognostic capacity, efficiency, power, impact of knowledge, evidence-based research, have gained in importance.
>
> (Keiner 2010: 159–160)

In addition to these general institutional constraints on critical scholarship, there is a further reason why anarchist perspectives in particular struggle to be heard within education departments. For the very focus on teacher education that allowed these departments, and the scholarship and research undertaken within the foundation disciplines of education, to flourish, also means that nearly all work within them is oriented towards the formal, institutional setting of schooling. Any academics researching educational issues in informal and non-school settings, let alone questioning the very institution of state schooling, are bound to be seen as something of an anomaly.

The neo-liberal education system

The institutional academic environment described above is symptomatic of the wider cultural and political forces of neo-liberalism, the ideological underpinnings of which have been rigorously challenged within the academy. Critical sociologists of education have analyzed and documented the socio-economic consequences of neo-liberal reforms in education, showing how, as Stephen Ball (1993: 12) puts it, 'the operation and effects of an education market benefit certain class groups and fractions to the detriment and disadvantage of others.' Ball (1993: 17) has argued that 'we have to understand the [education] market as a system of exclusion', where existing social inequalities are accentuated but remain hidden under the guise of 'choice'. This sociological analysis of the detrimental effects on socio-economic inequality of market-driven policy reforms is accompanied by philosophical critique of the way the language and conceptual underpinnings of the neo-liberal discourse signal a worrying shift in the way we understand the very meaning of 'education' and related concepts:

> Prospective students are represented as customers/markets in order to justify commodifying educational services. Knowledge becomes a product for individual students to consume, rather than a collaborative process for students and teachers. Individualized learning both promotes and naturalizes life-long re-skilling for a flexibilized, fragmented, insecure labour market. ... [and] a global competitive threat and opportunity is invoked to justify commodifying all institutional arrangements.
>
> (Levidow 2001: 16)

A related critique has been articulated by Emery Hyslop-Margison and Ayaz Naseem about the world of educational research, which, they argue, is dominated by the scientistic paradigm. They analyze the historical origins of this paradigm, its ideological underpinnings, and its pernicious effects on current debates about educational practice and policy. Specifically, they discuss how 'by blaming educational failure on "bad teaching" or "failing schools", any analysis of the structural inequities denying many students access to the intellectual capital consistent with academic success is avoided' (Hyslop-Margison and Naseem 2007: 106). The accumulation of a range of data and evidence of these systematic connections between structural inequalities and educational achievement is ignored, they point out, because it invalidates 'a conservative and corporate driven ideological agenda based largely on social Darwinian principles and micro-level accountability' (Hyslop-Margison and Naseem 2007: 106).

Defending education

In the climate described above, what chance is there for anarchist ideas to become a part of philosophy of education as a critical practice? The important criticisms of the neo-liberal discourse and its effects on education illustrate the climate within which educational theorists and practitioners are working, and suggest a possible answer to the question of why it is that the very model of state education is rarely problematized by contemporary scholars. For we live in a time when calls for 'rolling back the state' are coming from agents with agendas very different from the collective, egalitarian values of the social anarchists. In this climate, it is hardly surprising that those academics and teachers concerned to defend a vision of education as a public good and a commitment to social justice and equality, find themselves defending liberal state education against the forces of privatization and marketization. Within philosophy, as I shall discuss in further detail below, the implicit or explicit statism of both mainstream and critical positions is often accompanied by a kind of suspicion of the political. Contemporary philosophers of education have extended the sociological critique described above, focusing on the dominant language, logic, and conception of education implicit in policy and curricular documents and in popular discourse on education, specifically on the dominance of performativity in educational thought and practice (see e.g. Blake et al. 1998, 2000; Smith 2002; Standish 2007). In articulating an alternative, richer account of education, several philosophers have turned to the notion of education as a practice. Thus philosophers of education such as Joseph Dunne and Padraig Hogan (drawing on the work of Alasdair MacIntyre) emphasize the intrinsic quality of educational practices and relationships and have developed accounts of 'the goods internal to education' – accounts that go hand in hand with a concern that conceptualizing educational success in terms connected to the productive, political, and economic sphere runs the risk of subverting or displacing these intrinsic goods (see Dunne 2005; Hogan 2010, 2011). To the extent that politics appears at all in such work, it is as something 'external' from which the practice of education must be protected in order to preserve its integrity. Padraig Hogan defends this view particularly forcefully, arguing that educational practice needs to 'emerge from its historic subordination to paternalistic and bureaucratic masters, and to lay claim in an articulate and sure-footed way to its own identity as a human practice' (Hogan 2011: 30). From the perspective of this position, both work by philosophers of education defending the aims of education in a liberal society (White 1990, 2011; Levinson 1999; Callan 1997) and work within the critical pedagogy tradition that sees education as a means to emancipatory social change, runs the risk of 'subverting' education and distorting its internal goods, and suggests a dangerous form of closure (Standish 1995).

The contemporary landscape of work in philosophy of education, then, seems to present us with two sets of contrasts: one the one hand, the contrast between defending the internal goods of education as a human practice or subverting it by conceiving education instrumentally, as a means to achieving external social, political or economic ends; and on the other, the contrast between defending public state education as a guarantor of minimal social justice and equality, or undermining the value of equality and the notion of education as a public good through pursuing neo-liberal, marketized forms of educational provision. Both these sets of contrasts, however, represent what Dewey described as 'false dualisms'. Their hold on the way debates within the discipline are framed suggests, I argue, a serious lack of philosophical and political imagination, and the misleading models that they suggest can be fruitfully challenged by a serious engagement with anarchist theory.

The philosophical imagination

There is good reason to believe that philosophy is a discipline particularly suited to the kind of rigorous, critical exploration of fundamental ideas, values, and assumptions inherent in the anarchist position. Nathan Jun has defended this idea of philosophy from an anarchist perspective, pointing out that it goes beyond any superficial notion of 'critical thinking' (Jun 2012: 295). Alice Oancea and David Bridges (2010: 2) too note that it is in philosophy that processes of 'analysis, argumentation and critique are given most central, systematic and comprehensive attention'. One could also argue, as Oancea and Bridges do, that contributions to the contemporary field of philosophy of education are not completely governed by external policy agendas, so potentially have more space for imaginative engagement. Likewise, as they point out, there are many opportunities for philosophical teaching on the increasing number of BA programmes in education studies that are not tied to practical teacher training. Thus philosophy of education, one may think, is well placed to take up a role of critical reflection on central political questions, thereby challenging dominant assumptions, theoretical models and policy trends. Cris Mayo (2012) explicitly defends a radical, critical role for philosophy of education, arguing that:

> In times that demand easy answers that have been destructive, philosophy of education, I think, needs to maintain its problem-posing approach and encourage students to think through the dangers caused by certainty but to also maintain a curiosity about how to approach these problems.
>
> (Mayo 2012: 5)

In pursuing this project, philosophers of education, Mayo suggests, should form alliances with other critical movements and scholars. For

> it may be that our very marginality will give us renewed energies for problematizing education. Occupying our marginal position carefully and in concert with other marginal inquiries, I think, will do our field good ... [P]hilosophy of education is about holding concepts and movements in tension, bending the implications

of commonplace, commonsensical ideas about education, and carefully examining all of these manoeuvres for the exclusions they wittingly and unwittingly produce. Problematizing the certainties derived from majoritarian positions, be it whiteness, Westernness, or any other dominant perspective, can provide us with a diversity of claims to scrutinize and epistemological positions to be wary of .

(Mayo 2012: 43)

Richard Pring, while not necessarily endorsing this radical position, adds an important dimension to this rejection of the formal and narrow notion of philosophy as focused on the logic and analysis of concepts, and questions the simplistic model whereby philosophy, like other 'theory' produced by academic enquiry, must demonstrate its 'relevance' to improving the practice of education. As Pring argues,

We live in a world of ideas. These ideas shape thinking about practice (whether that be the practice of the teacher or the practice of policymakers) in unacknowledged ways. One function of philosophy is to make these ideas explicit, to subject them to criticism, and to influence practice, not by providing alternative theories or bodies of knowledge for the guidance of practice, but by ensuring that the assumptions behind practice are tenable and coherent.

(Pring 2010: 24)

While I would not disagree with this view, I would add, echoing Mayo, a more explicitly moral and political dimension to it: What is important is not just that the assumptions behind (educational) practice are coherent, but that they are morally and politically defensible. This is where the significance of an encounter with radical educational ideas, including those of the anarchist movement, can be seen to be crucial for anyone studying education, especially anyone interested in philosophical questions about the control and content of education.

Stuck with the state

In addition to the external constraints discussed above, there are internal constraints preventing philosophy of education from taking on the radical and intellectually critical role described here. These are hinted at in Pring's work where, immediately following his defence of a broad critical role for philosophy of education, he goes on to talk of the education *system*, as if the existence and form of this system were not in itself an assumption in need of questioning. Pring's comments are symptomatic of the assumption of statism that characterizes most contemporary work in philosophy of education. Roger Marples, in a standard introduction to the discipline (Marples 2010: 35), articulates a view common to most mainstream theorists in philosophy of education, who, whether or not they are working within the analytic tradition, still assume that a central task of the philosopher is to articulate a set of general aims of education, and that this, in turn, requires 'some attempt on the part of government ... to formulate a coherent and plausible set of overall aims'. A reluctance to question seriously the mainstream paradigms within which debates about education are conducted is evident even in work by philosophers of education that can be described as 'critical' in the sense that it articulates and defends accounts of educational equality or justice that imply serious challenges to current educational policies. Yet a lot of this work, most of which is conducted from an explicitly liberal egalitarian framework, assumes that a certain amount of socio-economic inequality is here to stay, an assumption which is of course inherent in the Rawlsian framework within which this work is positioned. So even philosophers of education who propose fairly 'radical' policy measures such as abolishing private schools and introducing rigorous systems of state intervention in order to minimize the effects of family background on children's educational opportunities, do not question the liberal statist framework, or indeed the liberal model itself. Yet as Charles Mills has argued, 'the abstractions of ideal theory are not innocent' (Mills 2004: 179), and theoretical accounts constructed on a model of the polity that is still thought of as essentially liberal-democratic can, as he points out, 'blind people to the serious failings of actual real political life' (ibid.). It is, I suggest, the assumption of the state and the institutional framework of state education as the conceptual territory on which all debates about education take place, and a connectedly narrow view about the meaning of and possibilities for social change, that lies behind the lack of philosophical imagination I refer to, and that thus prevents philosophy of education from fulfilling a more radical, critical role.

The (capitalist) state is there implicitly in the work of philosophers within the analytic tradition from the 1970s, and explicitly in the work of prominent contemporary theorists such as Harry Brighouse, Eamonn Callan, Richard Pring, John White, Patricia White, and Christopher Winch. Indeed one could argue that while this tradition was once centrally concerned with a defence of 'liberal education', it is now more accurately described as focused on 'education in the liberal state'. Yet the state itself is rarely argued for by philosophers of education who, like most political philosophers, seem to assume that, however imperfect, it is somehow inevitable. In short, while theorists have noted that most contemporary political philosophy suffers from a 'state fixation' (Miltrany, in Sylvan 1993: 215), this is doubly so in the case of philosophy of education, where nearly all philosophers of education assume that all questions about education are essentially questions about schooling in a universal, compulsory state-controlled system. The very fact that 'state education' does not appear as a theme in the survey of the most common themes featuring in publications in the four leading journals in the field over the past ten years is, I believe, testimony to the fact that the paradigm of state education is simply taken for granted (one of Mayo's 'commonsensical ideas') within the discipline (see Hayden 2012). The work of philosophy of education frequently referred to as the most 'radical' in recent years is James Tooley's (2000) *Reclaiming Education*, where he argues for completely removing state control of education. Yet while Tooley (1996, 2000) has made an important contribution to philosophy of education in reminding us that 'education' is not equivalent to 'schooling' and in questioning the monopoly of state education, he begins, like his opponents, from the assumption that the state is the framework in which we are operating. In Tooley's market-driven alternative to state schooling, the capitalist state is still very much there in the background – indeed, it constitutes the very structures and paradigms within which the market system can operate and within which the educational goods that it provides make sense.

Philosophers of education keen to defend a liberal idea of education and a commitment to social justice have attacked proponents of private educational provision such as Tooley. Thus Padma Sarangapani and Christopher Winch (2010), drawing on both conceptual analysis and empirical data, defend the notion of education as a public good and argue that market-driven educational reforms exacerbate socio-economic inequalities. However, Sarangapani and Winch, like other critics of market or quasi-market reforms or parental choice policies in educational provision, assume that the basic structure of the capitalist state will remain the same; all we can do is ameliorate its worst injustices. The main quarrel between Tooley and these critics is that *given the current political structure*, Tooley does not think that the socio-economic disparities produced by differential educational opportunities will be any worse under a market-driven system than they are in a state-controlled system. While I would not disagree that re-constructing educational provision along the market-driven lines Tooley suggests will both encourage the kinds of attitudes and individual propensities that will undermine humanistic values and entrench socio-economic gaps, I do want to reject the implication that there are only two options to choose from: either education provided and controlled by the liberal state, hopefully configured in such a way as to meet at least a minimum requirement of social justice, or educational provision within a private system operating on the logic of free-market capitalism. By focusing on the fact that 'It is unfair, then, if some get a worse education than others because, through no fault of their own, this puts them at a disadvantage in the competition for these unequally distributed goods' (Brighouse 2010: 27), defenders of state education, working with a Rawlsian model, divert attention from the point that the capitalist state is *characterized* by competition for unequally distributed rewards, with educational attainment causally linked to such rewards. Likewise, John White, whose recent work focuses on the notion of well-being as an aim of education, assumes the state framework, as indicated by his very focus on the question 'what schools are for', rather than what education is for. The state, in White's account, is a given; our task is merely to delineate its 'proper role' (White 2011: 48) in determining the aims of schools. Thus in arguing that schools 'have a contribution to make in encouraging young people to ... be sensible in managing money' (ibid.: 6), White fails to acknowledge the ways in which this very argument assumes the capitalist state structure.

The assumption of the state as the backdrop against which all contemporary philosophical debates about education take place is no less evident in work by philosophers of education sympathetic to poststructuralist approaches. Thus one finds repeated references to 'the system' in the work of philosophers who have developed an eloquent critique of 'managerialist assumptions' (Blake et al. 1998; Hogan and Smith, 2003) and of what Richard Smith (2002: 4) describes as 'the instrumentalism, the techno-rationalism that runs through education at all levels'. Yet the absence of any reference to the state in such work suggests a failure to seriously consider the ways in which it may be, in fact, features of the state itself that are bound up with the problems these theorists identify in their critique. In assuming the (capitalist) state as an inevitable feature of our lives – the worst consequences of which can, perhaps, be ameliorated through educational provision – such positions narrow the horizon of our political imagination. Effectively, they suggest that there are only two alternatives: state education constructed along egalitarian, liberal lines, or an educational market governed by neo-liberal regimes. Tooley (1996: 15) himself explicitly invokes this dichotomous model in stating: 'State education is so all-pervasive that at first it seems hard to imagine what the alternative – markets in education – could be like.' But while this may be *an* alternative, it is not *the* alternative. It takes an act of political and philosophical imagination to imagine a further possibility – the real alternative suggested by the anarchist vision of a stateless society. Articulating and defending this alternative involves not just offering a very different picture of the kinds of educational practices and processes that may be possible, but also challenging the dominant conception of the relationship between education and social change.

Utopianism and the anarchist imagination

How many philosophers have dared to think beyond the warning that 'Excessive positional advantage conferred by education may lead to outcomes that are harmful both to individuals and society through the production of excessive relative inequalities of income' (Sarangapani and Winch, 2010, p. 501) and to imagine a social world in which the very structures which give rise to 'positional advantage' have ceased to be relevant? How many have dared to imagine not just a world where poor or working-class children's educational opportunities would not be restricted by their parental background, but in which there was no poverty and where society was not characterized by hierarchical divisions of class? Many philosophers of education will question the legitimacy of a philosophical approach that begins from such a 'utopian' vision. Yet it is important to recall the history of derogatory use of the term 'utopian' towards anarchism, and to reject the misperception that anarchists have a naively optimistic account of human nature, thus rendering their position 'impractical' (Morland 1997; Suissa 2006). Likewise, the conflation (famously found in Popper and Berlin) of the term 'utopian' with the idea of a static state of perfection or a form of totalitarianism, can be rejected on the basis of a rigorous understanding of anarchist theory; specifically, the anarchist aversion to blueprints for revolutionary practice and social organization. In philosophy of education, this derogatory usage was famously invoked by John Wilson in his dismissal of the educational ideas of Plato, Rousseau, and Locke, who, he says, write 'as if education were not really a respectable *philosophical* topic at all, but just a stamping-ground for utopian theory or personal prejudice' (Wilson 2003: 280).

Saul Newman has described how, in the contemporary political landscape, dominated by implicit or explicit references to the 'inevitability' of capitalism, free-markets, and neo-liberal assumptions, 'the word utopia has a precise ideological function: it operates as a way of stigmatising alternative political and economic visions as, at best, unrealistic and naive, and, at worst, dangerous' (Newman 2009: 209). It is within this climate of 'no alternative' that anarchist utopian approaches can fill the important positive function noted by so many theorists of utopia, namely that of 'generating constructive and dynamic critical thought' (Goodwin and Taylor 1982: 27), and 'relativising the present' (Bauman 1976: 13). As Newman puts it, at a time when 'the very idea of utopia has been discredited', introducing a utopian dimension to political discussion can bring 'a kind of radical heterogeneity and disruptive opening into the economic, social, political and ideological constellation that goes by the name of global capitalism' (Newman 2009: 208). The anarchist idea of social transformation is one in which spheres of social action are gradually freed of relations of domination, a process which can go on within and alongside the existing structures of the state – as captured in the phrase 'building the new society in the shell of the old'. Thus anarchism, as Colin Ward explains, is 'not about strategies for revolution'; rather, 'far from being a speculative vision of a future society, it is a description of a mode of human organization, rooted in the experience of everyday life, which operates side by side with, and in spite of, the dominant authoritarian trends of our society' (Ward 1973: 18). So rather than see education – and schools – as either a process of preparing children for life in society as we know it, an inevitable reproduction of existing ideological structures, or a means to improving and strengthening liberal institutions through the nurturing of certain intellectual qualities or civic virtues, anarchism invites us to see educational activity as a site of social transformation. This view is connected to the key anarchist idea of prefigurative practice, for it is central to the anarchist view that the means for creating the alternative, stateless society be commensurate with the ends. And as we do not and cannot know the form of the ideal society, it is essential to enable the free interplay of human imagination and experimentation as far as possible. Engaging with the anarchist tradition thus not only constitutes an important act of political imagination that challenges both the statist position and the 'alternative' of neo-liberalism, but also offers a very different perspective to the dominant philosophical orthodoxy regarding the conceptualization of means and ends in education (Suissa 2006).

Reconfiguring the social

As discussed above, the philosophical critique of both neo-liberal and liberal accounts of education that suggests either an instrumental concept of education as serving national economic needs, or a fully worked-out set of aims from which curricular content can be analytically derived, often involves defending the idea of education as in intrinsically valuable practice. As Paul Standish puts this, 'the suspicion that emerges is that stating the aims of education may lead to a kind of stifling' (Standish 1999: 42). Yet an understanding of the anarchist view suggests that one can take seriously the point that education is bound up with political questions about the kind of social world we want without falling into the trap of seeing education merely as a means to bring about social change, or constricting the educational experience of individuals by imposing fixed ends and aims on the process. The choice is not between defending the integrity of educational practice or allowing education to become hostage to a kind of rational planning that runs the risk of subverting its integrity by rendering it subservient to political or economic ends. The anarchist position offers an imaginative, critical, and motivating vision of a good society, without proposing a programme of revolutionary social change that can be worked out in advance, or a total overthrow of the existing system. Anarchism, in fact, suggests a very different perspective on the relationship between education and social change. What this suggests is, in fact, a reconceptualization of the social: the fixation on the state and its logic, which, as I have argued above, characterizes most contemporary work in philosophy of education, gives rise to a narrow view of the political. Yet it is the state which is associated with what Martin Buber referred to as 'the political principle', and which he distinguished from the social principle. Whereas the political principle 'is seen in power, authority and dominion', the social principle is seen in 'families, groups, unions, cooperative bodies and communities' (Ward, in Wilbert and White 2011: 268). While it seems naive to conceive of families and communities as devoid of issues of power and authority, the point that the monopolizing of power by the state weakens society conceived of as a network of spontaneous human self-organization is an important anarchist insight. Concerns that thinking about the quality of educational practices in light of normative ethical ideas about the good society would somehow contaminate education, or imply a dangerous form of closure are, in light of the anarchist position, ill-conceived. Legitimate philosophical concerns about closure and perfectibility should not lead us to abandon the project of thinking about education as part of a normative, ethical project for transforming our life as individuals and as a society; for as Ward points out, 'The concept of a free society may be an abstraction, but that of a freer society is not' (Wilbert and White 2011: 97). Thus while I would not want to reject valuable philosophical defences of 'the virtues of teaching and learning' (see Hogan 2011), I would add that *the practice* of education always takes place in a social space which is itself reflective of and embodies particular modes of organization and forms of interpersonal relationships; there is no escaping the question of how these relationships are constituted and what qualities they embody; those of domination, hierarchy, and competitiveness, or those of commensality, mutual aid, and spontaneity? Buber's distinction between the political and the social is helpful in thinking about how an anarchist philosophy of education can not only transcend the dichotomy between 'intrinsic and extrinsic aims of education' (a dichotomy that has become something of an orthodoxy within the discipline), but can contribute to a theoretical and practical reclamation of and reaffirmation of the social. For the state fixation which characterizes so much work in political philosophy and philosophy of education has the effect not only of seriously limiting our philosophical imagination, but also of squeezing out the social in the sense that Buber and Ward talk about it.

This point is developed by Banu Bargu, as follows:

> From the perspective offered by traditions of mutuality, the crisis of modernity lies less in the invasion of the political by the social than in the flattening out of the social by the hegemonic construction of the autonomy of the political and the progressive destruction of the social by the incursion of a capitalist market whose primary form of competitive and individualist action has been detrimental to communal practices and relations.
>
> (Bargu 2013: 37)

Conclusion

In the current political climate, many philosophers of education will be uneasy with the suggestion that state education needs to be questioned. Siding with proponents of free educational experimentation outside the state system will be seen as a dangerous betrayal of the struggle for social justice that plays into the hands of neo-liberal reformers.

Yet I believe that to frame the debate as if one had to choose between a blanket defence of state education and an endorsement of neo-liberal, market-led forms of private educational provision is both to ignore the historical context of state education and to misrepresent the critical role of philosophy. Educational theorists on the left are almost universally united against current proposals for 'free schools'. Yet as the history of working class initiatives in cooperative education, free schools, and experiments in cooperative living reminds us, the alternative to a state monopoly on education is not just free-market individualism or for-profit schools. Indeed, the tendency to polarize debates on issues like welfare and education can be seen as symptomatic of the ideological anti-utopian stance described above. We need to revisit and re-examine the history of these debates as part of an attempt to reclaim a more critical, emancipatory position, particularly at a time when the traditional values of the socialist left are so under attack. Philosophers, sociologists, and historians of education can contribute to the project of reclaiming notions like 'community', 'freedom', and 'fairness' from the right and challenging contemporary ideological positions by articulating and documenting alternative ideas and experiments. Some philosophers of education have in fact been doing just that; yet even these theorists often overlook the anarchist position. Michael Fielding and Peter Moss (2011), for example, in their book *Radical Education and the Common School: A Democratic Alternative*, explore and defend the pedagogical practice of radical educational experimenters within the state system, such as Alex Bloom. Of course the book's title implies a tacit defence of the state (where, while the need for radical democratic education is rigorously defended, the need for *state* education is not). Yet even so, given that the notion of prefigurative practice features so centrally in their analysis, it is remarkable that the anarchist tradition, arguably the tradition most associated with this idea, receives not even a passing mention. Fielding and Moss, however, at least do an important job in reminding us that it is not state education as such that is a project worth defending, but only state education insofar as it instantiates human and social values such as justice, freedom, and equality. As discussed above, framing the discussion as if there are only two options: universal compulsory state schooling or a private market in educational provision, shuts down the possibility of imagining and allowing schools and other educational experiments where the utopian idea of a radically different society could be enacted freely through the kind of prefigurative practice so central to anarchist theory and practice. We do not have to choose between either daring to imagine and to prefigure a society radically different from the kind we have now, or trying to ensure that, given the kind of society we live in, educational provision is not shaped by policies that adversely affect certain groups and privilege others. We can do both. Indeed, as Chomsky reminds us,

> In today's world, I think, the goals of a committed anarchist should be to defend some state institutions from the attack against them, while trying at the same time to pry them open to more meaningful public participation – and ultimately, to dismantle them in a much more free society, if the appropriate circumstances can be achieved.
>
> (Chomsky 1996: 75)

It is important to note, though, that in the same way as worries about the excesses of neo-liberalism should not lead political theorists concerned with social justice into blindly defending state education, nor should anarchists assume that all 'free schools' are necessarily better than those provided by the state. The anarchist commitment to prefigurative practice is consistent with the commitment of many anarchist educators to working within the state school system (see Haworth 2012). Furthermore, it is vital that both philosophers and practitioners address the political context in which current possibilities for 'freeing' education from the state are being proposed. While an anarchist perspective demands that we reclaim and enact a multiplicity and plurality of spaces for 'the social', how, where, and to what extent this can be done in the current political climate is an open question. Certainly current UK Government policy on free schools and academies is very far removed from any truly social, grass-roots initiatives, and seems rather more like what Nikolas Rose (1996) has described as another form of politically centralized and hegemonic control by the state of spaces once thought of as 'social'. The individuals within such spaces are also subject to what Rose calls 'government by audit' – in this case educational forms of audit such as standardized testing and inspection regimes – which 'hold out the promise – however specious – of new distantiated forms of control between political centres of decision and the autonomized loci – schools, hospitals, firms, – who now have the responsibility for the government of health, wealth and happiness' (Rose 1996: 351). Most 'free schools' in Britain today are thus very different places from the original free schools of the 1960s and 70s, as Emily

Charkin (2011) reminds us. Yet nor should we be under the illusion that there was a golden age of 'free schools' in which such projects were immune to the kinds of entrenched privileges and social hierarchies which contemporary critics warn of. Jonathan Kozol talked scathingly, as early as 1972, of people who go out 'into the mountains of Vermont' to start 'an isolated upper-class rural free school for the children of the white and rich' while still profiting from the consequences of the deeply unequal and racialized power relations that characterize US society (Kozol 1972: 5–12). Free schools he says, 'cannot with sanity, or with candor or with truth, endeavor to exist within a moral vacuum' (ibid.: 10). Yet this is not to say that there were not then, or now, and that one cannot imagine, genuinely free schools that engage with these issues of power, through a form of prefigurative practice, while at the same time perhaps exhibiting the 'virtues of teaching and learning' that philosophers such as Hogan have described. The history of radical educational experiments is full of examples of such schools (see Smith, 1983; Shotton 1993; Gribble 1998; Avrich 2006), and the contemporary world of anarchist activism has yielded many similar educational experiments (see Haworth 2012, Haworth and Elmore 2017; Springer et al. 2016). Part of the role of philosophers of education, I have argued, is to explore and articulate different conceptual and practical possibilities from the ones dominating our political and academic discourse, thus contributing to the anarchist project of multiplying 'the political and also the social and imaginary ties people are subjected to' (Bottici 2013: 18).

References

Avrich, P. (2006) *The Modern School Movement: Anarchism and Education in the United States*, Oakland: AK Press.
Ball, S.J. (1993) 'Education Markets, Choice and Social Class: The Market as a Class Strategy in the UK and the USA', *British Journal of Sociology of Education*, 14(1): 3–19.
Bargu, B. (2013) 'The politics of commensality', in J. Blumenfield, C. Bottici and S. Critchley (eds.) *The Anarchist Turn*, London: Pluto Press, pp. 35–58.
Bauman, Z. (1976) *Socialism: The Active Utopia*, New York: Holmes and Meier.
Blake, N., Smeyers, P., Smith, R. and Standish, P. (eds.) (1998) *Thinking Again: Education after Postmodernism*, Westport: Bergin & Garvey.
Blake, N., Smeyers, P., Smith, R. and Standish, P. (eds.) (2000) *Education in an Age of Nihilism*, Abingdon: Routledge.
Bottici, C. (2013) 'Black and Red: The Freedom of Equals', in J. Blumenfield, C. Bottici and S. Critchley (eds.) *The Anarchist Turn*, London: Pluto Press, pp. 9–34.
Brighouse, H. (2010) 'Educational Equality and School Reform', in G. Haydon (ed.) *Educational Equality*, London: Continuum, pp. 15–70.
Callan, E. (1997) *Creating Citizens: Political Education and Liberal Democracy*, Oxford: Clarendon Press.
Charkin, E. (2011) 'For a Real Free School Look to Postwar Peckham', *The Guardian*, Comment is Free, 30 August.http://www.guardian.co.uk/commentisfree/2011/aug/30/free-school-peckham-education
Chomsky, N. (1996) *Powers and Prospects: Reflections on Human Nature and the Social Order*, Boston MA: South End Press.
Dunne, J. (2005) 'What's the Good of Education?' in W. Carr (ed.) *The RoutledgeFalmer Reader in Philosophy of Education*, Abingdon: Routledge, pp. 145–160.

Fielding, M. and Moss, P. (2011) *Radical Education and The Common School: A Democratic Alternative*, Abingdon: Routledge.
Furlong, J. (2013) *Education - An Anatomy of the Discipline: Rescuing the University Project*, Abingdon: Routledge.
Furlong, J. and Lawn, M. (eds.) (2010) *Disciplines of Education: Their Role in the Future of Education Research*, Abingdon: Routledge.
Godwin, W. (1986) 'Evils of National Education', in P. Marshall (ed.), *The Anarchist Writings of William Godwin*, London: Freedom Press, pp. 146–147.
Goodwin, B. and Taylor, K. (1982) *The Politics of Utopia: A Study in Theory and Practice*, London: Hutchinson.
Gribble, D. (1998) *Real Education: Varieties of Freedom*, Bristol: Libertarian Education.
Haworth, R.H. (ed.) (2012) *Anarchist Pedagogies: Collective Actions, Theories, and Critical Reflections on Education*, Oakland: P.M. Press.
Haworth, R.H. and Elmore, J.M. (eds.) (2017) *Out of the Ruins: The Emergence of Radical Informal Learning Spaces*, Oakland: PM Press.
Hayden, M.J. (2012) 'What Do Philosophers of Education Do? An Empirical Study of Philosophy of Education Journals', *Studies in Philosophy and Education*, 31(1): 1–27.
Hogan, P. (2010) 'Preface to an Ethics of Education as a Practice in Its Own Right', *Ethics and Education*, 5(2): 85–98.
Hogan, P. (2011) 'The Ethical Orientations of Education as a Practice in Its Own Right', *Ethics and Education*, 6(1): 27–40.
Hogan, P. and Smith, R. (2003) 'The Activity of Philosophy and the Practice of Education', in N. Blake, P. Smeyers, R. Smith and P. Standish (eds.) *The Blackwell Guide to the Philosophy of Education*, Oxford: Blackwell, pp. 165–180.
Hyslop-Margison, E.J. and Naseem, A. (2007) *Scientism and Education: Empirical Research as Neo-Liberal Ideology*, Dordrecht: Springer.
Jun, N. (2012) 'Paideia for Praxis: Philosophy and Pedagogy as Practices of Liberation', in R.H. Haworth (ed.) *Anarchist Pedagogies*, Oakland: PM Press, pp. 283–302.
Kaltefleiter, C.K. and Nocella, A.J. (2012) 'Anarchy in the Academy: Staying True to Anarchism as an Academic-Activist', in R.W. Haworth (ed.) *Anarchist Pedagogies*, Oakland: PM Press, pp. 200–217.
Keiner, E. (2010) 'Disciplines of Education: The Value of Disciplinary Self-Observation', in J. Furlong and M. Lawn (eds.) *Disciplines of Education*, Abingdon: Routledge, pp. 159–172.
Kozol, J. (1972) *Free Schools*, Boston: Houghton Mifflin Company.
Levidow, L. (2001) 'Marketizing Higher Education: Neoliberal Strategies and Counter-Strategies', *Education and Social Justice* 3(2), retrieved from http://users.skynet.be/aped/babel/english/
Levinson, M. (1999) *The Demands of Liberal Education*, Oxford: Oxford University Press.
Marples, R. (2010) 'What is Education For?', in R. Bailey (ed.) *Philosophy of Education: An Introduction*, London: Continuum, pp. 35–47.
Mayo, C. (2012) 'Philosophy of Education is Bent', in G. Biesta (ed.) *Making Sense of Education: Fifteen Contemporary Educational Theorists in Their Own Words*, Dordrecht: Springer, pp. 43–48.
Mills, C. (2004) '"Ideal theory" as ideology', in P. DeSautels and M. Urban Walker (eds.) *Moral Psychology: Feminist Ethics and Social Theory*, Lexington: Rowman and Littlefield, pp. 163–181.
Morland, D. (1997) *Demanding the Impossible? Human Nature and Politics in Nineteenth Century Social Anarchism*, London: Cassell.
Newman, S. (2009) 'Anarchism, Utopianism and the Politics of Emancipation' in L. Davis and R. Kinna (eds.) *Anarchism and Utopianism*, Manchester: Manchester University Press, pp. 207–220.
Oancea, A. and Bridges, D. (2010) 'Philosophy of Education: The Historical and Contemporary Tradition', in J. Furlong and M. Lawn (eds.) *Disciplines of Education*, Abingdon: Routledge, pp. 50–66.
Peters, R.S. (1977) Education and the Education of Teachers, Routledge Kegan Paul: London.

Pring, R. (2010) 'Does Education Need Philosophy?', in R. Bailey (ed.) *Philosophy of Education: An Introduction*, London: Continuum, pp. 21–34.

Rose, N. (1996) 'The Death of the Social? Refiguring the Territory of Government', *Economy and Society*, 25(3): 327–356.

Sarangapani, P.M. and Winch, C. (2010) 'Tooley, Dixon and Gomathi on Private Education in Hyderabad: A Reply', *Oxford Review of Education*, 36(4): 499–515.

Shotton, J. (1993) *No Master High or Low: Libertarian Education and Schooling in Britain, 1890–1990*, Bristol: Libertarian Education.

Smith, M. (1983) *The Libertarians and Education*, London: George Allen and Unwin.

Smith, R. (2002) 'Sustainable Learning', *The Trumpeter*, 18(1): 125–138.

Springer, S., Lopes De Souza, M. and White, R.J. (eds.) (2016) *The Radicalization of Pedagogy: Anarchism, Geography and the Spirit of Revolt*, London: Rowman and Littlefield.

Standish, P. (1995), 'Postmodernism and the Education of the Whole Person', *Journal of Philosophy of Education*, 29: 121–135.

Standish, P. (1999) 'Education without Aims?', in R. Marples (ed.) *The Aims of Education*, London: Routledge, pp. 35–49.

Standish, P. (2007) 'Rival Conceptions of Philosophy of Education', *Ethics and Education*, 2(2): 159–171.

Suissa, J. (2006) *Anarchism and Education*, London: Routledge.

Sylvan, R. (1993) 'Anarchism', in R.E. Goodin and P. Pettit (eds.) *A Companion to Contemporary Political Philosophy*, Oxford: Blackwell, pp. 215–243.

Tooley, J. (1996) *Education without the State*, London: Institute of Economic Affairs.

Tooley, J. (2000) *Reclaiming Education*, London: Cassell. Ward, C. (1973) *Anarchy in Action*, London: Allen & Unwin.

White, J. (1990) *Education and the Good Life: Beyond the National Curriculum*, London: Kogan Page.

White, J. (2011) *Exploring Well-Being in Schools*, Abingdon: Routledge.

Wilbert, C. and White, D. (eds.) (2011) *Autonomy, Solidarity, Possibility: The Colin Ward Reader*, Oakland: AK Press.

Wilson, J. (2003) 'Perspectives on the Philosophy of Education', *Oxford Review of Education*, 29(2): 279–293.

13 Anarchism and religious studies

Alexandre Christoyannopoulos

Despite the traditional anti-clericalism and frequent atheism of much anarchism, the intersection of religious studies and anarchism has proved a fertile ground for a variety of analyses, indeed with renewed attention in recent years (Christoyannopoulos, 2009; Christoyannopoulos and Adams, 2017). Students and practitioners of religion have taken anarchism more seriously, and students and practitioners of anarchism have taken religion more seriously. The encounter can lead to tensions and expose unbridgeable differences, but in most cases explorations have been fruitful, opening up and investigating new avenues of thought and practice.

This dialogue encompasses a variety of rather different conversations: sometimes anarchists are revisiting their assessment of religion; sometimes religious scholars are articulating a theology which engages with anarchism; sometimes the focus is on how specific anarchists approached religion; sometimes general parallels are drawn between anarchism and religion; sometimes religious scriptures are interpreted to point to anarchist politics; and so on. In other words, the encounter between religious studies and anarchism can concentrate on very different facets of either, and involves very different approaches and methodologies, very different modes and tones of enquiry. That variety reflects not just the different themes of interest to both anarchism and religious studies, but also different ontological, epistemological, and methodological approaches.

The aim of this chapter is to sketch out some of the ways in which anarchism and religious studies intersect and influence each other's imagination. The aim is not to systematically present all the scholarship there is in the area, although an effort was made to encompass a high number of sources to illustrate and compile an accurate map of the different *types* of scholarship buzzing around this topic. As often with typologies, the divisions and categories proposed might at times be rather arbitrary, so they should not be interpreted too strictly but rather heuristically, as an attempt to overview and catalogue the territory.

The chapter is structured in four sections: the first considers some classic anarchist quarrels with religion and its institutions; the second surveys the scholarship on anarchist interpretations (or in the religious jargon: 'exegesis') of founding religious scriptures and figures; the third discusses the growing interest in anarchist 'theology' as distinct from scriptural exegesis; and the fourth points to the variety of historiographical studies on specific religious anarchist thinkers, communities, and movements.

It will quickly become obvious that the dominant religion in the scholarship, and hence in this chapter, is Christianity. One reason for this might be that (at least according to the traditional narrative) anarchist thought and practice cut many of its teeth in societies in which Christianity and its institutions tended to dominate.

Nonetheless, even though the main religious interlocutor in this chapter is Christianity, other traditions are still cited whenever possible and appropriate, and the arguments which apply where anarchism and Christianity meet anyway often apply in comparable ways to other traditions too.

Anarchist quarrels with religion

It seems sensible to begin this overview by acknowledging the frequent suspicion of religion among many anarchists, and in some cases the outright hostility to all things religious (for helpful overviews of classic anarchist criticisms and their main proponents, see for instance: Ellul 1991; Walter 1994; Barclay 2010). There are a number of different reasons for these suspicions, most of which hold much validity but nonetheless require some qualification.

Firstly and fairly obviously, religious institutions have frequently and historically enjoyed comforts and privileges as central pillars of the establishment, legitimizing (even deifying) whatever regime happens to be in place and calling the oppressed away from insubordination in exchange for preferential support from the political authorities. Many anarchists have therefore understandably railed against this. (More generally, an element of anti-clericalism has often been present in progressive thought and movements given that religious institutions have often sided with conservative or even reactionary camps.) However, religious groups and institutions have not *always* colluded with political authorities: even at the height of the Middle Ages, various rebellious or subversive churches disputed precisely that cosy collusion of more established religious hierarchies with political ones. Many a religious movement has found itself repressed and persecuted by political authorities precisely for such subversion. Moreover, many *religious* anarchists have shared secular anarchists' anti-clericalism and denounced the conspiracy of religious and political institutions (see, for instance, Christoyannopoulos 2016). In any case, given this historical (and, in many parts of the world, contemporary) collusion, a lingering anarchist uneasiness with religion is not surprising.

It is also true that, historically, many anarchist thinkers and activists have been committed atheists. After all, if religion is at best a misperception and at worst a deception peddled by elites to keep the masses in stupefied submission, then it seems all the more important to denounce it. In the mind of some anarchists, the same consistent critical thinking which leads to anarchism must also lead to atheism (see for instance: Gibson 1994). Some go as far as to almost see an avowed anarchist's atheism as one of the measures of their commitment to an anarchist approach. Certainly atheists have been strongly represented in the writings of many classical anarchists and in many anarcho-syndicalist circles. At the same time, atheism is not a strictly necessary precondition for reaching anarchist conclusions: the two sets of conclusions do not depend on each other, and even though they can reinforce each other, a dismissal of all religion following atheist arguments is analytically separable from the dismissal of the religious, political, and economic establishment following anarchist arguments.

There is another argument which is implicit in the frequently-evoked 'No Gods, No Masters' anarchist motto, which is that gods (and their mediators) are erected by humans as the greatest masters of all (a sort of hyper-patriarch), and that the anarchist suspicion of authority must therefore extend to those patriarchal imaginaries as well as their real-world 'representatives'. Here again, though, significant currents within religious traditions have been critical of patriarchal structures even within their own tradition, and these ought not to be written out of history. Moreover, it should be noted that even within the self-understanding of religious traditions, 'gods' are not always or only defined as 'masters'. As Alexis-Baker (2005: 2) notes, in the Christian Bible, 'God is also identified as Creator, Liberator, Teacher, Healer, Guide, Provider, Protector and Love', so that anarchists and Christians *alike* who are 'making monarchical language the primary descriptor of God' in fact 'misrepresent' his 'full character'. To understand God as a male despot on a throne perched somewhere above the universe is therefore to misunderstand the varieties of the multifaceted understandings of 'God' even within the Christian tradition. (Hugo Strandberg (2017) also argues, using Max Stirner as an interlocutor, that it is a mistake to see religion as necessarily requiring servitude.) It may be that Christianity has produced enough proponents of precisely such a narrow view to explain the popularity of such a misunderstanding, but there are many other theological views about the nature of God too – an argument which seems to apply to the gods of most other religious traditions as well. In other words: God need not and is not always projected as a 'master', though when indeed so, the anarchist critique does have evident ground to stand on.

A further anarchist argument is that anarchism cannot coherently derive from divine command or authority, that determining 'truth' through 'revelation' is epistemologically suspicious, and that therefore anarchists who reject the state or capitalism because some divine figure 'told them so' are rather incoherent and selective. There are also questions about the authenticity and veracity of religious scriptures – based on decades of extensive scholarship, indeed especially within religious studies. Precisely for these reasons, however, most religious anarchists do not necessarily simply absorb scriptural instructions with no critical reflection, and instead engage in some hermeneutical discussion and reflection. Religious traditions, even 'sacred' texts, are rarely swallowed uncritically by their followers, but rather are engaged with, interrogated, reflected upon both individually and in community. At the very least, given that scriptures tend to reach us from distant historical contexts, some interpretation or hermeneutics (including what Muslims call *ijtihad*) is unavoidable, and this is precisely one of the main tasks which occupy religious scholars and students (anarchist examples are discussed in the next section). Therefore, even though in the final analysis, religious anarchists can often hold anarchist conclusions because they understand sacred texts and commands to imply such conclusions or because they otherwise embrace a theological worldview *a priori*, the process is not necessarily some blind uncritical obedience to divine command. Besides, even though secular anarchists might have legitimate concerns about anarchism deriving from a 'revealed' instruction, it remains the case that religious anarchists share the criticisms of the state, capitalism and the church that characterize the anarchist position. Whatever the source of their anarchism and its disputability, their political and economic stance remains closer to anarchism than any other main political ideology, thus the 'anarchism' label does seem appropriate to describe this religious position.

In any case, even though a substantial (though varied) hostility to 'religion' has long been present in anarchist milieus, many anarchists today nonetheless display considerable patience and tolerance of their religious comrades, an openness to respectful yet critical discussions of unfamiliar perspectives, and a willingness to leave some of their differences on religion aside in their shared contemporary struggles against various forms of oppression. Indeed, as Barclay (2010) shows, even several classical anarchists had some sympathy for some aspects of the religions they encountered – such as the emphasis on love and mutualism in the teachings of Jesus, the radical politics of some religious sects and movements, and so on. Kropotkin's (1910) famous entry on anarchism in the *Encyclopaedia Britannica* provides one example of this, and Gérard Bessière's (2007) *Jésus selon Proudhon* discusses Proudhon's productive fascination with the figure of Jesus and his conclusion that Jesus was a social and moral reformer whose message was corrupted and 'spiritualized' by Paul and his generation. John Clark's (2005) 'Anarchism' entry in the *Encyclopedia of Religion and Nature* also paints a detailed picture of 'anarchist tendencies across history that have held a spiritual view of reality', thus showing that the meeting of anarchist and religious currents is not new. Hostility to all aspects of religion, therefore, is not a trait universally shared by all anarchists. Rather, just as an anarchist impulse can be noticed in some 'religious' people, a 'religious' impulse can be noticed among certain anarchists.

Furthermore, as some scholars have argued, certain possibly unnoticed or unacknowledged parallels can be identified between anarchism and religion. For example: Aurelio Orensanz's (1978) *Anarquia y Cristianismo* discusses the strong similarities between several central Christian themes and values and those propounded by anarchists (in particular Bakunin, interestingly); Keith Hebden's (2009) 'Building a Dalit World in the Shell of the Old' examines the parallels between anarchism (as defined by Colin Ward) and Dalit values and practice; and Demetrio Castro Alfín's (1998) 'Anarquismo y Protestantismo' considers the parallels between the anti-clericalism of nineteenth- and twentieth-century Andalusian anarchist peasants and that of sixteenth- and seventeenth-century protestant agitators; Franziska Hoppen (2017) discusses the 'mystical anarchism' of Gustav Landauer and Eric Voegelin to reveal common threads in their vision of an 'anti-political community'; and Simon Podmore (2017) juxtaposes Søren Kierkegaard's theism with Proudhon's anti-theism to reveal surprising affinities such as a similar critique of the abuses of Divine Providence. In other words, certain views and practices can be found in both anarchist and religious groups.

Finally, it is worth atheist anarchists bearing in mind that too cavalier a dismissal of religion can have regrettable effects in alienating potential allies and comrades emerging from different journeys yet keen to share and build bridges. Erica Lagalisse's (2011) 'Marginalizing Magdalena' indeed examines some of the pitfalls of the typical anti-religious prejudice among anarchists by reflecting (from a feminist, anti-colonial perspective) on the marginalization of a female Oaxacan activist during a speaking tour in Canada. What can be dismissed as 'religion' includes many aspects and phenomena (beliefs, communal practices, moral commitments, etc.), and whilst anarchists might converge on denouncing domination and oppression where those are indeed displayed, it may be that today many of those facets of 'religion' are not the main sources of domination – indeed even that as many secular anarchists have recognized, there is much to respect and learn from religious comrades in the struggle against structures of oppression (including their own). Besides, if Paul-François Tremlett (2004) is correct that in early anarchist writings, 'religion' as a category was formed and functioned as 'a cipher for thinking about the past' (whether as something that was looked back at nostalgically or as something that needed to be overcome), then perhaps the broader context has evolved enough for the time to have come to leave aside this use of this category, reconsider the variety of facets and experiences of 'religion', and work with those religious people who share many of the goals of fellow anarchists.

Anarchist exegesis

Having outlined and discussed some of the traditional suspicions of religion among anarchists, it is time to look at examples of more favourable interactions. One example of a positive encounter comes from studies that interpret religious scriptures to advocate anarchism or to otherwise imply anarchist conclusions – that is to say, anarchist exegesis. Here, the 'anarchism' is in the political deductions of those scriptural interpretations, in other words in the criticisms of the state, capitalism, and other structures of oppression – including indeed many aspects of 'religion' – that these interpreters derive from major religious texts. This approach therefore refuses to dismiss all religion *a priori*, reads foundational religious texts, and finds their line of reasoning to lead to anarchist conclusions.

My *Christian Anarchism* considers many examples of notorious anarchist exegeses and weaves them together to present a relatively generic and systematic anarchist interpretation of the Christian gospels (Christoyannopoulos 2010a). Chapters 1, 2 and 4 in particular develop a detailed textual interpretation of New Testament passages based on the complementary work of writers such as Tolstoy, Ellul, Eller, Andrews, Elliott, and others. Here is not the place to discuss in depth the precise contribution of every Christian anarchist exegete, but a brief outline of the main interpretations might help illustrate some of the variety of styles and focuses involved.

The author who is traditionally cited in *anarchist* circles as the primary example of Christian anarchism is Leo Tolstoy, and the most frequently cited book is his *Kingdom of God Is within You* (Tolstoy 2001 [1893]). In it, Tolstoy covers at length topics such as military service, state violence, and revolutionary methods, and defends his interpretation of Christianity against what he sees as perversions of it. That book, however, was originally written in response to the reception of his earlier and more methodical exegesis published as either *What I Believe* or *My Religion* (Tolstoy 1902 [1884]), which therefore outlines Tolstoy's analysis of Jesus' teaching in more meticulous detail. Very interesting too is Tolstoy's harmonized and translated version of the gospels ('The Gospel According to Leo', as it were), which by what it includes and excludes illustrates how Tolstoy interprets the four canonical scriptures (Tolstoy 1895 [1881]; 1933 [1881]). As an exegete, however, Tolstoy was quite a maverick. He rejected and ignored everything he saw as irrational, and focused squarely on the moral teaching of Jesus. He also ignored much of the Old Testament, Paul's epistles, and the rest of the New Testament. Predictably, therefore, his exegetical approach has been widely criticized, and it may not be surprising that even in *Christian* radical circles Tolstoy tends to be approached with caution. Nonetheless, one of the merits of his exegesis is its stubborn refusal to shy away from the logical implications of Jesus' teaching with regards to the state's perpetration and legitimation of violence – a topic on which he writes as well as can be expected from the author of acclaimed works of fiction.

Less unconventional as an exegete and more respected as a theologian is Jacques Ellul. A prolific scholar, he wrote dozens of volumes several of which interpret specific books and passages of the Bible. He gained particular notoriety for his critique of what he called our *société technicienne* (usually translated as 'technological society'), a society in which the obsession with efficiency overrides ethical concerns. His most explicitly anarchist contribution to biblical exegesis, however, came in the chapter: 'Anarchism and Christianity' (Ellul 1998) and the short book: *Anarchy and Christianity*

(Ellul 1991). In those, Ellul offers an explicitly anarchist interpretation of several Bible passages, including some largely ignored by Tolstoy – such as the Old Testament Book of Samuel, 'render unto Caesar' (which Tolstoy deals with rather hastily) and the Book of Revelation. Although he does not match the piercing eloquence of Tolstoy's denunciation of state violence, both Ellul's coverage of the Bible and indeed his theological approach are more conventional than Tolstoy's, making him more amenable for contemporary Christians to identify and engage with.

Several other writers have published explicitly anarchistic exegeses of Christian scripture. One somewhat controversial example is Vernard Eller's (1987) *Christian Anarchy*, which, as discussed in my book (Christoyannopoulos 2010a), proposes a reading of Romans 13 which has not always been well received by Christian anarchists and poses problems for secular anarchists, yet nonetheless articulates clear criticisms of the state despite the counter-intuitive method it proposes to subvert it. Other anarchist exegeses include: Niels Kjær's (1972) *Kristendom og Anarkisme*, Michael Elliott's (1990) *Freedom, Justice, and Christian Counter-Culture*, Dave Andrews' (1999) *Christi-Anarchy*, Matt Russell's (2004) 'Anarchism and Christianity', Mark Van Steenwyk's (2012) *That Holy Anarchist*, and Paul Dordal's (2017) *In Search of Jesus the Anarchist*, each of which reflects on Jesus' teaching, often contrasts it with the mainstream church interpretation of it, and gives examples of Christian communities that have tried harder than the mainstream to remain faithful to it; David Alan Black's (2009) *Christian Archy*, which revisits the meaning of God's 'kingdom' in the New Testament; Tom O'Golo's (2011) *Christ? No! Jesus? Yes!*, which argues that Jesus and his first followers were anarchists and that Paul corrupted Christianity; Greg Boyd's (2008) 'The Bible, Government and Christian Anarchy', which comments on a variety of biblical texts in support of an anarchist interpretation; Nekeisha Alexis-Baker's (2009) 'The Church as Resistance to Racism and Nation', which looks to scripture to describe how the church can embody an opposition to both the idea of race and the nation-state; Peter Pick's (2009) 'A Theology of Revolutions', which analyzes Abiezer Coppe's use of the Bible as a weapon against the earthly authorities of his day; and Justin Meggitt's (2017) close reading of scriptural sources to interrogate the claim that 'Jesus was an anarchist'. There are therefore numerous examples of explicitly anarchist exegeses, many written relatively recently.

Also noteworthy because cited by contemporary Christian anarchists are exegeses which, even though not explicitly anarchistic, come very close to it because of their criticism of violence or of political elites, such as John Howard Yoder's (1994) *Politics of Jesus*, Ched Myers' (1988) *Binding the Strong Man* and Walter Wink's (1984; 1986; 1992) studies of the 'powers'. A further example worth a short discussion is Shane Claiborne and Chris Haw's (2008) *Jesus for President* with its associated website, YouTube clips, speaking tours and DVDs. Written primarily for US Christians and adopting a format which is quite lively and colourful (it is full of drawings, pictures, and other graphics), their book aspires to 'provoke the Christian political imagination' beyond the narrow confines of electoral politics. However, perhaps to minimize the risk of alienating its readership and maximize the chances of convincing it, the word 'anarchism' seems deliberately avoided. Yet its exegesis, its commentary on church history, and its reflections on the political engagement of contemporary Christians are all strikingly anarchistic, similar to and indeed often relying on the writings of several of the authors cited above.

Clearly, then, Christian exegesis has increasingly been bearing fruits coloured in anarchist themes and ideals. However, only fairly recently have studies aiming to map out the variety of Christian anarchist authors, exegeses, and arguments been published. Examples include short books, short online texts and chapters in edited collections (Russell 2004; Kemmerer 2009; Christoyannopoulos 2010b; Van Steenwyk 2012), but to the best of my knowledge, my book remains to date the most comprehensive book-length study (in English anyway) to weave together as many pre-existing publications which explicitly argue that 'Christianity' implies 'anarchism'.

It might be worth remarking that, in a sense, these exegeses tend to focus their direct criticism on the state, and to some extent the church, more than on capitalism – even though many secular anarchists today see capitalism as at least as dangerous as the state. Of course, the precise nature of the overlap, interaction, and mutual reinforcement of 'the state' and 'capitalism' is complex and evolving, and whether there even is a single and primary source of 'evil' in the global political economy is debatable. Besides, Christian anarchists do frequently interpret scriptural passages as challenging contemporary economic orthodoxies, and they do frequently criticize the capitalist system on that basis. However, their arguments from scripture to the state seem to require fewer logical steps than those from scripture to capitalism. It is presumably easier to interpret ancient scripture to denounce the political and religious establishments (although of course, the state today is a rather complex phenomenon too) than it is to denounce the complex web of interests and the instruments of oppression that form the 'establishment' in the globalized capitalist economy. Still, whether borrowing Hardt and Negri's notion of 'empire' in pamphlets such as Jason Barr's (2008) *Radical Hope* or in numerous Iconocast podcasts (Iconocast Collective 2013), denouncing responses to the financial crisis in Christian anarchist blogs and newspapers, or turning some classic submissive passages from the King James translation of the Bible into an empowering call to 'occupy the land' and 'cast wickedness into the furnace of fire' (Nemu 2012), contemporary Christian anarchists do spend much time denouncing the current economic order. To date, however, Christian criticisms of capitalism rooted directly in exegesis tend to be less ubiquitous and less developed than those of the state or church.

In any case, anarchist interpretations of religious scripture are not restricted to Christianity. In Islam, for instance, both Mohamed Jean Veneuse's (2009) *Anarca-Islam* and Abdennur Prado's (2010) *El Islam como Anarquismo Místico* demonstrate that the Koran can be interpreted anarchically as an anti-authoritarian, anti-capitalist and anti-patriarchal text – indeed also (just as the Christian gospel) as a text critical of the religious establishment. These studies, however, seem to be the first detailed attempts at such exegesis so far (at least in English). Outside monotheistic traditions, John Clark's (n.d.) *Master Lao and the Anarchist Prince* aims to show that 'the Daodejing is in accord with ... holistic ecological anarchism', and in *Zen Anarchy* Max Cafard (2013) (John Clark's alter-ego) similarly argues that Zen was always meant to be anarchic, indeed that it *is* 'the practice of anarchy', and demonstrates this through an interpretation of respected Zen and Buddhist writings and teachings.

In short, there are numerous examples of anarchist exegesis, in other words of interpretations of scripture that lead to anarchist conclusions. These examples do of course illustrate the paradox, mentioned in the previous section, of anarchism *derived from scriptural authority.* Even if the conclusion is an anarchist critique of the state, the economy or even of religion, secular anarchists may still justifiably denounce the 'revealed' point of departure as not very anarchist. Yet that is also the strength of that position. That is, within contemporary *religious* circles, appeal to scriptural authority can act as a theological trump card, and religious anarchists have sometimes used it precisely in this way. When a holy text can be convincingly and consistently argued to imply an anarchist position, this can help persuade coreligionists. Anarchist exegesis therefore provides an essential line of reasoning for religious anarchist arguments.

Anarchist theology

'Theology' is a term that can be misunderstood in non-religious circles, and sometimes the word 'theological' gets used almost as a synonym for 'religious'. Yet theology refers to a specific mode of inquiry and understanding, one that is more deeply rooted in religion than 'religious studies'. It follows a style of argument which is more contemplative, which often assumes 'belief', and which thinks within (and uses the language of) religious traditions. Compared to exegesis, therefore, theology is less concerned with scripture and its interpretation, and more with approaching specific questions and themes (such as war, evil, peace, justice, love) from a particular religious or cosmological understanding. Theology ultimately seeks to remain faithful to scripture, but not be reduced to it.

There is some debate within religious studies as to whether the term 'theology' should only be applied to Christian or at least monotheistic thought, or whether it can be used to describe the similar thinking and philosophy which can emerge from any religious tradition. Yet even though some religions have no deity ('theos') to 'reason' ('logos') about, Christianity is not the only religion to engage in the mode of reflection rooted within a religious tradition which is described by the term: 'theology'. Hence although somewhat ethnocentric, the word does name a type of investigation which is not necessarily restricted to Christian thought. Therefore, the label of 'anarchist theology' can similarly be applied to anarchist reflections rooted in any religious tradition, thus helping differentiate such a mode of thinking from a more exegetical one focused on interpreting foundational texts.

At the same time, the boundary between exegesis and theology is not a rigid one. Theological discussions are not necessarily directly and hurriedly rooted in scripture, but many ultimately are. Exegetical discussions can be quite narrowly focused on the specific verses they seek to interpret, but frequently evoke theological ideas and debates which have matured within their religious tradition. In short: 'exegesis' and 'theology' point to two types of analyses which are driven by different primary concerns, but are nonetheless complementary and often used together. For instance, Christian anarchists have contributed to theological discussions on restorative justice (theology), they have articulated a detailed interpretation of the Sermon on the Mount (exegesis), but they have also criticized mainstream theological developments such as just war theory on the basis of scripture (both).

I was very conscious, when publishing *Christian Anarchism*, that it concentrated on exegesis and contained little theology, an absence which has been noted implicitly or explicitly by some of the reviews emanating from religious (rather than anarchist) circles. To some extent, this absence simply reflected the literature the book was bringing together: many of the authors who had explicitly written on Christian anarchism had made scriptural exegesis a core part of their argument, so it seemed appropriate to emulate that in a study purporting to weave those authors together. Moreover, providing a fairly comprehensive panorama of Christian anarchist exegesis could then, in turn, enable others to both develop an anarchist theology which could build upon those interpretations, and deflect scriptural objections by pointing to the existing exegeses which already address them. Besides, theology with explicitly anarchist leanings was until recently a somewhat underexplored (albeit emerging) field, so it seemed sensible, in *Christian Anarchism*, to focus on exegesis.

However, not all Christian anarchism is merely about scripture, and several Christian anarchists have been articulating theological considerations of specific contemporary questions. For example: Claiborne and Haw's (2008) *Jesus for President* and Ted Lewis' (2008) *Electing Not to Vote* both address the themes of elections and voting; Ellul's (1970) *Violence* ponders the topic of violence from a variety of Christian perspectives; Keith Hebden's (2013) *Seeking Justice* blends personal experience and theology, and more broadly stories and theory, to explore ways in which activists can be inspired to challenge unjust structures today; and Ronald Osborn's (2010) collection of essays reflects from a radical perspective influenced by Tolstoy and Chomsky on a number of topics related to war and political power including Obama's Nobel Prize, the political contribution of the Seventh-day Adventist Church, and the Vietnam War. These publications all seek to address specific themes and debates grounded within an anarchist-leaning Christian tradition.

Such theological discussions often engage with and find support in existing theological schools of thought which, although not reaching explicitly anarchist conclusions, have developed arguments which are sympathetic to it. For instance, much 'theology of liberation' considers themes close to anarchism. Its critique of oppression and of the capitalist economy and its preference for grassroots and community-based forms of organization, for instance, chime with anarchism. Given liberation theology's indebtedness to socialist thought, this is probably not surprising. Rarely, however, is anarchism explicitly mentioned in liberation theology, and rarely is a specific criticism of the state expressed in arguments more familiar to anarchists. Indeed empowerment of the oppressed is often envisaged in statist terms. Yet just as anarchism is ideologically close to (indeed arguably a stream of) socialism, anarchist theology is not far removed from liberation theology. Linda Damico's (1987) *The Anarchist Dimension of Liberation Theology* explores precisely this ideological proximity, and Keith Hebden's (2011) *Dalit Theology and Christian Anarchism* illustrates this proximity in the particular postcolonial Indian context of Dalit theology.

Similar arguments can be made of pacifist theology. Indeed, one of the main reasons some Christian anarchists (Tolstoyans in particular) are anarchists is that they apply their pacifist rejection of violence to the state – they see their anarchism as a consistent and essential extension of their pacifism. Conversely and as already noted in passing, some Christian anarchists have found support in arguments made by leading theologians such as Yoder or Hauerwas who, although not anarchists, have articulated powerful theological cases against violence.

A more recent school of theological thought which at times echoes anarchist themes is Radical Orthodoxy, in particular in some of the writings of William T. Cavanaugh (1995; 1999; 2004). This theological current aims to return to and affirm 'orthodox' interpretations of Christian faith such that implicitly or explicitly, it is critical of contemporary ideas and institutions such as secularism but also of the modern sovereign nation-state established by the Peace of Westphalia in 1648. Even if its main concern is not necessarily with politics and even if its critical engagement with much secular thought brings it into direct philosophical conflict with much anarchist thinking, when some of its scholars engage with political questions, it can find itself close to an anarchist position. Richard Davis (2013) completed a doctoral thesis precisely on

Cavanaugh and Milbank (possibly the most notorious theologian in this school) which discusses their critique of the state on theological grounds, using the language of creation, preservation, and redemption to examine the origins of the state and present the church (in the 'radical orthodox' sense) as an alternative to it. Most secular anarchists will presumably reject the grounding in theology as well as the critique of secularism, but Radical Orthodoxy nonetheless does present an example of theology which leans towards anarchism in its critique of the state – in short, a kind of anarchist theology.

At the same time, even when the state or capitalism are criticized theologically, rarely do theologians openly adopt the 'anarchism' label. This reluctance might be driven by a degree of caution and distrust based on the perception that anarchists inexorably dismiss all things religious, or perhaps sometimes to avoid lengthy justifications of the appropriateness of the label. But this seems to be changing. In both activist and scholarly circles, there is a palpable buzz around religious (especially Christian) anarchism and in religious groups in particular an apparent desire to articulate and discuss it *theologically*. Whether in current research projects, online discussion fora, recent publications or conference papers, there is perceptible enthusiasm for more explicitly anarchist-leaning theology.

One example is the quality of theological discussions hosted on websites such as Jesus Radicals, whether in essays and podcasts (Iconocast Collective 2013 includes interviews with a substantial list of American theologians), at conferences convened through it, or in publications emerging from these (e.g. Van Steenwyk 2012). Also interesting and indicative of the up-to-date appeal of anarchist theology is Kevin Snyman's (2013) *Occupying Faith*, which is a collection of sermons, reflections, and other resources placing Jesus among the Occupy movement and exploring how Christians can respond 'though prayer, meditation, liturgy, stories, art, reflection and theological debate' to today's 'unjust economic and political systems'. Mohamed Jean Veneuse's (2009) ambitions for 'Anarca Islam' are similarly rooted in the contemporary political economy and blend exegesis with more theological considerations.

In any case, anarchist theology is not exclusively new. As already noted, several established schools of theological thought have hovered close to anarchist conclusions. Hundreds of articles printed in the Catholic Worker newspaper since its launch (in 1933) have echoed central anarchist themes using theological language. Moreover, most of the books mentioned above as 'exegetical' also at times engage in more 'theological' reflection and arguments, as do their authors in other publications. For instance, Ellul, Boyd, Wink, Yoder, and Andrews, to name but a few, have published theological works which lend themselves well to Christian anarchist arguments. As to Gary Snyder's (1969) *Buddhist Anarchism*, it also probably best comes under the category of 'theology' rather than 'exegesis' in that it articulates anarchist reflections from a Buddhist position. What examples such as these illustrate, therefore, is that the recent burst of scholarship on anarchist theology does have older foundations to build upon.

A further set of theological publications are the rather more controversial ones which might perhaps be qualified as 'polemics', 'tracts' or 'pleas' (a good but French term might be: *plaidoyer*). For instance, Jacques de Guillebon and Falk van Gaver's (2012) *L'Anarchisme chrétien* blends an avowedly selective reading of renowned French Catholic theologians with meandering discussions of anarchist themes and expected figures such as Tolstoy, Ellul, and Day, thus painting a deliberately controversial yet rich and stimulating canvas which for its authors captures the Christian anarchist imagination. Another example might be Paul Cudenec's (2013) *The Anarchist Revelation*, which journeys through the anarchism of Bakunin, Landauer, and Read, but also through esoteric forms of religion, psychology, and existential philosophy to present anarchism as a complete way of being in contrast to the alienating life of modern society. One could also mention Kerry Thornley's (1997) *Zenarchy*: unorthodox in its structure, provocative in its arguments, typical of its author, it describes itself as 'a way of Zen applied to social life', a 'non-combative, non-participatory, no-politics approach to anarchy intended to get the serious student thinking'. Such publications may not follow conventional or academic lines of argument, but they do offer thought-provoking contributions to anarchist theology.

Lastly, the recent work of Simon Critchley ought to be mentioned here because it engages with theology even though it is not 'theological' in the sense of speaking from within a theological tradition. Both his 'Mystical Anarchism' (Critchley 2009) and his *Faith of the Faithless* (Critchley 2012) journey through Schmitt's political theology, Rousseau's civil religion and medieval mysticism and millenarianism in order to reflect on the mystical, anarchist, and arguably millenarian potential for love of fellow humans to transform both the self and our understanding of the common. Critchley is not speaking from a Christian context, but his work is 'theological' in the sense that it contributes to what Schmitt understood as 'political theology' (which sees political discourses and institutions as secularized theological ones), and it discusses the theological work of medieval mystics and millenarians. Ted Troxell's (2013) 'Christian Theory' arguably adds to Critchley (and to the view that all politics is in some ultimate sense 'theological') by bringing into careful dialogue a number of postanarchist themes with theological reflections articulated by John Howard Yoder, thus presenting Yoder as a potential contributor to postanarchist theory.

In short, anarchist theology refers to diverse modes of analysis which are relatively distinct from anarchist exegesis, although complementary. As anarchist exegesis is gaining increasing recognition, so is anarchist theology. While the contribution of anarchist exegesis centres on the interpretation of religious scripture, anarchist theology addresses a variety of themes and discussions, broad or specific, often in response to contemporary challenges and debates, and in the language of its religious tradition. Several schools of theological thought have come close to anarchist territory in the past, but rarely have theological discussions explicitly embraced anarchist reasoning and conclusions. More recently, however, a number of scholars and activists have been developing theological reflections that are sympathetic to and driven towards anarchist themes and arguments, so it seems likely that anarchist theology will continue to bear a variety of fruits in the coming years.

Religious anarchist historiography

A third and more loosely defined type of scholarship in which anarchism and religion encounter each other is the one that presents and analyzes the thought and biography of specific thinkers and movements. This type of scholarship varies between the more biographical and the more discursive, some studies concentrating on mapping the lives and genealogies of individuals or movements and others more concerned with reflecting on or discussing their ideas and philosophies, perhaps drawing parallels and charting currents across different historical contexts. What is common to such studies despite significant variety is their concern to present (indeed often recover and affirm) the life and thought of religious anarchist figures – who did what when, how this was religious and anarchist, and why it matters for the broader histories of those contexts.

Examples of such studies abound, and include: studies of Tolstoyan colonies (e.g. Armytage 1957; Holman 1978); Charlotte Alston's (2013) monograph on Tolstoyism as an international movement; Valerio Pignatta's (1997) (Italian) book on sixteenth-century English religious revolutionaries; Bojan Aleksov's (2009) history of religious dissenters in early twentieth century Hungary; André de Raaij's (2009) account of Dutch Christian anarchists in the same period; Harold Barclay's (2002) short book describing various religious sects and his earlier article centred more narrowly on Muslim communities; Patricia Crone's (2000) presentation of ninth-century Muslim anarchists; Anthony Fiscella's (2009; 2012) panoramas of Islamic anarchist individuals and movements; Ruy Llera Blanes' (2017) discussion of the Tokoist church in Angola; Tripp York's (2009) biographies of Dorothy Day, Clarence Jordan and the Berrigan brothers; Terrance Wiley's (2014) reflections on the confluence of anarchism and religion in Thoreau, Day, and Rustin; the several studies chronicling the lives of Catholic Worker individuals and communities (e.g. Segers 1978; Coy 1988; Holben 1997; Ellis 2003; Zwick and Zwick 2005) as well as of course the autobiographical publications of some of those individuals (e.g. Day 1952; Hennacy 1994; O'Reilly 2001); John Clark's (2005) overview of anarchist-leaning and 'nature-affirming spiritualities' including Daoism, Buddhism, Zen, and many more; John Rapp's (1998; 2009; 2012) accounts of the anarchist impulse in the Dao De Jing, in Daoist philosophers and poets, and in more recent Chinese figures; Michael T. Van Dyke's (2009) chapter on Kenneth Rexroth's Zen and anarchist leanings and on the post-war spiritual counter-culture in San Francisco; and Enrique Galván-Álvarez's (2017) discussion of Shinran Shonin's Buddhist anarchism.

One could also mention Jesse Cohn's (n.d.) presentation of Jewish anarchists; studies of Jewish anarchists prior to the First World War in the United States (Biagini 1998), Central Europe (Löwy 1988) and London (Fishman 2004); Amedeo Bertolo's (2001) edited volume bringing together the proceedings of a conference on anarchism and Jews; research on the role of Judaism in the radicalism of anarchists such as Emma Goldman (Gornick 2013); as well as works by and about thinkers such as Martin Buber and Gustav Landauer, for instance. However, one difficulty here is that 'Jewish' is a label that is as cultural and ethnic as it is 'religious', and – apart perhaps from Buber – it is not always very clear how far Jewish anarchists are anarchists based on specifically *religious* arguments.

There are therefore clearly many examples of publications that have narrated and reinstated the histories of religious anarchist movements and activists. These studies are rarely *only* descriptive and biographical, but they do perform an important role in writing or rewriting oft-neglected religious anarchists back into their historical contexts, in presenting some of their original contributions and telling the story of their political and religious impact. They paint a rich tapestry of religious anarchist practice (and thought) across time and space, thus empowering contemporary practice (and thought) with historical perspective.

In addition to those publications, Tolstoy and Ellul are two particular Christian anarchist authors who have enjoyed significant attention over the years, with many publications providing relatively integrated studies of both their thought and biography. Predictably given his notoriety as an author of classic fiction, countless biographies and analyses of Tolstoy have been published in many languages. However and frustratingly, the specifically anarchist aspects of his later thought are rarely explicitly engaged with. Numerous studies discuss his unconventional religious views, but his political ones tend to be more quickly dismissed as too eccentric, or only described in passing or in rather vague terms. This applies as much to the scholarship on Tolstoy as to the many news articles, documentaries and other publications which commemorated the centenary of his death in 2010. Still, a few studies have nonetheless directly engaged with both his religious and his anarchist thought. I tried to list several of these in an *Anarchist Studies* article (Christoyannopoulos 2008), though a few others have come to my attention since. Colm McKeogh's (2009) *Tolstoy's Pacifism*, for instance, is one notable recent study which presents Tolstoy's religious and political ideas, including his anarchist thought, in significant depth. Rosamund Bartlett's (2010) recent biography also gives some space to Tolstoy's anarchism as well as his take on religion. By and large, however, the vast scholarship on Tolstoy tends to focus on other aspects of his writings than his anarchist thought, or if it does touch on the latter it does so in vague and frequently dismissive terms.

Jacques Ellul is the other particularly notable Christian anarchist whose thought has been the subject of a number of scholarly publications. One recent example is an issue of the *Ellul Forum* (Alexis-Baker 2011), which includes four essays devoted to taking seriously the anarchist dimension of his thought. In general, however, as with Tolstoy, the anarchist elements of Ellul's thought are rarely engaged with in much detail. Indeed Frédéric Rognon's (2012) *Générations Ellul*, which lists and briefly describes the various 'successors' of Ellul's thought today, only includes three 'anarchists', even though his *Jacques Ellul* (Rognon 2007) does include some discussion of Ellul's anarchist thought and its relevance for contemporary ecological and global justice movements. Of the biographies of Ellul, however, Andrew Goddard's (2002) is perhaps the one which analyzes Ellul's religious and anarchist thought in most detail. Still, most of the scholarship on Ellul's social and political work tends to engage with his analysis of the technological society more than with his (admittedly less abundant) explicitly anarchist musings.

In terms of historical figures and their thought, there are also well-known thinkers who are not usually identified as religious anarchists, but whose thought, some have argued, is closer to anarchism than typically acknowledged. For instance: Peter Marshall (1994) presents William Blake as a forerunner of modern anarchism; Christopher Hobson (2000) examines Blake's perception of Jesus and how it informs his anarchist-leaning politics; Mitchell Verter (2006) discusses Emmanuel Levinas' use of the term *anarchy* and the extent to which his thought resonates with that of classical anarchists; and Richard Davis (2009) argues that Søren Kierkegaard's call for indifference to the state makes him a peculiarly Christian type of anarchist.

As to histories of much more recent examples, I am not aware of any scholarship aiming to comprehensively map out today's religious anarchists. The religious anarchist community, however, still appears to be thriving. Religious anarchism seems particularly vibrant in North America, but significant communities are perceptible in the British Isles, in Australia and the South Pacific, as well as in continental Europe and beyond. Websites such as Jesus Radicals provide a hub and a source of information for religious anarchist networks, as do of course social media, online fora, and other online tools and campaigns such as Occupy Faith. Offline, these networks organize conferences and other gatherings, and religious anarchism is practised daily in communal living, in providing care and support for the victims of the global political economy, and in 'liturgy' and agitation against the powers and for a more just global society. For many, one important aim is to affirm, through practice, alternative traditions which are more faithful to scripture or to the origins of their particular religion, and in so doing to engage mainstream coreligionists as well as anarchist comrades and the broader citizenry. In any case and despite their similarities, today's religious anarchists are rooted in a variety of religious traditions and political contexts, and it will be a task for future scholarship to tell the history of their life and thought.

Conclusions

The above categories are not perfectly distinct from each other, many studies could arguably come under more than one category, and some publications which have not been cited – novels like Michael Muhammad Knight's (2004) *The Taqwacores*, for example, or more ecclesiological work such as Jonathan Bartley's (2006) *Faith and Politics after Christendom* – would not fall neatly into any of these categories. Nonetheless, this particular classification has its merits in that it illustrates some of the variety of publications touching on anarchism and religion.

The first type of scholarship shows that anarchists have articulated a number of criticisms of religion, but also that religious anarchists agree with many of these criticisms and that anyway some of these accusations, when unqualified, are too sweeping. Of course just as atheists can be expected to question religious assertions, anarchists can be expected to question structures of patriarchy and domination – not least those based on seemingly false premises. Critical anarchist questioning, therefore, *including* by religious anarchists, of dogmatic claims and oppressive institutions will continue, but religion is not the only target, nor is 'religion' necessarily the main or only problem.

Anarchist exegesis is a slightly different mode of analysis than anarchist theology. It is one thing to study and try to interpret faithfully the founding texts of a religious tradition, and another to ponder specific contemporary challenges and phenomena from within the language of a religious understanding (and without necessarily even having clear scriptural guidance to refer back to). As the more historiographical studies introduced in the fourth section show, the reading of founding religious texts has encouraged anarchist tendencies across the centuries, and the scholarship covered in the second section underpins such interpretations. The more intellectually innovative and challenging scholarship, however, is probably in anarchist theology, where sincere reflections and musings about various questions confronting the world are articulated in ways that seek to resonate within the authors' religious tradition.

The impact of 'anarchism' in religious studies is therefore varied: sometimes anarchism criticizes religion; sometimes parallels are noted between anarchist and religious ideas and practices; sometimes scriptural interpretations lead to anarchist conclusions; sometimes theologians lean towards anarchist themes in their religious debates; sometimes historical individuals and movements are studied and reinstated; and meanwhile many religious anarchists try to live out their religious anarchism. The intersection of anarchism and religion is an area of study that has been very vibrant in recent years, with much interest not only from academics, but also anarchists and religious people in the wider community. Yet many avenues of research remain ripe for original explorations in all of the categories mentioned above (and indeed others), not least in religions other than Christianity.

In a global arena witnessing what some scholars have described as a 'resurgence' of religion, anarchist encounters with religion are not likely to become rarer. In that context, the emergence of religious anarchism radicalizes religion and thus empowers religious people to join anarchist ranks, builds bridges with fellow travellers confronting similar anarchist struggle, and with a good balance of respect and critical enquiry can enrich both anarchism and religious studies with a better understanding of anarchism, religion, and religious anarchism.

References

Aleksov, B. (2009) 'Religious Dissenters and Anarchists in Turn of the Century Hungary', in A. Christoyannopoulos (ed.) *Religious Anarchism: New Perspectives*, Newcastle upon Tyne: Cambridge Scholars Publishing, pp. 47–68.
Alexis-Baker, A. (ed.) (2011) *Anarchism and Jacques Ellul*, South Hamilton, MA: The International Jacques Ellul Society.
Alexis-Baker, N. (2005) 'Embracing God, Rejecting Masters', *Christianarchy*, 1(1): 2.
Alexis-Baker, N. (2009) 'The Church as Resistance to Racism and Nation: a Christian, Anarchist Perspective', in A. Christoyannopoulos (ed.) *Religious Anarchism: New Perspectives*, Newcastle upon Tyne: Cambridge Scholars Publishing, pp. 166–205.
Alston, C. (2013) *Tolstoy and his Disciples: The History of a Tadical International Movement*, London: I. B. Tauris.
Andrews, D. (1999) *Christi-Anarchy: Discovering a Radical Spirituality of Compassion*, Oxford: Lion.
Armytage, W.H.G. (1957) 'J. C. Kenworthy and the Tolstoyan Communities in England', *American Journal of Economics and Sociology*, 16(4): 391–404.
Barclay, H.B. (2002) 'Islam, Muslim Societies and Anarchy', *Anarchist Studies*, 10(2): 105–118.
Barclay, H. (2010) 'Anarchist Confrontations with Religion', in N. Jun and S. Wahl (eds.) *New Perspectives on Anarchism*, Lanham, MD: Lexington, pp. 169–188.
Barr, J. (2008) 'Radical Hope: Anarchy, Christianity, and the Prophetic Imagination'. Online. Available at: http://propheticheretic.files.wordpress.com/2008/03/radical-hope-anarchy-christianity-and-the-prophetic-imagination.pdf (accessed 11 March 2008).
Bartlett, R. (2010) *Tolstoy: A Russian Life*, London: Profile.
Bartley, J. (2006) *Faith and Politics after Christendom: The Church as a Movement for Anarchy*, Milton Keynes: Paternoster.
Bertolo, A. (ed.) (2001) *L'anarchico e l'Ebreo: storia di un incontro*, Milan: Elèuthera.
Bessière, G. (2007) *Jésus selon Proudhon: la 'messianose' et la naissance du christianisme*, Paris: Cerf.
Biagini, F. (1998) *Nati Altrove: Il Movimento Anarchico Ebraico tra Mosca e New York*, Pisa: Biblioteca F. Serantini.
Black, D.A. (2009) *Christian Archy*, Gonzalez, FL: Energion.
Boyd, G. (2008) *The Bible, Government and Christian Anarchy*, Reknew. Online. Available at: http://reknew.org/2008/01/the-bible-government-and-christian-anarchy/ (accessed 9 August 2013).
Cafard, M. (2013) *Zen Anarchy*, RA Forum. Online. Available at: http://raforum.info/spip.php?article3503 (accessed 7 August 2013).
Castro Alfín, D. (1998) 'Anarquismo y Protestantismo: Reflexiones sobre un Viejo Argumento', *Studia Historica: Historia Contemporánea*, 16: 197–220.
Cavanaugh, W.T. (1995) 'A Fire Strong Enough to Consume the House: The Wars of Religion and the Rise of the State', *Modern Theology*, 11(4): 397–420.
Cavanaugh, W.T. (1999) 'The City: Beyond Secular Parodies', in J. Milbank, C. Pickstock, et al. (eds.) *Radical Orthodoxy: a New Theology*, London: Routledge, pp. 201–219.
Cavanaugh, W.T. (2004) 'Killing for the Telephone Company: Why the Nation-state is not the Keeper of the Common Good', *Modern Theology*, 20(2): 243–274.

Christoyannopoulos, A. (2008) 'Leo Tolstoy on the State: A Detailed Picture of Tolstoy's Denunciation of State Violence and Deception', *Anarchist Studies*, 16(1): 20–47.

Christoyannopoulos, A. (ed.) (2009) *Religious Anarchism: New Perspectives*, Newcastle upon Tyne: Cambridge Scholars Publishing.

Christoyannopoulos, A. (2010a) *Christian Anarchism: A Political Commentary on the Gospel*, Exeter: Imprint Academic.

Christoyannopoulos, A. (2010b) 'Christian Anarchism: A Revolutionary Reading of the Bible', in N. Jun and S. Wahl (eds.) *New Perspectives on Anarchism*, Lanham, MD: Lexington, pp. 149–168.

Christoyannopoulos, A. (2016) 'Leo Tolstoy's Anticlericalism and Its Contemporary Extensions: A Case against Churches and Clerics, Religious and Secular', *Religions*, 7(59): 1–20.

Christoyannopoulos, A. & Adams, M.S. (eds.) (2017) *Essays in Anarchism and Religion: Volume I*, Stockholm: Stockholm University Press.

Claiborne, S. and Haw, C. (2008) *Jesus for President: Politics for Ordinary Radicals*, Grand Rapids: Zondervan.

Clark, J. (2005) 'Anarchism', in B. Taylor (ed.) *Encyclopedia of Religion and Nature*, London: Continuum, pp. 49–56.

Clark, J.P. (n.d.) 'Master Lao and the Anarchist Prince.' Online. Available at: http://anarvist.freeshell.org/JohnClark/MASTER_LAO_AND_THE_ANARCHIST_PRINCE_by_John_Clark.html (accessed 9 August 2013).

Cohn, J. (n.d.) 'Messianic Troublemakers: The Past and Present Jewish Anarchism.' Online. Available at: http://www.zeek.net/politics_0504.shtml (accessed 14 February 2006).

Coy, P.G. (ed.) (1988) *A Revolution of the Heart: Essays on the Catholic Worker*, Philadelphia: Temple University Press.

Critchley, S. (2009) 'Mystical Anarchism', *Critical Horizons: A Journal of Philosophy and Social Theory*, 10(2): 272–306.

Critchley, S. (2012) *The Faith of the Faithless: Experiments in Political Theology*, London: Verso.

Crone, P. (2000) 'Ninth-Century Muslim Anarchists', *Past and Present*, 167: 3–28.

Cudenec, P. (2013) *The Anarchist Revelation: Being What We're Meant to Be*, Sussex: Winter Oak.

Damico, L.H. (1987) *The Anarchist Dimension of Liberation Theology*, New York: Peter Lang.

Davis, R.A. (2009) 'Love, Hate, and Kierkegaard's Christian Politics of Indifference', in A. Christoyannopoulos (ed.) *Religious Anarchism: New Perspectives*, Newcastle upon Tyne: Cambridge Scholars Publishing, pp. 82–105.

Davis, R. (2013) 'The Political Church and the Profane State in John Milbank and William Cavanaugh', PhD thesis, University of Edinburgh.

Day, D. (1952) *The Long Loneliness: The Autobiography of the Legendary Catholic Social Activist*, New York: HarperSanFrancisco.

De Guillebon, J. and Van Gaver, F. (2012) *L'Anarchisme Chrétien*, Paris: L'Oeuvre.

De Raaij, A. (2009) 'The International Fraternity Which Never Was: Dutch Christian Anarchism between Optimism and Near-defeat, 1893–1906', in A. Christoyannopoulos (ed.) *Religious Anarchism: New Perspectives*, Newcastle upon Tyne: Cambridge Scholars Publishing, pp. 69–81.

Dordal, P. (2017) *In Search of Jesus the Anarchist*, Pittsburgh, PA: Eleutheria.

Eller, V. (1987) *Christian Anarchy: Jesus' Primacy over the Powers*, Eugene: Wipf and Stock.

Elliott, M.C. (1990) *Freedom, Justice and Christian Counter-Culture*, London: SCM.

Ellis, M.H. (2003) *Peter Maurin: Prophet in the Twentieth Century*, Washington: Rose Hill.

Ellul, J. (1970) *Violence: reflections from a Christian perspective*, trans. C. Gaul Kings, London: SCM.

Ellul, J. (1991) *Anarchy and Christianity*, trans. G. W. Bromiley, Grand Rapids: William B. Eerdmans.

Ellul, J. (1998) 'Anarchism and Christianity', *Jesus and Marx: From Gospel to Ideology*, trans. J. Main Hanks, Grand Rapids: William B. Eerdmans, pp. 166–167.

Fiscella, A.T. (2009) 'Imagining an Islamic Anarchism: A New Field of Study is Ploughed', in A. Christoyannopoulos (ed.) *Religious Anarchism: New Perspectives*, Newcastle upon Tyne: Cambridge Scholars Publishing, pp. 280–317.

Fiscella, A. T. (2012) 'Varieties of Islamic Anarchism: A Brief Introduction'. Online. Available at: http://www.ru-a.org/2012/03/varieties-of-islamic-anarchism-zine.html (accessed 9 August 2013).
Fishman, W.J. (2004) *East End Jewish Radicals 1875–1914*, Nottingham: Five Leaves.
Galván-Álvarez, E. (2017) 'Why Anarchists Like Zen? A Libertarian Reading of Shinran (1173–1263)', in A. Christoyannopoulos and M.S. Adams (eds.) *Essays in Anarchism and Religion: Volume I*, Stockholm: Stockholm University Press, pp. 78–123
Gibson, T. (1994) 'Should We Mock at Religion?', *The Raven: anarchist quarterly*, 25: 10–18.
Goddard, A. (2002) *Living the Word, Resisting the World: The Life and Thought of Jacques Ellul*, Milton Keynes: Paternoster.
Gornick, V. (2013) *Emma Goldman: Revolution as a Way of Life*, New Haven: Yale University Press.
Hebden, K. (2009) 'Building a Dalit World in the Shell of the Old: Conversations between Dalit Indigenous Practice and Western Anarchist Thought', in A. Christoyannopoulos (ed.) *Religious Anarchism: New Perspectives*, Newcastle upon Tyne: Cambridge Scholars Publishing, pp. 145–165.
Hebden, K. (2011) *Dalit Theology and Christian Anarchism*, Farnham: Ashgate.
Hebden, K. (2013) *Seeking Justice: The Radical Compassion of Jesus*, Alresford: Circle.
Hennacy, A. (1994) *The Book of Ammon*, Baltimore: Fortkamp.
Hobson, C.Z. (2000) 'Anarchism and William Blake's Idea of Jesus', *The Utopian*, 1: 43–58.
Holben, L. (1997) *All the Way to Heaven: A Theological Reflection on Dorothy Day, Peter Maurin and the Catholic Worker*, Marion: Rose Hill.
Holman, M.J.D.K. (1978) 'The Purleigh Colony: Tolstoyan Togetherness in the Late 1890s', in M. Jones (ed.) *New Essays on Tolstoy*, Cambridge: Cambridge University Press, pp. 208–211.
Hoppen, F. (2017) 'A Reflection on Mystical Anarchism in the Works of Gustav Landauer and Eric Voegelin', in A. Christoyannopoulos and M.S. Adams (eds.) *Essays in Anarchism and Religion: Volume I*, Stockholm: Stockholm University Press, pp. 198–237.
Iconocast Collective (2013) 'The Iconocast', Jesus Radicals, Online. Available at: http://www.jesusradicals.com/category/iconocast/ (accessed 5 August 2013).
Kemmerer, L. (2009) 'Anarchy: Foundations in Faith', in R. Amster, A. DeLeon, L.A. Fernandez, A.J. Nocella II and D. Shannon (eds.) *Contemporary Anarchist Studies: An Introductory Anthology of Anarchy in the academy*, Abingdon: Routledge, pp. 200–212.
Kjær, N. (1972) *Kristendom og Anarkisme*, Aarhus: Self-published. Online. Available at: http://archive.org/details/KristendomOgAnarkisme (accessed 7 August 2013).
Knight, M.M. (2004) *The Taqwacores*, Berkeley, CA: Soft Skull.
Kropotkin, P. (1910) 'Anarchism', *Encyclopaedia Britannica*. Online. Available at: http://dwardmac.pitzer.edu/Anarchist_Archives/Kropotkin/britanniaanarchy.html (accessed 26 April 2007).
Lagalisse, E.M. (2011) '"Marginalizing Magdalena": Intersections of Gender and the Secular in Anarchoindigenist Solidarity Activism', *Signs*, 36(3): 653–678.
Lewis, T. (ed.) (2008) *Electing Not to Vote: Christian Reflections on Reasons for not Voting*, Eugene, OR: Cascade.
Llera Blanes, R. (2017) 'Mutuality, Resistance and Egalitarianism in a Late Colonial Bakongo Christian movement', in A. Christoyannopoulos and M.S. Adams (eds.) *Essays in Anarchism and Religion: Volume I*, Stockholm: Stockholm University Press, pp. 51–77.
Löwy, M. (1988) *Rédemption et Utopie: Le judaïsme libertaire en Europe centrale*, Paris: Presses Universitaires de France.
Marshall, P. (1994) *William Blake: Visionary Anarchist*, London: Freedom.
Meggitt, J. (2017) 'Was the Historical Jesus an Anarchist? Anachronism, Anarchism and the Historical Jesus', in A. Christoyannopoulos and M.S. Adams (eds.) *Essays in Anarchism and Religion: Volume I*, Stockholm: Stockholm University Press, pp. 124–197.
McKeogh (2009) *Tolstoy's Pacifism*, Amherst, NY: Cambria.
Myers, C. (1988) *Binding the Strong Man: A Political Reading of Mark's story of Jesus*, Maryknoll: Orbis.

Nemu, D. (2012) Mistranslation and Interpretation in the Service of Empire, Vimeo, Online. Available at: http://vimeo.com/50409919 (accessed 5 August 2013).
O'Golo, T. (2011) *Christ? No! Jesus? Yes!: A Radical Reappraisal of a Very Important Life*, St Andrews: Zimbo.
O'Reilly, C. (2001) *Remembering Forgetting: A Journey of Non-Violent Resistance to the War in East Timor*, Sydney: Otford.
Orensanz, A.L. (1978) *Anarquia y Cristianismo*, Madrid: Mañana.
Osborn, R.E. (2010) *Anarchy and Apocalypse: Essays on Faith, Violence, and Theodicy*, Eugene, OR: Cascade.
Pick, P. (2009) 'A Theology of Revolutions: Abiezer Coppe and the Uses of Tradition', in A. Christoyannopoulos (ed.) *Religious Anarchism: New Perspectives*, Newcastle upon Tyne: Cambridge Scholars Publishing, pp. 30–46.
Pignatta, V. (1997) *Dio L'Anarchico: Movimenti rivoluzionari religiosi nell'Inghilterra del Seicento*, Milano: Arcipelago Edizioni.
Podmore, S. D. (2017) 'The Anarchē of Spirit: Proudhon's Anti-theism & Kierkegaard's Self in Apophatic Perspective', in A. Christoyannopoulos and M.S. Adams (eds.) *Essays in Anarchism and Religion: Volume I*, Stockholm: Stockholm University Press, pp. 238–282.
Prado, A. (2010) *El Islam como Anarquismo Místico*, Barcelona: Virus.
Rapp, J.A. (1998) 'Daoism and Anarchism Reconsidered', *Anarchist Studies*, 6(1): 123–152.
Rapp, J. A. (2009) 'Anarchism or Nihilism: the Buddhist-influenced Thought of Wu Nengzi', in A. Christoyannopoulos (ed.) *Religious Anarchism: New Perspectives*, Newcastle upon Tyne: Cambridge Scholars Publishing, pp. 202–225.
Rapp, J. A. (2012) *Daoism and Anarchism: Critiques of State Autonomy in Ancient and Modern China*, London: Continuum.
Rognon, F. (2007) *Jacques Ellul: une pensée en dialogue*, Geneva: Labor et Fides.
Rognon, F. (2012) *Générations Ellul: soixante héritiers de la pensée de Jacques Ellul*, Geneva: Labor et Fides.
Russell, M. (2004) 'Anarchism and Christianity', Infoshop News. Online. Available at: http://news.infoshop.org/article.php?story=04/09/14/5885651 (accessed 7 August 2013).
Segers, M.C. (1978) 'Equality and Christian Anarchism: The Political and Social Ideas of the Catholic Worker Movement', *Review of Politics*, 40(2): 196–230.
Snyder, G. (1969) 'Buddhist Anarchism', Bureau of Public Secrets. Online. Available at: http://www.bopsecrets.org/CF/garysnyder.htm (accessed 9 August 2013).
Snyman, K. (2013) 'Occupying Faith: Resources for Worship, Meditation, reflection and Study', Smashwords. Online. Available at: https://www.smashwords.com/books/view/290593 (accessed 9 August 2013).
Strandberg, H. (2017) 'Does Religious Belief Necessarily Mean Servitude? On Max Stirner and the Hardened Heart', in A. Christoyannopoulos and M.S. Adams (eds.) *Essays in Anarchism and Religion: Volume I*, Stockholm: Stockholm University Press, pp. 283–307.
Thornley, K. (1997) 'Zenarchy', IllumiNet Press and Impropaganda. Online. Available at: http://www.impropaganda.net/1997/zenarchy.html (accessed 7 August 2013).
Tolstoy, L. (1895) *The Four Gospels Harmonised and Translated*, London: Walter Scott (reproduced by BiblioBazaar).
Tolstoy, L. (1902) *What I Believe (My Religion)*, trans. Mayo, F., London: C. W. Daniel.
Tolstoy, L. (1933) 'The Gospel in Brief', in *A Confession and The Gospel in Brief*, trans. A. Maude, vol. 11, London: Oxford University Press.
Tolstoy, L. (2001) 'The Kingdom of God Is within You: Christianity not as a Mystical Doctrine but as a New Understanding of Life', in *The Kingdom of God and Peace Essays*, trans. A . Maude, New Delhi: Rupa.
Tremlett, P.-F. (2004) 'On the Formation and Function of the Category "Religion" in Anarchist Writing', *Culture and Religion*, 5(3): 367–381.

Troxell, T. (2013) 'Christian Theory: Postanarchism, Theology, and John Howard Yoder', *Journal for the Study of Radicalism*, 7(1): 37–60.

Van Dyke, M.T. (2009) 'Kenneth Rexroth's Integrative Vision: Anarchism, Poetry, and the Religious Experience in Post-World War II San Francisco', in A. Christoyannopoulos (ed.) *Religious Anarchism: New Perspectives*, Newcastle upon Tyne: Cambridge Scholars Publishing, pp. 226–248.

Van Steenwyk, M. (2012) *That Holy Anarchist: Reflections on Christianity and Anarchism*, Minneapolis: Missio Dei.

Veneuse, M.J. (2009) *Anarca-Islam*, The Anarchist Library. Online. Available at: http://theanarchistlibrary.org/library/mohamed-jean-veneuse-anarca-islam (accessed 7 August 2013).

Verter, M. (2006) 'The Anarchism of the Other Person'. Online. Available at: http://www.waste.org/~roadrunner/writing/Levinas/AnarchismOtherPerson_WEB.htm (accessed 9 August 2013).

Walter, N. (1994) 'Anarchism and Religion', *The Raven: Anarchist Quarterly*, 25: 3–9.

Wiley, A. T. (2014) *Angelic Troublemakers: Religion and Anarchism in America*, London: Continuum.

Wink, W. (1984) *Naming the Powers: The Language of Power in the New Testament*, Philadelphia: Fortress.

Wink, W. (1986) *Unmasking the Powers: The Invisible Forces that Determine Human Existence*, Philadelphia: Fortress.

Wink, W. (1992) *Engaging the Powers: Discernment and Resistance in a World of Domination*, Minneapolis: Fortress.

Yoder, J.H. (1994) *The Politics of Jesus: Vicit Agnus Noster*, Grand Rapids: William B. Eerdmans.

York, T. (2009) *Living on Hope While Living in Babylon: The Christian Anarchists of the Twentieth Century*, Cambridge: Lutterworth.

Zwick, M. and Zwick, L. (2005) *The Catholic Worker Movement: Intellectual and Spiritual Origins*, Mahwah, NJ: Paulist.

14 Aesthetics of tension

Allan Antliff

Our current understanding of aesthetic experience first comes to the fore in Immanuel Kant's discussion, in the *Critique of Judgement* (Kant 1790), regarding an artwork's ability to trigger, through sensate experience, a 'free play' of understanding and imagination that we find pleasurable (Gero 2006: 4). 'In fact,' writes Robert Gero, 'Kant claims that the reason artworks can stimulate such enjoyable floods of thought is *because* that thought is not narrowly constrained within the boundary of a particular determinate concept' (Gero 2006: 5). In sum, aesthetic knowledge is a knowledge that can never be fully 'contained' within a set of precepts: it must always, by definition, remain unbounded. Subsequently, Kant's thesis led many to define aesthetic experience as perceptual-based and subjectively absolute. Idealized as autonomous from socio-historical factors in such treatments, aesthetics was cast as the key adjudicator of an artwork's worth, even its status as 'art'. Consequently, for much of the nineteenth and twentieth centuries, an artwork's significance was routinely adjudicated according to formal properties assessed in splendid isolation.[1] At the same time, however, the practice of art was becoming increasingly conceptual or performance-based, a development which led American art historian Hal Foster, in the early 1980s, to coin the term 'anti-aesthetic' to encapsulate the supposed renunciation of 'the conjunction of aesthetics and art' on the part of contemporary artists. Foster's thesis gained purchase in part because it offered a powerful anecdote to the lingering influence of formalist art criticism but, as Armen Avanessian and Luke Skrebowski point out, the case for an 'anti' aesthetic was misconstrued. An artwork and its aesthetic effect, though interrelated, stand at one remove from each other: arguably, then, the conditions of their conjunction are where we should focus our attention (Avanessian and Skrebowski 2011: 2). Indeed, this becomes imperative in a contemporary situation in which art production has decoupled from any obligatory medium specificity and artists are conceptualizing their work in terms that have more to do with relational situations than the art object as such.

This is where anarchism finds its point of entry. If, as Alejandro de Acosta argues, 'becoming anarchist has to be something on the order of a seduction, a passionate attraction, the feeling of anarchy's lure', then aesthetics is integral to anarchism's politics and art is an important site of enactment (de Acosta 2009: 27). This chapter explores anarchism's 'aesthetic of tension' in contemporary art. This tension involves self-actualization and transformative modalities. It thrives on qualities of contestation at the same time as it seeks to intensify ruptures that are generative, unleashing imaginative freedoms that find their indexical grounding in the artwork's relational power and communicative efficacy. What lies at the core of the anarchist tension? Alfredo Bonanno characterizes it as a relationship of engagement, 'a continual reversing of theory into action and action into theory' which refuses closure (Bonanno 1998a: 4). Arising from an ontological positioning that is self-constituted, dynamic, relational, and critical of authoritative origins, this tension aspires to extend the freedom it embodies into the world as a social force. Its paths are tactical and multiple: residing in the flux of contestation, it signals anarchism is an empowering idea, one that orients itself toward the future, rather than atrophying in the present, because the conditions for its realization are ever-changing (Bonanno 1998a: 8). Most importantly, it contributes to anarchism's allure, its means of building affinities that draw others toward a social vision that has no end goal or final reckoning: 'In a freed society where anarchy has been reached', writes Bonanno, anarchists will continue concerning themselves 'with perfecting the tension towards anarchy' – a social aspiration without limits (Bonanno 1998a: 30). Thus, anarchism's aesthetic of tension unfolds along social continuums we create, working within society from an engaged stance of immediacy that broaches no deferrals.[2]

Capitalism's primary site of reproduction is the workplace and this is the target of Au Travail/At Work, an 'anarchical' network characterized by its founder as 'wild in nature' by virtue of its organic, affinity-based, egalitarian structure (Badger 2010: 99–100). The organization hosts a website – http://atwork.enter1646.com/ – showcasing participants 'making use of, subverting, or undermining the cultural and technological means that are available to them in the workplace' to produce art (Au Travail/At Work 2010: 103). Following Au Travail/At Work's guidelines, artwork is constituted out of a relationship of antagonism towards workplace regimentation and the exploitive reduction of labour to standardized, capitalized activities. Here the artists of Au Travail/At Work find affinity with an important feature of anarchist activism born of necessity in communities that are largely impoverished, namely the appropriation of workplace materials, time, and resources for radical ends. Which is not to say that the activity of workplace subversion practised by Au Travail/At Work is replicating the instrumentalism of capitalist employer-labourer relations through a kind of perverse inversion: far from it. The more one brings the workplace in line with 'self-determination' – to quote Au Travail/Art Work – the more that site is aestheticized into a terrain of tension, where working can serve as an invitation to rebel, as opposed to acquiescence (Badger 2010: 101). This, to my mind, constitutes the anarchist aspiration in Au Travail/At Work's project, which comes into play as an inescapable component of its stated purpose. The challenge the collective poses is not to ape the exploitive agenda of the employer: it is to actualize freedom in the workplace as an extension of our social being, bringing work into the flux of rebellion and expanding our creative capacities. This is another way of de-alienating artistic activity through concrete means, a decoupling of art from the banal round of capitalization and spectacular consumption. While Au Travail/At Work's constitutes itself as an 'open' structure, its mandate has given rise to an internal 'core', an 'anarchist faction' that has responded to criticisms that Au Travail/At Work might evolve into a 'safety valve', making horrible jobs more endurable, by engaging in sabotage to create utterly dysfunctional workplaces (Badger 2010: 102). The anarchist faction positions itself as an antagonistic force without compromise: it 'seeks completely to abandon the merchant-utilitarian economic conception of labour, and considers the pursuit of human capacities for imagination and resilience as an end in itself' (Au Travail/At Work 2010: 103). Bringing the pleasure of creativity to its highest aesthetic pitch as a mode of being antithetical to workplace subjugation, the faction lends power to Au Travail/At Work's disruptiveness, its capacity to foment an anarchist tension.

In contemporary society, art is routinely commodified and museums tend to function like corporate entertainment industries, marketing culture for a profit. Wealthy collectors found museums to immortalize themselves and the work they have collected, while state entities use them to showcase national cultural accomplishments. The public museum, then, has an important aesthetic function as a pedagogical and political embodiment of ordering systems of value, constituting public consciousness along lines that reinforce the status quo (Preziosi and Farago 2004: 4–5). Its cultural aura is integral to its economic function, which, in turn, impacts on our conception of art's role in society. Working from a position of deliberative marginalia, Philadelphia-based Albo Jeavons' strategies for injecting tension into this scenario involve bringing to light the unspoken ways in which the corporate museum corrals and domesticates art through imaginative monkey-wrenching, beginning with the idea of what kind of artist merits institutional attention. Jeavons recently introduced himself to Saatchi OnLine, a website created and hosted by the Saatchi Gallery where artists are invited to 'profile' themselves and upload artwork for sale (the gallery gets a 30% commission). Saatchi OnLine is a branch of a privately-owned 'museum of contemporary art' located in London's exclusive Chelsea district which promotes itself as a 'springboard for young artists to launch their careers' (Saatchi Gallery 2013). In practice, since its founding in 1985, the Saatchi Gallery has served as a vehicle for showcasing the tastes of its owner, Charles Saatchi, who uses the institution to leverage the monetary value/cultural clout of his personal collection. Jeavons' page pokes fun at Saachi OnLine's typecast young, ambitious career-launcher. His 'bio pic' is a slumping child sporting an 'afro' wig. 'Future Shows' are 'coming to a lamppost or t-shirt near you'. Jeavons' 'About' profile is hardly calculated to elicit sales – '1959, Lower Marion PA USA. Anarchist, artist, pornstar, benefactor, criminal, pathetic toady, elusive, ineluctable, ineffable, thin, delicate, indestructible, well-meaning, smelly, trenchant, poised, deformed, disincorporated' – and none of the artwork showcased in his Saatchi OnLine 'Portfolio' is for sale (Jeavons 2013a). Tellingly, this portfolio features a web-based parody of a quintessentially corporate museum: the 'ArtJail' (2007).

ArtJail's subtitle: 'the Fine Art of Punishment on Philadelphia's Museum Row' (Jeavons 2013b) refers to the recent relocation of a famous art collection, the Barnes Foundation, from a converted mansion with an extensive garden in the wealthy suburban enclave of Merion to a newly built museum situated in the cultural hub of Philadelphia. Founded in 1922 by multi-millionaire Alfred Barnes with an educational mandate to introduce the working-class, and, specifically, African-Americans, to art appreciation, the Barnes Foundation's holdings include prized paintings by Pablo Picasso, Henri Matisse, Vincent Van Gogh, and many other canonical modernists. Barnes believed he had discovered the 'main principles that underlie the intelligent appreciation of the paintings of all periods of time' and his exhibition programme was designed to inculcate this aesthetic. Artists and art movements were ranked 'like school boys', in the words of one critic (among the modernists, Barnes ranked the Impressionist Pierre-Auguste Renoir highest) and artworks were exhibited in groupings alongside 'aesthetically instructive' colonial-era door knockers and other items (Hauser 1928: 289). When he incorporated his Foundation, Barnes stipulated the public could only access his collection in small groups twice a week (with free admission for workers) and that the Trustees were to maintain the museum as an educational facility.

The Barnes Foundation is a classic case of museum as pedagogical tool for working-class cultural uplift (in this instance racially-inflected), propagating the aesthetic tenets of an immensely wealthy eccentric.[3] Moving the collection to downtown Philadelphia's museum row involved a series of hotly contested court battles over nine years pitting 'Friends of the Barnes Foundation' against its Board of Trustees, which the 'Friends' accused of being more interested in exploiting the collection than managing it for educational purposes. The Trustees gained legal sanction to dissolve limited access stipulations and move the collection by committing to reconstruct Barnes' original exhibiting schemes and fulfil the Foundation's educational programme (three-hour workshops – $300 US per participant for four sessions – and courses in art appreciation – $900 US per participant for fourteen lectures – are now offered after closing hours). The sumptuous new Barnes Foundation museum (with a vegetated roof, solar panels, and water conservation system) projects an image of a wealthy institution with a venerable collection and a social conscience, a message the Foundation's website emphasizes. In its video chronicling the ecologically-friendly building's construction on the former site of a detention facility for juvenile criminals called the 'Youth Study Center' ('a Juvenile prison' in the words of Executive Director and President Derek Gilman), much is made of how the Trustees have conscientiously strived to renew Alfred Barnes' philanthropic civic vision (Barnes Foundation 2013).

Jeavons' ArtJail website parodies this rhetoric of renewal by imaginatively combining the new museum with the now demolished facility to create a hybrid fusion of the Foundation's cultural mandate with capitalist profiteering in the raw. Rebranded as 'a franchise in the for-profit My First Prison® chain, a division of Poorhauser Inc.', ArtJail educates by putting its young, predominantly African-American criminals to work (at an hourly wage well below the minimum) for the Barnes Foundation cultivating organic vegetables in the roof-top garden adjacent to the 'New Plantation Café' or manufacturing museum-related merchandise for purchase (Jeavons 2013b). Integrating prison cell ranges and barred classroom units with exhibition galleries allows ArtJail's incarcerated juveniles (sporting striped prison uniforms) to gain an appreciation for art as dictated by Alfred Barnes alongside the paying public who, in turn, 'get a rare glimpse of the education of some of our culture's most under-privileged young people'. This 'innovative synthesis of two educational institutions maximizes educational opportunities for all' while new profit streams fill the Barnes Foundation's coffers. ArtJail features an array of Barnes-branded slot machines; a twenty-four-hour Barnes Foundation Shopping Channel promoting 'My First Prison' products on a gigantic exterior wall screen; an exclusive condominium complex on the top of the building; and a multiplex movie theatre. Jeavons also pokes fun at Alfred Barnes' aesthetic principles of art appreciation by displaying up-to-date aesthetically-complementary artifacts – 'cell phones, music players, televisions, and designer clothing and weaponry' – alongside collection paintings. Most devastatingly, he mocks the Barnes Foundation's articulation of a philanthropic social consciousness through architectural design while preserving the 'feel' of Barnes' original galleries by calling attention to the demolished 'Youth Study Center's' ad hoc function as a shelter for the homeless in the heart of Philadelphia's cultural epicentre, a function Jeavons integrates into the ArtJail to combine preservationist virtues with social responsibility:

> For many years Philadelphia's Museum Row has offered visitors a cultural experience not featured in most cities' cultural districts: the long-term encampment of homeless people living inside bundles of plastic tarps along the Parkway facade

of the Youth Study Center. Many are essentially permanent residents, using the scant protection that the overhangs above offer from the elements. Since many of these people will not fit into crowded city shelters or have refused placements, the ArtJail will 'bring the mountain' to the homeless by turning the old Youth Study Center building into a combined multiplex theater/homeless shelter. For homeless people who don't want to enter the shelter, the areas between the two layers of the high-tech facade that surrounds the ArtJail will be left open at ground level and will offer greater protection from the elements than the Youth Study Center facade.

(Jeavons 2013b)

The Barnes Foundation's institutional coherence gives way to deep contradictions revealed through a round of playful web-based mimicry deploying irony, mockery, inversion, satire, and so forth. ArtJail's lovingly detailed website is a supremely funny means of truth-telling directed at cultural systems of authoritarianism, racism, and class inequality which depend on the erasure of historical memory, in this instance, the memory of a jail that called itself an educational facility and an educational art facility that is now a museum, both touting socially-beneficent missions that belie their shared function as cultural pillars in the state capitalist status-quo. Aestheticizing anarchist analysis to create a satirically-infused tension, ArtJail marshals critiques in the guise of serial jokes that induce a perspective utterly antithetical to the museum's elitist norms. This comic presentation of the Barnes Foundation's makeover is a rich, multifaceted analysis which seduces its audience into anarchism by utilizing the website's interactive technologies to create participatory roles in the final reckoning.

Considering the artwork as a site of prefiguration alongside critique invites other considerations related to the aesthetic of tension's potential as a focal point for affinity, nurturing diversity and inclusivity without hierarchy. These are the preoccupations of Peruvian-Canadian artist Luis Jacob who, based on first-hand involvement in anarchist gatherings and free schools, characterizes anarchist organizing as 'a realm of togetherness based on participation' where you can 'enact your agency without the coercion of authority' (Antliff 2007a: 239). Jacob came of age during the renewal of gay radicalism in the 1980s and 1990s, when groups such as the Radical Faeries began using the term 'queer' to imbue their sexuality with a socially libertarian intent. 'The experience of marginalization for one's sexual orientation can make one try to challenge this marginalization in all its forms or to simply join the ranks of power that determine such marginalization', Jacob observes: 'Queer identity mark outs the choice not to join power's ranks' (Antliff 2007a: 247). The anarchist challenge is to transform queerness into a staging ground whence to struggle for a non-hierarchical, anarchist society based on love, mutual aid, and trust. 'Being queer and being anarchist is intimately linked', argues Jacob:

Anarchism has long identified that liberation must also address our own fullness as human beings – not only our status in terms of social and economic class, but also in our various identities as persons who love and desire, persons who experience fear and shame, and persons with the capacity for pleasure and joy. For anarchism, liberation must also entail liberation at the level of these dimensions of being human.

(Antliff 2007a: 247)

Embracing the status of 'not-normal', queer anarchism combats the homophile ideology of normalization, creating a 'lived' tension aspiring toward an egalitarian society wherein difference is celebrated as an expression of self-fulfilment.

Jacob credits his involvement in the Toronto Anarchist Free School with the original impetus to politically 'out' himself on these terms in the art milieu. Inspired by the school's open and participatory structure, he asked its founders if he could exhibit the minutes of their organizational meetings as art works in a number of university galleries. Each installation ('Anarchist Free School Minutes,' 1999) included activist/anarchist publications for people to peruse and take away, a feature which exposed the tension between the values the exhibit propagated and capitalized learning (Antliff 2007a: 240). A second education-related work was an outgrowth of a class Jacob facilitated on 'Art and Collaborative Approaches' at the Free School's successor, Anarchist U. This work documented one of the class's collaborative performances – a sandwich-making party on the Toronto Subway, during which food was distributed to participants and passengers alike. As Jacob relates,

> I invited the participants of the original action on the subway to help make the documentary drawings [five large-scale artworks created with coloured pens]. Produced with the assistance of people who may or may not identify as artists, the variety of mark-making gestures and pen colours that were used become the manifest traces of the various hands at work in producing each drawing.
> (Antliff 2007a: 243)

Taking collaboration to the next level, he then arranged for a number of host galleries to organize bread-making workshops facilitated by local bakers as part of the exhibition. Openings for the 'Anarchist Sandwich Party' (2003) took the form of potlucks emulating the anarchist tenor of sandwich-making on the subway: in effect, each time participants re-enacted the fun-filled economics of generosity celebrated in the drawings they intensified the installation's antithetical relationship to capitalism.

A third project commissioned as a public outdoor sculpture by the city of Toronto developed this participation-based tension further by galvanizing play and spontaneity into an ecological action. Jacob's 'Flashlight' (2005) installation included a playground for children, a rotating disco ball powered by a solar panel, and an L.E.D. sign suspended over the play area. Anyone who wanted could illuminate the sign using pedal-powered electrical generators to create energy free of the central power grid (which depends in the main on fossil-fuel powered plants). The sign's ecological message, 'Everybody's Got a Little Light under the Sun', excerpted from a famous dance song, 'Flash-Light', by the 1970s Funk band Parliament, is the artwork's signature statement. The sign celebrates Funk culture's stress on egalitarian sharing and self-expression through joyous dancing that can never be channelled or forced into existence. Similarly, the playful spirit of Flashlight calls attention to the ways in which anarchism might help us overcome the authoritarian institutions and exploitive economics that separate us. Everyone, Jacob suggests, carries an 'innate agency or power' analogous to the sun's freely shared energy, a natural life force antithetical to the capitalized present (Antliff 2007a: 239). 'It is in the ever-new excitement of play, quite the opposite to the alienation and madness of capital', writes Bonanno, 'that we are able to identify joy. Here lies the possibility to break with the old world and identify with new aims and other values and needs' (Bonanno 1998b: 28). Flashlight awakens us to the natural aspects of our being and the anarchic forces innate in life itself, creating a tension that is fun-filled and profoundly adversarial.

In 2007 Jacob was invited to participate in the 12th Documenta exhibition in Kassel, Germany, an event held every seven years which profiles artists from around the world. His installation, 'Album III' (2004), consisted of hundreds of mass media derived images, loosely ordered into themes of dance, movement, and social participation; rigidity and open form; the standardization of the build environment; passive and active roles in experiencing art; masking; and the juxtaposition of social 'fabrics' with textiles (Jacob 2011: 2). In Album III images flow in undifferentiated associations that seemingly defy any unitary aesthetic, though the process of selection implies one. What we are presented with is a fecund image bank that mitigates definitive interpretations as thematic motifs dissolve and re-emerge in dynamic configurations which confound visual privileging. Eluding expectations of a fixed order, the Album suggests co-extensiveness between us and Jacob, the environments we create, the cultural practices we engage in, and our collective ways of understanding. The world as presented by Jacob is heterogeneous, multiple, and unpredictable. Continuously forgoing closure, it maps out zones of free association where photographs separate out into discrete representations before re-entering imaginative associative networks adjudicating meaning. On one level then, the artwork enacts its aesthetic of tension as a set of metaphorical possibilities within a field of imagery that is extra-discursive and experiential, rather than predetermined. But there is also a more pointed, proscriptive critique embedded in this aesthetic. Presenting authority-inflected images (Adolf Hitler overlooking a Nazi Party parade ground, for example) amongst the arrested fragments of life he inventively assembles, Jacob cancels out implied relations of domination by subsuming representations of power over others into larger associative frameworks. Album III posits freedom anarchically, as an already realizable goal in which reality is simultaneously presented as deeply familiar and intensified by a succession of associations that stimulate our perceptions. Appreciating Jacob's pictorial ensemble, we discover social structures manifest as autonomous from yet intimately related to our agency. Contiguous with reality, the photographs become a frame for reality's recapitulation as a field of creativity that is indivisible from our selves.

At Documenta, Album III was accompanied by a video, 'A Dance for Those of Us Whose Hearts Have Turned to Ice, based on the Choreography of Françoise Sullivan and the Sculpture of Barbara Hepworth (With Sign-Language Supplement)' (Jacob 2007) which presents a spontaneous dance performance by Keith Cole, a queer artist from Toronto. Small TVs on either side of the video screen feature hand-signers for the deaf who communicate a series of statements in French and English. These statements are also reprinted in a bilingual brochure which Jacob made available as part of the installation. Françoise Sullivan worked with painter Paul-Emile Borduas to further anarchist politics in the 1940s and 1950s while Barbara Hepworth was a close associate of Britain's pre-eminent anarchist art critic, Herbert Read. The brochure reproduces statements by Sullivan, Hepworth, Read, and Borduas, creating a reading experience that unfolds like a dialogue. The text critiques social authoritarianism while calling attention to freedom's immanence throughout nature and our expressive capacities to connect with one another through the arts. These statements effectively frame the work of Hepworth, who distilled the organic rhythm of growth forms in abstract sculpture, and Sullivan, who danced without predetermination, as anarchist and the video, in turn, reconfigures these same values through a queer lens, bringing sexual otherness into an anarchic discourse signed back to the gallery on-lookers in silence.

Jacob summarizes the politics of his intent:

> The very presence of the sign-interpreters addressing us suggests that 'it is the audience that lacks'. It is all of us in the art gallery who are 'deaf', who are unwilling (or simply unequipped) to hear what the dancer is trying to say in his cold and desolate environment. Will the expressive *élan* of the dancer and sign-interpreters – their *need* – arouse in illiterate viewers like ourselves the need to try and somehow come to understand those strange and foreign gestured words uttered by bodies truly not unlike our own?
>
> Is there a point or dimension within us all that is the universal root of all flowing, of all openness and connection from one to another, of all transmission across distance and across separation – and that is also the bare-life resource of heat, contact, pleasure, vitality and joy? I am convinced there is something profoundly anarchist in posing these questions.
>
> (Antliff 2009: 130)

This artwork positions itself as a site of tension seeking to foster recognition within a contemporary art world largely ignorant of or hostile towards such values. Jacob has gone so far as to characterize the current cultural-economic art system as 'anti-life'. Hence the video, 'A Dance for those of us whose hearts have turned to ice'.

The aesthetic of tension figures in other projects as well. Jacob's (2011) recently published anthology, *Commerce by Artists* explores the realm of economics, focusing, specifically, on relationships of exchange that are rife with counter-capitalist promise. Announcing, 'I want to concentrate on artists' projects that do not so much represent commercial transactions as they *enact* them', Jacob serves notice that *Commerce by Artists* deals with sites of engagement, where 'the artistic project *itself* takes the form of a transaction of some kind' (Jacob 2011: 2). The anthology is all about loosening up capitalism's ideological hold on the concept of exchange: documentary selections are organized into four primary categories – 'Art, Economy, Goods, Value' – which generate their own unique subsections. Jacob reproduces photographic and print documentation of the artists' works, sometimes with a related article, letting each piece and/or accompanying essay speak for itself. To take one example, the 'disruptions' subsection of 'Economy' includes an article on Mexican artist Teresa Margolles' forensically preserved 'ready-made' sculpture, 'Lengua (Tongue)', which was extracted from the corpse of a drug-war victim and acquired through an exchange with the diseased man's impoverished family – body part traded for coffin to enable the family to avoid the economic humiliations of Mexico's legal bureaucracy. A coffin gave them the right to claim the remains for burial; without it, the body, now property of the state, would have been dumped in a common grave or used as a practice corpse in a medical school. We then track the tongue's subsequent elevation as art object, from exhibition in a high-end Californian commercial gallery to inclusion in a State-sponsored survey of contemporary Mexican art staged at Mexico City's Fine Arts Palace. From its inception, Tongue grates against the status-quo in a multitude of contexts, calling attention to class inequality and related social perversions embodied at their point of origin in a grotesque cycle of artistic capitalization. Ownership as such is also critiqued. Under the 'land' subsection of 'Goods', Jacob presents Indigenous artist Edward Poitrus' installation, 'Offensive/Defensive' (1988), in which Poitrus cut out two strips of grass, one from the grounds of the Mendel Art Museum in Saskatoon, Saskatchewan and the other from the reserve lands of the nearby George Gordon Nation (Saulteaux [nākawē] and Cree [nēhlyawēwin]) and exchanged them (Reed 2011: 286–287). The transaction refers to the Canadian government's imposition of legal property relations on Saskatchewan's original inhabitants, who were forced to sign away 'ownership' of their traditional lands and then penned into reservations. Defying this history, Poitrus buried lead moulds spelling out 'offensive' 'defensive' underneath each strip of grass to signify that Indigenous resistance against such state-imposed theft is far from over. Foregrounding anarchist values in such a wide range of artwork, Jacob intensifies the radical efficacy of the aesthetics of tension by revealing its capacity to foster networks of self-liberation among the oppressed.

Anarchism entails continual self-reflection and questioning (Bonanno 1998a: 4) and this is the focus of Montreal-born anarchist Freda Guttman's work. Guttman grew up during the 1930s in the Outremont district of Montreal, Quebec where 99 per cent of the students in the public schools were Jewish (she describes her pre-World War II community as 'boxed in') (Christoff 2008). Nazi Germany was a source of considerable anxiety. One of Guttman's earliest memories is of her father listening intently to a speech by Hitler on the radio. World War II and its aftermath weighed heavily on her as she tried to comprehend what forces led millions to participate in the mass slaughter of her people (Guttman n.d.: 1). On a more personal level, discovering the history of Jewish anarchists such as Emma Goldman provided a compelling counter-identity to the stifling patriarchal Judaism of Outremont. Reflecting on her sense of Jewishness once she broke free of religion, Guttman relates, 'the feeling of victimization [associated with the Holocaust] gradually transformed into an awareness and identification with all oppressed people ... the Jewish experience of not belonging anywhere and crossing cultures and not having an allegiance to any group or nation state' became a core part of her self-identity (Maestro and Horne 1990: 62).

Guttman's artistic practice, which is deeply personal, highlights tensions arising from our capacity to critique oppressive social forces which seek to shape the future by manipulating our consciousness of the past. In this regard, some of her most powerful statements concern processes of Israeli nation-building, which she reconfigures around her own responsibility as a Jew to undo the consequences (Christoff 2008). An exemplary instance is her family's complicity in the creation of 'Canada Park' under the auspices of the Jewish National Fund (JNF), an organization originally founded to purchase land for Jewish settlements. Since the founding of Israel in 1948, the JNF has been given supervisory control over lands expropriated from Palestinians and, in the early 1970s, the Canadian branch of the JHF raised $15 million (in tax-deductible donations) to develop the park, which now serves as a recreational destination for visitors from Jerusalem and Tel Aviv. What goes unacknowledged is that it is built on the ruins of three Palestinian villages – Imwas, Yalu, and Beit Nuba. During the 1967 war, the Israel army forcibly expelled over 5,000 inhabitants from these communities and then razed them to the ground. Photos taken by an Israeli soldier who participated in the expulsions left a visual record of the process (village descendants still languish in West Bank refugee camps) (Cook 2009). Guttman first visited the site in 1991. There, she discovered her parents' names amongst the list of Canadians who had donated money towards planting trees in the park. After returning to Montreal, while flipping through a family photo album of her parents on vacation in Israel in the late 1970s, she came across pictures of her mother and father at Canada Park. In response, Guttman created a complimentary album dedicated to the people whose lives Canada Park attempts to obliterate by tracking down photographs of Imwas' Palestinian inhabitants. She assembled these portraits in a weathered book documenting life before the photographed individuals could ever have imagined being driven from their ancestral homes (Antliff 2007b). This became part of an installation, 'Canada Park: Two Family Albums' (1998), featuring four digitized wall photos (all taken from the same viewpoint) of the village of Imwas. The first depicts the village before it was destroyed; three successive photos, taken in 1968, 1978, and 1988, document the ruination of the village and the creation of Canada Park. Guttman pairs her Imwas 'family album' with the album of her parent's trip to Israel during which they photographed themselves at the park, oblivious to its history and the politically-charged complicity of their own contribution to 'forgetting' (Guttman 2005: 49–50). Thus, the artwork bears witness not only to the artist's family's involvement in Israel's racist programme of nation-state building through war and forced expulsions: it creates a critical tension which resonates outward from a specific place and time to encompass Guttman's own life. In sum, Canada Park: Two Family Albums underlines that for Jewish anarchists in Israel and globally, activist solidarity with Palestinian liberation necessarily entails a personal struggle for 'self-liberation from a militaristic, racist, sexist and otherwise unequal society', i.e. Israel (Gordon 2008: 150). Internalizing this insight is an inescapable facet of freeing oneself from the falsifications of history, a productive tension that opens the future up to other possibilities.

Anarchism's aesthetic of tension, then, constitutes itself within the 'inner life' of an artwork as a socially transformative force to be taken up and developed in a myriad of ways. Autonomous from but intimately connected to the artwork and the artist's creative agency, this tension binds qualities of critique and pre-figuration together so as to further an adversarial power contiguous with anarchist politics. The artwork escapes the threat of aesthetic closure within the system it challenges by activating our desire to go beyond it, to enter the future society of anarchy fully cognizant that that society will, perforce, give rise to many more tensions.

Note

Completion of this chapter was supported by a visiting research fellowship at the Edith O'Donnell Institute of Art History, University of Texas at Dallas.

Notes

1 The American art critic Clement Greenberg was an influential spokesperson for this point of view in the 1960s and 1970s.
2 Understood as a site of tension, aesthetics escapes Marxism's closure-inflected argument that art's reifying role within the pre-revolutionary capitalist totality (as cultural commodity alienating us from our own creativity) necessitates that art's 'realization' (creativity permeating everyday life) can only unfold after the anti-capitalist revolution represses 'art' – a paradigm that has haunted our understanding of radicality in art.
3 On the history of museums conceived as educational institutions to raise the cultural level of the lower classes see Bennett (1995).

References

Antliff, A. (2007a) 'Queer Art/Queer Anarchy: An Interview with Luis Jacob', in J. McPhee and E. Reuland (eds.) *Realizing the Impossible: Art Against Authority*, Oakland: AK Press, pp. 236–249.
Antliff, A. (2007b) 'Interview with Freda Guttman', unpublished.
Antliff, A. (2009) 'Anarchy at Documenta: Interview with Luis Jacob', in M. Behm and Y. Dziswoir (eds.) *Towards a Theory of Impressionist and Expressionist Spectatorship*, Köln: Verlag der Buchandlung Walther König, pp. 47–52.
Avanessian, A. and Skrebowski, L. (2011) 'Introduction', in A. Avanessian and L. Skrebowski (eds.) *Aesthetics and Contemporary Art*, Berlin: Sternberg Press, pp. 2–12.
Au Travail/At Work (2010) 'Au Travail/At Work: Manifesto, 2010', in M. Jahn (ed.) *Byproduct: On the Excess of Embedded Art Practices*, Toronto: YYZ Books, pp. 103–105.
Badger, G. (2010) 'There Are Shitty Jobs Everywhere; That's My Freedom – An Interview with Bob the Builder of Au Travail/At Work', in M. Jahn (ed.) *Byproduct: On the Excess of Embedded Art Practices*, Toronto: XYZ Books, pp. 99–102.
Barnes Foundation (2013) Homepage. Online. Available at: http://www.barnesfoundation.org/about/press/media-info/leed (accessed 9/10/2013).
Bennett, T. (1995) *The Birth of the Museum*, London: Routledge.
Bonanno, A. (1998a) *The Anarchist Tension*, London: Elephant Editions.
Bonanno, A. (1998b) *Armed Joy*, London: Elephant Editions.
Christoff, S. (2008) 'The Art of Activism: Interview with Freda Guttman', Online. Available at: http://hour.ca/2008/09/25/the-art-of-activism/ (accessed 8/14/2013).
Cook, J. (2009) 'Canada Park and Israeli "memoricide"', The Electronic Intifada. Online. Available at: http://electronicintifada.net/content/canada-park-and-israeli-memoricide/8126 (accessed 15/10/2013).
de Acosta, A. (2009) 'Two Undecidable Questions for Thinking in Which Anything Goes', in R. Amster, A. DeLeon, L.A. Fernandez, A.J. Nocella II and D. Shannon (eds.) *Contemporary Anarchist Studies: An Introductory Anthology of Anarchy in the Academy*, London: Routledge, pp. 26–34.
Gero, R. (2006) 'The Border of the Aesthetic', in J. Elkins (ed.) *Art History versus Aesthetics*, London: Routledge, pp. 3–20.
Gordon, U. (2008) *Anarchy Alive! Anti-Authoritarian Politics from Practice to Theory*, London: Pluto Press.
Guttman, F. (n.d.) 'Artist's Statement: Exhibition Submission for "Notes From the 20th" to A Space Gallery, Toronto'.
Guttman, F. (2005) 'Imwas 1967, 1968, 1978, and 1988 Canada Park: Two Family Albums', *Positions: East Asia Cultures Critique*, 13(1): 49–50.
Hauser, J.R. (1928) 'Review: The Art in Painting by Joseph Barnes', *The Art Bulletin*, 10(3): 288–290.
Jacob, L. (2007) *Album III: Image Bank*, Köln: Verlag der Buchandlung Walther König.
Jacob, L. (2011) 'Introduction: Commerce by Artists', in L. Jacob (ed.) *Commerce by Artists*, Toronto: Art Metropole, pp. 2–15.
Jeavons, A. (2013a) 'Artist Albo Jeavons – Saatchi On-Line', Online. Available at: http://www.saatchionline.com/albojeavons (accessed 8/14/2013).
Jeavons, A. (2013b) 'Art Jail', Online. Available at: http://www.artjail.org/intro.htm (accessed 9/10/2013).
Kant, I. (1790) *Critik der Urtheilskraft*, Berlin and Libau (Liepāja): Bey Lagarde und Friederich.
Maestro, L. and Horne, S. (1990) 'Interview with Freda Guttman', *Harbour Magazine*, May: 61–64.
PreziosiD. and Farago, C. (2004) 'General Introduction: What are Museums For?' in D. Preziosi and C. Farago (eds.) *Grasping the World: The Idea of the Museum*, Aldershot, UK: Ashgate, pp. 13–22.
Reed, J.W. (2011) 'Offensive/Defensive', in L. Jacob (ed.) *Commerce by Artists*, Toronto: Art Metropole.
Saatchi Gallery (2013). Homepage. Online. Available at: http://www.saatchigallery.com/gallery/intro.htm (accessed 8/15/2013).

15 Conclusion in three acts
False genealogies and suspect methodologies?

Carl Levy

Act One: Anarchist encounters in a hall of mirrors

In this conclusion, I return to the questions of genealogies and methodologies, which shape the various encounters of anarchism with the humanities and the social sciences. I will knit together key themes and unresolved problems. I identify these as the problems of the boundary between 'small-a' anarchism and Anarchism as used in the humanities and social sciences, the identification of false genealogies by those who want the anarchist tradition to be relevant to the humanities and social sciences, and the epistemological claims of conflicting advocates for the use of anarchism as a methodology in the humanities and social sciences.

Let us start with the question of the anarchist canon, the struggle between the supporters, roughly speaking, of the continuity of the classical anarchist tradition, and those advocates of postanarchism (Jun 2012; Evren 2012; Kinna and Evren 2013). But even within these broad schools, these are differences of interpretation, which concern identifying what is inside and what is outside the anarchist canon. Thus in an often cited example, Michael Schmidt and Lucien van der Walt, have a rigorously selective definition of what anarchism is and isn't (van der Walt and Schmidt 2009). In their very informative overview of varieties of syndicalist and peasant movements in the Global North and the Global South from the 1870s to the 1940s, anarchism is defined as a form of class-struggle Bakuninism and revolutionary 'anti-landlordism' with an anti-statist flavour, which disposes with Proudhon (the first thinker to coin the term 'anarchy' in its modern connotation), and dismisses outright the impact of Godwin and Stirner on their subjects of study. On the other hand, their capacious review of 'legitimate' movements includes organizations and social actors who never considered themselves anarchists and at times were rather hostile to those who identified themselves in that way, certain figures close to the De Leonites, while the IWW, a favourite, was far more divided over embracing anarchism than they suggest. Nathan Jun, a critic of this approach, adopts a fine-grained method in which anarchism is either an historical movement or a philosophical or theoretical orientation, a methodology to be read anarchically: 'the hermeneutic practice of discovering anarchistic attitudes, ideas, and thoughts in literature, philosophy, and other venues' (Jun 2013: 115), whereas the highly politicized approach of Schmidt/Van der Walt cherry-picks from both of Jun's categories. Another example is the previously discussed connection between 'capital-A' Anarchism and the 'small-a' anarchism of the practices of horizontalism and consensus democracy identified in the Global Justice Movement and the Occupy/Square waves of radical mobilization (Graeber, etc.), despite the fact that the most successful classical anarchists ('capital-A' Anarchists), the Spanish CNT-FAI, did not practise consensual democracy as understood and practised by these post-Cold War movements (Cohn 2006: 207–209).

The fraught nature of genealogies can also be found in Geography. Thus interactions between geography and anarchism, discussed in Ince's chapter, are misleading in the estimation of Pascale Siegrist (2017). Anarchism, as the epistemological point of departure for geography, is undergirded by historical studies of the interaction of Reclus and Kropotkin. But for her, 'anarchist geography is largely a modern construct' which 'obliterates much of the way in which Reclus and Kropotkin thought about the relationship between science and radicalism' (132). According to her reading of both nineteenth-century geographers, neither ever spoke of 'anarchist geography' or 'in their strictly speaking geographical works, the anarchism is subliminal at best' (132). And thus questioning Federico Ferretti's (2018) interpretation, 'even the private correspondence between the anarchist geographers yields no sustained reflection on how to invigorate geography through anarchism' (131). From Siegrist's perspective, Kropotkin and Reclus' contemporaneous fellow geographers did not take their anarchism seriously and concurrently Kropotkin and Reclus did not address their fellow anarchists in their role as geographers. Unlike the present-day anarchist-geographers discussed in Ince's chapter, Kropotkin 'was more interested in transforming anarchism than he was in turning the epistemic foundations of geography upside down' (140).

I will now turn to two remaining examples in this 'Hall of Mirrors'. First, the variety of uses the anarchists make of anthropology and the complex interaction of the professional anthropologists to anarchism. Secondly, the contested linkages of biology, altruism, human language, and anarchism.

Act Two: Anarchism and anthropology

Anarchism and anthropology have been in conversation with each other since the nineteenth century. Kropotkin's concept of mutual aid relied on the concept of altruism (more below) and ethnographic and historical studies, which 'proved' the viability of mutual aid. He reported lengthy accounts of the Siberian Buryat, the Algerian Kabyle, the European medieval city, and his hosts, the watchmakers of the Jura in Switzerland. He was interested in the creative genius of people living in the 'clan period' of history and identified in all these examples the promotion of social individuality which avoided the false 'individualism' of Victorian capitalist society. Elie Reclus' (1903) *Primitive Folk* stressed the moral and intellectual equality of all cultures. Celestin Bouglé, famous for a study of Indian caste society, was shaped by Proudhon. Marcel Mauss' (1990, first published 1925) *The Gift* has functioned both as an anarchist text (more below) *and* a primer for anthropologists (one sees the effect on the captivated David Graeber 2001). A.R. Radcliffe-Brown, the Oxford anthropologist, was known in his early years as 'Anarchy Brown' for his attraction to the works of Kropotkin. Evans-Pritchard's (1940) study, *The Nuer*, described their political system as 'ordered anarchy'. The American anthropologists Paul Radin and Dorothy Lee drew insight from the sense of community, egalitarianism, and reciprocal behaviour found in their studies of Native Americans. The list can go on, and other examples will appear in my discussion in due course (Morris 2005; 2015). Long before the current intense exchanges between anarchists and anthropologists, Brian Morris and most particularly, Harold Barclay (1982), described the anarchic societies of hunter-gathers such as the Inuit, the Bushmen, the Yaka Pygmies, and the Australian Aborigines, but also tribal societies in

Africa and in southern India, which sported much higher population densities and therefore were closer to the daily realities of inhabitants of the modern state.

Anarchists have always been attracted to anthropology, because the anthropologists' studies of so-called primitive indigenous societies showed that hierarchical societies were not necessary and that alternatives to the state and hierarchy were workable and had worked and were working in the past and the present. In the literature of the new anarchism,

> a continuity is established in which indigenous examples appear alongside historical anarchist struggles, contemporary autonomous forms of organisation such as social centres, and southern autonomous social movements such as Argentinian recuperated factories. The point is that indigenous groups provide practical rebuttals of capitalist naturalisations and practical alternatives to dominant practices, and the explicit use of the examples is for the purpose of showing that anarchism is practically possible.
>
> (Robinson and Tormey 2012: 146)

In short, anthropology has been mobilized and deployed in a strategic fashion by anarchists because these accounts validate their narrative of an alternative order based on statelessness, horizontal modes of organization and non-hierarchical forms of social cooperation, which are non-monetarized and in turn generate solidarity, friendship, and reciprocity.

The French anthropologist Pierre Clastres (1977) concluded from his studies of Amazonian peoples that primitive societies were not embryonic versions of later states but societies based on different first principles, alien to the ethnocentric views of the European anthropologists, namely, so-called primitive societies implanted mechanisms based on exchange and reciprocity, which embraced technological change to reduce work and not increase production, but which also prevented tribal leaders from exercising autonomous and self-aggrandizing power, which arose from these societies' fear of domination. For the anarchist enthusiasts of Clastres, the French anthropologist's findings validate the anarchist concepts of temporary functional leadership or followership (Ehrlich 1996), as well as post-scarcity anarcho-communism. For Clastres, the shift to the state occurs when the activity of production aimed at satisfying the needs of others, is replaced by the tyranny of debt, thus the difference between the Amazonian and the oppressed Incan farmer lies precisely here. But countering the then dominant Marxist interpretations, this social transformation was caused by a political revolution not the transformation of the economic base, which replaced 'primitive communism' with a slave or feudal society. Indeed, Clastres proposed an anarchist-like reading of the Marxist base/superstructure couplet, similar to Banaji (2011) on the origins of Asian capitalism, namely, that if one wants to preserve the Marxist concept of the base, perhaps the superstructure should be economic and the base political! In a similar vein, anarchists have been keen to cite the latest evidence from Eastern Turkey, which indicates that temples preceded the statist structures of power, that urban habitations were the result of shaman-cults and religious devotion, which encouraged the collection of wealth and power to guarantee good weather, a healthy world, and an untroubled afterlife. Thus status accumulation and symbolic power were more important than economic power for proto-states, power flowed from the gods not the 'gun', that massive structures preceded cities, that 'the concentration of spiritual power enabled a concentration of political and economic power' (Gelderloos 2016: 197).

Anarchists are also attracted to the latest finding by anthropological archaeologists who insist that the universality of the state is a very recent event, that until 10,000 years ago human life was carried out in small nomadic bands of hunter-gatherers, and even the first states were unsteady institutions, which were followed by long periods of non-state societies – not 'Dark Ages' – but the self-reliance of societies counter-acting the dysfunctionality of these early states, which had failed to withstand the pressures of famines, epidemics, and continual warfare. The retreat from the 'ruins' may have been an enlightened and sensible reaction by those who fled these failing states (Scott 2009; 2017). The sum total of much of human history demonstrates non-linear societal change and a diversity of structures (clans, trading confederations, religious fraternities, etc.), that point to a complexity in which hierarchy and stratification are largely absent or at least not prominent features: the hegemony of the state-form is only obvious from the seventeenth century onwards (Levy 2010: 6–8; Ince and Barrera de la Torre 2017). But as James Scott has argued, this alternative take on the state in history has been obscured by the predominance of statism in the social sciences: 'Aside from the utter hegemony of the state form today, a great deal of archaeology and history throughout the world is state-sponsored and often amounts to a narcissistic exercise in self-portraiture' (Scott 2017: 13).

Primitivist anarchists may take heart in the arguments put forward by Yuval Noah Harari, who discusses Neolithic hunter-gatherer post-scarcity Stone Age economics, originally advanced by Marshall Sahlins in the 1960s (his domestic mode of production, a species of anarchy), and argues in a popular history of homo sapiens, that 'the essence of the Agricultural Revolution' was 'the ability to keep more people alive under worse conditions' (Harari 2014: 83) and thus the advance of infectious diseases, animal cruelty, and the enslavement or near enslavement of farmers; or as Scott puts it, the state domesticated humans but if one wishes to compare the fate of hunter-gatherers to early farmers and urban dwellers, 'in terms of their diet, their health, and their leisure', hunter-gatherers win hands down (Scott 2017: 10), and thus to return to Harari, '[T]he discrepancy between evolutionary success and individual suffering is perhaps the most important lesson we can draw from the Agricultural Revolution' (Harari 2014: 97).[1]

Besides Clastres' and many other studies of 'primitive stateless societies' (Overing 1993; Gibson and Sillander 2011), anarchists have been inspired by Mauss' treatment of the gift relationship, and Graeber's (2011) treatment of debt joins the two streams together. But well before Graeber, Clastres showed how the Amazonians anti-power mechanisms were underwritten by the logic of a gift society in which self-aggrandizing 'leaders' 'all end up competing to see who can give the most away' (Graeber 2004: 22). The Situationists (part Marxist, part Dadaist and part anarchist), the subversive force in Paris' May 1968, used the concepts of the gift exchange and the potlatch (binge gift-giving) as a lens to 'reveal social relations' in the era of spectacular capitalism and they came 'to see as the main arena of revolutionary struggle; the tendency of commodity exchange (not production per se) to reify social relations and hide their interconnectedness' (Martin 2012: 129). A reading of Mauss revitalized the French libertarian left in the age of the mass consumer. Thus the African American rising in Watts, Los Angeles in 1965 could be seen, according to the Situationists, as an assault on the Society of the Spectacle, and thus the Situationists were twenty years in advance of what anthropologists term 'gifting', the transformation of commodities into gifts, because 'very few ethnographers talked about the coexistence of the gift and commodity exchanging until the 1980s' (132). The Situationists also anticipated Pierre Bourdieu in 'the possibility that unequal access to commodities is a source of humiliation and social hierarchy that are central to the constitution of social class in western societies (well before the publication of works such as Bourdieu's (1984) *Distinction*)' (137).

But this complex and long-lasting interchange of anarchism and anthropology has not gone unchallenged by anthropologists today, even those who evince sympathy to anarchist cross-traffic. Anthropologists are wary of the cherry-picking and 'weaponizing' of their academic studies, thus: 'The approach is typically pragmatic, a kind of prospecting through the ethnographic record for those elements that were useful for a political platform without taking on most of the discipline's key preoccupations' (High 2012: 98). The 'anarcho-sympathetic' Robinson and Tormey (2012) warn about a simplistic projection of the Western narrative on 'Others': 'Statements from people identified as indigenous, and sometimes also from anthropologists, are taken at face-value in this literature, rather than as strategic claims or attempts at cultural translation' (146). Thus it is has been argued that Scott's treatment of Zomia may be an anachronism, especially his employment of the word 'state' to describe what the highlander 'Zomians' were fleeing (High 2012: 99). Holly High cautions about the 'promise and pitfalls of mutual prospecting' (99). In the current anarchist literature which depends on a certain reading of the anarchic anthropologists, the stakes are high, because in these debates, 'if it can be shown that there is no necessity for antagonism and conflict' between humans 'then this opens the possibility for more harmonious, cooperative and autonomous forms of life to emerge' (Robinson and Tormey 2012: 151, also see Birmingham 2013). This erects, a critic argues, a false dichotomy between the free space, the shatter-zone, and the 'Zomias' of this planet ('this binary of pure natives and oppressive state' (Jonsson 2012: 161)), or again more forcefully: 'Zomia offers no place for the Asian Highlanders on whatever have been their own terms, but instead is a vast playground for Western libertarian distraction and delight' (167).[2]

Thus this dichotomous reading of the pre-state condition can lead to differing and mutually opposite if misleading interpretations as a 'morally desirable refuge, freedom and resistance', but equally as 'violent, lawless and chaotic' (here Holly High is referring to a treatment by Tess Lea (2012) of the periodic moral panics in contemporary Australia about Aboriginal self-government) (High 2012: 102; also see Johnson and Ferguson 2018). Primitive anarchists and their friend-enemy social anarchists (Price 2018), may take heart that a popular study of the history of humanity, such as Harari's cited earlier, seems to endorse respectively their conflicting concerns, the dangerous legacies of the Agricultural Revolution and the emergence of mutual aid, but Harari twists these statements in uncomfortable directions for the anarchists. Disregarding Graeber's idea of the communist baseline of exchange in market societies, Harari (2014: 180) argues that money is the most efficient source of trust ever devised, and that mutual aid is value neutral, anticipating a discussion I will address very shortly, so that mass networks of cooperation are seldom altruistic, voluntary, and egalitarian: 'Even prisons and concentration camps are cooperation networks, and can function only because thousands of strangers somehow manage to coordinate their actions' (Harari 2014: 104). There is also the assertion by Steven Pinker (using a controversial methodology) that the per capita murder rate was higher in pre-state societies than in modern day societies, even comparing the bloody twentieth century to the Neolithic past (Pinker 2012). Harari cheekily adds that an urban dweller living during Brazil's military dictatorship (1964–1985) would have been less likely to be murdered by the state, than a male in 'stateless' Amazonian Yanomami society (Harari 2014: 367). In a similar spirit to Siegrist's (2017) critique of a false genealogy of contemporary anarchist geography, Robinson and Tormey (2012) warn that the studies of the anthropologists can be interesting for the anarchists, but anthropology is not anarchist (150).

I would like to end this discussion with a qualified defence of the anarchist anthropologists and some of the self-taught anthropologists amongst the anarchists. Brian Morris (2005), for example, never argues that anthropology can be read as anarchism *tout court*; his aim is to highlight the elective affinities between the two. He also notes some differences between how one uses an anarchic methodology to explain pre-state societies in the works of Clastres and Barclay (mirroring the various and contending applications of anthropological evidence by the Primitive Anarchists (Robinson and Tormey 2012: 147)). Thus for Clastres social hierarchy creates the state but for Barclay power is an agent, which creates the state. 'For Clastres', Morris argues, 'social hierarchy engenders the state as a political institution, which separates from and dominates society; in Barclay's terms, the state is able to exercise "authority" because it is recognised as a "legitimate" agent of coercive power' (Morris 2005: 8). Barclay recognizes the numerous oppressive features which inhibit free expression in stateless societies. Even in a society free of police, 'the reliance on customary sanctions can be unforgiving and cruel' (Barclay 1982: 127). And he continues, the 'Big Man' and the shaman, whose functions are to soothe the disruptions of personal feuds and anxieties over mortality, could be parlayed into state leadership through the growth of informal clienteles and the monopoly of religious knowledge. Graeber cautions against the dichotomous reading of state-less societies previously discussed in reference to the work of Lea. 'Primitive societies' were and are neither heaven nor hell on Earth. In this sense he argues that Clastres was naïve and romantic since he did not highlight in his studies the ways men had threatened women with gang rape (Graeber 2004: 22). We never lived in the Garden of Eden and conversely '"modern societies" still possess "primitive" cosmologies and kinships systems' (Graeber 2004: 54–55; also see Lagalisse 2018). The stateless societies of the Orinoco in Venezuela, the Highlands of Madagascar or the Tiv of Nigeria, did not dispense with certain forms of dominance, 'at least of men over women, elders over juniors' (Graeber 2004: 31).

Thus anarchist anthropologists and self-taught anarchists have arrived at a far more nuanced approach than many of their critics realize. Morris argues that we should avoid rigorous and self-excluding typologies. There have been areas on the Earth where the state and stateless societies have lived together. There is a spectrum of examples in which societies without government – bands and tribes – become centralized into chieftaincies (Morris 2015: 115–117). Graeber argues that some apparently stateless societies are nothing of the sort: 'one of the most striking discoveries of evolutionary anthropology has been that it is perfectly possible to have kings and nobles and all the exterior trappings of monarchy without having a state in the mechanical sense at all' (Graeber 2004: 67). Graeber advances the project 'to reanalyse the state as a relation between a utopian imaginary, and a messy reality involving strategies of flight and evasion, predatory elites, and a mechanics of regulations and control' (68). Graeber wants to rescue anthropology from 'its squalid colonial history' and wishes it to 'become the common property of humankind' (94). Anthropology's 'vast archive of human experience, of social and political experiments' (96) should be employed in carefully calibrated discussions which dispense with over-eager essentialist logic or politically motivated wishful thinking, much in parallel to the spirit of Eric Olin Wright's (2010) 'Real Utopias Project' (indeed Graeber (2004: 76) calls his quest 'a kind of sociology of micro-utopias'), and thus he concludes, 'I think Mauss and

Clastres have succeeded somewhat despite themselves, in laying the groundwork for a theory of revolutionary counterpower' (24).

But for those who want to chart the emergence of the state form in human history, a careful dosage of anarchist sensitivities may pay dividends. Thus Scott's latest work charts how key components of the state (irrigation, alluvial fishing/agricultural communities and communal forms of slavery) are formed before the arrival of the state, but a monoculture, which is easily legible by the proto-state will be also easily taxable: 'You can have a grain-producing non-state alluvial community but any state needs an alluvial grain-producing population – therefore the state has parasitized them' (Scott 2017: 117). Therefore the state, where a captive population is more important than mere territory, erects barriers and walls not to keep the barbarians out but to keep former pre-state populations within the recording, registering, and measuring machine that is its essence (139), and so dispensing with any Edenic projections of the pre-state realities, Scott asserts that states did not invent slavery but they invented 'large-scale societies based systematically on coerced, captive human labor' (169). Thus as states are established, a zone of non-state rule by the 'barbarians', as the Han Chinese or Romans might describe them, by raiders who seek rent from sedentary farmers within the state's walls and outside them is established: as the Berber saying goes, 'raiding is our agriculture' (241). Thus, the tribal societies of the Mongols and Ottomans, states-in-waiting before they became full-fledged horseback states, replaced the more lucrative protection rackets of those walled states' trading partners/adversaries, which had earlier exiled them to the hinterlands, Scott asserts. Thus we can see the helpfulness of the anarchic approach to the evolution of empire, state, and tribal horseback societies and their predatory relationship with farmers: 'If we step back and widen the lens, barbarian-state relations can be seen as a contest between two parties for the right to appropriate the surplus from the sedentary grain and manpower module' (242).

The self-taught polymathic anarchist anthropologists have also contributed to this innovative approach. Murray Bookchin (2005) comes to mind, but even in our era of pervasive credentialization, Peter Gelderloos (2016) has produced research reliant upon a careful sifting of the research of the historical anthropologists of the state. His aim is to present an anarchist theory of state formation which discards or revises the legacies of dialectical materialism (Marxism), environmental determinism (Jared Diamond), and the previously mentioned anarchist primitivists (agreeing with Barclay or Graeber, he argues that the primitivists cannot account for hierarchy in hunter-gatherer societies and they tend to Orientalize their subjects of study) (11).[3] In a parallel fashion to Scott's previously cited critiques of statist accounts of the rise of state, he criticizes the academics of the Early State Project who recognized the concept of multilinear evolution of the state but still could not wean themselves from assumption that the state is the most advanced form of organization available to human society (Gelderloos 2016: 76), and thus are silent on the anomalies of the Indus Valley civilization, which was probably stateless with little evidence of religious practice or slavery (143). Therefore, Gelderloos argues societies without economic stratification can be formed in hundreds of different ways and state forms can happened through many different pathways: the sacred commerce state based on the consolidation and centralization of interregional networks of commerce and spirituality; reluctant client states formed by former stateless societies in response to an imperialist interloper; imitative states in which local elites existing in former non-state hierarchies are impressed by the power of a neighbour and copy its methods; the progressive state where a popular revolt forces the formation of a state to oppose a more oppressive state- interloper; the conquest or colony state in which a warrior brotherhood takes over a larger population and creates a state; the Greek-type democracy in which a state-forming warrior elite is modified by a form of stateless consensus; the royal court state, in which the state is a creation of an alliance of nobles and a charismatic warrior who establishes a line of descent; and its transcendence by the Holy Father State in which family/clan worship is transformed by major religions (Confucianism or Hinduism) (160–182). But as I mentioned previously, central to his anarchist understanding of the rise of the state is a form of status accumulation based more on symbolic rather than economic power: 'Spiritual power played a role in engineering a rupture with the value systems of earlier, non-state societies' (201). Pyramids preceded cities, but they also generated the demand for more trade and more warfare, creating a truly autonomous elite of priests for example (and architecture, astronomy, mathematics, and medicine) and their receptacle, the state (204).

Act Three: Humanity, language, and altruism and final thoughts on methodologies and epistemologies

Noam Chomsky is perhaps the most famous academic who has self-identified with anarchism since the Second World War. But his more diffuse criticism of US foreign policy and his notoriety in the field of linguistics, are the real pathways to his political fame. Chomsky's anti-imperialism (Vietnam, Latin America, Indonesia, War on Terror, Iraq, etc.), and his dissection of the mass media's collaboration with the US foreign policy elites, do not immediately draw on anarchist sources, albeit a forensic examination can reveal some of the connections, the explorations of media power appear more Gramscian than strictly anarchist. Chomsky is a self-declared anarcho-syndicalist whose attraction to this doctrine began with his childhood fascination with the anarchists and syndicalists of the Spanish Civil War (1936–1939). Chomsky's anarchism is gradualist, non-sectarian, and linked to the unorthodox Marxism of the council communists. His anarchism is class-based and underpinned by his belief in the innate goodness of human beings. He is a firm advocate of the values of the Radical Enlightenment (especially the work of Wilhelm von Humboldt), taking on the mantle of Rudolf Rocker (who also influenced his adaption of anarcho-syndicalism), and therefore an advocate of the scientific method and human rights, both of which does not predispose him to Foucault's methodology and more recent iterations in varieties of postanarchism (Elders 2011; McGilvray 2014; Edgley 2015). The most controversial, interesting, and relevant aspects of Chomsky's intellectual biography are the connections or otherwise between his theory of language acquisition and his anarchism. Chomsky has been coy, admitting that there are loose and tentative connections between the cognitive sciences and his anarchism (Rai 2015). But a deeper discussion is needed and serves as a startling case study of both the 'Hall of Mirrors' in anarchist genealogy and also the methodology behind Chomsky's major contributions to linguistics.

Chomsky argues that we do not need to explain the historical origins of language because human nature is qualitatively different from animals. Language cannot be taught but is awakened in humans. Chomsky advances the concept of a Language Acquisition Device (LAD), which arose in the human brain due to a cognitive leap, caused by a random genetic mutation some 50 to 100,000 years ago: thus Chomsky's study of language is a form of natural not social or historical science. The task of the science of language is to postulate a computational theory, 'that describes its actual nature and explains on the basis of evidence why it has this nature' (McGilvray 2014: 123). Chomsky's approach does not feed into a direct endorsement of his anarchism, but he does argue that human nature can be studied scientifically, whereas the study of government or economics does not sanction the use of the methodology of the natural sciences. Thus it can be argued that his project is biological humanism: his quest is to understand human beings as natural subjects with language (rather like the role of 'reason' in Descartes, separating them from other species). Unlike Foucault who argued in their famous televised confrontation in 1971 that 'justice' was merely an instrument to acquire forms of power and economic supremacy, Chomsky claimed that human justice was grounded in solidarity and sympathy, which could be underwritten by empirical proof arising from the use of the scientific method. The target was not merely Foucault's Nietzschean approach to power but American Cold War social science (Elders 2011).

Thus gradualist approaches to the appearance of language should be abandoned and the science of the mind should abandon the reverse engineering of the compelling 'just so stories' of Evolutionary Psychology or Social Biology. Both disciplines, Chomsky argues, have not produced the evidence that a natural scientist should take seriously. He uses a natural scientific approach to undermine the political messages of Stephen Pinker or the earlier B.F. Skinner, but: 'the connection between Chomsky's natural science of human nature and in particular the natural science account of language embedded within it and his anarchosyndicalism is not a tight one. It is a matter of deduction' (McGilvray 2014: 135).

This process of deduction is rather complicated to unravel. Whereas Chomsky believes Social Biology and Evolutionary Psychology are too ideological and reduce human behaviour to genetic determinism, Chomsky's Cartesian innate-ism is more open-ended. Thus Chomsky argues,

> The normal use of language and the acquisition of language depends on what Humboldt calls the fixed form of language, a system of generative processes that is rooted in the nature of the human mind and constrains but does not determine the free creations of normal intelligence or, at a higher and more original level, of the greatest writer or thinker.
>
> (Chomsky 2013: 137–138)

So the free will expressed through human intelligence nevertheless obeys the innate rules of the LAD. Chomsky continues:

> The normal creative use of language, which for the Cartesian rationalist is the best index of the existence of another mind, presupposes a system of rules and generative principles of a sort that the rationalist grammarians attempted, with some success, to determine and make explicit.
>
> (Chomsky 2013: 138)

So within Chomsky's idea of a libertarian form of freedom, exists the constraints of nature, 'without this tension between necessity and freedom, rule and choice, there can be no creativity, no communications, no meaningful acts at all' (138). And he concludes by returning to his champion from the Radical Enlightenment:

It seems to me fair to regard the contemporary study of language as in some ways a return to the Humboldtian concepts of the form of language: a system of generative processes rooted in the innate properties of mind but permitting, in Humboldt's phrase, an infinite use of finite means.

(Chomsky 2013: 140–141)

But from whence did Chomsky's idea of the LAD, and its subsequent iterations arise? In a fascinating, in turns flawed and valuable book, the unorthodox Marxist anthropologist, Chris Knight (2016), presents us with a genealogy of the Language Acquisition Device, which reveals deeper anarchist roots, other than the libertarian affinities of Humboldt. I will not enter into the merits or demerits of Chomsky's theory of the LAD, which has generated much heat. I am also highly sceptical of Knight's psychological account of Chomsky's research. Knight argues that Chomsky attempts to present his linguistics as 'dispassionate, value-free, insulated from social fashion, as well as from his own or anyone else's political agenda or needs' (234). He believes that Chomsky has run a cult, which defies the strictures of the scientific method. His theories are implausible and incredible. Unlike Galileo or Einstein, 'when their theories were taken up by others and tested, it turned out they worked' (180), there has been no empirical testing of Chomsky's theories. For Knight, the basis of Chomsky's academic fame, his 1954 PhD, later published as a monograph (*The Logical Structure of Linguistic Theory*), is gratuitous and mathematically illiterate (53). For Knight, Chomsky does not engage in experimental science, but makes a series of deductions without showing his 'workings' and thus his theories were characterized by a lifetime of zig-zags and rethinks, from the concept of 'deep structure' to 'universal grammar' to 'merge': for Knight, Chomsky is the Picasso rather than Einstein of linguistics. Thus his work is governed by a form of artistic license not science. For Knight it is madness to assert that language occurred because of one moment of mutation: it is madness to imagine that language can be conceived without a discussion of previous Darwinian evolution, and on this, more further on (210). What drove Chomsky's increasingly ornate and confused research, according to Knight, was a guilt complex, because 'state-funding provided the institutional framework needed to ensure the cognitive revolution success. If there was a political will in operation here, no matter how unconscious, it was indisputably that of the state' (234). In short, he had to convince himself that 'his linguistics, had no connection with military priorities, nothing to do with the Pentagon-funded academic establishment [so prominent at his institution MIT: CL] ...' (140–141).

Returning to an earlier theme of Chapter 1, which will pop up again in the discussion of anarchism's role in the search for the 'altruism gene', namely, the curious pairing of anarchist approaches to the history of the American Military Industrial Complex, the immediate origins and funding for the LAD are found in the quest by the Pentagon for a machine-translation device necessary for the command and control systems of the USA's nuclear arsenal. As mentioned in previous encounters of anarchism with the military-industrial complex (the Rand Corporation and 'swarming'; techniques of mass civil disobedience, the Colour Revolutions and the Square Movements, etc.), both anarchism and the Military Industrial Complex adopted a universalist worldview (for diametrically different reasons, naturally): the immediate background to the Pentagon-funded universal translation machine project can be found in the 1940s in the ideas of Warren Weaver, who also anticipated Chomsky's work on 'deep structure' and universal grammar, and who was motivated by the desire to promote world peace, not ICBM command and control systems (Knight 2016: 53).

However, the intellectual and practical origins of machine-translation are intimately tied to anarchist sources stretching back to pre-revolutionary Russia. In this regard Knight has provided an invaluable service to intellectual history; his psycho-history, however, is very dubious. Knight argues that Chomsky denounced the Mandarins of the social sciences and the humanities and seemed to forget his natural science colleagues at MIT busy devising the architecture of MAD or working on fuel-air explosives, the most powerful form of conventional armaments on Earth. But although he documents them, Knight does not try to square Chomsky's brave stances against the Vietnam War, his arrests during many protests, and his putative lifetime of academic evasion:

> Unlike his ordinary social intelligence, Chomsky's *scientific* intelligence had been shaped since his student days within a culture heavily dependent on state sponsorship, particularly by the US military; because these sponsors wanted practical applications, Chomsky had to take care to avoid violating his conscience. Taking no chances, he divorced the very concept of 'language' from *all possibility* of practical use. While accepting the funding, he would retreat into a space of his own in which language was not public, not social, not communicative – and not even capable of making reference to anything in the world, whether real or imagined.
>
> (Knight 2016: 147–148)

But isn't Knight's psycho-intellectual history the very example of the 'just so stories' he lays at Chomsky's feet? How does he know what is going on in Chomsky's head? Did Chomsky leave diary evidence or oral testimony of his grand strategy?

Let us now turn to Knight's intellectual history of the LAD, which is of far greater merit and links directly to the themes of this chapter. Chomsky's theory relied upon the concepts of deep structures advanced by Claude Levi-Strauss and Roman Jakobson's concept that sound patterns not language are hard-wired in the human brain. Jakobson was a Russian exile who had direct links before 1917 with Russian Futurians, the Russian anarchist Futurists (also see Gurianova 2012). The central influence was the poet and thinker, Velimir Klebnikov and his concept of *zaum* ('transreason' or 'beyondsense'); inspired by the role of Einstein's reconstruction of the concepts of time and space, the Russian Futurian

> had the idea of a universal language from the equally elemental 'atoms' of meaning, Klebnikov's notion of *intrinsic* [italics in text] meaningfulness, and this was an attack on the Saussurean idea that speech sounds are only arbitrarily connected with their meanings.
>
> (Knight 2016: 89).

Jakobson's linkage to the Russian Futurists is reflected in Chomsky's belief that linguistics was a natural science, which had its own internal laws not merely social conventions, and that here was an underlying 'deep language'. Thus the central claim of Klebnikov was 'to have discovered a lost alphabet of sounds – a universal language rooted not merely in habit or convention but in the laws of nature yet to be fully understood' (95). In other words 'every sound is *intrinsically* significant, retaining its meaning across all languages of the world' (97), and therefore like the anarchist advocates of Esperanto but using a different approach (Levy 2012), he aimed for the unity of the world's languages. Thus Jakobson's concept of a universal alphabet can be detected originally in Klebnikov's concept of the 'strings of the alphabet' (Knight 2016: 97). And like the advocates of Esperanto or indeed the later thoughts of pacifist Warren Weaver, Klebnikov's universal language would abolish all political borders and restore 'the planet to its former unity' (98). Whereas Jakobson was less dreamy than the Russian poet, the influence of anarchist Russian Futurism was reflected through Jakobson and also the quest of the previously mentioned Warren Weaver, whose concept of the universal translation machine, his self-described 'New Tower of Babel', had its own Russian Futurist influence through the anarchist turned Bolshevik, Vladimir Tatlin's proposed Babel-like tower of the Third International, which found its original inspiration not only in the Communist internationalism of the early 1920s, but also in Russian myths which claimed that Slavic tongues were chosen by God to unify the world.

Thus to summarize the ornate dance between anarchism and the world of calculated nuclear annihilation, this strand of Formalism, and the genealogy of Chomsky's thought, Knight reaches a startling conclusion about the quest for a universal 'deep language': 'invented by revolutionary anarchists, communists and war-resisters [it] ended up being sponsored by the US military in the hope of enhancing their weapons command and control' (112). But of course Chomsky's concept of the LAD and its successors seemed to be the 'secret of human creativity and freedom' (114), and meant that humans had a deep-seated instinct to rebel and therefore tell right from wrong. As I mentioned before (in his disputes with Social Biologists and Evolutionary Psychologists, Chomsky disavowed forms of Hobbesian behaviouralism), certain qualities were innate, such as language, and thus he disavowed the Left Liberal Mandarins' technocratic managerialism, which was founded on the belief that humans were blank sheets malleable through social engineering. His work, he argued, was based on natural science, not social scientific speculations by unqualified humanists and social scientists who were not capable to intrude on, or form a clear judgement of, his theories. This of course leads us to the debate about the so-called altruism gene and the legacy of Kropotkin. And the bridge to that discussion is constructed by examining Knight's counter-suggestions to Chomsky's claim that the language acquisition device in all human beings arose from a random mutation 50 to 100,000 years ago.

Knight's approach has curious parallels with Clastres' suggestion that the state arose through a political rather than economic revolution. Like Harari, Knight suggests that a social-cognitive revolution occurred in which human beings could project empathy and imagination, thus unlike chimpanzees, human beings can put themselves in others' shoes. At some point, human primate culture was overturned, and hunter-gatherers developed an assertive egalitarianism, not present in troops of baboons, for example, who live under the despotism of alpha males. Thus in our ancestors, mutual gazing, babbling, kiss-feeding, the sharing of children amongst mothers to protect them from the predation of males (female bonding) created the background for human language. This reading of others' intentions by our ancestors, Knight relates, occurred over 500,000 years ago and the development of language arose through early human beings' growing ability to develop a cooperative capacity and to infer meanings from context, 'to recognise common ground and to remember past communications to build upon' (224). In short, Knight dismisses Chomsky's mentalism and stresses, instead, the role of sex and gender in shaping the framework of cooperation, of a sort of cooperative mind-reading in which language slowly developed in social contexts. Cooperation is based on trust, the grounds for altruism, and thus we turn to that topic, but as we will see, tensions persist between the forms of social biology and political anthropology advanced by Knight, and the role of a pure computational natural science advanced by Chomsky, and the position of anarchism and the anarchists in all of this.

The question of altruism has haunted the social and natural sciences since the nineteenth century. We can summarize the present-day discussion in three camps. In camp one, the theme is the process of group selection. Altruism within a group helps the species survive, advanced by Darwin and more importantly for our purposes, Kropotkin. One of the most important new treatments can be found in David Sloan Wilson's (2016), *Does Altruism Exist? Culture, Genes, and the Welfare of Others*. The second camp argues that altruism is hard-wired into our brains, not that dissimilar to Chomsky's argument that we possess a LAD (Donald Pfaff (2015), *The Altruistic Brain: How We Are Naturally Good*). The third camp approaches the subject by discussing the management of altruism using utilitarian logic, most famously by Peter Singer (2015), *The Most Good You Can Do: How Effective Altruism is Changing Ideas about Living Ethically*. In a parallel fashion, Michael Taylor (1976; 1987) argued that positive altruism and voluntary cooperation atrophy in the presence of the state and grow in its absence. He argued that the state released the need for individual to cooperate. Thus the state destroyed the basis of altruism, whilst small voluntary organizations stimulated altruism.

But here I would like to return to the discussion featured in our review of Chomsky: the tensions between the contributions of the social sciences and the humanities and the natural sciences in understanding human behaviour. The 'science' of altruism began with the dispute between the Social Darwinism of Huxley and the Social Anarchism of Kropotkin, but as Lee Allan Dugatkin (2006) argues, their diametrically opposed political and philosophical views can be lumped together in their failure to present empirical proof, by which he means, computational, equation-based evidence, not (when it came to human beings) archaeological or ethnographic data, or naked eye observations of animal behaviour, the sort of 'just so stories' derided by Chomsky in his duels with the Social Biologists and the Evolutionary Psychologists. So as in the case of Chomsky's humanist biology, the sources of altruism can only be found in natural science using the accepted protocols of the natural sciences. Central to the definition of altruism advanced by evolutionary biologists today, is the link between altruistic behaviour and blood kinship. The present-day scientists would disagree about the gladiatorial behaviour of insects advanced by Huxley or Kropotkin's suggestion that the original source of altruism was not the family but the tribe or group (Dugatkin 2006: 30). Modern day evolutionary biologists have a baseline definition of altruism which, Dugatkin argues, invalidates Kropotkin's altruistic mutual aid, thus:

> Cooperation and altruistic acts are typically defined in modern-day evolutionary biology as behaviors that benefit others but entail a cost to the individual performing them. For Kropotkin, by contrast, group life per se and indeed almost every sort of action involving members of the same species – with the possible exception of aggression, which he hardly ever recorded [recall Harari's use of the term in this regard: CL] – constituted altruism.
>
> (Dugatkin 2006: 28)

Thus for Dugatkin, both Kropotkin and Huxley were nineteenth-century purveyors of 'just so stories'. Not a single experiment was generated by the feuding pair and 'neither of them ever formalized a theory of the connection between blood relatedness and altruism, let alone developed a mathematical model amenable for testing' (35). Therefore, although classical anarchists such as Errico Malatesta and postanarchists, such as Saul Newman, fault Kropotkin for his scientism, that is confusing biology with political ethics, Dugatkin faults Kropotkin for his lack of scientific rigour!

It was only in the twentieth century that the first controlled experiments on animals were carried out and only in 1973 that Tinbergen, Lorenz, and Von Frisch won their Nobel Prize for their work which initiated the contemporary scientific study of animal behaviour. But the influence of Kropotkin's imagination, the anarchist imagination, was not absent, as can be seen in W. Clyde Allee, an American Quaker ecologist working in the 1920s, influenced by the Russian anarchist, and sharing his belief that kinship had nothing to do with mutual aid and altruism, that humankind was not innately warlike and that cooperation was the definition of life itself. But in contrast to the Russian, he tried to use scientific protocols to operationalize Kropotkin's findings. He tried to show how organisms who were not kin could control water in dry environments. He wanted to create a grand theory of cooperation beyond kin by scaling up from fast producing and rapidly generation-forming isopods to human beings. Similarly, using mathematical modelling, Sewall Wright argued for group selection which transcended kin (Dugatkin 2006: 52–55). Dugatkin argues that modern genetics owes a great deal to Sewall Wright, but on the whole does not endorse his concept of non-kin cooperation. But neither Sewall Wright nor later, Haldane or Fischer, leaves us with a mathematically based linkage between kinship and altruism. In the 1960s Bill Hamilton (without any political or religious leanings) addressed the issue of 'whether natural selection worked via kinship to produce altruism' (Dugatkin 2006: 94). But at this point the argument comes full circle and returns us to some familiar, recurring themes of this chapter and my introduction.

George Price was an American scientist who led an intriguing and tragic, professional life, spanning the 1940s to 1970s and shaped by our old acquaintance, the American Military-Industrial Complex. Price worked on the Uranium Enrichment Project in Chicago and the Manhattan Project which produced the first atomic weapons, and he became obsessed with the threat of mutually assured destruction. Like Hamilton, whom he worked with at the end of his life in London, and who introduced him to game-theoretic logic (in which the influence of one the 'fathers' of the H-Bomb, John von Neumann, is important), and applied it to the protocols of Evolutionary Biology, both men investigated the role of goodness in nature (Harman 2011: 360). Price believed that one of Hamilton's most important papers could explain altruism and spiteful behaviour (109). Using covariance analysis, Price claimed to show that altruism was genetically coded. Price argued that kinship did have an effect on altruism: when 'individuals were in groups with lots of blood kin' he argued, 'then a gene coding for altruism had a positive covariance with the number of off-spring an individual produces. Altruism could evolve', but on the other hand, 'that if the average genetic relatedness within the population – that is when the individuals in groups are "negatively" related – then spiteful behaviour can evolve' (110). But the result for Price meant that biological altruism need not generate universal goodness:

> Whether altruism came about at the altruist's own expense because it helped shuttle related genes into the next generation, or because it somehow ended up paying for the altruist later in his life, there were always an interested logic involved. Even when 'truer' altruism evolved under group selection it could only work if the good of one group was to triumph over the good of another, whether conscious or brainless, intended or instinctual, altruism was never truly 'pure'.
>
> (Harman 2011: 362–363)

Price experienced Asperger's Syndrome, depressions, and finally, after his work in London, delusions, and in the end he found the Good Samaritan's ideal of self-sacrifice as a route to the pure altruism, which his biological experiments had blocked. At the end of his life he sought to help the victims of spousal abuse and abandoned his worldly possessions and was found dead in a squat in London's Camden Town. A group of tramps and two fellow biologists, Hamilton and Maynard Smith, attended his funeral, but the after-effect of his work, ironically for him, was the incorporation of his and Hamilton's work in Richard Dawkins' (1976) *The Selfish Gene* and E.O. Wilson's (1975) *Sociobiology* in which 'altruism was the manifestation of the hardworking selfish gene' (!) (Dugatkin 2006: 116).

But the merry waltz of anarchism, genes, and altruism does not end here. Psychology and anarchism are the linkage (Fix 2011), and Abraham Maslow's hierarchy of values, in which my former PhD student, Michael Babula (2013: 4–5), has suggested there emerges a third level of values beyond baseline instinctual needs, which he terms, exocentricism, whose 'types' exude the values of peace, charity, and redistributive justice. Babula engages with research in the natural sciences too, thus, he argues that 'the newly emergent neurobiological research seems to confirm cognitive empathy as underlying exocentric altruistic behaviour' (15). And in our age of populist uncertainty, Babula pleads for the need for exocentric altruistic value-type leaders who argue for cooperation and do not prey and thrive on the fears of the populace (174–175). In a similar vein Stephen Nugent (2012: 212), a sceptical but sympathetic observer of the anarchism/anthropological exchange,[4] suggests that the theoretical linguistics of Chomsky, although side-lined by the 'anthropological commitment to constructivism' and suspicion of his innatist arguments, deserve more recognition by his fellow anthropologists than they have received. Nugent argues that the Chomskyan revolution should be revisited, particularly in light of the genomic paradigm of the selfless or cooperative gene because the human language facility could supply valuable evidence, 'and it is in this regard that anthropological interest in anarchism seems to have missed a crucial opportunity' (213). Thus like his former colleague at Goldsmiths, University of London, David Graeber, but with different first premises, he wishes to rescue anthropology from its discredited past, and reassure his fellow academics that they would not be venturing near racist, eugenicist, and crackpot stories, and he suggests that they moderate their prospectivism, in short, 'to factor out anything which has an implication for the biological basis of social behaviour in order to defend the field diminishes anthropological authority' (213). But unlike, Knight, he does not dismiss Chomsky's biological humanism thus:

> Chomsky's anarchism is meaningless without acknowledgement of the biological endowment as well as socio-historical formation of humans, but in the context of a discussion of anthropology and anarchism, there is an impediment generated

within the discipline itself that forestalls fruitful engagement with these compelling arguments.

(Nugent (2012: 213))

The challenge thrown down by Nugent has recently been taken up by a neuro-linguist, Elliot Murphy (2018), who mounts a strong case in his chapter in the *Palgrave Handbook of Anarchism* for the connections between that 'latest neuro-biological research', to recall Babula, and the question of altruism, and its fresh encounters with anarchism in the twenty-first century.

Perhaps for the anarchists a degree of humility is required and requested: they have warned about science being a machine, or a form of colonial violence, or ploy of pure objectivity to win resources from the state or even as a house of worship, but the anarchists also incorporated science into their worldview to help defeat a gamut of metaphysical propositions, the Church, the State, Capitalism, and Marxism. With all its limitations, the modesty bestowed by the 'anarchist squint' is required. An 'anarchist squint' does not fall victim to the nihilism, cynicism, and despair characterized by certain readings of 'the postmodern condition', but embraces contingency and an imagination which postmodernists applaud, which is alert, in a Popperian way (Stevens 2011), to the limits of large data sets, that can foster a science, reinforced by universal scientific literacy and practices of citizens' science (Thorpe and Welsh 2008), but which nevertheless respects probability and embraces the linkages between science, technology, and human freedom (Restivo 2011).

Notes

1. Of course it is one thing to invoke the golden past and another to wish it on the Earth in the twenty-first century: Noam Chomsky has taken issue with the mass genocide needed to reduce the Earth's population to the numbers suited for Neolithic post-scarcity anarchism!
2. Hjorleifur Jonsson (2012: 169) states that 'it is historically inaccurate to declare that Southeast Asian highlanders were created and shaped by deliberate separation or escape from the state'.
3. Or as James Birmingham (2013: 167) argues: '…For every example of a seemingly as-good-as-it-gets egalitarian pastoral or foraging society, there usually exists a counter-example of a group using virtually the same subsistence strategy with very different results in the social sphere. The evidence just does not support the technological base creating the superstructure of a society'.
4. Thus Nugent (2012: 211) endorses Morris' elective affinity argument (of anarchism and anthropology) but thinks many of the new anarchist anthropologists overstate and romanticize their case, so that, for example, the anarchism/pre-state formations arguments of Clastres and others are 'based on questionable anthropological generalizations about core features of pre-class societies'.

References

Babula, M. (2013) *Motivation, Altruism, Personality, and Social Psychology: The Coming Age of Altruism*, Basingstoke: Palgrave Macmillan.
Banaji, J. (2011) *Theory as History: Essays on Modes of Production and Exploitation*, Chicago: Haymarket.
Barclay, H. (1982) *People with Government: The Anthropology of Anarchism*, London: Kahn and Averill (with Cienfuegos Press).
Birmingham, J. (2013) 'From Potsherds to Smartphones: Anarchism, Archaeology, and the Material World', in J.A. Meléndez Badillo and N.J. Jun (eds.) *Without Borders or Limits: An*

Interdisciplinary Approach to Anarchist Studies, Newcastle-Upon-Tyne: Cambridge Scholars Publishing, pp. 165–174.
Bookchin, M. (2005) *The Ecology of Freedom: the Emergence and Dissolution of Hierarchy*, Oakland: AK Press.
Bourdieu, P. (1984) *Distinction: A Social Critique of the Judgement of Taste*, London: Routledge.
Chomsky, N. (2013) *On Anarchism*, New York: The New Press.
Clastres, P. (1977) *Society against the State*, Oxford: Blackwell.
Cohn, J.S. (2006) *Anarchism and the Crisis of Representation: Hermeneutics, Aesthetics, Politics*, Selinsgrove: Susquehanna University Press.
Dawkins, R. (1976) *The Selfish Gene*, Oxford: Oxford University Press. Dugatkin, L.A. (2006) *The Altruism Equation: Seven Scientists Search for the Origins of Goodness*, Princeton: Princeton University Press.
Edgley, A. (ed.) *Noam Chomsky*, Basingstoke: Palgrave Macmillan.
Ehrlich, H. J. (1996) 'Anarchism and Formal Organization', in H.J. Ehrlich (ed.) *Reinventing Anarchy, Again*, Edinburgh: AK Press, pp. 56–68.
Elders, F. (ed.) (2011) *Human Nature: Justice versus Power. The Chomsky-Foucault Debate*, London: Souvenir Press (Originally published 1971).
Evans-Prichard, E.E. (1940) *The Nuer*, Oxford: Oxford University Press.
Evren, S. (2012), 'What is Anarchism? A Reflection on the Canon and Constructive Potential of its Destruction', unpublished PhD, University of Loughborough.
Ferretti, F. (2018) *Anarchy and Geography: Reclus and Kropotkin in the UK*, London: Routledge.
Fix, D. (2011) 'Anarchism and Psychology', *Theory in Action*, 4(4): 31–48.
Gelderloos, P. (2016) *Worshipping Power: An Anarchist View of Early State Formation*, Edinburgh: AK Press.
Gibson, T. and Sillander, K. (ed.) (2011) *Anarchic Solidarity: Autonomy, Equality and Fellowship in Southeast Asia*, New Haven: Yale University Press.
Graeber, D. (2001) *Toward an Anthropological Theory of Value: The False Coin of Our Own Dreams*, Basingstoke: Palgrave.
Graeber, D. (2004) *Fragments of an Anarchist Anthropology*, Chicago: Paradigm Press.
Graeber, D. (2011) *Debt: the First 5000 Years*, Brooklyn: Melville House.
Gurianova, N. (2012) *The Aesthetics of Anarchy: Art and Ideology in the Early Russian Avant-Garde*, Berkeley: University of California Press.
Harari, Y. N. (2014) *Sapiens: A Brief History of Humankind*, London: Harvill Secker.
Harman, O. (2011) *The Price of Altruism: George Price and the Search for the Origins of Kindness*, London: Vintage.
High, H. (2012) 'Anthropology and Anarchy: Romance, Horror or Science Fiction', *Critique of Anthropology*, 32(2): 93–108.
Ince, A. and Barrera de la Torre, G. (2017) 'Future (Pre-) Histories of the State. On Anarchy, Archaeology, and the Decolonial', in F. Ferretti, G. Barrera de la Torre, A. Ince and F. Toro (eds.) *Historical Geographies of Anarchism: Early Critical Geographies of Present-Day Society*, London: Routledge, pp. 179–194.
Johnson, K. and Ferguson, K. E. (2018) 'Anarchism and Indigeneity', in C. Levy and M. Adams (eds.) *The Palgrave Handbook of Anarchism*, Cham: Palgrave Macmillan, pp. 697–714.
Jonsson, H. (2012), 'Paths to Freedom: Political Prospecting in the Ethnographic Record', *Critique of Anthropology*, 32(2): 158–172.
Jun, N. (2012) *Anarchism and Political Modernity*, New York: Continuum.
Jun, N. (2013) 'Rethinking the Anarchist Canon. History, Philosophy, and Interpretation', in R. Kinna and S. Evren (eds.) *Blasting the Canon, Anarchist Developments in Cultural Studies*, 1, Brooklyn: Punctum Books, pp. 82–116.
Kinna, R. and Evren, S. (eds.) (2013) *Blasting the Canon, Anarchist Developments in Cultural Studies*, 1, Brooklyn: Punctum Books.

Knight, C. (2016) *Decoding Chomsky: Science and Revolutionary Politics*. New Haven: Yale University Press.

Lagalisse, E. (2018) *Occult Features of Anarchism - with Attention to the Conspiracy of Kings and the Conspiracy of Peoples*, Oakland: PM Press.

Lea, T. (2012) 'When Looking for Anarchy, Look to the State: Fantasies of Regulation in Forcing Disorder within the Australian Indigenous Estate', *Critique of Anthropology*, 32(2): 109–124.

Levy, C. (2010) 'Social Histories of Anarchism', *Journal for the Study of Radicalism*, 4(2): 1–44.

Levy, C. (2012), 'Gramsci's Cultural and Political Sources: Anarchism in the Prison Writings', *Journal of Romance Studies*, 12(3): 44–62.

Martin, K. (2012) 'The "Potlatch of Destruction": Gifting against the State', *Critique of Anthropology*, 32(2): 125–142.

Mauss, M. (1990) *The Gift: Forms and Functions in Archaic Societies*, London: Routledge.

McGilvray, J. (2014) *Chomsky*, 2nd ed., Cambridge: Polity.

Morris, B. (2005) *Anthropology and Anarchism: Their Elective Affinity*, London: Goldsmiths Anthropology Research Papers, GARP 11, Goldsmiths, University of London.

Morris, B. (2015) *Anthropology, Ecology, and Anarchism: A Brian Morris Reader*, Oakland: PM Press.

Murphy, E. (2018) 'Anarchism and Science', in C. Levy and M.S. Adams (eds.) *The Palgrave Handbook of Anarchism*, Cham: Palgrave Macmillan, pp. 193–210.

Nugent, S. (2012) 'Anarchism out West: Some Reflections on Sources', *Critique of Anthropology*, 32(2): 206–216.

Overing, J. (1993) 'The Anarchy and Collectivism of the "Primitive Other": Marx and Sahlins in the Amazon', in C. Hann (ed.) *Socialism: Ideals, Ideologies, and Local Practice*, London: Routledge, pp. 43–58.

Pfaff, D. (2015) *The Altruistic Brain: How We Are Naturally Good*, Oxford: Oxford University Press.

Pinker, S. (2012) *The Better Angels of Our Nature*, London: Penguin.

Price, A. (2018) 'Green Anarchism', in C. Levy and M.S. Adams (eds.) *The Palgrave Handbook of Anarchism*, Cham: Palgrave Macmillan, pp. 281–291.

Rai, M. (2015) 'Chomsky and Revolution', in A. Edgely (ed.) *Noam Chomsky*, Basingstoke: Palgrave Macmillan, pp. 165–184.

Reclus, É. (1891) *Primitive Folk: Studies in Comparative Ethnology*, London: Walter Scott.

Restivo, S. (2011) *Red, Black, and Objective. Science, Sociology, and Anarchism*, Farnham: Ashgate.

Robinson, A. and Tormey, S. (2012) 'Beyond the State: Anthropology and "Actually-Existing Anarchism"', *Critique of Anthropology*, 32(2): 143–157.

Scott, J. C. (2009) *The Art of Not Being Governed: An Anarchist History of Upland Southeast Asia*, New Haven: Yale University Press.

Scott, J. C. (2017) *Against the Grain: A Deep History of the Earliest States*, New Haven: Yale University Press.

Siegrist, P. (2017) 'Historicising "Anarchist Geography". Six Issues for Debate from a Historian's Point of View', in F. Ferretti, G. Barrera de la Torre, A. Ince and A. Toro (eds.) *Historical Geographies of Anarchism: Early Critical Geographers and Present-Day Scientific Challenges*, London: Routledge, pp. 129–150.

Singer, P. (2015) *The Most Good You Can Do: How Effective Altruism Is Changing Ideas about Living Ethically*, New Haven: Yale University Press.

Stevens, J. (2011) 'Anarchist Methods and Political Theory', in J.C. Klausen and J. Martel (eds.) *How Not to Be Governed: Reading and Interpretations from a Critical Anarchist Left*, Plymouth: Lexington Books, pp. 1–18.

Taylor, M. (1976) *Anarchy and Cooperation*, London: John Wiley and Sons.

Taylor, M. (1987) *The Possibility of Cooperation*, Cambridge: Cambridge University Press.

Thorpe, C. and Welsh, I. (2008), 'Beyond Primitivism: Towards a Twenty-First Century Anarchist and Praxis Science', *Anarchist Studies*, 16(1): 48–75.

Van der Walt, L. and Schmidt, M. (2009) *Black Flame: the Revolutionary Class Politics of Anarchism and Syndicalism*, Edinburgh and Oakland: AK Press.
Wilson, D. S. (2016) *Does Altruism Exist?: Culture, Genes and the Welfare of Others.* New Haven: Yale University Press.
Wilson, E.O. (1975) *Sociobiology,* Cambridge, MA: Harvard University Press.
Wright, E.O. (2010) *Envisioning Real Utopias*, London: Verso.

Index

Note: Information in figures and tables is indicated by page numbers in *italics* and **bold**.

Abensour, Miguel 89
Ackelsberg, Martha 104
activism 69
activist fatigue 152–153
Adams, Jason 174–175
Adorno, Theodor 99
aesthetic of tension: defined 229–230; inner life and 238; museum and 231–233
aesthetics: anti-aesthetic and 229; in Kant 229; knowledge in 229
Agamben, Giorgio 66
Agricultural Revolution 243–244
'Album III' (Jacob) 235
Aleksov, Bojan 221
Alexis-Baker, Nekeisha 215
Alfin, Castro 213
Allee, W. Clyde 253
Alston, Charlotte 221
alterity 169
altruism 13, 247–255
American Political Science Association (APSA) 96
Amnesty International 69
anarchaindigenism 124–125
anarchic subject 85–86
anarchism 76n5
Anarchism (Woodcock) 1
Anarchist Developments in Cultural Studies (journal) 51
anarchist-feminism: anti-racist 122–123; bodies in 117–118; capital in **114**, 118–120; colonialism in **114**, 122–128; defined 110–113; gender in **114**, 115–118; global 122–128; governance in 120–122; immigration and 123; power in 113–114, **114**, 118–119; and public vs. private spheres 116–117; race in **114**, 122–128; sexuality in **114**, 115–118; state in **114**, 120–122
anarchist geographies 241; autonomy and 150–153; history of 147–149; renewal of interest in 149–150; spatialities and 155–157; statism and 153–155; territorial imagination and 153–155
anarchist imagination 4–6, 13, 20, 73, 203–204, 253
Anarchist Sandwich Party 234
Anarchist Studies Network (ASN) 50
Andrews, Dave 215
ant-aesthetic 229
anthropology 241–247
anti-colonialism: postcolonialism vs. 163; theories 175–177
anti-discipline: anarchism as 81–83
anti-landlordism 240
Antipode (journal) 148–149
anti-politics 88–90
anti-Semitism 99
Antliff, Alan 22n5
Anzaldúa, Gloria 140–141
APSA *see* American Political Science Association (APSA)
Apter, David 1
Arab Spring 30–41, **32**, **37**, 127–128, 138, 174, 177n3
Arendt, Hannah 89
Argentina 138
Arrighi, Giovanni 167
ArtJail 231–233
Ashley, Richard 45–46
ASN *see* Anarchist Studies Network (ASN)
atheism 210–212
authority: organic anarchy and 34
autonomous geographies 150
autonomous spaces 141
autonomy 150–153
Au/Travail/At Work 230
awareness 132
axiom of liberty 87–88

Index

Babula, Michael 254
Bacon, Francis 101
Bakunin, Mikhail 6, 54, 70–71, 73, 81, 83, 88, 100–101, 103, 220
Ball, Stephen 197
Bamyeh, Mohammed 22n5
Barber, Benjamin 9
Barclay, Harold 221
Barents, Jan 99
Bargu, Banu 205
Barnes, Alfred 231
Barnes Foundation 231–232
Bartlett, Rosamund 222
Bartley, Jonathan 223
Bayat, Asef 32
Bell, Daniel 9
Berkman, Alexander 70–71, 183–184
Berneri, Marie Louise 10
Bessière, Gérard 213
Beveridge, William 97–98, 107
Bevir, Mark 99
Bey, Hakim 54, 83
Bhabha, Homi 166
Birmingham, James 255n3
Black Bloc 13, 74–75
Blake, William 14, 222
Blanes, Ruy Llera 221
Bliss, W.D.P. 107
Bloom, Alex 206
Bonanno, Alfredo 229–230
Bookchin, Murray 10, 48, 53, 83, 103–104, 246
Booth, Ken 62, 64, 68–69
Borduas, Paul-Emile 235
Bouglé, Celestin 241
Bourdieu, Pierre 243–244
Boyd, Greg 215
Brennan, Robert 172, 177n2
Brighouse, Harry 201
Brown, Gavin 141
Brown, Sarah 116
Brown, Wendy 139
Buber, Martin 76, 221
Burke, Edmund 49
Butler, Judith 66, 137

Cafard, Max 216
Callan, Eamonn 201
Calvino, Italo 140
'Canada Park: Two Family Albums' (Guttman) 237
canon 240
capacitación 120–121
capital: in anarchist-feminism **114**, 118–120
capitalism 33, 133–134, 148, 230
Carter, Alan 4
Cavanaugh, William T. 218

CCD *see* culture of critical discourse (CCD)
Charkin, Emily 206–207
Chomsky, Noam 10, 46, 206, 218, 247–252
Christianity 210–211, 214–215
Christoyannopoulos, Alexandre 22n5
CIRCA *see* Clandestine Insurgent Rebel Clown Army (CIRCA)
citizenism 2
Claiborne, Shane 215, 218
Clandestine Insurgent Rebel Clown Army (CIRCA) 75–76
Clark, John 102, 213, 216, 221
Clastres, Pierre 242–243, 245–246
climate change 104
Cloward, Richard 11
Cohen, Stan 7
Cohn, Carol 65, 76n5
Cohn, Jesse 221
Cold War 45, 165, 248
Cole, Keith 235
Collectif de recherche sur l'autonomie collective (CRAC) 112–113, 128
colonialism 154–155; in anarchist-feminism **114**, 122–128
Colson, Daniel 151
Comfort, Alex 7
complexity theory 11
Comstock Law 184
conceptual radicalism 35, 56
Cooppan, Vilashini 164
Copernican Revolution 84
Coppe, Abiezer 215
Coser, Lewis 9
Cossacks 11
Cox, Robert 45
CRAC *see Collectif de recherche sur l'autonomie collective* (CRAC)
Crain, Martin 118
Crenshaw, Kimberlé 10, 112
Critchley, Simon 47, 220
critical jurisprudence 181–189
critical radicalism 56
Critical Security Studies (CSS): anarchist response to 67–76; emergence of 63; journals relevant to 63; securitization theory and 64–65; Welsh School and 64
Crone, Patricia 221
CSS *see* Critical Security Studies (CSS)
Cudenec, Paul 219–220
Cudworth, Erika 48
culture of critical discourse (CCD) 10

Dabashi, Hamid 177n3
Damico, Linda 218
Darwin, Charles 6
Davis, Richard 218–219, 222
Day, Dorothy 221

Day, Richard 69–70, 72–73
de Acosta, Alejandro 229
de Cleyre, Voltarine 6, 10, 111–112
decolonized planetarity 168
Deep Green Anarchism 10
de Gaulle, Charles 4
de Goede, Marieke 70
de Heredia, Marta Iñiguez 127–128, 129n1
Deleuze, Gilles 183
de Raaij, André 221
Derrida, Jacques 66, 82, 188–189
Diamond, Jared 246
diaspora 171–175
Dillon, Michael 73–74
Dixon, Chris 11
Dordal, Paul 215
Douzinas, Costas 181, 186
Downes, David 7
Dugatkin, Lee Allan 252–253
Dunne, Tim 69

Easton, David 99
education: as central theme 194; defending 198–199; free schools and 206–207; managerialism and 202; neo-liberal 197–198; and philosophical imagination 199–200; practical turn in 195; Research Excellence Framework in 196–197; Robbins Report and 194–195; state and 200–202; utopianism and 203–204; 'what works' discourse in 196–197
Egypt 34–36, 41n1, 127–128
elites 9
Eller, Vernard 215
Elliott, Michael 215
Ellul, Jacques 214, 221–222
End of Representative Politics, The (Tormey) 2
enemy ideology 133–134
England, Lynndie 65
epistemological anarchism 84–85
epistemologies 247–255
Eschle, Catherine 110, 116
ethics: postanarchism and 89
exegesis 214–217, 223

Fabbri, Lorenzo 188
Falk, Richard 47
Farrow, Lynne 111
feminism 10; and Critical Security Studies 65–66; Third World 176; *see also* anarchist-feminism
Ferrell, Jeff 22n2, 146, 156
Ferrer, Francisco 6
Ferretti, Federico 241
Feyerabend, Paul 5–6, 84, 103, 105
Fielding, Michael 205–206
Fiscella, Anthony 221

Fitzgerald, Mary E. 184
'Flashlight' (Jacob) 234–235
Food Not Bombs 73
Fordism 7
Foster, Hal 229
Foucault, Michel 66, 81–83, 85, 91–92, 92n1, 113–115, 118, 120, 122–123, 175, 190
Frank, Andre Gunder 167
Frankfurt School 45, 64
Franks, Benjamin 92n8
Freeden, Michael 13
French Revolution 87
functionalism 1
Furlong, John 194
Futurists 250–251

Galbraith, John Kenneth 10
Galván-Álvarez, Enrique 221
Gandhi, Leela 165, 169–171, 177
Garden City Movement 148
gay rights 134–135
Gearey, Adam 181
Geddes, Patrick 6
Gelderloos, Peter 246
gender: in anarchist-feminism **114**, 115–118; performativity of 137
genealogy 51, 53–54, 82, 85, 92, 165, 167, 240
geographies *see* anarchist geographies
Gerbaudo, Paolo 2
Gero, Robert 229
Gilman, Derek 232
Gilman-Opalsky, Richard 75
Gilroy, Paul 172
GJM *see* Global Justice Movement (GJM)
globalization theory 163, 167, 172
Global Justice Movement (GJM) 2, 4, 11, 127, 240
global warming 104
Goddard, Andrew 222
Godwin, William 49, 91, 110, 194
Goldman, Emma 6, 70–73, 110–111, 137–138, 183–187, 189–192, 221, 237
Goodman, Paul 9, 11, 15, 22n2, 101
Goodrich, Peter 187
Goodwin, Adam 48, 53
Gordon, Uri 11, 112, 121
Gorz, Andre 174
Gouldner, Alvin 10
governance: in anarchist-feminism 120–122
Graeber, David 3, 9, 13, 22n5, 75, 81, 134, 243, 245, 254
Gramsci, Antonio 8–9
Grayson, Kyle 70
Greed radical thought 10
Greenway, Judy 141
Gross, Otto 8

Growing up Absurd (Goodman) 9
Grubačić, Andrej 11
Gunnell, John 52
Guttman, Freda 237–238

Habermas, Jürgen 92n7
Harari, Noah 243–244
Hardt, Michael 5, 164, 168, 172, 216
Hassan, Budour 127–128
Haw, Chris 215, 218
Hawley, John 167–168
Hebden, Keith 213, 218
Heckert, Jamie 72–73, 117, 129
hegemony 69–70
Heidegger, Martin 83
Heller, Hermann 96–98, 106–107
Hepworth, Barbara 235
High, Holly 244
Hill-Collins, Patricia 10
historiography 220–223
Hobbes, Thomas 47, 90, 187
Hobden, Stephen 48
Hobsbawm, Eric 14
Hobson, Christopher 222
Hogan, Deirdre 111
Hogan, Padraig 198
homosexuals 134–135, 137–138
Honeywell, Carissa 22n5
hooks, bell 133, 142
Howard, Ebenezer 148
Huerta, Carmen 111
Huxley, Thomas 147, 252–253
hybridity 171–175
Hyslop-Margison, Emery 198

Iannello, Kathleen 112
ideology: analyses of 13–14
Illich, Ivan 6
immigration 123
individuality, queer 137–138
informal networks 32–33
International Relations (IR) 42–58; anarchism and 46–48; anarchy in 44–46; critical turn of 45; empirical theory in 55; historical turn in 52; liberalism in 44–45; morals and 54–57; myth of 52–54; normative theory in 55; post-positivist turn of 45; realism in 44–45; Ruggie in 45–46; social science and 42–43
intersectionality 10
intifada 31
IR *see* International Relations (IR)
Iraq War 76n2
Islam 212, 216
Ismail, Salwa 32

Jacob, Luis 233–237
Jacobs, Jane 6

Jaggar, Alison 112
Jakobson, Roman 250–251
Jameson, Fredric 165
Jeavons, Albo 231–233
Jeppesen, Sandra 173–174
Jesus Radicals 219, 222
Jiwani, Yasmin 122–123
Joll, James 1
Jonsson, Hjorleifur 255n2
Jordan, Clarence 221
Jun, Nathan 195, 199, 240
jurisprudence 181–189

Kant, Immanuel 45, 92n7, 229
Kantorowicz, E. H. 92n6
Kazmi, Zaheer 11
Keiner, Edwin 197
Kersner, Jacob A. 190–191
Kibbutzim movement 73
Kierkegaard, Søren 213, 222
Kinna, Ruth 22n5, 49
Kissinger, Henry 50
Kjaer, Niels 215
Klebnikov, Velimir 250–251
Knight, Chris 249–252
Knight, Michael Muhammad 223
Krishnaswamy, Revathi 167–168
Kropotkin, Peter 3, 6, 11, 13, 30, 47–48, 54, 73, 84–85, 92n3, 95, 103, 106–107, 146–148, 158, 183, 187–190, 213, 241, 252–253
Krøvel, Roy 104–105
Kuhn, Thomas 40

La Boétie, Étienne de 92n4
LAD *see* Language Acquisition Device (LAD)
Lagalisse, Erica 124–125, 213
Landauer, Gustav 47, 73, 86, 102–103, 157, 213, 220–221
Landstreicher, Wolfi 102
Lane, Rose Wilder 49
language 247–255
Language Acquisition Device (LAD) 247–249, 251
Lasch, Christopher 9
Lasch, Scott 5
Lasswell, Harold 9–10
law: critical jurisprudence and 181–189; in Kropotkin 189–190
Lazarus, Neil 168–169
Lea, Tess 244–245
Left and Right: A Journal of Libertarian Thought (journal) 49
Le Guin, Ursula 136, 138
'Lengua (Tongue)' (Margolles) 236–237
Levinas, Emmanuel 83
Levi-Strauss, Claude 250
Levy, Carl 22n5, 46, 48

liberalism: in International Relations 44–45
libertarianism 49
liberty: postanarchism and 87–88
Libya 31, 36, 41n1
Liesegang, Jerimarie 117
Linebaugh, Peter 11
Loomba, Ania 165, 167, 175
Lorde, Audre 119
loving politics 142–143

MacDonald, Dwight 9
MacIntyre, Alasdair 198
MacKinnon, Catharine 116, 119–120
Mair, Peter 2
Malatesta, Errico 70–71, 92n3
managerialism 202
Manning, Chelsea 65
Margolles, Teresa 236–237
Markovic, Svetozar 176
Marples, Roger 200
marriage, gay 134–135
Marsh, David 96, 100
Marsh, Margaret 110, 114, 116, 129
Marx, Karl 8–9, 102, 110
Marxism 1, 3, 8, 14, 70, 85, 103, 151–152, 165, 238n2, 242, 246
Maslow, Abraham 254
Mauss, Marcel 3, 241, 243
May, Todd 87, 92n5, 113, 172, 178n14
Mayo, Cris 199–201
McKeogh, Colm 222
meditation 132, 136
Meggitt, Justin 215
Melucci, Alberto 174
methodology 1–6, 10, 14, 16–17, 43, 52–55, 82, 84, 96–99, 106–107, 176, 240, 247–255
Mills, Charles 201
Mills, C. Wright 5, 9, 95, 105–108
Morris, Brian 241, 245, 255n4
Morris, William 14
Moss, Peter 205–206
Mott, Carrie 157
Mouffe, Chantal 90
Mueller, Tadzio 174, 178n15
Mufti 34
Mujeres Libres 111–112, 119–121, 127, 129
Mumford, Lewis 6, 101–102
Murphy, Elliot 255
Murray, Daniel 47–48
museum 231–233
mushrooms 139
Muslims 212, 216
mutual aid 141
mutualism 33–34
Myers, Ched 215

Nancy, Jean Luc 188
Naseem, Ayaz 198
NASPIR *see* Network of Activist Scholars of Politics and International Relations (NASPIR)
nationalism 169–171
Negri, Antonio 164, 168, 172, 216
Negri, Tony 5
Neocleous, Mark 73
neo-elitism 9–10
neoliberalism 33, 163, 197–198
network analysis 11, 22n10
Network of Activist Scholars of Politics and International Relations (NASPIR) 50
New Anarchism 6–7
New Class Theory 9–10
New Criminology 7
New Left Marxism 1
Newman, Saul 22n5, 46, 75, 103–104, 113, 187, 203, 253
Newton, Herber 95, 107
Nietzsche, Friedrich 82–83, 97, 182–183
Nomad, Max 9, 22n8
Non-Violent Communication (NVC) 140, 143
normative political theory 91
Noys, Ben 92n10
Nugent, Stephen 254–255, 255n4
NVC *see* Non-Violent Communication (NVC)

Obama, Barack 218
Occupy (movement) 4, 11, 88, 133, 136, 138, 158, 174
Occupy Wall Street 4
'Offensive/Defensive' (Poitrus) 237
O'Hearn, Denis 11
ontological anarchism 83–84
Orensanz, Aurelio 213
organic anarchy: Arab Spring and 31–32; authority and 34; basic features of **32**; defined 30; pragmatic radicalism and 35–36; self-conscious anarchism vs. 33; sociology and 36–41, **37**
Orientalism 169
Ostrom, Elinor 6
Otpor! Movement 13

Palestine 31
Pareto, Vilfredo 97
Pateman, Carole 6
Paterson, Isabel 49
People's Global Action 174
Perlman, Fredy 105–106
Peterson, V. Spike 66
Pick, Peter 215
Pignatta, Valerio 221
Pinker, Steven 244, 248
Piven, Frances Fox 11

Pi y Margall, Francisco 30
Podemos 2
Poitrus, Edward 237
Political Opportunity Structures 11
political science: anarchism and 104–107; history of 95–100
Political Studies Association 50
politics: invisible 138–139; loving 142–143; postanarchism and 88–90; of representation 135–137; representation of 133
Popper, Karl 5
populism 2–3, 54
postanarchism: and anarchic subject 85–86; and anarchism as anti-discipline 81–83; axes of 83–87; and epistemological anarchism 84–85; ethics and 89; insurrection and 86–87; liberty and 87–88; misinterpretations of 82–83; and ontological anarchism 83–84; and political theory 90–92; politics and 88–90; revolution and 86–87
post-autonomism 151
postcolonialism 13; alterity and 169; anarchism and 168–175; anti-colonialism vs. 163; diaspora and 171–175; hybridity and 171–175; nationalism and 169–171; periodization of 164; subalternity and 169
postmodernism 1
Power Elite, The (Mills) 9
Prado, Abdennur 216
pragmatic radicalism 35–36, 40
pragmatism 9
Price, George 253–254
Prichard, Alex 2, 46, 51, 53–54, 58n12, 95–96, 100, 108
primitivism 10
Pring, Richard 196, 200–201
Prison Solidarity 11
Proudhon, Pierre-Joseph 19, 22n6, 46–47, 49, 53, 83, 241
Putnam, Robert 11

queer anarchonormativity 135
queer individuality 137–138

race: in anarchist-feminism **114**, 122–128
Radcliffe-Brown, A.R. 241
Radical Enlightenment 247–249
radicalism: conceptual 35, 56; critical 56; pragmatic 35–36, 40
Rancière, Jacques 87
Rand, Ayn 49
Rand Corporation 13
Rao, Nagesh 166
Rapp, John 221
Read, Herbert 235
realism: in International Relations 44–45

Reclaim the Streets 158
Reclus, Elisée 146–147, 155, 241
Rediker, Marcus 11
REF *see* Research Excellence Framework (REF)
Regulation Theory 152
Reich, Wilhelm 7–8
Reid, Julian 74
religion: anarchist quarrels with 211–213; exegesis and 214–217, 223; historiography and 220–223; state and 247; theology and 217–220
Research Excellence Framework (REF) 196–197
Resource Mobilization 11
Rexroth, Kenneth 221
Rice, Condoleezza 50
Robbins Report 194–195
Rocker, Rudolf 48, 71
Rognon, Fréderic 222
Rose, Nikolas 206
Rosenberg, Marshall 140
Ross, Dorothy 50
Rossdale, Chris 22n5, 47
Routledge, Paul 154
Ruggie, John 45–46
Russell, Matt 215

Saatchi, Charles 231
Saatchi OnLine 231
Sahlins, Marshall 243
Said, Edward 164, 166, 170
Samuel, Raphael 7
Sandoval, Chela 176
Sarangapani, Padma 201–202
Sartre, Jean Paul 99
Schmidt, Michael 82, 240
Schmitt, Carl 48–49, 54, 89
School of Oriental and African Studies 164
Schürmann, Reiner 83–84
science 100–104
Scott, James 11, 14–15, 49, 56, 172, 243–244, 246
Seattle 1999 13, 150
Second Wave feminism 10
securitization theory 64–65
security: defined 65; obedience and 66; state and 74
Security Studies: realism and 62; *see also* Critical Security Studies (CSS)
Seeds of Hope 69
Selective Service Act 183, 185–186
self-conscious anarchism: basic features of **32**; defined 30; organic anarchy vs. 33; sociology and 36–41, **37**
Sennett, Richard 6
sexuality: in anarchist-feminism **114**, 115–118

Shannon, Deric 110, 118, 122
Shonin, Shinran 221
Shulman, K. 184
Siegrist, Pascale 241, 244–245
Singer, Peter 252
Singerman, Diane 32
Situationists 243–244
Skinner, B.F. 248
Skinner, Quentin 13, 58n12
Skrebowski, Luke 229
Slater, Philip 9
Smith, Adam 4
Smith, Andrea 169
Smith, Tuhiwai 124
Snyder, Gary 219
social capital 11
Social Darwinism 147, 252
social history 13–14
sociological imagination. 5, 105
sociology 36–41, **37**
Sorel, Georges 97, 134
Soyinka, Wole 171
Spain 30, 148
spatialities 155–157
Spencer, Herbert 6, 8, 147
Spivak, Gayatri 166
Standish, Paul 204
Starhawk 121
state-centrism 55
statism 47, 55, 68, 147, 153–155, 157–158, 198, 243
Stirner, Max 49, 72, 82–83, 86–87, 91–92, 212
Stoker, Gerry 96, 100
Strandberg, Hugo 212
Strauss, Leo 52
subalternity 169
Sudan 31
Suissa, Judith 22n5
Sullivan, Françoise 235
Syria 31
SYRIZA 2

Tatlin, Vladimir 251
Taussig, Michael 4
Taylor, Ian 7
Taylor, Laurie 7
Taylor, Michael 252
Temporary Alternative Zones 2
territorial imagination 153–155
theology 217–220
Third Wave feminism 10
Thompson, E. P. 14
Thornley, Kerry 220
Tolstoy, Leo 71, 214–215, 218, 221–222
Tooley, James 201–202
Tormey, Simon 2
Toronto Anarchist Free School 234
Tremlett, Paul-François 213
Troxell, Ted 220
Tucker, Benjamin 49

utopianism 203–204

van der Walt, Lucien 240
Van Dyke, Michael T. 221
Van Steenwyk, Mark 215, 219
Veneuse, Mohamed Jean 216
Voegelin, Eric 213
von Humboldt, Wilhelm 247
von Neumann, John 253

Waever, Ole 64
Waldo, Dwight 98–99
Wallerstein, Immanuel 167
Ward, Colin 7–8, 11, 15, 22n2, 49, 73, 141, 203–204, 213
War on Terror 163, 168
Warrington, Ronnie 186
Weaver, Warren 249, 251
Webb, Beatrice 98
Weber, Max 8, 37, 101
Weiss, Thomas 47
Welsh School 64
Wendy, Alexander 56
Wheeler, Nicholas 69
White, John 201–202
White, Patricia 201
WIley, Terrance 221
Williams, Dana 3
Wilson, David Sloan 252
Wilson, Matthew 92n8
Winch, Christopher 201–202
Wink, Walter 215
Woodcock, George 1, 4
World War I 43, 50, 70–71, 184
World War II 98–100
Worth, Owen 2
Wright, Eric Olin 245–246
Wyn Jones, Richard 64

Yates, Luke 22n9
Yi, Jin 126
Yoder, John Howard 215
York, Tripp 221
Young, Jock 7
Young, Robert 165
Young, Robert 178n17

Zapatistas 11, 13, 73
Zhen, He 115, 126

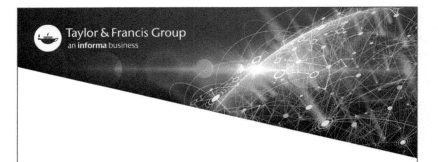